13. 11

50p

THE
SKI TEACHER

John I hope its a good
enough birthday present for

you

Yours Aye

Frith.

August 1997,

First Published 1997 by Culross

Copyright 1997 Frith Finlayson

Printed and Published in Scotland by
Wm. Culross & Son Ltd.
Coupar Angus
Perthshire
Scotland PH13 9DF

ISBN 1 873891 28 8

THE
SKI TEACHER

An Autobiography

by

FRITH FINLAYSON

*The story of British Professional Ski-ing
and development of Ski-ing in Britain*

DEDICATION

TO JEANIE:
> Bonie wee thing, cannie wee thing,
>   Lovely wee thing, wert thou mine.
> I wad wear thee in my bosom:
>   Lest my Jewel it should tine.
>
> Wishfully I look and languish
>   In that bonie face o' thine:
> And my heart it stounds wi' anguish
>   Lest my wee thing be na mine.
>
> Wit and Grace, and Love and Beauty,
>   In ae constellation shine:
> To adore thee is my duty,
>   Goddess o' this soul o' mine.

When Robert Burns wrote these lovely sentimental words, so appropriate to the Celtic heart back in the 1780s, he perfectly described how I have always felt about Jeanie Irvine Finlayson.

Without her, I could never have been part of the long story I am about to relate.

When we were getting started and experiencing great economical difficulties, never once did she complain.

It was I who was getting to do the skiing. It was always me in the limelight. But with her ever present steadfastness she remained a quiet pillar of strength in the background.

All our dear friends who lived through these wonderful times with us don't need to be told how fortunate I am in my partner.

How to thank you, Jeanie, is past my ken.

CONTENTS

ACKNOWLEDGEMENTS

A special thanks to Willie "Smiler" Wilson who one noon-time took me to his home in Aviemore where he produced a complete computer system and told me to start writing – something I should already have been doing. At home he gave me a crash-course on how to put words on paper.

Thanks also to four newer friends in my life, Rosemary and John McKendrick and Hazel and Robbie Allan, all of whom added to my now considerable computer capability. For their dear and true interest in all I have undertaken this past few years and, more importantly, for their friendship, I thank them.

Grateful thanks to Ian McKie for undertaking to tidy up written memories and opinions on life, for inserting words I had omitted and deleting extra wordage. Ian is as different from me as black is to white. Although pragmatic by nature and one of the world's more gentle people, his temper has a tidy "Wee Bite" to it. He has taken a long look at the world and how it works and I was sure his kindly philosophy of life would help him understand the text. The fact that Ian is neither a skier nor a man of the mountains served to leave his mind clear for tidying up my many mistakes. Thank you Ian.

My luck held out when my publisher put forward Robert J. Benzies to do the final edit. Bob is a well kent skier from the Dundee Ski Club stable and his knowledge of most of the people in British skiing since 1950 is as sound as my own. Early on, Bob became a firm favourite of my own club, Glencoe Ski Club, where he was held in high regard. His natural good humour would play a big part in this and it all came back to me when we got together to put this monster "to bed." Watching the Old Pro working, I learned so much and thought how valuable this knowledge would have been had I known it before I started writing. Thank you, Bob.

An Aviemore Man, Born and Bred–In December 1962 a curious and courteous teenager appeared, as if from nowhere, and seemed to become part of our scene. Unobtrusively, he became very close to our family and, at 18, came with me for 2 weeks skiing in St. Moritz – certainly the first Speyside butcher's apprentice to ski with the jet set! When we started to golf together, he became good whilst I became average. In the production of this work he made a considerable contribution to its completion. Thank you, Fraser Sharp.

Not all photographs have been acknowledged. Thanks to all photographers I could not trace. I have quoted poetry of Chris Lyons here and there and thank his family for this privilege. Extracts are marked CL.

Frith Finlayson.

FOREWORD

This is a timely story to tell; in any field of human activity, as the pace of change grows, there is always the danger of losing touch with the roots that link past and present. To know where we are going, we need to know where we came from and in the context of Scottish skiing, there can be no-one better placed to write such a chronicle than Frith Finlayson. It is, however, not only a book about the development of skiing in Scotland; because it is also a personal account, the story becomes a semi-autobiography of the author, whose life has been inextricably bound up with the sport. Frith has become something of a legend in skiing circles, a Glaswegian shipyard worker, who took to the hills to walk and to climb and then turned to "the skiing." He is one of those people about whom there is no indifferent opinion. When rumours were rife that Frith was writing this personal story of Scottish skiing, (a BOOK, no less!) the numbers who counted themselves likely to feature in it were in no doubt that it would be "a most interesting" tale.

It was as a young and enthusiastic weekend skier in the Cairngorms that I first met Frith Finlayson, whose Ski School D'Ecosse was by then already established. I have vivid memories of his team of ski teachers, swooping down the White Lady ski run, professionals all, smartly turned out in their distinctive red uniforms, made by Jeanie, Frith's wife. I may have been impressionable, but the inkling of an idea began to take form–I wanted to become a ski teacher!

Frith's dream of training and qualifying indigenous ski teachers had already begun to materialise and I was fortunate enough to be one of the first of this new breed of Scottish skier. We learned also (some would say it was drummed into us) standards of professionalism that would influence us for the rest of our working lives. Although I personally entered this story much later on in the scale of Frith's account of the birth of Scottish skiing, many of the tales which I heard from him at first hand as a trainee were of the great and famous skiers, foreign places and stories of the Alps, which fired the imagination. Frith even then was aware of the importance of acquiring a wider view and experience than our own home-spun skiing could offer us. He widened our horizons. In due course, this meant that I too fled the nest at Aviemore and headed for the Swiss Alps.

Anyone who is a skier–recreational, aspiring teacher or racer–or anyone indeed, who simply enjoys a good story about a period of our skiing past, full of anecdotes which though accurate, are written with colour and more than a touch of irreverence, will enjoy and appreciate this book. I would like to take this unique opportunity to give him my personal vote of thanks.

Alasdair Ross

Strathpeffer. October '96.

INTRODUCTION

This is an autobiographical story outlining the beginnings of most of the Main-Stems of todays' organised skiing in Britain.

It would be true to say that a great deal of the impetus for this discipline came from Scotland, the reason being the advent of ski lifts and resultant development of Scotland's ski areas.

The "British" part of skiing had been for years well represented by English ski clubs in Wengen, Murren and other Alpine resorts. The growth of the Scottish Ski Industry began to produce people who skied throughout the winter, many of whom became members of the S.C.G.B. in places like Wengen and Murren. Included in these numbers were most of the Main Players in both the Scottish and English side of skiing who, through the Clubs, participated in the common denominator of ski racing. These ski race events took root from 1956 onwards and, in time, the interests of Alpine and Scottish skiing would work in close harmony for the general good of British skiing.

The need to organise ski-teaching on a national scale was the beginning of this co-operation. Working in national ski racing followed soon after. Inevitably, this ultimately embraced and brought together a good cross section of the nation's skiing population. This was good for skiing.

At this time the growth of all aspects of skiing in the U.K. was at its peak and there appeared to be no end to the possibilities. This of course changed when each different faction started to look out for its own personal end – "Human Nature always dominates." As a result, the two most prominent sectors of skiing – racing and instruction – are less well organised than they should be at present.

Where is skiing today? Is it like the rest of the world, trying to find something "decent" to do with its deep, intricate knowledge? Or is it stagnating and becoming blase in that knowledge?

After reading this story, you may perceive and understand my reason for making these observations about organised skiing as it stands today in the U.K.

1. The Outdoors

For quite a number of years now, many of my friends in skiing have been asking me why I have never written about my almost forty years' experience in British skiing. In particular, the professional teaching. Until recently, I have always taken the considered view that any experiences I or my family have had in skiing, be they either successful, joyful, or sad, were the private property of ourselves or our close friends. However, on looking around lately, and seeing that some of the very special people are no longer with us, and some are not as well as we would like them to be, it got me to thinking that soon there might not be many people around with the knowledge, experience, or the authority to write on the subject and to try and put down on record a part of how British skiing arrived at where it is today from the early 1950s. If I do it well, it is my tribute to all the tremendous people from the most varied walks of life, imaginable, as you will see!

Without them being a part of it, I most certainly could not have been. They gave it its warmth, its interest, its colour, its excitement and its occasional pain. Without this, it would have had no soul, and therefore, no value. I will do my best not to miss out too many people of importance. If I do miss the odd one, it will be the fault of memory, it will not be because I wanted to. I'm sure, to my knowledge, that there has never been a reasonable account of the build-up to all the representative groups that exist in British skiing today. In the early fifties, there was the S.C.G.B. and the Scottish Ski Club. Both of these were established before the first world war. The former looked after the British skier abroad. And most of the Scottish were also loyal members of the British. There were other British clubs based in different Alpine villages. There was the Dundee Ski Club, which was very strongly led.

In most of the Alpine villages the Ski Club of Great Britain maintained Reps. These Reps looked after the needs of club members on holiday, and also first-time skiers. This they did with flair and aplomb. First-time skiers became second-time and so forth. I'm sure there are thousands of people, who, if they read this, will have fond memories of happy days skiing with the Reps. It was around the late fifties that skiing started to change dramatically. There was more spending power, and flights became available, and travel agents made all arrangements very simple. Ski resorts in the mountains were waiting. They'd been waiting a long time, and were ready and willing. It was in the low countries of Europe and America that this new demand started. In the United Kingdom, new ski clubs sprang up all over the country, and the same thing happened in the USA. The sport of skiing was becoming available to anyone who was prepared to get up and go. With all the clubs, the travel agents, and in the four different countries of the UK, and with the emergence of ski teachers and other fractious persons, it was obvious that some controlling body, or bodies, would need to be established. Easier said than done! The fun was just about to start, and so is the story.

The story starts with the beginning of an enterprise which would organise British Skiing into the future. It would become a challenge for those who would be at the centre of it. I'm sure those who were at the centre knew, and fully understood, what was happening. There were dozens of others who were not so close to the centre, but were contributing in many ways, and without their unstinting endeavours, the work at the centre would certainly have taken much more time to achieve. They possibly never realised just how important a part they played. They who remember being a part of it, should do so with pride.

Here was a first-time, never to be repeated part of the history of skiing in the UK. These are the kind of people who create national bodies and make them work, which in turn are used by beginner ski club skiers, and non-club skiers. "They are about." And in particular, racers of all standards, who in most cases take the organised skiing in all its forms for granted. This is not only the habit of British skiers, it happens all over the world. It is the culmination of a natural chain of events. Racers do this without thinking. This can be understood. From the first stirring of thinking along these lines in the late fifties, it took until 1963 to get it up and going. This may seem a long period of time to have accomplished this, as things are today. Even in hindsight, I'm sure it could not have been done any quicker. In those days, each small club, and the big clubs, held their independence dear. And rightly so. There were other individuals and organisations to be considered, and taken along, with as much harmony as possible. It would become apparent in the years to come, how easy it was to rattle the cages of some of the most mild and tranquil folks on this earth. If they thought the powers that be were in anyway interfering with their rights or privileges, they could, and did, cause Cain. Sometimes not without reason. Out of the needs of events taking place and by common consent the following National Bodies were set up:-

The British Association of Professional Ski Instructors, later to be changed to *The British Association of Ski Instructors*, January 1963.
The Scottish National Ski Council, May 1964.
The National Ski Federation of Great Britain, formed in 1964. Changed to *The British Ski Federation* in 1981.
English, Welsh and Northern Ireland *Ski Councils* were set up at later dates.

It is worth taking a look at the different groups that made up these bodies, remembering that big changes were taking place in skiing all over the world at that time. It was true to say, that most British skiers, at that time, were either professional or business types, and people of reasonable means. This was normal. It was more or less the same in Europe and other countries where skiing was being practised. Even mountain people, if they skied, did it in some form of employment, such as ski teaching, which is work, contrary to common belief. Because you live in the mountains did not make you a skier, nor, for that matter, a climber. This would change as we moved into the early sixties.

Where did British ski teachers come from? I'll tell you how I managed to become one, and, in the process, describe how others did, at about the same time. In the process I will explain the necessary cooperation that took place between full-time skiers, part-time skiers and others.

The story starts for me from a tenement in a north western district of Glasgow, called Maryhill, from where I discovered the completeness of the outdoor life. I would probably have been eleven or twelve. At the same time, many others from Glasgow were finding their way out of the city in different ways. Little did we know, how most of our lives would come together in the future, and lifelong friendships would grow, that would last into the twilight of our lives. Through the district of Maryhill flowed a river called the Kelvin. A lovely name for a river, it was my first river, the first of many to come. It flowed from the northeast to the southwest, where it spilled into the river Clyde at the famous ship building yards at Govan. When I was a boy, the old people of Govan called it Sunny Govan pronounced with a French accent. You can't keep these Glaswegians down! I understand that the first ships built on the Upper Clyde were on the mouth of the Kelvin. The Kelvin river ran from its mouth up through the city for some seven to eight miles to the open country. One of the main features of the Kelvin is that the bed of the river runs deep to the lay of the land, and, as a result, its banks are wooded for most of its course through the city. This was a place for adventure, exploring, and getting into trouble. If your mother knew you had been anywhere near that river, you would have been *in real trouble*! In those days, mothers had their hands full, just running their very poor homes, to have any time to keep their eye on the likes of us!

There was waste effluent flowing into the main stream from paper mills, and other industrial discharges, fouling and polluting to such a degree that it no longer looked like water. It must have been pure poison. No one seemed to know about toxins in those days. On the odd occasions we had a swim. We also swam in the Forth and Clyde canal. Gone are the mills, and the waters are running clearer. I understand the salmon are trying to run back up to their old spawning grounds, as they are now doing in the River Clyde. There's hope for us yet. The banks of the Kelvin look much better now, with the water running cleaner, and they are also physically unchanged, apart from the new richness of the water flow.

There was another, much easier way out of Glasgow. That was by tramcar. But it was by no way as exciting as the river route. The tramcar passed by the street where I lived. It cost three half pennies each way, half fare, in old money. The car terminus was at an old country town called Milngavie. Of all the old country towns that surround Glasgow, Milngavie is most handsome. It is here that the north western highlands of Scotland start to rise up and present to the traveller a delight to be remembered. And also a scene that only improves when you move into the depth of its vastness! The country round Milngavie is delightfully varied. There are farms with open grazing, little rivers, wee burns, streams, lochs, small wild glens, hilly woodlands and, with the Campsie Hills rising above the surrounding landscape, they seem to frame the whole picture as an idyllic place where you could live in complete contentment. Once again, here is another place from my youth that has almost not changed.

From my first early explorations in and around the Kelvin, I eventually found myself in Milngavie. It was in the early years of the 1939-45 war, and during the school holidays. On my first visit, the weather was very warm. It would have been early July. Not far from where the tram stops, a small river, called the Allender, flows by. Within sight of the tram stop, there's a pool in the river. In warm weather, it used to be full of kids swimming in the heat of the day. These would be Glasgow youngsters, even though Glasgow had public baths, at three pence for a half hour. You could swim all day in the Allender for three pence! The difference between the Allender and the Kelvin was that you could more or less drink the Allender water. I wonder if the children still swim in that pool.

As I look back on those few balmy days, in what was probably the last year of my teen age before starting to work, it comes back to me how simple life was in those days. However, what is strong in the memory, was always being hungry. There were no pack lunches nor money to buy food in those days. Shortage of food was something that was present in many of the homes in Glasgow tenements. Not starvation, just plain shortage of food. When we started to work, this improved a little. I'm sure that none of those screaming kids had an idea of the horrors that were happening around the world, under the guise of making this world safer and better for all of us. We would find out in the next few years just what war was all about.

From the swimming, which probably only lasted a few days, I started to wander out into the surrounding countryside. This wandering became a great source of joy, although I don't suppose I would have described it that way when I was thirteen years of age. It became a great need, to be there. Over the next year or so, at every opportunity, the wanderings continued, and, with my wandering, knowledge of the area grew. The discovery of a place the size of a small country, or so it seemed at the time, filled me with wonder. It was different from the paradise that was the Kelvin, confined as it was by a large city. The countryside around Milngavie excited me. It afforded the possibility to range right, left and forward, and to keep doing it. How much bigger things seem to young eyes. In the quiet times of war, the countryside was short of its usual complement of menfolk, therefore it was much more open to people like me to come and go as we pleased.

As I found my way deeper into the Land, and became more intimate and comfortable with the ground, the small secret places gave themselves up to me. Places where you felt at home. Places you felt were *yours*. Places that, when you were there, were yours. I would have been around thirteen when I found my way into this boys' paradise. I learned to camp without tents, to light fires, no matter how heavy the rain, or how wet the wood. I had some cold wet nights before I learned how easy it was to light a fire, to make a shelter, or find one. Learning these skills is an age old process of trial and error. That practice makes perfect. This is something you can learn yourself. I knew deep inside of me that the land must be left as near as possible to how nature means it to be. In so doing, the people who control it may leave you alone. I say people who *control* the land, not *own* it. Much of this was wild land. Many, like myself, sincerely believe wild land should not be owned by any individual. That is not to say it is up for grabs, or that it should be abused in any way. When you think that this wonderful paradise we call the world we were born into, has been raped and pillaged since man started *to get his act in gear*, it is a wonder that little enclaves, as described above, can still exist so close to a town, despite man's rapacious behaviour.

Primitive cooking was learned with whatever food was available, or came to hand. Here was a place for wandering, exploring, and finding out how the real things in this world worked. To be free to enjoy life as it has evolved to be enjoyed. Another skill that came to me, was the ability of keeping out of the way of people who did not want you to be there. This was a skill I acquired quickly, and one I had to use many times since.

It was around this time that Jim and Willie Purves and I met up. Jim was my age, Willie some two years younger. From this meeting grew a lifelong friendship. We lost Willie a while past. Even worse, Jim has been a victim of multiple sclerosis for long years now. The awful tragedy was that Jim, like his brother, was an outstanding hill walker. What a terrible thing for Jim to be confined to a wheelchair. From these weekends in the Milngavie area, we somehow found our way to the south eastern shores of Loch Lomond, to a place called Balmaha. It was here we started the next part of growing up. Loch Lomond was called by weekenders "The Loch." I'm convinced The Loch was one of the most impressive parts of my growing up. If there is any supreme Deity who made this possible, who or whatever that may be, he made one hell of a wonderful job of it!

Jim and I started full-time working when we were fourteen. In those days, it was out of school and into work. Not many tenement boys got to go for further education. It seems a great shame that someone like myself, who had very high marks going into secondary school, could not go on to a better education. But there it is, your *karma*. Even so, life has to be lived as it comes to you. Wasting time bitching about it may well leave you *behind the pack*. Life, as it did come to all of my friends, brought many rewards which bypassed the average person. So, maybe after all, we did get to university, the University of Life. And we should be more than thankful for all the richness of what we have had together, and over long years. Loch Lomond was some playground for growing up in!

Willie, Jim and I probably found our way to the Loch by wandering ever more northward from Milngavie. It would be a natural route to take, if you were looking for newer and more exciting terrain, even if you did not know the Loch was there. If we thought the country north of Milngavie was special, we were to find a dream world, which would make Mark Twain's boyhood on the Mississippi fade into small beer by comparison. As we started to find our way into and through the intricacies of this geographical wonder, we knew, even in our tender years, how lucky we had just become.

To try and describe the beauty of Loch Lomond in any way, has never been done adequately. Leastwise, I have never read anything that comes near to imparting to your imagination what is really there. Even Robert Burns, with all his unbounded talent for using words to please the Scottish ear, never, ever took on Loch Lomond. I have read and listened to poems singing praises to Scotland's other bonnie places. There are few about Loch Lomond. I wonder why. You would need to see Loch Lomond in all its different moods. Summer, winter, storm or calm, or on its very special days, it is special. When you have lived there and seen it at its possible best, you can then start to understand what the Loch is all about. Anyway, I'm not a poet. What I will do is tell you how it appeared to three impressionable young boys, who wanted to believe all they saw straight off!

Balmaha was a small community in a sheltered bay on the south east corner of Loch Lomond. There was an old boatyard belonging to the McFarlanes, who were reputed to be descendents of the local clan. The mouth of the bay is protected by large, long island called Inchcailloch, "Nuns Island" or "Old Woman." Oaks, pines and many other trees indigenous to Scotland, cover the island in luxuriant profusion. It has a sheer cliff, of around eighty feet in height. A climber fell from the top of it and broke his back. He lived to climb again, emigrated to Australia, and prospered. On the west end of the island was a beautiful shallow sandy bay. In the sunlight, when you row into the bay, the golden sand on the bottom can be seen shining back up at you, through the clear water. In the heat of the soft summer day, that is how I remember it the first time I was lucky to be there. It could have been a Pacific atoll. It was on such a day that Jim, Willie and I first landed on the beach, on sandy bay. Looking south and north on that golden day gave you a feeling that you were the first to have stood there. Such is how young heads take to fancy. This would be our first *feel* of the Loch.

It's just about now, in the tale, that we would meet the first of the outstanding characters in our lives, who, without us knowing, introduced us to a clearer way of looking at the world and how to deal with it. To go about explaining what all these completely different men were like is something I will not attempt. That would be a story on its own, the putting of which on paper would take a bold person. A task I'm not even thinking of. What I will do, is give a simple description of some of them. They were all from different parts of the Glasgow area. Most of them had been weekending since before the war, and many made their start during the depression in the mid thirties, when unemployed men went out onto their nearest hills to find some sort of solace from the heartbreak of unpaid idleness. How many did this is unknown. What is known, is that many who did, eventually left their mark on the world, the world being the better for it.

The different groups went under different names. But they were all known as "The Boys." To be called one of The Boys was an accolade. I was proud to become one of The Boys. Most of these men were socialists, and, if not, they were certainly of that persuasion. Their background would be the reason for this, having came from poor housing, and heavy industrial working conditions. The popular press of the time loved to call them "the Red Clydesiders" and they were proud to answer to this. They were not, however, mindless wavers of the Red-Flag. They were too clever and astute for such stupidities. For the most part, they were clear thinkers, and as open minded as their circumstances would allow. It was their sense of justice and fair play which stood out, and their concern for the underdog. That I learned to appreciate. This seems to me to be a by-product of tenement living.

From this group, into society came some very fine men. They all prospered in some of the most varied careers, considering the commonality of their backgrounds. Here is a selection of some of them.

Jock Nimlin

A crane driver from a Govan shipyard. The first man from his background to become famous as a rock climber and mountaineer in Scotland. Many would follow Jock. He wrote about his experiences, and when you read what he had to say, you can almost *feel* what he was talking about.

Back in the middle sixties, Jeanie and I camped next to Jock and his wife, Jenny, in Glenmore campsite. It was the first time I'd had the privilege to have had long conversations with Jock. It was more like listening sessions for me. Over some long wet days and nights, in a caravan, we heard him tell of his memories of his mountain activities. In his fine self educated Scots Burr, as he spoke, you could see the man in his youth. He did a lot of fine things in his life, too numerous to tell here, even if I knew of them. From the cabin of his tall crane in the Govan shipyard, he could see the peaks of his beloved "Arrochar Alps." Can you imagine how he must have felt on the beautiful days, sitting above the appalling noise and pollution, dreaming of where he should have been?

During the last part of Jock's life, he worked for the National Trust for Scotland. This work involved him in moving about in Scotland's fair land. He must have enjoyed that.

6

Sir Robert Grieve

A friend of Jock's, another from the tenements of Glasgow. A university man, our only one. He was an internationally renowned urban planner. The first chairman of the Highlands and Islands Development Board. I always thought how fine a choice he was, to be the first Chairman of a job he so well suited.

Like most of his kind, he was a philosopher, a humanist, who seemed to understand there are others in this world who need consideration. He was a natural raconteur with endless stories. More of Bob later.

Tom Weir

Tommy told me once how he worked as an assistant in a grocer's shop in the north part of Glasgow. Early one morning, for some reason or other, the owner started to remonstrate with Tommy about late coming. Some minutes. He said the boss went so far as to be offensive. Despite the fact Tommy is a Glasgow man, he is, by nature, a mild man. He said that, as the boss kept raving on, he calmly removed the blue stripped apron, folded it carefully and placed it on the shop counter. Then did the same with the white coat.

He then told the upstart what he thought of his behaviour, then told him that he, Tommy, would never, ever work for anyone for the rest of his life. And he never did. Never judge a book by its covers.

He became what you call a "free spirit," doing what he wants. He has climbed all over the world. He is a very well known writer and the darling of the "*Scots Magazine.*" He is one of the knowledgable experts on the mountain geography of Scotland. An honoured man in the Scottish climbing world. From Glasgow's tenements, to a lovely wee village on the shore of Loch Lomond, Gartocharn.

Calum Finlayson

Chief Superintendent of the Glasgow police. He came from the Isle of Skye, as did my grandfather. He was brought up in Glasgow. As you see, he was a very successful policeman. He was in charge of the northern division of Glasgow, Maryhill. With his singing voice came a fine speaking voice, which he used skilfully when telling stories, something he was also good at. A member of the police choir, with these two talents, he was always more than welcome round anyone's campfire. He was always to hand for any friend who needed his special kind of help.

John Kay

A one time design engineer. A man of outstanding intellect, a natural entertainer. A talker of manipulative ability. He had a deep sense of fair play and an understanding of others' needs. He was a devoted communist. He was the chairman of the Scottish Communist Party for a number of years. John is one of the most impressive people I have ever had the pleasure to be with. He definitely was a "Red Clydesider."

Christopher MacGregor Lyons

Chris to his friends. Probably the epitome of "the Clydesider." He worked all his life in John Brown's ship building yard. I think he went to sea as an engineer for a short period of time. He worked on the Queen Mary, the Queen Elizabeth and

7

the QE2. He was a ship's engineer. During the latter part of his working life in charge of all the labourers in Browns, a tougher job it would be hard to think of, with three hundred-odd unskilled workers. Three hundred "Red Clydesiders," and women amongst them. He was the greatest hustler I've ever seen in action. He was also a powerhouse at any kind of work. As a poet he has written a history of the Glencoe Ski Club. A fine teller of stories. We will hear of Chris later.

Peter McGeogh

From the same background as the others, made his career in engineering. Became the managing director of a chain-making firm that had factories in Glasgow, the Midlands, and America. He became the Scottish *Hornet* sailing champion at over forty years of age. I understand this was an achievement. I have skied with Peter on many occasions. He was never short of guts. A little short on skiing ability, but that was all.

Once skiing became organised, Peter became the independent chairman of an important national body called The British Ski Instruction Council. This body's task was to keep the peace among those of us who were involved in ski instruction. Jesus could not have kept the peace. Peter did a very good job. He carried this off with consummate skill, while dealing with some of the most difficult people in the world. I was one of them. Some of us were a bundle of trouble. Watching Peter dealing with some of the outrageous behaviour was classic, and very educational.

I've highlighted these extraordinary men to let readers know a little of the type of people who helped create the physical and intellectual climate in which we all thrived. Many more made up and contributed to all the different fabrics that made weekends so important to us. They will come into play as the story grows. Now we had discovered the Loch, we started to explore it. If you can think of how it looked to our eager young eyes, it being there, the size of it. An almost empty place, apart from around the town of Balloch, the Loch has very few houses. The hills on the west and east rise up quickly, they are covered with Oak, Birch and in places some imported Spruce. The peaks above the tree line run north, the Loch narrows, and with this it becomes like a heavily timbered gorge. Where the river Falloch runs into the Loch, the road starts to climb quickly up onto the high moorland above. The waters of the Loch are some 22 miles north to south. The wide part in the south is around 7 miles. In the narrows, below Ben Lomond, the water is around 550-odd feet deep. There are some fifty islands and islets. There's farming on two of the bigger ones. Yew trees grow on the island of Inchlonaig. It is said they were planted by some ancient Scottish king, the reason being that never in the years to come would Scottish archers be short of Yew for their bows again. I have a fondness for reading British history, in particularly Scottish history, but I've never got the impression that Scottish kings gave much thought to the future of their "poor wee" country. However, mountain countries all over the world are good at producing similar wee *folklore gems*.

Our first weekend wanderings on the Loch were up from Balmaha to a sandy bay with good camping. This got our first attentions. Farther up, the shore is steeper and rockier. In times earlier some of the worthies I've been speaking about had dug out in these high banks, making cave-like overhanging shelters. Talk about Mark Twain! On many splendid nights, in the pouring rain round roaring fires, we sat listening to these old Clydesiders curing the world of all its strife and troubles. With eyes wide and ears open, we sat and heard the saviours of the world explaining how easy they could undo all the unfairness and injustices that take place in the name of humanity every day. The detailed measures that would be taken were explained. It was simple. I for one, with the wisdom of my fourteen years, approved with all that was said. The "sicking world" has lasted well. We must have got it wrong. It's a fine thing to be young.

Years later, I learned that some of these men had been in the International Brigade, during the Spanish Civil War. Now that was putting yourself where your mouth was! In 1950 I met one of them who was not long released from a Spanish Algerian prison. He was a sad man, and he did not look too well. I do remember his spirit, and the look of compassion in his eyes. He did not live long after that. These men were talkers, but, as you see, some were doers. Camp fires like these were not too common, probably three or four, and they seemed to be used by different groups as if by arrangement. There was never any dispute about who used these camp sites. They also moved about on the weekends to other parts of the Highland area, where they had other established camp sites. It would appear that things worked out.

There was one exception to this. One group, who went by the name of the Barroom Mountaineers, seemed to have a site to themselves. They were in age a bit older than the others, and their unelected leader was an imposing figure of a man. Tall, in a society which tended, at the time, to produce smallish men. He was a blacksmith by trade, a poet and song writer by nature and choice. His name was David R. Clark. In a forest full of tall trees, he stood tall. By pure chance I have a self handwritten copy of some of his work. It is dedicated to Frank Galbraith, his friend. Here is the dedication...

A bottle for this book you said
I'll hold you to the letter
And if the whisky's bad my lad
You'll find the book's no better.

It seems that societies like these have a habit of producing folklore poet types such as Big Davie Clark, who are capable of expressing the innermost thoughts of how the whole of their society feel about the culture they live in. There was singing of songs, old favourite's like *"The Red Flag"* and *"When The Don Bas was Raided."* Songs of rebellion seemed to be the in thing in our youth. Resistance to the Establishment is still here, it's more subtle and sophisticated. I never really understood, at the time, what prompted this powerful fervour, I only wanted to be there, with these strong men. It was in the years coming, when the world and its problems started to press on me, that I began to realise there were reasons for these sentiments, that helped create the use of these nationalist songs. On reflection, listeners to songs take from them what they think they need! We had singers who could sing the Scottish songs so well, they could *wring the tears out of your working jacket.* Such were their talents.

Lady readers may ask, "where were the girls?" Well, there were not many about in 1943. I think it was considered *infra dig* for girls to go camping with boys in those days! It was also a male world, the words "male chauvinist" were not in vogue, and the powerful force of chauvinism was accepted as a correct concept we lived by in our everyday lives. I never ever saw the right of it. As the

9

number of weekenders grew after the war, so did the number of females. There were couples weekending. On looking around all of those couples seemed to have got married.

It took our little band quite a few weekends to find our way in and out and around our new fiefdom. This we established about two miles north of Balmaha. We made a marvellous wee camp just up from the shore, in a broad wooded gully, with a nice burn running by. We made shelter from a tarpaulin we nipped off one of the temporary ammunition dumps that were scattered through the Trossachs and the lochside at the time. Always build with local material! We were in the Oak woods, and there was ample windfall wood for fires. Oak makes good, long burning fires. If you're a real weekender, you call the firewood "timber." You had to get the jargon right! That was us fixed for the coming winter. And as Burns said to the mouse, as he his ploughed the field...

An' weary Winter coming fast,
An' cozie here, beneath the blast,
Thou thought to dwell.

Well, like the mouse, we were fixed for the coming blast. Unlike the mouse, we kept our shelter. And the "establishment" had accepted us as being part of "The Boys." We felt terrific! Independent, grown up.

You may wonder why the powers that be left these merry wanderers alone. It was simple. This is a sparsely populated area, and, with the war, the younger men would be off doing their bit. So, there were no able bodied men to disturb us. Once in blue moon, a patrol boat from McFarlane's boatyard, with a searchlight, would patrol up the shoreline, with a loud-hailer complaining about the lights of the campfires. Nobody bothered. I'm sure it was part of the local Dad's Army. They most certainly knew who we all were.

A Stirling bomber, coming back from a raid on Europe, crashed on the hill, high above where we camped. I remember as we walked up to take a look at what it was all about, rain pouring down, the midges out in force, and, in the distance, we saw this group coming down towards us. It turned out to be the recovery team, later to be the RAF Mountain Rescue Team. I would never have thought, at the time, how much of their work I would see in the long years coming. The recovery team were carrying the bodies of the bomber's crew. The pathos of the moment, the awfulness of the weather, the quietness of the team carrying the remains of the crew. Some of that crew would not be much older than we were. As Marlene Dietrich sings in her famous song, *"When will we ever learn?"* The plane was in bits in the peat of the bog. The tail was the only part of the plane in one piece. The scene is clear to me now. The Browning machine guns had been removed. I wondered, at the time, what was the importance of the reason for this. Strange, the thinkings of the youthful mind.

Our first winter was a rich and wonderful experience. It seemed to me, through the memory of my rose tinted spectacles, to have been cold and snowy the winter long. Probably like in northern Canada. During the cold of the long winter night, with our oaken fire burning all night, keeping us snug in our shelter, we were in a dreamland just made for 14 year olds. It was a great gut satisfying feeling. Something I still get today, when the moments are right.

Early on a cold clear crystal winter morning, standing by the lochside, the Loch was like a burnished mirror. There was no movement in the air. It was then

I had one of the many joys of my life. I heard pipes start up and play a lament. The music came out of the islands on the west side of the Loch. As music drifted about in the air, it created a sensation of completeness to the whole scene. Not long after this event, I saw a film. In the film, that fine actor Harry Andrews had a line, "I'm sorry for a man who hears the pipes and is'na born a Scot." I feel that way myself!

That spring, we took to the boats. The boats were the key to the Loch for us. The boats let us find our way into the heart of the Loch and its islands. Without these, it would be more or less a great screed of water. Instead, it has many lovely islands of all different shapes and sizes. Many are timbered. Near to Luss, four large islands form a beautiful lagoon-like anchorage. This is a sheltered haven that can be seen from the main road north. The Loch, with its size, and the variety of its geography, must be unique in the UK, so that, within its shores, on the islands and its waters, it can present to you all the joys and pleasures that much larger land masses would find it hard to match. Around this time, Ian Alan joined up with us. He was Willie's age. A big, strong, wilful boy of reckless courage, much more grown up for his age than was normal for those times. I did my first climbing with Ian. Ian was of the same way of thinking as ourselves, so we all got on well together. Ian died in a very long fall on the Buachaille Etive Mor in Glencoe, in 1949. At the time I was serving in the army in Malaya. From time to time, others joined up with us, and this made the hire of the boat cheaper for us. These rowing boats were from MacFarlanes. They cost eight shillings a weekend. Weekends started on Saturday afternoons. No five day week in those days! We used to row long distances. We would have four oars, and a half oar for a tiller. We became skilful in handling the boats. Because of the late starts on the Saturdays, we would have to row often at night, sometimes in pitch darkness. No compasses, we seemed to manage by feel. No life jackets, we even kept our heavy boots on. The inane stupidity of youth takes some believing. We were to find out later, just how clever we were *not*.

After some long pulls up the Loch, the pulls became something we learned to enjoy the physical challenge of. During the rowing, we would we sing rowing songs and songs suitable for rowing. The man on the tiller would call the beat. On clear or storm blown nights, the challenge was constant. It was the boat, the Loch, and us for it. There are goals to be had in all endeavours. At the end of the pull, the reward was the landing, the lighting the fire, and the warmth of the camaraderie round the fire in the cooking of the meal. You couldn't buy this with a fist-full of dollars! On the rainy nights, of which there were many, we would pull the boat up on the shore, prop it up on its side, and light the fire beside it as a real good shelter. On clear nights, we'd sleep round the fire in our sleeping bags. Great nights, wet or clear. On clear calm mornings, the Loch has to be seen to be believed and, I would say, the winter scene had the edge on the summer.

There was a wee cracker of an island called Buck Inch. It was about three hundred yards across. It stuck its head out of the Loch around fifty feet, and was covered with Pines. A fisherman's hut, with an external veranda, sat on its south shore. We had good nights under that veranda.

Not far from Buck Inch was the island of the Yew trees, by the name of Inchlonaig. Red deer used to swim over to it in winter. Some trees grew onto the shore line. We camped under one, a big old thing that graced the campsite and gave it the feel of permanence. I don't know if any of the Yew wood ever became bows! I do know we burnt some of its dead branches and, like all of the old hard wood, it burned well. Being a hopeless romantic, I thought of those French Canadian Voyagers of the seventeenth century, with all that northern wilderness, to range and wander in. How free they must have felt, how fulfilled and contented on those dreamy campfire nights, and long exciting days of complete freedom, wandering free. That is exactly how we felt. When you think we were only a little more than an hour and a half from the city of Glasgow, and here we were having experiences certainly similar to those Voyagers of old! That is the Loch at its most benign. Here is another side of the Loch's nature and of young boys with a bent to natural stupidity.

On a stormy winter weekend in 1946, we decided on a long row up to Inverbeg. This is some twelve miles from Balmaha on the Loch's west side. It's a small steading at the mouth of Glen Douglas. We had decided to spread our wings and camp the night, then row back in the morning. The weather was not too good. So what! With being good at rowing, and fireproof, the weather made no difference to us. We had a man in the boat who had crippled legs. This made walking very difficult, but sitting in the narrow bow of the boat with his powerful upper body he could pull on two oars all day. He was peerless. We shall call him Bow Man. It would be worth looking at the map of Loch Lomond to see the lay of the land, as this would let you see what was involved. We rowed up through islands, past the village Luss, where the TV soap *Take the High Road* is filmed. The rowing was hard, and, with big waves and heavy rain, we reached the lee of the west shore, where the comparative calm made the going easy, and the spirits rose. We camped at the mouth of the River Douglas. The big mistake was next morning, when we messed about round the fire, so we never left till after noontime. By the time we left, the wind was making up from the west, as it has the habit of doing. Down in the lee of the west shore was easy. We started our crossing from near to Luss. It so happened I was on the tiller. As the boat came round on its new course, we found the wind, and, with the wind, came big waves. Down out of Glen Luss it came, venting through the narrow mouth of the Glen, as if it were coming for us personally. I turned the boat east on the shortest distance to the other side. The boat was now running before the weather, and it seemed to us that the weather could bring the water into the boat. We put two rucksacks and a groundsheet as a wave-break. This made us feel more secure. Without this, I'm sure we could have taken the deep six. What did help, was the three good oarsmen, two in the middle and the cripple in the bow. The oars gave us the feeling we could handle the power of water, and had something going for us. As we came into the shore, the boat grounded and filled with water. All able bodied men ashore! The Bow Man went ashore in style, as he had to be carried. There is no way he could have made it on his own. We got the rucksacks out and the boat up onto the shore, clear of the waves. I wonder where the Bow Man is today. We still had a good couple of *Scotch country miles* to go for the bus and we covered this at a jog-trot, eating raw kippers and taking turns, two at a time, more or less carrying the Bow Man. He earned his carry by the way he had pulled his two oars! I suppose we were quite pleased with ourselves. McFarlane got his boat back, eventually. We lost our deposit. A lot more could have been lost than ten bob. But that's what life is all about!

There would be many times, in the years to come, when, with close friends, we would be faced with what can only be called "moments of danger." These would come, almost without exception, on the mountains. These happenings did not in any way worry us, or make us change the paths we had chosen. It is later, in moments of reflection, when you look back, such as for the purpose of writing this, or for whatever other reason, you may be forced to analyse the importance of these peaks of adventure in life. If there was danger, so what! That is all very much a part of the whole enterprise. I know for sure, I never did anything for the danger. The graveyards have many residents who pulled that one too often. Like most human enterprises in the outdoors, tragedy can occur. Not long after this, we lost two friends one night, from a canoe. It's a wonder there were so few accidents. No life-jackets, no head protection for climbers or motor-bikers. And no one gave a damn.

Before we move on from Loch Lomond, I would like to comment on how fortunate our small band had been, in finding our way into this boys' paradise, at a time when you could, without halt or hindrance, use the quiet peacefulness of its moods of weather. The way the seasons change, so subtly, made its environs so desirable to be in. All but the southern side of the Loch are encompassed by wild mountainous terrain. In the west are great sea lochs, and in the east are many freshwater lochs, some of which are large by most standards. The northern end of the Loch reaches into the lower half of the western Highlands. All of this country in sparsely populated. This is where we ventured, as curiosity got us on the move again. We were in no way abandoning our beloved Loch.

Aberfoyle, in the Trossachs, was our next venture. It was here we saw our first climbers. We were sixteen at the time, and most impressionable. The climbers were older and they were bigger. Their boots had steel nails round the soles, and big ropes hung from their rucksacks. They looked different. They looked confident. To us, they looked *terrific*. We found our way to a famous wee rock peak, by the name of Ben A'nn. You could camp high up, right under the climbs, and light fires (important to us, as we had not yet got Primus stoves). On its rock faces are shortish climbs, to suit all climbers. Here is an excellent place for beginners. Not only do you have short simple climbs that go all the way up the scale of difficulty. The last climb ends on the summit. A nice touch to finish on. Here we met and spoke to some real climbers, and, of all things, we met the climber who fell off the island on Loch Lomond. He was called Jimmy Strachan. He climbed with Bob Cathcart and Jim Jackson. Jim and I would become very close friends. There were others climbers on the hill. It was so very easy to fit into this society of what turned out to be an elite part of the climbing world. Jim Jackson took an interest in us and it was suggested we come and climb on the Cobbler at Arrochar the following weekend. Arrochar, a village at the head of the sea loch, Loch Long, is some two miles from Loch Lomond. A story goes that, in the Viking times, a longboat sailed up Loch Long. The Viking boatmen pulled the longboat over to Loch Lomond on rollers, and proceeded to sail round the Loch, raping and pillaging. The pickings must have been very slim in those days.

The following weekend saw the rain bouncing off the pavements in Arrochar. All was not lost, as our mighty leader had a first reserve up his sleeve. The caves in Glen Lyon. Our disappointment turned into delighted amazement. The caves were wonderful! They were obviously the remnants of what had been an ancient cliff, or large buttress, broken down by natural processes, leaving a number of cave-like chambers, which made fine shelters. These caves were some 500 feet above Glen Lyon, and, when you stood looking down over the glen, you felt good. You felt secure when you saw the glen laid out below. It's always a fine feeling, when you look down off a high mountain place. The caves were located among the massive blocks and small rock faces. Some of them had names like the "Star Chamber," and the "Lomonds." This was called after the Lomonds Mountaineering Club, who made the most use of it. If others knew the Lomonds were coming up, they would leave it free. That's how things were done in those days. Our first night was in the Star Chamber, with a big fire, the rain pouring outside, adding to this fairy place. The talk round the fire was naturally led by the older ones. This was all right with us. Another *Shangrila*. We'd done it again, we were in! Men could never have created a place like this. It was a gift of nature. Here was shelter in a situation which suited the way we wanted to commune with each other. There would be few places in the country where people were passing their time as we were. What man did manage to do in and around this beautiful glen was as follows.

The whole area around the Caves was cloaked in a lovely stand of native oak trees. They were old enough to have trunks two feet in diameter. In their location, they made a beautiful picture. In 1950 the Forestry Commission planted over the whole area with Norway spruce. Then, in their effort to encourage the growth of the spruce, they "ring-barked" all the standing oaks. Hundreds and hundreds of trees. It was sickening to look at. You would have thought they'd have left the old oaks to take their chance among the spruce. I'm sure that when the spruce were cropped, the oaks would still be standing amidst the debris of harvesting. Shortly after this criminal vandalism had taken place, a group of us were making our way up through the ruined oaks to climb. We were accosted by two forestry workers in a most offensive manner. In normal circumstances this would not have gone down too well. But here, amid the destruction of the oaks, was not the place for them to be giving us lectures about doing damage to the environment. We made it clear to these two what we thought of the methods used by the Forestry to get what they thought was success. This went right over their heads. Private estates would never have been so uselessly stupid.

Big Strachan introduced us to abseiling, "sliding down a rope under control." This is a method used for escaping quickly off long cliffs. There was an old Rowan growing right out of the lip of a 70 foot overhang. When beginners learn abseiling, they start on slabs. Not us, we started at the deep end, or should I say, the top end! Strachan, our mentor, started us off the Rowan gibbet. Getting off that gibbet when you are a beginner is not too easy, if you are honest with yourself. But the Piper must be paid! Big Strachan was the Piper. He helped me with my first abseil. Once you get your first one over, you can't get enough! That was my first introduction to the technical side of climbing.

It was round about this time the Purves's decided that climbing was not for them, and, as a consequence, our weekending together dropped off. We stayed lifelong friends and the future saw to it that we would have many more wonderfully exciting times together, as you will hear. Around this time, Blackie Currie joined us. His hair was jet black and curly. A man of short and quick temper. Highly intelligent, he was a friend to be trusted. A plumber by trade and Communist by conviction, which he kept private to himself. It never bothered any of us. None of the rest of us thought much about those things. We were too busy trying to dodge working, in our effort to get more time on the hills. Blackie went to America, where he was a "money success." He seemed to hold true to these political values. This said a lot for him, during the years of the McCarthy stupidities. He was a "closet Commie." If you do not allow free speech, you tend to get people being secretive about what they believe. They will not give up their right to think. Not the best way to run any society, communist or democratic! Ideology seems to cloud our minds at times, and makes us behave in the most perverse ways, and do things that are not really us. Blackie was a very complex man. When I look back at his many talents, I'm sure climbing would not have been one of them. Maybe, like the rest of life, it would not have been complicated enough for his way of thinking. He is someone who always comes back to my mind when I think of those early days, when we were starting to learn to think, which I'm sure effects some of our behaviour today. We lost Blackie some years ago.

Before leaving the Caves, I'd like to take you over across the Glen, about a quarter of a mile, to a glade of trees called The Pines. They really were Larches. Despite all the street wisdom of the weekenders, we called them The Pines. It was years later we learned the difference. These trees were magnificent giants of their kind, in their full grown glory. We used to camp up here in off weekends. We would light big fires under the tall trees and look across to the Caves. The was a fair sized cave above the campsite, where, on wet nights, you could set a fire and sit in comfort, and look out into the downpours, which could be considerable, on our west coast. How these great trees survived through the war was a mystery. Maybe, hiding up that glen, they escaped notice. They are gone now. I have never seen the site since, and I prefer the memory. We know that, in the modern world, trees become a crop, when full grown. At least the Larches were full-grown, unlike the Oak trees on the other side of the glen. The people of the west coast of Scotland have the gift of taking moments of sadness, and, with words, turning them into songs of nostalgic beauty. To quote two lines from one of them:-

Oh gone alas are my joys for ever,
like bubbles bursting on yonder river.

The bubbles will be back on the river before the Larches. But, in truth, I'm sure those Larches were man planted. This is how people like us feel about the wild places. Though it would be unseemly to say it to each other. I'm proud to say we still have many, many places like this is Scotland. So here we were, two miles from Loch Lomond, within one mile of the Cobbler, the Caves, and the Pines. Not bad, so near to Glasgow.

None of us knew it at the time, but we were about to embark on a path which would last for the rest of our days. The companions we would share these times with are special. We'd weekend, climb, ski, and sometimes work together, as the years grew in number. There were times when sadnesses would be shared by all of us. Some of the group would be larger than life, some smaller, or just plain normal. Best of all, we shared these common interests, which has kept us all friends over the long years, from then until these present days.

The Climbing and some of what it taught us.

Climbing. We were to learn rapidly just how hard a task master climbing and its demands could be. We found there were ground rules. These rules work the same for all. Also, that no one man made the rules. I would imagine the demands of the beast that is climbing, made the rules, those being:-

15

The difficulty of the places and the terrain, where climbing takes place.
The fitness you needed, to take you to the hills.
The weather and your personal attitude was of great importance, all to be
learned the hard way.

We had our baptism in finding out what this meant, on that first night, padding up to the Caves through the pouring rain, behind Jackson and Strachan. We had been in the pub in Arrochar, all nice and cosy. Then it was out into the west coast rain. You have to have carried a pack up a hillside in these conditions to know that gritting your teeth is not much help. Getting used to being in the harness comes first.

As we set off in the dark, heading for Glen Lyon, it was the impact of the pace that the climbers set, that I remember. The pace did not slacken as we got onto the steep path up to the Caves. I'm sure the pace picked up as the ground got rougher, and you were worried stiff that you could not keep up with these animals that were screwing you into the ground. In your efforts to be a big strong man, you knocked lumps out of yourself. As a result, you became over stressed "between the ears," quite unnecessarily. That's your first lesson. The way to handle the fatigue, is to "keep the heid," and you will come through the pain barrier! After all, the others are going through the same thing. You find out later that it's a matter of getting used to it. One of the unspoken rules is that you don't drop out. Drop behind, and you can catch up later and be none the worse for it. This hang-in attitude would stand you in good stead in times to come. You kept up for yourself. No one told you there was a reason. If you had to be told, you were in the wrong place.

We learned, as time went by, that the standards we seemed to work with were a by-product of our own unwitting efforts to do things well. There were no tests, no examinations. If the will was there, you were there. No medals, no prizes, nobody to say how good you were. Membership by choice. The cost? Total effort, good or bad. And I can't recall anyone dropping out. It must be presumed that what has been said above had a direct bearing on the actual climbing of those who stayed with climbing. Such preparation could only have a good effect on the ultimate performances of people so conditioned, as the years coming would show, by producing some very fine climbers from this country. In the time I speak of, climbing was rock, snow and ice. They were, for the most part, summer and winter pursuits. The climbing part of the whole enterprise is where your personal endeavour had to be of the highest order, if you hoped to achieve. You almost always had a partner, whose safety at all times depended on you. And yours on the partner. This is seldom a solo pastime. The very nature of the beast ensured that you gave it your respect at all times. Many well known Scottish skiers came out of this background.

You hear a lot of talk of the dangers of the mountains. Mountains only become dangerous to us when we start to use them for our pleasure. For centuries man has worked and raised stock on mountains, and managed without bothering too many people. The trouble starts when man, (I say "man" because it's usually the male of the species who upsets the apple-cart), attempts to stretch the physical bounds, which tend to rule in these high places, where life, at best, is on the margin. Nature, in all its inanimate power, is there when you make your mistake, and then the laws of nature come into play. And you may have to "pay the final piper." Somewhere inside all of us, there's a primitive force to pace us towards goals that seem futile to the average way of thinking. If so, I'm sure the interest it creates is certainly worth the little trouble it may cause. I have just used the phrase "little trouble"- a little understatement!

Rescues in this country are carried out by local mountain rescue teams, whose members are certainly all mountain lovers. You don't hear them bitching about restricting people going to the mountains. I know for sure, that mountain types seldom have any trouble with the rest of society. It goes without saying, that youngsters, who find their way into the hills, are so tied up with their good luck, they've no time to find trouble. Earlier, I used the word "mistake," when accidents happen on mountains. It is almost certainly caused by human error, negligence, or a little carelessness. After it happens, it doesn't matter. Most accidents are very serious. Not many minor mishaps take place on steep hills. There are also the real bad luck happenings. You've done every thing to the book, and you still have trouble. Here are two different examples.

Ian Alan and I were winter climbing on a ridge close to the Cobbler, in January 1946. Our equipment was as follows. Woollen mitts, I had my working boots, Ian had dug up a pair of old climbing boots, (the fact they were too big for him never kept his head down to its correct size), and home-made anoraks. But the crowning glory must have been the First World War puttees wound all the way up to our knees! We actually used these for walking, and where we got them from is a mystery. My ice axe was home-made in the shipyards. Also from the yards, was our 100 feet of creosoted "climbing rope." It stunk! If, by chance, we had been lost, (which was on the cards), all the rescuers would have needed to do, was to follow the brown creosote marks in the snow! Snow conditions were good, but the visibility was zero. We had, of course, no compasses. If we had, we would not have known how to use them properly. Otherwise, we were fully equipped. The only solid thing about us would have been our enthusiasm.

We had been up here with the Big Boys the weekend before, so we knew our way about! What we did know was that a steep face was close by. We had seen, in an old climbing book, how you should rope up and belay in difficult terrain, etc. This we duly did, I'm glad to say. Ian was belaying me, as I aggressively moved forward. Before I could do anything, I was dropping. The drop was arrested by the shipyard rope, creosote and all. Classic stuff! After a bit of shouting, to see how we were all fixed, I climbed with the aid of the rope back up to Ian. We were chuffed with ourselves! This was how it was done! After this, we made our way down to the bottom of this wee broken cliff that caused the mishap, and proceeded to climb a nice steep cut, that took us back up. If I remember, we called this short climb "Avalanche Gully." Thinking back on that incident, makes it impossible for me to remark, on how young people of today go about taking their pleasures on the hills. Mind you, the shipyard rope was well utilised.

This next episode happened in early April of the same year. Ian Alan, the Purves and myself were taking a good pad. A "pad" is the jargon for a "long walk" The walk starts in the lovely town of Callander, up north through Bonnie Strathyre, past Kingshouse, then Balquhidder, where we slept out round a fire on Saturday night. On Sunday morning, when we left, the weather was glorious. The route was through the large, empty Glen Finglas. It's not empty now. They flooded it to help supplement Glasgow's water supply. There was no shelter in this glen. The walking is straight forward, up and over into the head of the

Finglas. The highest hills around here are about 2,500 feet. The fine weather made for easy walking. As we were crossing over the watershed to the heads of Glen Finglas, from out of nowhere, the sky seemed to go as black as the Pits of Hell. With the blackness came the cold wind that precedes these quick flash storms. From a beautiful spring day into the winter. And, with our "Auld Enemy" the wind, came snow to keep it company. Since then, and in all these years, the wind has been a pain in the arse! I have to put up with it. This was my first big storm, with wind and snow, so it sticks in my mind. From the flat calm to a hellish howling vortex. Walking became more than difficult, and something told us this could not go on. There was no discussion. We moved as one down into the bed of the young river Finglas, that lay below the surrounding hillside. Here, nature was good to us. In a treeless land we found a Mountain Rowan, sometimes called the Mountain Ash.

There was a famous writer, called Robert Service. He wrote about the Yukon, in northwest Canada, during the gold strikes. Born in Preston, England, and educated in Hillhead, Glasgow, he wrote of miners and trappers. One of his excellent short stories was called "To Light a Fire." He tells of a miner who, when he was walking over to the next valley, in temperatures of under 50 below, was followed by a dog. As he walked, it got colder. It got so cold he knew he had to "make a fire." The message of the story is that he never made his fire. The end is that he never got to the next valley. We decided to "make a fire." To make a fire in these conditions was no mean feat. The fire got going, but it took the sacrifice of two oilskin coats as firelighters. A crime! Man-made fire lighters! This was beyond the pale! We kept the fire going through the night with the living branches of the Rowan. No matter the awful wetness of the camp, the fire, as usual, was man's friend.

Before dawn, the wind, the bane of the mountain traveller, had gone. It left in its place, a majestic silence, that often follows a storm. The snow cover left by the storm reflected the starlight of the night's end. The combination of this natural phenomenon, seemed to prolong the coming of the new day. Even in our youth, we were deeply affected. No one moved about much, and the usual banter was absent. When you thought of the terrible world nature had just shown us, it was as if to say, this is also nature. Time, it seemed, had stopped. How fortunate to have experienced so much in so little a period of time, and to be so young in the seeing of it. As the euphoria wore off, we saw what we had done to the Rowan. In our need for a fire, we had destroyed a thing of beauty. It stood in the fresh pristine newness of the coming day, stripped bare, naked. It stood out black and ugly. If this was a picture, the caption could have read, "man was here." However, nature, in its usual charity, in the coming spring, would start to repair the damage of our dreadful act. And the Rowan would be green again. Unlike the trapper, we made our "fire." Even though, we still had a very long walk to Aberfoyle. The food was finished, and we had little money between us. What was new!

These are two good examples of what can happen to people who go to the mountains for pleasure. The first escapade was on the high tops, where danger is ever present, particularly in the winter. The second started as a simple hillwalk and, I'm glad to say, ended up as it did. We would have many more rich experiences like these in the years to follow. People with long years of going to the hills, know that experience, plus reasonably good behaviour on the hills, will keep you safe. *Plus a good chunk of luck!*

So far, these are two of the more memorable steps in our becoming *journeymen*. Anyone who says we were lucky to be so young, and had such a good start in this wonderful way of life, is right. It would also be right to say to say that no one gave us this opportunity. We made it ourselves. While we doing our thing, other small groups from Glasgow, Edinburgh and Aberdeen were doing the same things. Northern cities in England had similar groups. You would wonder what would trigger these spontaneous events in the different locations!

Anyway, here's a humorous cheeky ending to this expedition. After the long, hungry walk to Aberfoyle, we found we had missed the bus back to Glasgow, and the next bus was late that night. The trains still ran from Aberfoyle to Glasgow. There was one ready to leave, and we decided to jump on the train as it was leaving the station, and worry about the tickets at the other end. This we did. After all, we had pulled many better stunts in our time! The train got a mile or so down the line, stopped, and reversed back into the station, where we were duly pulled off and ejected into the street in Aberfoyle. The gross indignity! You win some, you lose some! We got the late bus back through Callander and from there to Stirling. We gave the conductress our wee story, and how hungry we were, and how we hadn't really eaten since the storm. The soft hearted Angel gave us sixpence each to buy chips from the chipper in Stirling. You got a awful lot of chips in those days for a tanner!

At the same time as you got a lot of chips for a tanner, the industrial cities still suffered from the terrible fogs. As the bus got nearer to Glasgow, we ran into one of these. It was a very heavy one. After the weekend we had just "enjoyed," all we needed was a week of fog, before we could escape again! Most of us would eventually escape permanently, and live in places of our choosing, where you would wake each morning knowing how well you had done! I'm delighted to say, weekends like this are still being enjoyed by friends of mine, who still live in "the Big Smoke." They are also yet available to those who may want them. And they are free.

To finish this part of the story, I should tell you of our next adventure. In the UK climbing world there are climbing Meccas in Scotland. There is Glencoe, Ben Nevis, and the Cuillins on the Isle of Skye. In England there's the Lake District. And North Wales. In the Easter of 1947, we planned a weekend on Ben Nevis. As I have explained, travel was difficult, but we had *an ace-in-the-hole*. Big Jim Purves worked on the railway. He acquired privilege tickets for us, and these very reduced priced tickets made it possible for us to go, otherwise none of us could have afforded the trip. The Purves's were making the trip for the hill walking. Blackie, Ian Alan and I were the climbers! I did mention, early on, that weekending was male dominated. It was. Well, in our case, the ladies had arrived! There was Suzy Newlands and Jeanie Irvin Neilson. Jeanie and I have been married since 1951.

This trip was a tremendous event for us. It was like going abroad. The rail trip was up through Stirling, Callander, Tyndrum, the Pass of Brander, to the west coast up past Benderloch, through Morven then to Fort William. What a journey! You can't do it now. Part of the line has been lifted. The countryside is still there and unchanged. You can drive, or, better still, you could walk. It is

19

certainly a match for the West Highland Way. Unfortunately, that Easter the Scottish weather was shocking. Our friend the wind, with its companion the rain at eighty miles an hour, came boring down Glen Nevis, and made our wee tents a poor place to cook in, far less sleep in. We got into the big Achentee barn in Glen Nevis. In weather like that, it was better than the Dorchester! There was no climbing on Nevis that weekend.

In the barn were other young people like ourselves, who were finding their way into the climbing world. They were some of the Glasgow Craig Dhu Club. I met John Cunningham for the first time. In years to come, John become a dear personal friend to our family. To his own credit he would become one of the foremost rock and ice men of the 50s, 60s, and 70s. He made some epic dog sledge journeys in Antarctica, for which he was awarded the Polar Star and the Perry Medal. Not many have achieved those two distinctions. Later on, John would partner up with Willie Smith. Between them, for some fifteen or more years, they took the accepted standards of the day, and raised them in quite a dramatic way. John died saving the lives of two of his climbing students. The irony of it was, the accident took place on a sea cliff. John was never found. This was a terrible loss to all of us. There were others in the club, who climbed more or less to the same standard. But John and Willie always seemed to set the pace, as the Glencoe guide book will show. Willie might agree that he is a taciturn kind of a person at times, yet, at all times, more than able to be articulate in the most lucid and humorous way. I have never met anyone who had anything but the deepest respect for Big Willie. And he is very much a part of this story.

At the same time as John and Willie were setting the pace for the new standards being established in Scotland, Joe Brown and Don Willans, from Manchester, were doing the same thing in the Lake District and in Wales. This just seemed to be a natural train of events. It is possible the five year gap of the war let these events take place simultaneously. It so happened I gave Joe his first ski lesson on Cairngorm. I don't know if he pursued skiing, but he most certainly had a good talent for it. When I think back to that weekend, when we never got to climb Nevis, what an impertinence! We never even had a guide book, our equipment was a joke, and the only thing of quality we had was our youth, confidence and bravado! I never got back to Nevis until 1954.

Climbing and skiing up to the 1950s was pursued by a small section of the UK population. However, tremendous changes were about to take place. These changes would, in time, be important to a very diverse cross-section of the country's active types, the *get-up-and-go-and-take-it* types. The fertile grey area left between the war and the recovery years, must have stored a human energy-field that, having been held in check for a long number of years, when it went, went with a *bang!*

The changes we were experiencing were taking place in the rest of the western world. These changes would open up a new world of physical and intellectual opportunities for all of the country's population. Hitherto they would have had little chance of participating fully in them and therefore, never able to produce their full potential. Those days are gone, to the good and betterment of climbers and skiers everywhere. This new set of circumstances helped in the of mixing of all the cultures from within the UK, and, as a result, it most certainly enriched the lives of those who enjoyed being part of it. At first, most people involved would not see what was taking place. How could they, the results were

20

not yet there to be seen! I know, from my own part in this evolutionary process, that it was years later before it came to me. In this I was lucky, because I was all the time in the middle of the national bodies, which were blessed with some of the finest people, from all possible walks of life, who were working like pioneers, breaking new ground. What adventurous times we all had together! When the growth of skiing and climbing peaked out, there were many more skiers than climbers, the reason being, that skiing is a pastime more easily learned than climbing. This is certainly the case with family groups. The danger climbing presents may not have been acceptable, as a family activity.

Like all enrapturing pursuits, climbing and skiing have exciting goals to offer, for people of all standards. These two mountain sports tend to establish lifelong friendships. It did for my family, and consequently, here, in the lateness of my life, I have many, dear, special friends, with whom I have travelled through most of life. The time of weekending for me was to stop for almost three years. I was inducted into the British Army. In the correct parlance of the day, "I was conscripted."

2. The British Army

What can anyone of my background say about the British army of 1947? In my opinion, it had all the poor quality of the pre-war treatment of the common soldier. Poor pay, at one pound seven a week. That's 135 pence in today's money! Even in those days, that was nonsense. The food was mostly poor. Worse, no real freedom of thought. The one redeeming feature about the whole thing, was the senior NCOs, who, for the most part, were very professional. When you got one of these, you were lucky, and knew where you stood. There were, of course, fine officers, but the gap between them and the *other ranks*, (that's how we were referred to), was like a void! The number of times I have heard grown men making the statement, "the best years of my life!" None of my friends ever came to that conclusion about the British Army. The army has changed dramatically since those days. I have worked with the army as a ski-teacher during the last ten years, and found the army of today to be a place of opportunity for those who are prepared to pull their corner!

Basic training in Cameron barracks, Inverness, was my introduction to the basic-ness of barrack room life. This in no way put me up or down, as I had lived and enjoyed much more spartan conditions. There were almost a hundred eighteen year old boys in that intake. Right after we were in uniform, we underwent an introductory pep-talk. The talk was given by no less a personage than the camp adjutant. I can see him as clear as day, tallish, fair, longish hair, (not allowed for us), a curled up military moustache, kilted, the kilt hanging down at the back, and two labradors. What an army officer needed two dogs for, was beyond me! The long shepherd's crook was an appendage that went over my head. He wore suede bootees. Not, of course, proper dress for the kilt! He had the most disdainful look I had ever seen on anyone. I've seen plenty since. His opening gambit was that army discipline demanded that its personnel did what they were told when they were told. Simple, but what's new? We all did that, at work, anyway.

He pointed out that, because of our background, we might be used to doing what we wanted. In the army this would be mutiny. All of this intake was from the Clydeside around Glasgow. Its name must have gone before it. I bet none of those young men were in a trade union. I for one, was not, nor was I interested. This was my first encounter with the *class barrier*. From the sheltered, free thinking society of the Red Clyde, we had never been exposed to such stupidities. Everyone was too busy trying to get by, and live decently. I wonder what background this pathetic pseudo-highlander came from.

After my service in a Highland regiment, I knew quite a lot about the class system, something I've never seen any value in. During my long life in the mountains, where everyone starts even, the class system does not operate. To be a leader of men in the mountain world, you must stand above your peers. This did not necessarily mean you were the best performer, and you only stay there as long as your peers wish you to be there. Leaders in the natural world, are there by stint of their ability! All these eighteen year olds must have looked a dangerous lot of anarchists. What I did see was a nasty piece of work. He would not have lasted ten minutes out of the cocoon he was born into, in my world. Since those days, I've always found education was an ongoing process of priceless value, to those who pay attention to other's opinions. I can honestly say, this was my first experience of a bigot in action. Of course, it's very easy to force people to listen, and make them do what you say, if they are in no position to disagree. I'm sure that, in later years, memories like these tempered my rebellious nature. A little! It seemed completely alien to me that here was one of our leaders, speaking in an accent created by a different culture from the one which we came from. There was no way he could start to understand anything about us. We had been, up to this, only exposed to the fair practical mind of the working man. This came out of the blue. Later in life, I had great fun working with some of these types, on equal terms. Very few of them, it seemed, ever learned to "box clever." At this stage I'll include two anecdotal happenings in the middle 1950s.

Loch Lomondside January 1948 – Absent from the Army
left to right – Willie Purves, Ian Allan, Self, Jim Purves

One day, about five miles north of Balmaha on Loch Lomond, some friends of mine came down out of the hills on to the lochside on a pouring wet day. They had come a very long way, and were soaked to the skin, waterproofs not being what they are today. In a county council workmen's lay-by, they lit a fire. A council lay-by is where road rubble and such is kept. There is always a fire spot, used by road workers. As the fire came good, so did the humour. The tea drum was steaming and so were their clothes. No matter, it was a soul warming time. Up drove the latest status symbol, a Land Rover, out of which stepped an absentee land owner. He had two labrador dogs, and he had the other necessary badge of rank, the three piece plus-four tweed suit, with specially designed pattern tweed, which indicates which estate he came from. He wore a wee pair of rubber bootees. He also had the shepherd's crook. He looked the part.

What he faced, in these men, would have been a force-majeure in any circumstances. However, he seemed to think he had the right to rant and rave

23

about the abuse of private property, and the decline in discipline among the young people of the day. Discipline? I always thought that one of the main things about it was self control and good behaviour. He continued with how the working classes were coming into the countryside and abusing it. Strong stuff. He had just put himself *beyond the pale*. There was one of the group, a fearsome fellow, with a very a short fuse, who was ready to deal with the halfwit. Jim Purves, the self-elected leader, a gentle soul by nature, told the fearsome one to hold fire and wait and see how far Big Mouth would go. He then made his second blunder. He took their silence for sign of submission. When he ran out of vitriol and exhausted his stupidity, Purves had him lifted up, and held over the fire until the seat of his estate plus-fours were almost burned through! His vitriol had turned to whining, his haughty arrogance gone. He would not have made a good leader of men, despite his obvious ex-army and public school background. He was very poor at picking his ground and assessing his opposition. His biggest problem was his "2" IQ! Surely there were not too many like him on the field of Waterloo?

In Lighter Vein

Near Fort William, on the hills above Spean Bridge, stands a monument to British Commandos, who trained in this area during the last war. Close by to the monument, by pure chance, is another county council lay-by. Once again, some friends had made a fire. In this group were some of those who had been involved in the above incident. Along came a kilted gentleman, with two labrador dogs, a shepherd's crook, and soft suede desert bootees. The kilt was hanging down at the back. How this effect is achieved has always puzzled me, however it's a style often affected by such personages. He became greatly agitated about the fire, and remonstrated with them for their misuse of the area. He came away with all the usual guff. He was so out of touch with present day realities, that he made this statement in all its crass stupidity, "I want you to know that my forebears fought for this land." If that was another way saying that they stole it from people like himself, well, fair enough. My friends were hard to surprise, but, here in the middle of the 1950s, was a reject from three centuries in the past, talking like a child. Hector MacDonald took him at his word and suggested that it might be a good idea if they fought for it here and now! The kilt did not see the humour in that suggestion. Hector went on to explain, as best he could, "as these people often find reason difficult to understand," that it was possible the council lay-by might not be in his ageing *fiefdom* any more, and therefore, the joust may not be necessary. If so, it was *honours even*. The Kilt took his twa dugs, and left. I wonder if he was any the wiser. If people had to work the land they so jealously claim as their own, without servants, and not being able to escape to their London houses when they were bored, would they be so zealous about *our* Highlands? I'm sure the answer begs the question. These two happenings may sound fanciful to anyone who has no experience of such people and their nonsense. Unfortunately, they are still about. If they were not so pathetically unnecessary, they would be a great joke!

After basic training, I was posted to Redford Barracks in the outskirts of Edinburgh. There were two barracks, the Infantry and the Cavalry. The food in the Cavalry was terrible, while the food in the Infantry barracks was very good. How this was managed took a bit of understanding. One day, on the rifle range,

I saw a young nineteen year old officer breaking every rule in the book. It was late in the year, and a skein of geese were making south over the Colinton hills. The officer took a rifle from a trainee and had a few shots up into the geese. What would have happened if we had all followed his pointless example? The NCOs just looked at each other. I wonder what they thought of this behaviour. Not the best example of "good order and military discipline." He was fresh out of Sandhurst. As chance would have it, he had a public school accent. It would look as if there were two sets of rules that day.

We had a regimental sergeant major. He was the epitome of all that a soldier should be. He stood head and shoulders above most others in that great barracks. It would have been interesting to see what he would have done if he had witnessed the goose-shoot. He was the holy terror of the new young officers. Just as well. We all need our mentors. No one seemed to care about how the common soldier felt or what he thought, and there did not appear to be any concern about his general well being. This could have been brought about because the war had not long ended, and the most of the army was made up of conscripts. Politicians of those days were no different from those of today, and were not interested in the army. It is possible that, at the time, I did not realise what caused my resentment to the situation I was in, because I was too young to understand how the world worked.

At Christmas 1947, I was given seven days leave, and this did not suit me. All my friends had their holidays over the New Year period. There was not much I could do about that. Instead of reporting back to barracks on the 30th of December, I left Glasgow for Loch Lomondside. The Purves brothers, Ian Allan, my wife to be and two others made up the party.

We had acquired an old sailing dingy, which had been abandoned during the war, called the "Dusty." It was a hand knitted thing, held together by whatever we could scrounge or nick. None of us had a clue how to handle the sails, such as they were. Having the boat, we decided to spend some nights on "our" little island of Buck Inch. As we were carrying heavy packs we decided to ferry most of our gear up to Buck Inch on our sailing boat! This was our first mistake. The big one was the condition of our craft. Anyway, this was to be our camp for that night, but not for all of us, as it turned out.

The rigging on the Dusty was not of the highest order. As a matter of fact, I've seen a better rigged boy-made raft on the Forth and Clyde Canal, in Glasgow. If the Dusty had been the best set-up craft on the West Coast of Scotland, our sailing ability would have been grossly inadequate. We had none. There's a fine book, by Jack London, "*Two Years Before The Mast*." The story's set in the 19th century. The captain and the bos'n are a pair of bastards. I know a few of those. But anyway, they were good at whipping the pressed crewmen into shape. Even all their skills, would have been of no avail, in our case. Willie and I set off and eventually arrived at Buck Inch, after much trial and error. When I later learned a little about how rigging was run on sailing craft large and small, I shudder to think of how we managed on that winter's day. Willie started to set-up camp. I left the island to sail the mile or so to pick up the others.

"Dusty" was a centreboard dingy, and, of course, the centreboard was missing! I was trying to sail before the wind. My rudder was a broken oar. As I left the shelter of the island, the weather, which was bad, decided to get worse.

There was no way I could control the boat, as I was rudderless and keelless. "Dusty" leaked a little, also. How I managed to get myself, far less that wee boat, to where I wanted to land, I'll never know! It was a very trying time. I got the sail down and fought it out with the broken oar. While this was happening, my memory went back to the time we got caught on that Inverbeg weekend. At least then I was in strong company and in a sound rowing boat. Despite the weather, I beached the boat more or less near to where I should have met the rest of the group. The boat filled with water as it beached and it was impossible for me to pull it clear.

The others had decided it was too rough for the boat to cross, and had gone to Galbraith's farm. This farmer friend of ours had let us use his barn in bad weather for some years now. It was here I found the others all snug and comfy. Needless to say, I was soaked to the skin. Being wet through was part of weekending. Our Scottish weather proved its fickle reliability. During the night, the sky had cleared, the wind had dropped, and heavy frost whitened the landscape. The lochside was fringed with young ice, and the Loch was a mirror, in which the surrounding hills and mountains were depicted as clear as where they stood. The poor wee boat was nowhere to be seen. We found her offshore in about six feet of water. Willie was out on Buck Inch on his own, with our gear, and no means of transport. There was nothing for it, so, stripped down to the knickers, we four men left our boots on to give us a grip on the bottom. I was cold the day before, but that was in hot blood, this was cold-turkey. *It was freezing!* Down into to the water through the thin sharpness of the ice, a deep breath, down to the boat and start working it along the bottom. This was very strenuous, between the cold, and the heavy physical endeavour, it nearly beat us. When we got the foredeck out, we rocked her beam to beam, to slop some of the water out. We started to win. We also made a fire. We needed it! During the process of the task in hand, my wife Jeanie made a humorous remark about swimming. Big Purves made it quite clear that she would be swimming shortly with her clothes on. The humour stopped. We noticed Willie was up and about, as we could see the smoke from his fire. This was easily seen in the clear morning light.

Because the Loch was so calm, we all fitted into the now sea-worthy (?) "Dusty." On Buck Inch, Willie was recumbent in his sleeping bag by the fire. His opening remark was, "what kept you?" What he really meant was that he was glad to see us! When he heard all that had happened, he knew Mother Luck had been smiling on us again. We stayed on Buck Inch a few days, to bring in the New Year. During this time, it came to me how much the army did not suit me. This was more like it, being back in the Happy Land again, and to have escaped from the mundane, awful pointlessness, of being an unwilling soldier. Being back was like discovering the Great Outdoors again. It stays with me that, having been removed from what was so important to my well-being, then getting back to it, I now saw its value with much more clarity. As a consequence, the world, as I saw it, was more exciting and even more necessary to my well-being. As I was the first from our group to be in the army, you can understand the interest of the others, as we sat round the fire, and I told them what takes place in the new strange ways of the British Army. It must be remembered that, at that time, none of us were yet 19. I had not yet made up my mind as to what I thought about the army. By the time I was released, I certainly had. The conscript army could not have been ideal for the professional soldiers. At least they *wanted* to be soldiers.

26

We sat there, hour after hour, the night sky ablaze in the starlight, the heavy frosts, the still air leaving the Loch's waters reflecting the stars, whose light seemed to turn that part of the lochside into something ethereal. You could feel the power of it. Sitting round the fire we were all at peace with the world. None of us were in any way religious. If there are gods or deities in this world, they were abroad that night, doing their work beautifully. What a dreamy tranquil world we were in, sitting in our own privacy, on Buck Inch.

The world was at peace after the long war. Another war to end wars. Little did we know what the next 50 years were to bring.

As Robert Burns said, all those years ago:-

The best laid schemes of mice an' men gang aft, a-gley
an leave us nought but grief an' pain for promised joy.

As the "Dusty" was too small to ferry us about the islands all at the one time, we moved to the east shore, to a place called Ross Point, five miles from Balmaha. This promontory stands into the Loch with a small island at its point, another place of wonder. There is rock formation and a cave you can sleep in. There was plenty of firewood. We spent the rest of our week wandering around the empty countryside, using it as our own. How pleasant the memory. And how perfect the land that made the memory possible. All good things come to an end, and I made my way back to Redford Barracks. I had no idea what I would have to face. I presented myself to the guardroom, where they gave me a "bed" for the night.

Next morning, the guard sergeant told me to make my way back to my company, saying "don't get lost again," laughing. It was the company sergeant major who confronted me. He was a very small man in stature, but big in essence! A Seaforth Highlander professional of 30 years, and he looked it. His very demeanour spoke volumes. His first words were, "where have you been, boy?" I could sense there was no animosity in the man. How many times had he seen this sort of thing in the past? He said, "that's a good man in there." He meant the company commander. "Tell him a good story!" I was marched in, with all the ceremony of being on Company Orders. The commander was a major, a tall thin man, and one side of his face had been badly damaged. It looked as if he had a glass eye, this, no doubt, from the war. He looked bushed and weary. When all the stamping of feet and shouting was finished, and the charges had been read out, the major asked me, "where have you been?" I told him the truth. I replied quickly, "climbing, sir!" "You must have climbed a helluva bloody height! Five days to barracks and five day's pay!" It was about-turn and out of the office. The sergeant major said, "you did well there, now get back to soldiering!"

To my great relief, I found out that if I had been two hours later in getting back to barracks, I would have been up in front of the colonel, and received the statutory thirty days in the "Slammer." Old Lady Luck again! Almost a week extra for so little retribution! It was good fortune that I managed these two weeks in my old stamping grounds, where I learned so much of my early thinking and understanding of the physical world. I was to be posted overseas to Singapore. I got a long weekend's leave, then shipped out from Southampton. The train journey to London was terrible. There were so many standing, that it was difficult to move about on the train.

27

The troopship, SS Strathnaver, was another experience. First impressions on going aboard, was the feel of it. She was alive. She was shiningly clean. You felt the organisation. For me she breathed excitement! You had the feeling she was loved. I wondered, at the time, what kind of bos'n was on board. This was a boy's dream, thirty days, which seemed to last for ever! Then it was over! Our draft of young conscripts was made up out of six Highland regiments. This was a bizarre bunch of hooligans. They took over the ship and *caused Cain*. So much so, we ended up doing all the shipboard duties. We left in the winter, and, crossing the Bay of Biscay, there was a enormous swell running. Sea sickness ran amuck through the ship, but an old Lomond sailor like me had no trouble!

Past Gibraltar, and then I had my first sight of big mountains. The Sierra Nevadas, on the south coast of Spain. 11,420 feet. They were covered in deep, heavy snow. There was no way, at that time, I could have envisaged how such mountains would dominate my life to come. Seeing these great natural wonders left me spellbound. As the ship made *easting*, taking me farther away, it was as if I was losing something. For days to come, the sight was constantly in my mind's eye. It's possible that was another part of the turn-on for me personally, and took me back to think and compare them to our own Scottish mountains. Today, young and old are still going to mountains all over the world, to take the pleasures people like us have been enjoying for years. When you hear foolish blethers about controlling the right to climb or walk on our mountains, it makes the likes of me smile. Our country has many more pressing problems.

Our first stop, Port Said, was a culture shock! The dockland seemed to be peopled by thieves, pimps and cutthroats. Glasgow's docklands were like churchyards, by comparison. On thinking back, I now understand it was the dreadful poverty of a large part of the population that caused all these problems, in this part of the ancient world. To blame the poor locals for all the bad things we saw, would have been a cop-out. I now know better. We sailed through the Suez canal during the night. The Stars, in the clear desert air, were something to behold. They seemed enormous.

I had found a small place, under a stairway, by the ship's rail. I would stand there for hours. This Wee Golden Bubble, a place of contentment. As I write, it makes me think this was possibly one of the most tranquil times I have enjoyed in my life. As the story unfolds you may agree. It was in this wee *cubby hole* that I first met Jimmy Mitchell, from Glasgow. He squeezed in, and asked me if I minded him joining me. Contrary to what people may think, Clydesiders are the most civil souls you can find. That day started a friendship that enriched us both. The conversation naturally turned to what our interests were. He was amazed when I told him about weekends. He could speak well, and he had a good presence. You felt at ease with him, and his intelligence was apparent. To my amazement, he had no interests, other than going to work. So the conversation fell on me. His questions were interesting and therefore, in the coming days, being used to speaking, I slowly and carefully described the outdoor life I'd enjoyed since my early days on the banks of the Kelvin. Up to my "five days to barracks and five day's pay." The effect was mesmeric. He was enthralled. Shortly after, we gathered another new friend, a Denny Devine, from Govan, where the Kelvin runs into the river Clyde. Denny had a very different background from Mitch and myself. He came from what would be called a "hard case" street, in Govan. He was interested in the weekending, but he was a real *Townie*. Like most Glasgow men, he had an enquiring mind, and used it !

We passed through the Red Sea, where we stopped at Aden for a day. Bombay was next, with a two day stop over. If we thought we had seen poor people in Port Said, we had our eyes opened in Bombay. Among all the majestic buildings, and other edifices the British Raj left, as monuments to having been there for more than two centuries, were some of the most wretched creatures on this earth. And this in a country that had been at peace for long, long years. We were the first troopship into the port since the country gained its independence from the British. Ceylon was the next stop, a much different place. They now seem to have the oldest sickness in our tiring world: *religion*. In that rich, beautiful island! Again, *"when will we ever learn?"*

The last leg, of what was a peaceful journey, crossed the Bay of Bengal, down past the island of Sumatra, through the Straits of Malacca and down the Sea Roads, off Singapore Island. Here indeed was a new world, almost on the equatorial line. The climate never really changes. You can almost see things growing. In the town of Singapore, and it was only a town in those days, the shops were full of every conceivable luxury you could imagine. Back in the UK, almost everything was on ration. Here was a country, just out of occupation in the hands of the barbarian Nipponese? And their shops were stuffed full of goodies! The two hundred odd Highlanders in our draft had to spend a week in Nee Soon transit camp. Most of the draft "Highlanders" were from the central belt of Scotland. Some Highlanders! In the transit camp we were in the charge of a professional longtime Royal Artillery warrant officer, a "Gunner," as all artillery men like to be called. The bunch of Bandits made the man's life a misery, for which we would all pay. Even if you took no part in messing the man about, you were guilty. Maybe that's where I learned not to like team games!

Before we were due to leave for the first Battalion Seaforth Highlanders, this bunch gave this warrant officer a hard time when and if he could be heard during catcalls. Some of us heard him say he was to be a guest for dinner that night in the senior NCOs' mess in Gillman Barracks, the Seaforth headquarters. This was to be my early lessons about *the abuse of power*. It is a two-handed-sword. It cuts both ways.

Next morning, two colour sergeants from the Seaforths came to collect us. They were something most of that group of draftees had forgotten about, the real world. The fun was over. I never thought it was much fun messing people about because you have the upper-hand. It doesn't prove much. My weekend experiences sorted that out early on. These two hardcases enquired if we had been enjoying ourselves and if not, it was all right. They would arrange for us to have a real good time where we were going! They said other things, about being soldiers, and letting the side down.

How quiet it was. When the poor Gunner sergeant major was talking, no one could hear a word he said. These two fellows had no trouble being heard. As they say in Glasgow, "the mouths were shut!" And tight! Gillman Barracks was obviously new not long before the war. It stood on a hill overlooking the small islands that surround the entrance to Singapore harbour. It was a super looking set up. Each company was housed in its own block, and each floor had a balcony that seemed to catch the lightest sea breezes. It sported a large swimming pool, a movie house, a big canteen with a bar, palm trees, banana plants and orchid trees. It looked like a movie set.

There were, however, the two colour sergeants, who were to introduce us to our respective companies which we would serve in, with whatever recommendations they felt like giving us. It would have been interesting to have heard what these two colour sergeants had in mind for this bunch of miscreants. I'm sure it would have been humorous banter, as to how they'd sort us out. I was in for a real shock. The acting sergeant major, in charge of my new company had good reason to dislike me. A lot! He had been a corporal in Redford Barracks, Edinburgh. Unfortunately I had messed him about in a big way, and made him look very stupid. He was now holding the big cards. He was in fact holding the full deck. What to do? The two-handed-sword was now his. This can happen when you sail too close to the wind. To say that a company sergeant major has power is a gross understatement. When I saw who it was I could not believe my luck. My luck had just gone on holiday! There he was, with his officer's balmoral, that warrant officers get to wear.

When I spotted his wee fat body first, I nearly died! I wasn't dreaming, I was having a nightmare. I tried to hide amongst my fellow miscreants. He started to lay off about the bad behaviour we had all been guilty of. He was running on two back-burners. Having a good time. Then he spotted me. So much for my hiding! Here was me, who never took part in the abuse of the gunner sergeant major, in the "deep stuff," deeper than all the rest of the draftees on parade. I had to stand there and listen to a load of puerile gibberish. A week in the Yards would have fixed his lip. I was now in deep trouble, completely in this cretin's power. Then luck changed again. He turned out to be a real half-wit, as we'll see later. He had me cold-decked, and he blew it.

At first he seemed to leave me alone. He must have been away somewhere out of barracks. Singapore was full of large storage dumps, of every imaginable commodity you could think of. The Chinese, being some of the finest entrepreneurs in the world, had to be prevented from supplying themselves from these goodies. This task was given to the army. I was on this duty, with live ammunition. We were given instructions as to how the Chinese came through the barbed wire to help themselves. The procedures for challenging these baddies was explained to you, then you were left to get on with it. Out in pairs, two hours on, two off. My first guard was a food store night duty. It was fun, exploring to find the goodies. Tinned peaches and pears and cream. And even large sealed tins of sweeties. There were large rats running everywhere. That was a bit off-putting, but we soon got used to them. There was a fetid stench caused by the awful heat. This would take around six months to acclimatise to. In the middle of the night, with our youthful minds, we spotted someone sneaking about near the wire. First thing was, one up the spout, *load the rifle*, move in close, and catch the bastard! All went well till we got close. Whoever it was had made away, and made good their escape. Well, you can't win them all!

Later on, we remembered we still had loaded rifles. In unloading, I must have made a mistake, because my rifle went off and the round went between the other guard's legs. Some shock! The corporal of the guard came running. He was great about it. He got me a round to replace the one I had just used. He told me, "let that be a lesson to you!" What a fair man. We had, up to this time, a total of 12 weeks training, yet we were let loose to try and be soldiers.

When the cretin reappeared, I was the first thing on his agenda. He was bound to get back to me anyway, now he had new grist to screw me with. You'd have thought he had won the pools! He told me how lucky I'd been that he'd been away when the shooting had taken place. I was not fit to be on guard. He was right, I wasn't! He assured me it would not be long before he sorted things out. I was quite sure the whole battalion were waiting to find out what was coming to me. This new draft had only been in Gillman a week or so when these events took place. It was shortly after me shooting off the rifle, that he had me on a charge for being late on parade, the easiest one in the book. I had not been late. This was the start of more to come.

The prewar army in India had local natives working in their barracks. They would shave you in bed, in the morning. There were tea and fried egg Wallas. Wallas who kept your boots, webbing, shoes and other bits and pieces. All for a few bob a week. The night before I was due to go on company orders, I went to get my shoes from the boot Walla. He told me the sergeant major took them to wear to the sergeants' mess. I never figured out why. The Indian boot Walla had explained to this clown that they were mine. He had just made a serious blunder, his first mistake. His second was thinking he could bully me into letting him off the hook! I had the boot Walla as a witness, plus another pal of mine. When I turned up for company orders next morning, he said I was late and he'd be putting me on another charge next morning. I was not late. He was up and going, and needed stopped! When he was finished yapping, I told him I wanted to see the company commander about him stealing my shoes. He still had them. I thought he'd blow a gasket! He blustered. He threatened what he would do to me. He saw he was getting nowhere, and it was then he showed his true colours. He said he'd give me another chance. This was a breathing space he needed. Me too!

An historic event took place within a day or two. The Malayan emergency started. This was caused when Malayan Chinese communists took up armed rebellion in their effort to take over the government. The very next day, a detachment of some thirty of us were posted to guard an ammunition dump. It's not often you get your bacon saved by an historical event on this scale! I never got back to the Seaforths, so I don't know what happened to this poor excuse for a man. Imagine a sergeant major not being able to contain an eighteen year old boy! *With karma!* Our detachment was sent to the north side of Singapore Island, to guard an ammunition dump. This was located in what had been a large rubber plantation. There was a system of dirt roadways through this very big area. There were sheds a hundred feet long, containing the *materials of war*. It was here I met soldiers who were completely different from what I had seen so far. The Ordnance Corps men went about the camp as if they were at everyday work.

On our arrival at the camp, in the late afternoon, we discovered some of us were going out on 24 hour guard patrol. Let me explain the situation. Here were a bunch of poorly trained 18 year olds. Before leaving Gillman, the powers that be made one of our older conscripts into a corporal. He was a very nice, quiet man, not one you would have thought was suited to command. Out of that lot, who could they have picked? As it turned out, the rest of the motley crew gave him complete cooperation. It was as if we all knew he'd been lumbered! The Seaforth battalion were immediately sent up country into Malaya for jungle patrol. So you could see why they would not be leaving any of their good NCOs,

31

to be in charge of a bunch of conscripts! I'm making all these comments in hindsight.

Denny Devine and I were picked for that first epic duty. Out we went to a hut. There was a staff sergeant there to brief us, and give us advice on getting on with our duties. You would not have believed your eyes. This man wore a big sloppy bush-hat, a holstered handgun at his waist. Slung over his shoulder was a stengun. To top it off, he had a Japanese cutlass stuck through his "gunbelt." He was tall and had a tremendous face. I don't know what he thought he was, but he certainly was right out of the book! He knew we were green. So, we were green, but not *that* green. The Hollywood star told us how these thieving Chinks were coming in and helping themselves to what they wanted. He said how dangerous they could be. He went on about the different kinds of poisonous snakes that crawled all over the place. He was going his duster, and starting to get through to me! Scorpions, all sorts of other nasty things. You wondered how the locals got by, living in such a dangerous environment!

It was getting dark. He showed us where we worked in twos. One went down one track, one went down another. He said we would pass each other, and arrive back where we started. In so doing we would cover all the ground. Out we went, children in the wilderness! The plantation was almost back to jungle. The night noises were frightening at first. The pep-talk we just had, left the morale less than one hundred percent! I was having kittens and seeing *bogeymen*. After what seemed hours, I spotted one of those dangerous Chinks. I was too afraid of snakes to take cover in the trees. In the moonlight, I was sure I stood out a mile. I cocked my rifle. After the food dump business, you would have thought I'd be a bit wiser. Since those days, I've come to understand, after much trial and error, that learning is a slow process. The dangerous Chink I saw, was Denny coming from the other direction. I think we were the dangerous ones. After that, we joined up and finished off patrol together!

Malaya 1948, Self with Chinese Woodcutters

Next morning, the locals came in to work in the dump. Sometime later, two Chinese came out of the trees carrying a six foot Cobra, dead, of course. Only the night before, Denny had assured me "the cutlass nutter" was talking crap! So much for the well informed jungle expert from *sunny Govan*, Glasgow! Reading this, you may think I'm knocking the British. That's not intended. After the War, the world was in an awful mess. China was shaking loose its ancient chains, using communism as its flagship. We were starting to face up to the communists here in Malaya. It took a long time to resolve this problem. Powers like ours the world over, were going through the same. It would be easy to look back and say, "here's where we went wrong." It appears the leaders of the world are poor learners.

This camp was designated as "443 B.A.D." A tidal creek ran into it from the Straits of Johore on the mainland. It was a sort of limbo place to be as an infantry soldier. Our job was to guard this great, sprawling place. During the day, when the ammunition was being worked, there was little to do. Night-time was ours. As I have already said, these young conscripts were left on their own. Hard to believe, but there it was. The living area was almost in the middle of the plantation. Drinking water was brought in by Water Garrys, an Indian name for a truck. Washing water was pumped out of a well. There was a Naafi they called a club. We used to swim in the creek, and the water was not too good. Mind you, I used to swim in the Kelvin! It would be hard to say something good about this place. However, for myself, the long nights walking the guard-patrols gave me, at times, a good feeling. A feeling of peace and solitude. I came to accept the night sounds as part of the whole of this experience. In time, I found a certain beauty in all of it. Learning can be humbling, and that's good for you. Those far off days is maybe when we started to appreciate how the natural world around us worked. That would be when the seeds set themselves, as to how we feel and think of such things today. There was the flash lightning, on some of the dark nights. It made no noise. It would start to flash and grow in the distant skies. The great clouds would grow like mighty mountains, as the flashes grew into their vastness. I would watch for long periods of time. These would go with my already rich store of life's good things. In a place I did not even like, here was nature reminding me of its power and majesty. Looking back, these scenes come very clearly to mind. They are some of the strong memories of that past time.

Another memory from the patrols was that Mitch used to get tired easy. He'd say "I'm having a kip," and doss down on the dirt track, without a care for the creepie crawlies, while I stood guard over him. What are friends for! Our weapons were always loaded on patrol. In the beginning, we were very careless. We played with them like toys. Two of our patrol came into the shelter hut for their rest period, in the wee hours of the morning. Sleepie time. Clowning had started. A rifle had been pointed at someone's head, and fun made about pulling the trigger. In a quiet voice, someone said, "that's loaded!" The one with the rifle laughed and said, "its not!," pointed it up, pulled the trigger and made a hole in the roof, and a lot of noise! Not much was said for some time. I don't remember anyone messing with weapons after that.

It would be round this time I got the news of Ian Alan being killed. It happened in Glencoe, on a mountain called Buachaille Etive Mor, *The Big Shepherd of Etive*. This was the first time I would have the experience of having someone die like this. I cannot remember how I felt, being so young and inexperienced to appreciate the value of deep friendships. It takes long years of close association to create the bond that would make grief possible. It was the middle of the 1960s before I had to face up to this sort of thing. As the years march on, sadly it happens more often.

I've spoken about luck and close shaves. My luck was about to run out. It could be said some of these young soldiers from Clydeside could be wild at times. One pay night, there was a disturbance in one of the living huts. When it was over, I had been charged with assault of a senior officer. I was court martialled and found guilty. Six months detention. The president of the court said they were being lenient. I could have got six years, as we were on active service. A sobering thought. This verdict would never have stood up in a civilian court of law.

Ever since that happening in my life, now, if I see a military junta taking over a country, it gives me thought to wonder what sort of justice takes place. In the detention camp, there certainly was no justice. And brutality was common place. The detention camp was in Ipoh, in the centre of Malaya. They sent a sergeant and private to escort me. They were armed, not to keep me from escaping, but for protection in the event of the train being attacked by "bandits." A piece of nonsense for propaganda reasons. It was political. They were communists trying to take over the country. It took long years before the might of the fading British Empire managed to destroy these so-called "bandits." The private escort was wearing sandshoes. He had foot rot. We all had it, at one time or another. The humour of the situation was the stengun. I noticed, when he was playing with his, there was only two rounds in the magazine. I hoped the sergeant had more in his. Just as well it was not on the return journey, as the train was attacked by the "bandits"! And, for some reason, they let me travel back without a weapon. Maybe they thought my skin was less valuable now my "time" was served. No matter how boring 443 B.A.D. was, it sure was better than Ipoh detention camp!

Soon after returning to my camp, a job with the regimental police came on offer. Never being one to hide behind a bush, I applied for it. The camp adjutant was amazed. He said, "you've a bloody cheek! Just out the Slammer, and looking to be put in charge of good order and military discipline!" I pointed out that, with my recent experience, I'd be ideal for the job. And got it! I never looked back. I was up and running! No more patrols in the sweating jungle night. The rank of corporal came with the job. Life was much more comfortable!

About this time we all got a real fright! The new rulers of China, the communists, had taken over most of that vast land. They were converging on Hong Kong. The western world presumed they'd go the whole way and take Hong Kong. This was a natural assumption. What else could they think? Malaya was stripped of all its loose manpower. Remember, it was in a full blown emergency. I was sick. What if this became a war! I was not interested in what happened in the Far East. History has proved no one really was. All we wanted, was back home. We had no money invested in the Orient. We had no money in our own country! The whole thing beggared your imagination. We had no stake in Hong Kong's wheeling and dealing. As it turned out, the Chinese were much shrewder than the West gave them credit for. They stopped. They could not afford a war.

The march of time brought us all nearer to "going home." The closer our respective release dates came, the longer the days became. The long peaceful nights were quite private times, when I thought of our past achievements and new ones to come. This is what went through my mind, in the small hours of the morning. It possibly was the stirrings of manhood. We were nearly 21 years. Getting shot of the army, the grumbling and bitching eased. All was forgotten. As the conscripts left, with their kitbags, and each with their handmade suitcases, the rest of us started to count our days. My day was not far off, but the system was not through with me yet. I was called to the company office and told my *demob* was put back six months! The reason being, the time I spent in detention was nonrecoverable service. This did not make for a very happy soldier. My first serious lesson on "The Rules," and the people who make them, and apply them. If you have any brains, you'll live by them. That philosophy should be written in stone. This was the situation I had to live with, for the six months Time is a healer, and, in due process, I was loading my kitbag and handmade suitcase onto the truck. For reasons unknown, we stood on the dockside for hours in the heat of the middle of the day. Even after all the time I'd spent out in the sun, I ended up with a blistered face.

Years after, as I started to mature, naturally I thought of Singapore and Malaya. In thinking of it, I came to realise how much I had missed because of my resentment at being there. My eyes were only half open. What a waste! Even though, I did see enough to remember the people who lived there. The dignity of the Malays, and the smooth beauty of their women. They seemed to be a passive people, who lived contented lives, happy in their soft verdant land. As for the Chinese, you have to have lived close to them to appreciate their strength of purpose, their zest for life, and their efforts to improve their lot. They have a code of honesty peculiar to themselves. When I was in detention, there was a big fat RAF fellah, a Billy Bunter. He was in for thieving. He had worked in an electrical stores. I asked how much money he bagged. I nearly fainted. He said his share had come to 35,000 pounds! In 1948! I found out later he was quite a celebrity. I asked him if he had any of it left. He said that he still had the lot. Next question was how had he managed that, and it seems that his Chinese partner had it invested for him. With my smart Glasgow mouth I said that he could kiss that goodbye! Billy was not in the least worried. He was getting dishonourably discharged, and sent home. He only got nine months. I got six months for stupidity. It's an ill-divided world! Billy Bunter had made arrangements to come back out to settle in Singapore. He seemed to think it was a land of opportunity.

I have been asked if I'd like to go back and see it. The answer is "no!" I have never been one to over romanticise the past. It's best you remember the sweet things, and how you saw them in your youth. The trooper home was the "S.S. Devonshire." She was built as a trooper of 11,000 tonnes. This ship was not a "Strathnaver." When you went aboard, there was no special feeling. It did not have "the feel." It was just a thing. Nevertheless, it was taking me home. Better still, there were only two hundred troops on board. Our first stop would be Port Said. Being a corporal, I was in charge of a mess deck of 24 men. All the way across the Indian Ocean, there was an enormous sea running. The seasickness amongst the troops was horrendous. Men lay where they fell. The vomit was everywhere. Men were so ill, they could not help themselves. Imagine if the ship had been full! I managed through without sickness. Loch Lomond experience - there's no substitute for good training! As the ship came about northward, into the Gulf of Aden, we sailed out of that gigantic beast of a sea, and then it became glass calm. Nature had again treated us to a splendid spectacle. For the whole of the next day the ship was surrounded by thousands of dolphins circling the ship as far as the complete horizon. Surely this must have been as great a moment in the wildlife world as at anytime. It most certainly would be today. The journey back, strange to say, did not excite me. I was on my own, which suited me at that time. The ship took on board 1500 men at Port Said, and this made life difficult. There were still a few places to get peace and quiet, where you could contemplate in your mind, the pleasant thought that soon you'd be free. There was almost a sensual touch to it.

I spent many hours in a little corner, up in the bow of the ship, wondering what this had been all about. To this day, I never got it sorted out in my mind. This was possibly part of the reason for my morose frame of mind these last weeks. Perhaps the culmination of the whole event was having its effect, now I was going home.

Passing the south coast of Spain, the weather was bad. I was disappointed not to have seen the high Sierra Nevadas. I have never seen them since. I have, however, seen many other beautiful mountains - and the Sierras are still there! We rounded out of the Mediterranean, and into the cold of the Atlantic. That is, cold by comparison, even though it was summer. With our thinned blood, we felt it. Liverpool was our port of disembarkation. A Dirty wet day. It could have been Glasgow. A pity it wasn't! I was discharged with something like two weeks pay, and thirty pounds I had saved. Around forty pounds. Not bad for thirty months service! Some of the best years of your life? They had even stopped giving out demob suits.

3. The Alps

Glasgow in 1949 was a dull, tired city. It looked as if it needed a long vacation. My eyes were fresh from being away for so long, and it was like seeing it for the first time. Clearly I knew little of other cities. However, the impact of looking at my city, as if for the first time, and recognising the results of long years of neglect, when over these long years, the wealth that was earned by most of the citizens was taken by a small number of the citizens, was immense. My mind went back to my thoughts and silent opinions when I first saw Port Said and Bombay. But who was I to think bad of other cities, and their cultures, and their living conditions, when here, in a part of the world that had enjoyed industrialisation for a hundred and fifty years, we had a city where the working people lived in the worst living conditions in Europe! What was not tired there, were the irrepressible people who populate this fine city, who give it its heart, its kindness, its strength and above all its *humour*. This is Glasgow - not its then decaying façade of bricks and mortar. The *citizens* are Glasgow!

On the credit side was coming back after a long period of time and basking in the rich warmth of the people and their speech, the sound of which can grate in the ears of those not born in this Dear Green Place. If you listen to Glaswegian, in its full flight of fun conversations, you will find the interplay of the dialectic language used a subtlety of wordplay that's hard to match! To take part in one of these discourses, you must know the people and the language, and, above all, be sharp with it. From the age of fourteen I had been living more or less on my own, which meant, when I got back, I had to find a place to live. This was difficult, as there was a tremendous housing shortage. So from then, up until the time of getting married, living conditions were poor. If this event happened in these present times, the returning hero would take a six month sabbatical as his right, and good luck to him! With forty pounds, this was not possible. How well six months roaming in the north west Highlands would have suited me. In years to come, I would be compensated beyond my wildest dreams. I would get to live in the mountains, but on my terms, and also be able to come and go as I pleased.

We worked a five and a half day week, at that time. Transport out at the weekends for us, was by service bus. This limited our movement very much, by present day standards, but, as always, there were goodies in the bag. The Creah Dhu Climbing Club ran buses some weekends. These took us to "Far Away Places." It was still a man's world, in those days. Unattached ladies were not allowed on the bus. Ladies with serious gentlemen friends travelled on the bus with their gentlemen. That's how it was. Club buses got us to places like Glencoe. Now here was a place of dramatic proportions. Your first visit was something to remember. The deep slot that is the Glen cuts its way through those massive granite mountains that start high up on the Rannoch Moor, and run down to the sea at Loch Leven and Loch Linnhe. The Glen starts where Glen Etive comes up to Buachaille Etive Mor, which is the *Prince of the Forest of Buachaille*, a name given to groups of mountains here in Scotland. Ben Nevis is *the King of the Forest of Mamores*. A nice romantic turn of phrase. This is one of the most impressive parts of our most impressive country. No matter how often you travel through Glencoe, it never fails to command your total attention.

37

The Club Bus, apart from getting you to new exciting places, had a social side, which was so good that travelling on the bus became a mentally stimulating experience, never to be forgotten. There was choir singing of a reasonably high order. For a group who held individuality dear, they allowed themselves to be organised by a nervy wag, Bob Harper, called Haps. His name was his badge of rank! Haps conducted our efforts like a martinet, and he was good at it. If you carelessly struck a wrong note, as punishment, he put you out of the choir during for next few songs. It was a tough place *to turn a buck*. This bus had more than its share of extroverts, most of whom were very good raconteurs. Billy Connelly would have been busy keeping his head up in this company! If you had a joke or story to tell, you stood in line to wait your turn. There were no behaviour rules on the bus, but if you came late for the departure time, you missed the bus. Without being a silly old fart, a little of that might be a good thing these days.

In the opening pages, I spoke of men who started their outdoor lives during the pre-war depression. Some of them used the bus. For some reason, I can still see them clear in my mind's eye today. The choir master, Haps, was one. Another was a wee man, by the name of Bill Caur. Because of his wartime experience, he was sometimes called Herr Caur. Jeanie and I climbed Mont Blanc with him in 1950. He was a master of bullshit, and we all enjoyed hearing a master at work! Wags like this must never be discouraged! There's not many of them in a pound! He was great company and he just loved being *one of the boys*.

There were others of the same calibre and background. They seemed to be at peace with the world. This could have been the result of the privations of the depression, linked to the fact that most of them had been through the depression and the war. Not everyone on the bus were climbers. There were hillwalkers, "padders," capable of walking long distances on high ground. This they could do at speed. The climbers, of course, could move at speed over any ground. There were those who took part in both pursuits, the common bond being the love of Our Mountain Country, which nature had so fortuitously placed on Glasgow's doorstep.

The Club Bus was responsible for a number of friends becoming bigger and more solid groups. This in itself enriched us all, and, as the years came on, we found this would benefit us in no small way, when we matured, and started to find our way in the world. It was not long before we started to lose friends. These were lost to Scotland's old sickness, emigration. As always, it was the strong and the best that went. From the early fifties to the sixties were the years when we, who got married, spent establishing our families and homes. That was a much more difficult undertaking during that decade than in those to follow. They were uncertain years, that being the reason for all the emigration.

While Jim and Willie Purves and I were marauding in our early days on Loch Lomondside, we discovered late running salmon, in a wee burn that ran into the Loch. We were thrilled to find fish that size in our wee burns! This took us by surprise, which never lasted long. Here was food, free food. In our panic to get the fish out before they escaped, we got soaked. Our performance very quickly improved and we made a lot of the fish, as long as they lasted, but nature, being what it is, took its course, and the silver bars went back to trying to achieve passage back to their true environment, in the Northern Seas. I was pleased to find they had improved their skills during my absence. They had learned to get fish out of big rivers by the use of nets. Even better, they had added to their skills by finding how to get venison off the hills by the use of the long-gun. The Purves's had not been indolent, when I was away defending the nation's rubber supplies! Here was another challenge, taking on the Establishment. By that I mean, we went to the hills and rivers, where we took our share of that which nature had produced, in what used to be a natural wilderness.

Most of my friends believe that the wild uncultivated land of our country should be available to all of the citizens, in a fair and equal manner, having the most stringent regard for all of its flora and fauna. It should not, under any circumstances, be held in bond for a handful of the privileged few. We all know that this country is a long way from being anywhere near to fairness in this matter, but anyone with honesty in their heart, must know that the *status quo* is dishonest. People have been taking wild game from the land "illegally" since the first Lords and Robber Barons claimed dominion over all of nature's bounty. When I said it was a challenge going to the hills and rivers for the deer and the fish, that was not quite true. We did it also for the flesh and the meat. The pursuit of these prizes could be dangerous. For instance, when going after salmon, it is necessary for someone to cross the river with the "long-end" - a rope to pull the net over. If the river was running high, I used to make the crossing with Big Jim Purves, who, for some reason, seemed to think that I was good at crossing, and, if the water was high, he'd use me. He was a lot taller than me. When the water was up to his shoulders, it was going into my mouth! A good thing some would say! Kidding apart, we were almost washed away a couple of times. I wouldn't have missed it for the world! *The nut is the sweeter, the harder it is to crack.*

One memory that stands out. Mitch and I had been taking a few fish out of a west coast river on a weekend. In the pre-dawn light, we were driving from the hills down through the glen on a motor bike. There's a phenomenon that happens when there is no air movement at around this hour. You can hear the silence and feel as if the world is private to yourself. On the moor, where the salmon river was still a burn, we drove past a herd of Red Deer. Further down, as the birch and oak started to form into lovely little glades, there stood a family of Fallow Deer. As we collected our rewards from the river in the old oaken woods where the river ran deeper, the little darling Roes welcomed the coming dawn with their quick throaty barks like as if to welcome the richness of their new day. Mitch thought it was the keeper's wee yappy dugs. Roe sound a bit like dogs. And what a way to start our new day. Silver bars of salmon were a nice added extra. The barking *prong-horns* helped get the adrenalin going, A good pump of adrenalin will not do you any harm, and it's also cheaper than drink!

Winning the Red Deer was different. I'll not demean the majesty of the noble beast by calling the winning of them a sport. To take a rifle and all the advantage of the human brain to kill this defenceless animal, and have the effrontery then to call it sport, is past my ken. If the beasts could shoot back, it might be sporty. No, it's in no way a sport! Stalking the beasts is reasonably skilful. Care and patience is the keynote to success. It takes place on high open ground that is called a Deer Forest. Another nice touch of playing with words. The fact that much of the ground was timbered in the not-too-distant past may have influenced this most unsuitable and misleading name. I have always wondered why we were so seldom disturbed in pursuit of this naughty pastime, considering the openness of the ground where the whole thing took place. As I said early on, many of us learned how to move about on the more heavily populated ground around Milngavie.

Having been part of this in the early fifties has always given me a nice warm feeling. It's something very few people have experienced. Like all good things, they usually take a wee bit of achieving. Motor bikes had just happened to us. They gave us mobility. Jeanie's and mine was a 1936 model. All the Highlands became a playground for us. You could please yourselves when and where you went. The bikes gave you a feeling of personal freedom, of mobility, which in turn changed your whole outlook, as to how you sorted your life out. Considering our already free thinking approach to what we were due out of society, the bikes certainly widened our scope.

Mitch started weekending as soon as I returned. He fell in love with our way of life, and was immediately accepted by our old friends. He found climbing well within his capabilities, as he was, by nature, very athletic. Our winters produced some hellish weather. With the coming of the season's change, we would take to the railway bothies, our *aces in the hole*. When the Victorians built the railways in the Highlands, they put in small shelters, every two miles or so along the line. They were used for keeping tools and as tea bothies. When the weather was real bad, like foxes, we'd go to earth and hole-up in them. There were open fireplaces, and lots of coal, that fell from the steam engines, onto the line. The bothies were built with railway sleepers, and were usually slate-roofed. They were of different shapes and sizes, likely whatever took the fancy of the linesmen who built them. The linesmen never seemed to mind us using them, the unwritten law being that they were left spotless, the way you found them.

How many wonderful nights did we sit round roaring fires fuelled by high quality British Rail coal! The more it stormed outside, the more comfortable our cosy bolt-hole became. It was our friendship that made times like these a great comfort. We would yarn away into the wee hours of the night. Bothies were an institution in weekend life at that time. They are a thing of the past. Mitch and I had our first Glencoe climbing on Buachaille Etive Mor. This peak is one of Glencoe's most impressive. Mitch and I had climbed on the Cobbler, the Arrochar Caves, Ben A'an in the Trossachs, and all the usual boulders problems. But the Buachaille is the pride of this Mecca. John Cunningham and Willie Smith were on the bus that weekend. They were already the biggest names in our climbing world, having established new rock climbs which would spur young "Tigers" onto greater heights. "Tigers" is the name given to good climbers. Johnnie and Willie showed us about the hill, and suggested several routes suitable for us. This was big stuff. The routes they suggested, we managed comfortably. Next day, we got a few more routes in. What a super way to start on the Buachaille, being helped by the two top climbers of the day! What a standard these two set for a hard nosed bunch of independent extrovert bastards!

It would be an understatement to say we were privileged, having been involved with men of this calibre. Being so close to these men, over this long period, makes it difficult for friends such as myself to say how good they were. Well, I'll say it now. The campsite we used lay directly under the Buachaille. That mountain seems to influence and dominate everything around it. That's in a landscape *full* of wonders. We constructed a very fine and large bothie on this site and, wonder upon wonders, it still stands today! It goes under the name, "Jacksonville," and is a famous place in the British Climbing. It was named after

Jim Jackson. He was always called "Jackson." I, for some reason, always called him "Jim." Jim is dear friend to our family. Jim and I spent many fine nights in railway bothies during the back-end of the year. Often we sat through long, wild, stormy nights, putting the world to rights. The world was always a better, kinder place when we were done with it. Jim and I did a fair bit of poking about rivers and deer forests, and, in the doing, we became easy in each other's company. We lost him to Seattle, where he was most successful. Like so many others, he's a sad loss to us. Out of Jacksonville developed a cadre of very good climbers. I have often wondered, if they had all gone fulltime with their climbing, how far could they may have gone. Maybe it's more exciting as it is.

I've always been more than grateful that I got my chance in professional skiing. It would be in the winter of 1950 that Willie and I were climbing in Crowberry Gully, on Buachaille. The snow conditions were good, and the weather was perfect. This was my first good snow gully. After coming out of the gully, at the summit cairn, eating my first Penguin biscuit, Willie casually remarked that we had climbed the gully in so many hours faster than the first ascent. It was quite a big difference in time. However, I never attached any importance to this, and I know Willie didn't. That was not the reason for being there. During the climb, I had been using a set of hand-made crampons. To save bit of time, Willie and I were using combined tactics. That means, I climbed up on Willie's shoulders to get over a wee hard bit. *Not* to be recommended when you are using crampons! Willie was facing out from the gully, and I had to get my left foot high. As I reached and stepped up, my left foot scarted off the rock wall and just missed Willie's face by not too much. When I looked down, before I could say anything, he said, "Don't do that again!" Willie was never long on words! I did say he could be taciturn at times......

4. Growing Up and Skiing

Not long after Willie and I had our good day, Jeanie, Mitch and I went into Crowberry. I had explained how good it was. We had stayed overnight in Doddie Cameron's barn that weekend. This was a good doss in wet weather, and it was wet that weekend. We left the comfort of the barn, made our way along the Coupall river, a short walk to the climb. Mitch and I were all "steamed up" and couldn't wait to get at it. As we started up towards Crowberry, we noticed it was very warm, passing the running water-slab. This is a big steepish rock slab which guards the way into the Crowberry gully and the fine high rock cliffs, that hold some of the best rock climbs in the country. We noticed a trail of avalanche rubble that ran from the mouth of Crowberry gully, right down the water-slab. That should have told us something. We were well into the gully when the first ice came down the gully. If you have not experienced this, don't try it! Mitch said he'd read that a Alpinist had seen debris in the Alps, the size of pianos! That may have been so, but a piece half the size of a tennis ball will kill you just as quick. There were fair size lumps coming down on us. The climb is a thousand feet, so you will understand that conditions like these can be very stressful. By this time you will have come to the conclusion that we should never have been in the gully. Try telling that to young men out to prove themselves. We arrived at the crux, three hundred feet short of the top.

The gully forks here, and any debris falling must come through here. You can't move about quickly to dodge the lumps of ice. That would have made the crux a nightmare, so, with tail between the legs, we started down. Getting down is not as simple as it sounds. With three people, it's much slower. With us having to keep our eyes peeled for the small pianos, it slowed us up. With all my experience (?), I came down last. From time to time, ice screamed down through the gully. We got to a thirty foot rock wall. I lowered the other two down, and while working out the best way down for myself, a lump of ice took me right on the bum. That worked out my way down - I was airborne! I managed to land on my feet. Mitch held me on the rope. All was well. We were, of course, soaked to the skin. No Goretex in those days! As we came out of the gully, we started to feel a lot easier. Walking back along the river to Doddie's, there was little said. We were possibly in some sort of shock, after the experience we had just been through. And in our youth we did not understand how dangerous the situation had been. This was a rather different finish to Crowberry from Willie's and mine, on the summit on our lovely day. A hard way to learn. If you survived *the learning curve*, you were doing well. It would be easy to criticise this sort of episode. In reality, it is an age old, well proven, trial and error method of finding out how far we puny humans can extend ourselves. The trick is not to pull it twice. Having said that, in the world of today, young people have easy access to the mountains, and equally, to the best of the excellent modern equipment. Is it surprising they get carried away with all the excitement of the challenge? We did, without the fancy gear. It's a commonly held belief, in my circle of friends, that up and coming climbers should be left in peace to get on with learning to enjoy the mountains, and thereby, their trade.

Chamonix, in the French Alps, was a big step for us. What a place for you first Alpine experience! Zermatt would be the other mountain village, which would be of the same historic quality. Mont Blanc and the Aiguilles of Chamonix tower over and dominate the village. In 1950 it was still an old Alpine gem. The Bossons glacier comes almost into the village. The first thing you notice are whole trees in the broken tumbled ice near to the bottom of this mighty chute of ice. Another memorable sight is the glacier stream through the centre of the village. In the heat of the day it runs much faster. It's little wonder, when you think of the two enormous glaciers, Mer de Glace and Bossons, that feed this river. When you stand by its side in the 80 degree heat, it feels quite cold.

Bill Caur, who organised the trip, told us how fortunate we were to be seeing the high Alps for the first time. He said it was never the same second time round. He was right. Here was one of your dreams come true. Everything was just as you expected. I thought back to the Sierra Nevadas, only this time I would get up into these sought after goals. The whole setting was idyllic, its very newness and strangeness adding a sweet charm to the scene. Gone was the austerity of home. Shops were full of consumer goods. At home, we still had partial rationing. In the village there was open trading stalls, where they had big fresh peaches, cheap. It was the first peaches I'd ever had. The shame of it was, we only had eight days. Part of our holiday was used by two days travel, each way.

We camped in the woods, five minutes from the village. There was a wee burn close by. Local urchins seemed to get good sized trout from it. It was not long after this the Aiguille de Midi cable car system was built, right over our lovely campsite. We even had camp fires. Not so today. When you first see these mountains close up, the scale of them gets your mind going. There are features on them, like outcrops, that are much bigger than Ben Nevis. Corries like glens. In your imagination, you start to plan how you will do this and that. Then you read the signposts. The huts can be twelve or fifteen hours walking. Most peaks require an overnight stay in a hut.

Nobody moves about these "hills" at speed. You soon learn the hard way to move as the locals have learned to do over long years. The altitude, the scale of the whole entity, and the power of nature. This you very quickly learned to keep in the forefront of your thinking. The hard lessons of home are soon brought to mind. Those blunders made at home, in your early days, may have been good for you. Mont Blanc is the highest mountain in western Europe, at almost 16,000 feet. When the weather is fair, it's a straightforward, simple undertaking. Like all big "hills," in bad weather, they go rogue. Mont Blanc, in poor and bad light, would return little pleasure for any energy expended. There were six in our party for the summit. Bill Caur, Jeanie, three others, and myself. We decided on the route from the cable car up from below Chamonix. The Piste Verte runs down close by. This downhill course has stopped being used some years since, being considered too dangerous for present day ski racing. My son had raced in it, and said it was frightening.

From the cable car, up an old rack and pinion steam railway. Something right out of the past. At a steep part of the track, near the end of the line, the old engine never made it. No wonder! The poor thing was so overloaded, it could have been somewhere in India. From the railhead, there's a fair long slog up to the Tete Rouge hut. This was the first time I'd seen mountain paths prepared and kept in good order. This, I found out, was the work of climbing club members. We slowly gained height, on our way up to the Tete Rouge. The aspect of the massive glacier system, of the western flank of Mont Blanc, was awesome.

1950 Bill Caur on way to Mont Blanc Summit

Looking down gave you a very different perspective of their layout and their size. It made you want to go down and explore them. Bill Caur explained there was no time. He was certainly right. Just under the Tete Rouge, there was a short rock face, and the path went up round the back to the hut. I took a shortcut and climbed up toward the hut. Under the steepest part of the wee climb, a man was upending a big wooden tub down where I was climbing. I was forced to make a detour. The tub contained accumulation of the produce of hut users. Human waste! They don't have water closets in a mountain refuge. The French sometimes call their huts by that name. They also call them "cabins." These names have a nice ring to them.

From our austere little island, not yet recovered from the war, nor indeed from the depression of the 1930s, to this cosmopolitan world of new excitement! Another door opened. Here we found a mixture of folks from all over western Europe, enjoying common communion with each other. French, Belgian, Italian, Germans and others. And us. Bill Caur, who had been through the war, made some remark. What was war about? A good question. What stood out was how the continentals were dressed and equipped. The latest vibram soled boots, climbing breeches, fancy patterned stockings, factory made anoraks, and the same with their ice-axes and crampons. Mountain rucksacks. They just looked the business! I had Australian army boots, the same as British, only brown, with my socks tucked in, see photo. I had an anorak made by Jeanie. A Clyde-built ice axe. The Europeans were greatly taken by this. Bill Caur, who had pre-war Alpine experience, was not much better turned out. At least we were there! This situation, with equipment and the approach to climbing, would change rapidly, through the endeavours of the newly emerging groups, and differently motivated

44

1950 Mont Blanc Summit
left to right – Bill Caur, Self, Jake Reynolds – Quality Equipment?!

mountain users. The changes they effected would be applauded, and welcomed, by the established climbers of the day. And of yesteryear!

Jeanie and I were short of French money. The guardian of the hut took two Scottish pound notes. We were short of money, period! We only had twenty four pounds between us. We had to buy a meal in the hut. I don't remember what it was. Who cares, there was more important business afoot. Sitting outside the Tete Rouge that night, watching the sun westing at the end of day, at that altitude, precludes all conversation. To describe it would be futile. It's a feeling that is personal to the individual. The phenomenon of the setting sun seemed to last a long time. This must be part of "the great adventure" mountains give, at magic moments like these at home. But this was a first in the Alps.

An early morning start is of premier importance. You save the time in the morning you may need in the afternoon. With our early start, we were treated to a high altitude sunrise. With the Alpine chain running away from Mont Blanc to the east, it gave the rising sun a tremendous foreground. Unlike the sunset, you are seeing the new day with fresh eager eyes. If you were still fuzzy headed from your night in the over heated refuge, this sight cured it. From the Tete Rouge to the summit, on a morning like this, we had what was a deluxe introduction to any Alpine summit, far less the historical Mont Blanc.

For readers who have no knowledge of climbing, and the effects of altitude on the climber, it's worth knowing, that the frail human body slows down the higher it goes. Some are affected much more readily than others. It was here that I discovered that I acclimatise quickly. This is good luck for someone who may have to expend a lot of energy above the normal altitudes where people live. I know a top class professional climber who was on a big Everest expedition. Everest was well within his capability, but he could not acclimatise. What a shame. Here we were at about half that height, and some of our party had it. Rather than hold back the group, they waited at the High Valour refuge. When we made the top, I don't remember feeling all that excited. Pleased, but not excited. If this sounds arrogant, it is not meant to be. In those days, like the rest of my peers, I was in a hurry for the next piece of the pie. We took success for granted, and ignored failure. We were also tinged with a little arrogance. A shortcoming of most young men involved in manly pursuits. At the time, we would have refuted such a suggestion. This is a statement made in long distance hindsight! We were like that. From what I see today, it's still the same. Human nature does not change in the short time of forty odd years! We met back at the Valour. The Valour is not far below the summit. Next to the Valour was the original wooden hut, which was locked. Inside the new aluminium monstrosity, it was "as cold as a lady of the night's heart." Not bad for the French! The war's not long over and they can fill their shops with goodies, and erect new mountain huts, so soon after. Of course, they did not tie their future to America's shirt tail. From the Valour, we made our way back to the Tete Rouge. As I said, below the Tete Rouge the path is steep and in good condition. It was our habit to run off the hills in those days. Jeannie and I ran all the way down to the railway. Jeannie was so dehydrated we had to buy a very expensive bottle of lemonade. A bottle of wine would have been much less. But, as I was the cause of the dehydration, I had to *pay the Piper!* Looking back with wiser heads, we can value some of our experiences and achievements, and, with some modesty, can say we were successful. And how fortunate we were to have found the way of getting to that stage.

On the other side of the valley, the mountains do not climb to the same heights as on the southern side. Here there's a peak called the Bravant. This peak is about four thousand feet above the village. A cable car runs to the summit. It is used by skiers in winter, and tourists in summer. In my opinion, it's too steep for the average skier. In a place where the mountains overwhelm your imagination, this peak holds its own. Its summit sits on a vertical rock face. A climber's paradise. The cable car goes onto a lesser peak, then crosses over to the Bravant. For some distance before it arrives on the summit, it traverses along this super rock face that supports the summit. From the cable car, you can see the climbs, the great long cracks and chimneys that flute the cliff face. You see the climbers doing their business. It was a great sight for anyone to see, climber or not. There was no one in our group who rock climbed seriously who wanted to climb on this face. It was not the place to be messing about. The day Jeanie and I walked down to Chamonix, it was in the warm dry Alpine air. The tall pines seemed to be taller, the way they climbed away from the very steepness of the slopes. The trees hung with mosses, the first time I had seen this in these natural surroundings. We saw a wood carver working outside his chalet. The place was hanging with dozens of baskets of geraniums and other flowers. I thought, here was man at peace with the world. He was young, stripped to waist and brown with sun. He could well have been a ski teacher. The picture of him comes back to me. I wonder how his life has been since that happy day, as I remember it. The holiday seemed to be over before it began. I later found that three weeks filled the bill in lieu of "three months." We had a stopover in Paris, on the way home.

It was here I got a horrific fright. Our government had got us into the Korean war. I was sick, here was me, just out, and it certainly looked as if I was back in it again. The news came to us, sitting in a café next to the Gare du Nord railway station.

There was a big Glasgow Commie *headcase*, shooting his mouth off about how we would show these capitalists bastards how to run the world. Well, they have had the opportunity and not done too well. Of course, the capitalists are not doing so well either. Anyway, this big commie *headbanger* had managed to get through the war in a reserved occupation. No fighting for him! It's interesting how these would-be leaders of revolution manage to keep their heads down when "the stuff hits the fan!" All mouth and no brain. Extremists, no matter the colour of their politics, are a waste of space. If nutters like these get control, its the likes of me they put against the wall! My brother was conscripted into the Kings Own Scottish Borderers. He had a real bad time in Korea. He was never the same, after he came back. Jeanie and I never knew it at the time, but we would be back to the Alps on very many occasions in the years to come. These future visits would be under much more comfortable circumstances. In a new world of skiing. My next visit to Chamonix would be to start the high level route to Zermatt.

5. Our First Ski-Lift

Jackson and I arrived at Buachaille. It was the middle of April 1950. The West Highlands was giving of its best weather. When it's like that, there's no better place to be. The climbing did not attract us. Jackson suggested we go and take a look at the skiers. The ski hill was some four miles from the Buachaille. We didn't favour walking the road, so we took a direct approach up and over the moor. Onto the Massif of Meall a' Bhuiridh, which means, "*Hill of the Roaring Stags.*" It is one of three peaks that go to make up a great horseshoe ridge called the Clach Leahad. This is a great lump of mountains. The skiing slopes are on the east side and overlook Rannoch Moor, which at times is extremely beautiful. It can be a lonely, haunting, peaceful place. As the mood takes you. I don't know what I expected to see. I had never thought I would ever be involved in skiing. What I did see excited me. In years to come I would get to know all there was to know about the "*Hill of the Roaring Stags.*" Or nearly?

It was here I would start to break the back of my *ski learning curve*, and, in the process, acquire the challenge to ski well, which I still have to the present day. Seeing skiing for the first time, it crossed my mind that it was a novel event for me. I had only found out there was skiing in Scotland, when I returned from the Far East. When I saw one of the skiers coming down the hill, my first reaction, was *to get a shot!* Most of those skiing were off the Club bus. John Cunningham gave me a shot of his skis and a one minute ski lesson. That was me off, I was hooked! I skied in my nailed climbing boots. The next weekend I had procured a pair of skis of my own. I dread to think what they were like. I'm sure they were no worse than all the rest were using. As it was now the middle of April, we got a few more days skiing until the following winter. The summer passed, with its passing we became more involved in climbing and wandering the hills. The New Year holiday was to take place in the Cairngorms, in Glenmore, where we would bring in Hogmanay. Where I would have many more Hogmanays. A late train to Aviemore. Jeanie, Blackie and myself. With "THE BIG CROWD," that's what the older ones were known as.

Despite all the many times I've been to exciting places since those early days, the first are still fresh in my memory. Nevis, Glencoe, Chamonix. Now Glenmore. This first visit to "The Gorms" could not have been better. The area presented itself perfectly to me as a Scottish winter mountain scene. It was under heavy snow. The temperature was away down 30 cent. below. The country looked spectacular. You could have well been in one of the Scandinavian countries.

The luxury of Scotland's different mountain places is, they never paint the same picture twice. This is what we found when arrived in Speyside, in the almost New Year of 1951. The train from Glasgow got into Aviemore at 4 am. The ticket collector brought large shovels of red hot coals and set fires in the general waiting rooms, Ladies and Gents. The frying pans were soon going great guns. You could smell the goodly fare of bacon, eggs, black pudding and potato scones, fried in butcher's dripping. Railways are run a wee bit different today. It's a pity. The price of progress! There were about forty of us, Lomonds, Creag Dhu and others, all of them weekenders, climbers and skiers of sorts? We rented the only transport available, a 20 cwt lorry from Hays local garage, at a shilling per head. We bought two bags of coal from the same garage and were off up to

Glenmore. The poor wee lorry was slightly overloaded. Talk about trains in India! We had all to get off and push the old motor up the hill at Altncapper. Glasgow people erroneously called it the "school house brae." All of us stayed in the Norwegian huts, where, in the large main living quarters, two big pot-bellied stoves held pride of place. At all times they glowed red. I wondered why they never melted.

In the evenings, the atmosphere was always full of expectations. There were some of the most exciting characters I have ever had the privilege to be associated with. They were so different from each other. But so much alike in their zest for life. The real play actors of the group were older than us, so we played more or less a listening role, or a learning role. Each night was hilarious. You had no clue what might happen next. This was the Club Bus Crowd and "Wee Crowd of the Lomonds Club," close friends of the Creag Dhu. We only had a week of these nights. The rapport never lost its sharpness.

At that time in Glenmore, an embryonic establishment was being created. It was known with affection as "the Lodge," and still is. In those days the Lodge was learning to introduce outdoor pursuits to children. It has long since became the "National Outdoor Training Centre." Today it deals with adults. Much of its responsibility is in training instructors in outdoor pursuits. Some extremely fine people contributed so much to what the Lodge is today. One of those, a Clydesider, Jack Thomson, was already working there as an instructor. He was to spend most of his working life there. At the end of our holiday, two of our group would stay and work as instructors, John Cunningham and Tom Paul. They, like Jack Thomson, were members of the Creag Dhu Climbing Club. These men became more than notable in the mountain life in this country. This story, in its telling, will illuminate how and why these men could be called famous.

Being part of this scenario was a strong stimulant. This would be the by-product of so many clear thinkers being together in social interplay, which in turn resulted in an unintended competition of brain, wit, joking and play acting. This was interspaced with fine debating and carried off with good humoured liberal thinking. The quality of this was possibly born out of their deprived backgrounds, which in turn made them what they were. The sorrow here would be, that this was the last time all these wonderful people would be together. We would lose some of them to Scotland's old sickness, *emigration.*

The week passed with its usual haste. With its passing we had seen the end of an era. Never again would all these people be under the same roof at the same time. I'm sure we were seeing a part of our personal culture at its peak. With the ending of that week, it would be fair to say some of us were beginning our adult lives in earnest.

Jeanie and I got married in 1951, as did many of our close friends. It must have been the marrying time. We were considered to be very lucky, we had a house to move into. At that time in Glasgow the housing shortage was horrendous. It was a serious social problem. Our little paradise was a two room flat. It was the place I had lived in during the war. How special we felt, with our own place. We had little money, no furniture, but we had this *bolthole*, our life in the hills north of Glasgow. We also had our 1935 350cc motorbike. Our needs were simple. We certainly had not developed expensive eating habits. What you're not used to, you'll never miss. We had a kitchen table, four straight chairs and a bed, an old open coal cooking range and two gas rings. The big thing was, it was private to us! This was a tremendous start. Two wages, however small, gave us an advantage. Like all youngsters, we were full of hope. The ambition would come when the newness of being together wore off. This was a new adventure, one that would last a long time. A constantly changing chain of events, most of which would be sweet. The normal share of not so sweet and luckily, in our case, not too many of sadness.

Before Christmas 51/52, snow came early. Mitch and I went skiing on the Campsie hills near Milngavie, a short run from our "house." Two pairs of skis were slung from our shoulders, as we drove out on the solo bike. I wonder what the police might have to say about that today! The memory of this is important, the reason being, it would be years before any of us would be having dinner in our homes after skiing all day! It's worth remembering that skiing, for us, was just another facet of mountain pursuits. You went skiing, or climbing, as your moods took you. On many occasions we went skiing out of tents. This was a treat for us. In the course of time, our son Iain came along. Weekending for us, as we pursued them, were not suitable for babies and certainly not in the winter. The following summer we got a stronger motorbike with sidecar. We were up and running again. Cars were in short supply in the early 1950s, and very expensive. For some years the Creag Dhu had a shelter below the Meall a' Bhuiridh. We also had a small one. For some reason the Black Mount Estate, whose land the shelters were on, left us alone. This was surprising. Here is a tale of what happened a few years before. It might explain why leaving the shelters standing was surprising.

Two miles south of where we had the shelters, there was an old coaching inn, on the original Wade road. It was called Ba Cottage. It lay in Corrie Ba. The Corrie had been declared a deer sanctuary many years back. It was used as a bothy by walkers, climbers and, on occasions, deer poachers. One weekend the head stalker and the landowner came into the cottage. In the cottage were poachers. The stalker and owner knew those in the cottage had been at the poaching. The owner remonstrated with "the hunters home from the hill." He was treated with jocular ribaldry and a unnecessary *spiel* that went for humour. The landowner was a fine gentleman of the old school. He was far from pleased with what had transpired on the hill. On the following Saturday night, as users of the cottage arrived, it was a dirty wet Rannoch Moor night. They found the smouldering remains of the cottage. This fine man was so incensed, he got rid of what he saw as a *canker*. He timed the *act* to make the biggest impact on those who he thought behaved so badly towards him.

I found out later that he hated doing what he did. He exercised his power to get back at others who had seriously upset him. Everyone lost in this unnecessary gross abuse the poachers had heaped on the owner. There must be a lesson there for all of us. It was a sad, stupid event. The cost was a lovely old historical building, and the loss of a fine shelter. This event took place in the forties, yet our two shelters were safe. A box of matches could have removed them. The owner had let them be. Here was the thinking of a fair man. Any of these shelters could have been used for poaching, "which they never were." They had lasted two years. With this in mind, and the need for a decent place to take our son where he could stay in comfort in winter, I put it to several friends that we enlarge the small shelter. This was done. For the next ten years, what we built became a haven for a mixed group of people who were more than "Friends." The shelter became known as "The Doss."

The permanent residents had their own reserved areas. We put up shelves and wee dookets. We left bits and pieces, and this made moving up at weekends easier. During the week anyone could walk in. At no time did we ever lose anything, nor was there any vandalism. When you have skied out of small tents when it's been snowing, you will know the difficulty of packing when they are frozen. You will understand how big a step up the comfort ladder this was. It was like having a stake in the system, and made it possible to enjoy the environment to a greater extent. Like having your own country cottage.

Inside the Doss –
Self with Willie Smith

The Doss
Glencoe 1954

The Doss was built low and sheltered, behind a glacial ridge. This was just as high as the roof. The winter storms can be tremendous. To have constructed it to a full height would have taken much more material than we could lay our hands on. There was a large entrance porch, an important feature during the regular wet stormy weather. Outdoor clothes and other ancillary necessities were easily kept there. This kept the main "chamber" much more comfortable. The living quarters were most salubrious. As I said, we all had an area which we fixed up to suit ourselves. There was a wooden floor.

Our pride and joy was a cast iron Queen Anne coal stove. It was a most decorative item. How we got it, I can't for the world remember. Its big feature was the opening doors which let us see the fire. How many long, soft, intimate and comfortable nights we had, and blethered away our precious weekends into the *wee hours*. In the early days of the Doss, the shareholders were Willie Smith, Maggie Dunlop, Johnnie and Nan McLennan, Mitch and Harry McKay, of whom you will hear much more. The Doss was much bigger than was necessary in the first instance. As time went on, others were accepted and, by their efforts, earned a place in the main chamber. It would be hard to number how many nights of complete contentment all of us experienced under that low tarpaulin roof. How many dreams were planned in the snugness of that happy sanctuary. None who were part of the Big Doss can complain of our lives since those halcyon days. All my dreams came true. There evolved from under that same tarpaulin roof a number of skiers, young and not so young, who in time would become notable in British skiing.

At this time there was only the odd rope tow in use in Scottish skiing and none on Meall a' Bhuiridh. Trouble is never far away. One warm spring day I was having fun by the side of a wee burn with my son. He was three at the time. We were a good distance from the Doss, and near the main road. The day was beautiful. All was well with the world. Iain, my son, was learning to swim and splashing about. We had been there some time, when a estate Landrover appeared. Out of it came the famous Jimmy Menzies, the head stalker of the Black Mount Estate. This was a man of calibre. He had a young ghillie with him. They were dressed in estate tweeds. It was some time before the great man spoke. I say "great man" with respect. First of all, he had, over long years, earned a big reputation in the district. He had in his charge, possibly the largest privately owned estate in Scotland. Jim Purves said it was "a long day's walk for a good hill man." Jimmy Menzies' remarks were most pleasant, then out came the Sword of Damocles and for several weeks, it *was* a Sword of Damocles situation. He asked if I was in "the bothy." He knew I was from the bothy. He said we had made a good job of building it.

He went on about being there without permission, which was fair. He said, for himself, he did not mind, and pointed out that it helped to keep poachers away. As he spoke, he looked at me very directly, and suggested we keep our eyes out for such goings on. I'm sure there was a hidden message in that request. Then he said it would be better if we cleared the whole matter up with the estate factor. To do this we would have to go to Killin, some fifty miles from Meall a Buiridh. He advised us to be careful with this man as he's English, whatever that meant. There are plenty of difficult Scots men in the world. I think the factor's name was Shelton. Willie Smith and I went to see him one Saturday morning, by appointment. We drove over by motorbike. Mr Shelton's office was in a very large handsome house, "Dall Lodge," as I recall.

52

The factor was something else. He was "*right out of the book.*" The curled up military moustache, short clipped speech, the disdainful look that goes with the rest of the façade. There was a short desultory conversation, the highlight of which was the state of the country because of the socialists. I don't remember who was in power at the time. I had more on my plate, dealing with him. His political outlook was not important to us. His unjustified power was. It is amazing how that breed of humanoid seems to be mesmerised by communists and socialists. The moment they hear what they think is a working class accent, they see the hammer and sickle. I don't know why. Some of the most unreasonable right wingers are working class people who are what's called, successful. I'm sure that, in totalitarian states run by headcases, whether right or left wingers, they get shot of free thinkers like me, *toot sweet*, I mean we get "shot!" Anyway, we were supplicants bearing a begging bowl, therefore the "Fifth Amendment" was the order of the day. When you think back on it, there was a kind of prosaic humour in what was taking place. The outcome of this bit of playacting was that the factor got to show his power, and we got what we wanted. I would imagine that was the first time Big Willie and I ever really bit our lips. Without Jimmy Menzies being in the background, and him having the ear of his boss, the estate owner, our Shangrila would have *gone for a burton!* He was a wee round roly poly man, with merry shining eyes that displayed a natural good humour, that he most certainly had. We had a lot to be grateful to him for. The land owner's name was Major Fleming. I believe he was related to the author of the James Bond sagas.

Now we had some sort of security of tenure, the Doss became more personal to us. We left tinned food, spare wet weather clothing, and other bulky things. When skiing became as important to us as it did, without the Doss, our participation in it at our level would have been well nigh impossible. The expense free permanence and comfort of the Doss, plus the strength of friendships contained within the Doss, gave us a power base from which we supported each other, as we will see. During the early fifties, there was a fresh influx of younger men into our small group. They were from the climbing world where they probably found skiing. Peter Simpson and Andy Scott were friends. Andy became Scottish Ski Champion and Peter became a well respected ski teacher. There was Jimmy Ellis and Tommy Lawrie. Tommy was known as Sunshine. The last two have been in Canada since the early sixties. Ellis, as Jimmy is known, worked on the high steel in many of the big American cities. He worked on the World Trade Buildings in New York. His climbing must have helped in this endeavour. At this time none of the Red Clydesiders skied well. This would come later, for the lucky ones. The attributes these small groups like ours had in common, was the total effort they invested in all their outdoor activities. No physical undertaking daunted them.

For instance, one New Year holiday, whilst staying in the Doss, I awoke very early. I knew Willie was awake. I suggested a snow gully. Willie, of course, thought it a good idea. I heated two large tins of soup for our breakfast and we were off. It was still some time before daylight. We drove down past Buachaille on Willie's motorbike, to the Gorge in Glencoe. The Glen looks splendid from here. It looks splendid from most places. On the west side of the Glen, behind Gearr Anoch and Anoch Dubh, is a very fine peak called Stob Corrie nan Lochan. There's two good snow gullies, Twisting Gully and South Centre. It was

53

to these we were heading. As we left the Gorge, Willie got out in front. The mountain goat was off, head down, arse up, nothing you can do, get your head down and your bum up and go. Not as if we were short of time, it was still a wee bit dark. It is not too far up to the gullies, as the terrain rises very steeply. With the big horse in front, you're there before you know it. As we were roping up in the bottom of the gully, the early morning light was just starting. No wind to spoil the morning. Calm stillness gave the high steep cliffs and the narrow gully a friendly atmosphere, something the wind and storm will not do. In those days the hills were secret lonely places. As fair minded people (?), we liked these climbs to ourselves. As we started into the gully, we found old steps had been cut. This was not on. *How dare anyone go in front of us.* But they were old steps, and we did, at that moment, have that forest of mountains to ourselves.

Like Crowberry Gully, the crux in South Centre is near the top. In climbing, partners take the lead pitch turn about. It so happened that I arrived up below the Crux first. Willie reminded me that I got to lead the Crowberry Crux, so it was his turn. Unfortunately, one must be fair. Especially with Willie. We came out of the gully, fine pleased with ourselves. It was so early. For those who have never been on the tops of our high mountains, the thing you notice is how clear the tops are of debris. Our westerly winds see to that. I remember thinking that at the time. It's strange how your mind works and why. We debated doing Twisting Gully. For some reason we reneged. I later regretted this but it's easy to be clever in hindsight. Our descent took us down by the Lost Glen. This is a lovely high place where climbers camp. It gives off this lost feeling, because of the great boulder field that blocks the entrance. The wee Fairies probably stay up there. Back up to Meall a' Bhuiridh and a big fry up breakfast. The rest of our group had gone up the hill skiing. After breakfast we headed up for a day's skiing.

The "Plateau" Meall a' Bhuiridh
left to right – Harry McKay, Jeanie, Maggie Dunlop, Self, Iain, Willie Smith

The rest of the crowd were surprised to see us. I would point out that there were no ski lifts on the ski hills in these days. It was considered to be a long walk to the ski slopes even then. It's still a long walk to the skiing there today. Only there are lifts. The lift goes up "Thrombosis Slope." It's steep! I'll go forward some twenty five years to highlight the difference in the thinking in general of people's approach to difficult physical problems at fairly high levels. It concerns two top performers in British ski teaching. In early February 1978, there was a tremendous snow storm in the Cairngorms, which lasted two days. When it was over, all the roads into Aviemore were blocked. This lasted most of a week. Electric power was cut off for three days. Houses were buried. This was the deepest snowfall I have seen on Scottish hills. Speyside looked wonderful.

As director of National Ski Teacher Training, I was running a course in Glenmore Lodge, Glenmore. The two trainers for this course were the two men I have mentioned above. They had missed the one day of training because of blocked roads. I had arranged with Fred Harper, the principal of the Lodge, to have the two classes to practice ski teaching outside the Lodge. This could be handled without the two trainers. As the course was not long under way, it was essential the trainers be back at the Lodge for the rest of the course. As I expected, the Chairlift Company would be making a big effort to open the road through Glenmore up to the chairlifts. It so happened, by this time, Willie Smith was now a senior manager with the lift company. It was he that was in charge of clearing the road up to the chairlift.

With the two young trainers and a well winterised mini bus, I set off for Glenmore. We got about three miles up the glen to where Willie Smith, with his digger and driver, was trying to cut through. The drifts were above the height of the machine. After a long period of time, Willie told me the obvious. The road's knackered! The trainers had to get to the Lodge and carry on with the full BASI programme. There was no shortage of snow outside the Lodge. At this juncture, a misunderstanding took place. Without thinking, I said, "right men, off you go!" What transpired shook me to the core. They seemed to think they were going back to the village. However, I quickly explained what the score was. If they had been less experienced I would have been more gentle with them. Instead I treated them as full grown mountain men. It seemed it was too far to walk to the Lodge, the snow was too deep. In my usual tolerant way, I pointed out, it was only three miles to the Lodge and they could ski through the deep snow and consider this a helpful part of their learning curve. It was then things took a more serious turn. It was suggested, as a question, what would happen if they refused to walk to the Lodge. Who would take the classes? This was said in half and full earnest. I said I would walk to the Lodge and finish the job. They would still have to walk back to the village. I also told them they'd never work for BASI ever again. And I was full serious! It so happened I was recovering from a very serious lung condition, and I did not need this. As they left on their way to the lodge, I did mention that there would be liquid refreshment in the Lodge. The question of women was up to their own personal endeavour, and their luck, which after this could only improve! If I remember, Big Smith heard this and in his usual quiet way he had a *wee smile.*

These young men were not the run of the mill youngster starting into ski teaching. They both had good tough backgrounds. One ended up as a trainer to the British Team. One season he was top ski teacher in Australia and has done special teaching in Japan. He is Jimmy Smith. The other started skiing aged three. Ski racing at six. Won the Scottish Senior & Junior Championships at sixteen. Ninth in French National Championships at eighteen. Twenty third in slalom in the 1972 Sapporo Olympics, Japan. His name was Iain Finlayson. Our son.

The reason this happened was not because they were less able, or weaker, than we had been. The thinking had changed, and life was more comfortable. Of course there will always be people who will drive themselves beyond the beyond. What Willie and I did on Stob Corrie nan Lochan and Meall a' Bhuiridh all those years ago was how those particular persons pursued their pleasures. It was normal, I think. Going back in time before that short anecdote, and remembering there were no ski lifts, ski racing was timed by hand held watches. We had racing points tables. Clubs were well run. There were not so many clubs. Skiing was progressing if by nothing else but by its own momentum. This momentum was created by certain stalwart members of the Scottish and Dundee Ski Clubs. To name all who took part and contributed in the build up to what is now organised national skiing, I will not even try. Instead I will give pride of place to Lewis Drysdale. Who could deny Lewis, and all the others who helped Lewis, to do what he did in the timekeeping, and in general firing up, the boiler, of what became Scottish skiing, which in turn contributed so much to British skiing nationally. There were also giants in the Ski Club of Great Britain and Alpine Clubs. We will get round to them as time in the story moves on. At this time our small group were using skiing as adjunct to our own mountain activities. I knew nothing of the Ski Club of Great Britain, nor the Scottish Ski Club. This was about to change.

The first time I saw a *good skier*, (that's a description to remember, it will come up again), was in 1953 on Meall a' Bhuiridh. It was a race day in spring. His name was Allan Crompton. He was British Ski Champion. It's clear in my eye today. He came boring out of Dead Man's Gulch in Glencoe about fifteen feet in the air, and turned in mid air at high speed! You did not need to be a skier to recognise the smooth fluid movements of the naturally gifted skier. Here it was in the flesh! I don't know what seeing him did for me, but half an hour later I was lying with a broken leg. A broken leg might not sound like much. To people like us it's very serious. The first concern is there any permanent damage to your future physical possibilities? Because, let's make no bones about this, people like us were very jealous of fitness. Almost to being childish about it, or that's how I felt about it. Then there is six months incapacitation, when income is reduced to a pittance. This screws up your economics. Fortunately, like all unpleasant things, they usually come to an end. Our weekends were all right. Mitch drove our motorbike combination. Iain and I in the sidecar, Jeanie on the pillion. A full leg plaster precludes walking, and all that goes with immobility. For people like us, it's a bind. There are others permanently much worse off! Advice for addicted skiers. If you must break your leg or legs, (you *can* break your two legs), do it at the end of the season!

That summer a lot of our weekends passed at Jacksonville. It was suited to my immobility. We, as a family, used a tent. In the evenings we had the "Ville" to socialise in. Unlike the Doss, the conversation was predominantly climbing. Our Iain was very lucky being there during this period of his growing up. He had the fantastic surroundings. He was also gifted by having many adopted Uncles,

left to right
Mitch, Bobbie, Self in Glen Orchy

On the West Coast
left to right
Peter, Maggie Porteous
Neil, Self, Iain, Jeanie, Jim Jackson

1954
Summer Activities

57

who were some of the finest men you would find in the world. They made a lot of him, in a sensible way. Iain, in time, would become an adult friend of all of these men. This was something I was privately proud of. These men were my good friends for the most of our lives. And still are. To come further South for a story. At the head of Loch Long, the mouth of which is at present being desecrated by building the Trident submarine base, is the village of Arrochar. Rising above are the Arrochar Alps. This is what the Glasgow climbers from the depression affectionately called these lovely Wee Mountains.

Here's one you'll like. It involves Willie Smith, plus me! The river that flows past the Caves and the larches in Glen Lyon, runs into Loch Long at this point. Because it is at sea level, and because of Glen's narrowness and the steepness of the mountains, it gives off an impression of being of greater scale than it is. There are two bridges where the river runs into the loch. One old and one not so old. They are called the "Shire Bridges." An old habit, the name has stuck. The Auld Brig is a high arched affair of locally cut stone, obviously very old and consequently very handsome. Like all those bridges, they are used by climbers to practice their climbing moves. The added attraction of these bridges was that, when the tide was in, if you had to jump off because your fingers gave out, instead of landing on the gravel, you got a good wetting. It always had spectators, your pals. Only the bold practised when the tide was in. Between the two bridges was a county council worker's layby. This was good for climber's fires. With, I am glad to say, no absent landowners. Late one afternoon Willie Smith and I had a good fire going, when up arrived the RAF Mountain Rescue Team. They were just making their way in the climbing scene at that time. For some reason they worked their way into the limited space between the bridges. Luckily, we were not landowners. From the campsite you can look right up into Corrie Grogan. A fine sight, especially in winter.

There were two or three of these RAF bods. They never had much to say. They set up a great searchlight, and pointed it at Corrie Grogan. They started a generator, switched on, and sent a monster beam of white light up toward the mountains. It was most impressive. It was getting dark and that made it look even better. Still not a word from The Bod. Willie's not long on words. Well, I'm not shy, and I asked The Bod what the idea of the light was. He quite seriously told me, it was a homing beacon for the practising rescue party. Now Arrochar's lit up like a Christmas tree. Well I suppose practice is practice! The RAF Bod went off somewhere. Our noses started to bother us, so we started to investigate what made the light so bright. This was an arc lamp. I lost interest in it. Willie's not so easily put off, and he kept at it. After a while, the light went out. Try as we may, it would not go back on. It must have been junk war surplus. It could not have been Willie's big horny working man's hands! Not a highly skilled Clydeside *artisan*. Never! All was not lost, the practice team could get a bearing back to base, from the lights of Arrochar.

Another short story on the subject of lights on and around the mountains of the Arrochar Alps. In the early fifties one of the first hydro dams since the 1900s was under construction at Loch Sloy. High above the glens there were temporary lights strung over parts of the hills where work was taking place. It was quite a site in the dark of night. It was my brother in law's lucky weekend. Jackson and I were taking him on his first mountain outing. We would bivouac under an overhanging rock face, high on the twin peaked Cobbler. This is a famous rock climbing mountain. Its real name is Ben Arthur. The bivouac site was not the best mountain shelter in the world. My "Guid Brother," was a Townie, a non-weekender. He had no mountain walking experience. Jackson and I were breaking him in the easy way, by giving him our personal attention. There's an old saying *"the Lord protect us from our friends."* Here was a case in point.

Not far from the Shire Bridge is the start of the way up to the Cobbler. By some perverse twist of the unhinged brain, it is called the Green Road. It's a vertical mud slog . On a good day it's bad. A good place for a début. It was pouring rain, west coast style. The midges were wearing crampons. It was muggie warm, not congenial to a hardened mountain traveller, let alone a badly led pilgrim. There is nothing worse than the unintended intolerance of well meaning friends introducing skills that take normal humans ten years to assimilate, and them having complete confidence in them pulling it off right away. At least you don't start at the bottom of the ladder.

The hydro people had put in a cable hauled tramway up through the Green Road. It was the first time we had seen it. Man's works are truly a profound beholdment. It's amazing how things get done when there is a political will. At the head of the tramway was a fine new hut. We could see a bright glowing fire through the windows. On investigation we found the door unlocked. The hut had electricity. The place was thumping with dryness and warmth. Gibby was spell bound. I think he thought we had planned this surprise. He was no more pleased that we were. The hut was near to thousand feet above Arrochar. Arrochar looked terrific when you looked down, with its lights blinking away, a fine sight from warmth of a newly found New Doss! There was a lot of switch gear and a large transformer. Smith, our light specialist, was not there, so lights were safe. Still, it was understood, hands off the gadgets! What made the Wee Palace even better, was the fire place. It had been hand made and was open fronted. Kings and Princelings never had it so good. As it was Saturday night, there would be little chance of us being disturbed by such a mundane nuisance as workers coming to their work. There's a sweet feeling you get when you hear and feel the rain pounding on the roof of a dry warm Doss. Gibby, by this time, thought the weekends were Big Time. Who could blame him? We settled down, got to smoking pipes, and the talk was of how good luck followed the Just!

Drinking at that time was not a big thing, but with my experience in later life, I know now a bottle of fine whisky would have added handsomely to the ambience of the occasion. Tea heavily sweetened and thickened with tinned carnation milk had to fill the bill. Suddenly, darkness! The lights went out. Jackson and I turned round. There he was, in the glow of the firelight. The guilty one, Gibby, the Guid Brother. He had been messing about with the gadgets. Hanging was too good for him! He was speechless, for once in his life. The consequences were too horrendous to contemplate. Not only were the lights out in the hut, they were out all over the hill. I could see it in my mind's eye. The men that ran the place, turning up and throwing us out on our backsides in the pouring rain. We would find out how the Wee Mouse felt when Burns destroyed its "Wee Bit Housie" before the coming winter. All was not lost. Clydesiders to the rescue! In our panic, we got the lights back on. Just as well it was a Saturday night, the people responsible for the system never noticed. What was said to the Guid Brother will go uncommented on.

Before we go on in time, here is another shortie from this period. One back-end of the year, on a very wet weekend, Big Willie, Jeanie, my son, and myself, were staying in the outbuilding of the cottage at the Gorge in Glencoe. The lady who stayed there let certain climbers use it. Its great attraction was the open fireplace. This made it very comfy. Glencoe can be a rain factory at this late time of the year as it was that weekend.

The Gorge of Glencoe is in a spectacular situation. It lies in the narrowest part of the Glen. Along its eastern side runs the Aonach Eagach Ridge. This can be a fine winter outing. On the western side the peaks of Gearr Aonach and Aonach Dubh climb straight up above your head. Here is an area of unbounded rock climbing opportunity. These two peaks were very handy in the rain storm that was taking place that day. Having a good fire to come back to makes the soaking you're going to get seem not so bad. With that in mind Smith and I were off. We did not have far to go to find a cliff that presented a challenge to our skills. I knew the skills we had, but we certainly were short in the brain department. The rain was belting down so hard there were wee *ad hoc* waterfalls steaming off the rockfaces all round us. Apart from the water running out of our knickers, it was a fine display of nature working at its best. Willie picked a fault and started to make his way up. Climbing conditions were crap. Directly below us, about 1500 feet, we could see our wee lum reeking its spume up into the steaming air. It was comforting to know that it was our Shangrila that the smoke was spuming up from. Jeanie would be thinking of the headcases high above her. If she had seen us sometime later, she would have known we were headcases!

Willie climbed about eighty feet over quite easy rock with good grips. They had to be. My leader then arrived at one of the wee waterfalls, where he made a belay and brought me up. Here we had a bit of bother. Willie tried to work his way round the gush of water, however there were no grips big enough to make the moves possible. The strength of Willie's climbing is his safety factor, and in the conditions prevailing that day, small grips were not justified. He had to climb up through the wee waterfall, the first I had seen this, he made a belay. This manoeuvre was not so simple as that sounded. Before I started, I made the following declaration that there was no way I was climbing through that water. Willie said something like, "do you think so?" Like Willie, I climbed through the wee waterfall, and was glad to. And I had the comfort of the rope! Some you win, some you lose. I don't know where I got the idea that I could find a way past the waterfall, when Willie could not. Such stuff are dreams made of. It seems this route was not recorded. I asked him some years later what he would have called it. He said, "Salmon Leap!"

Weekends like this happened all the time. How fortunate for us we had complete access to them at all times. We learned early how important this environment was, and treated it with care. The back-end of the year, weekends like these, when nothing serious took place, were great. "Nothing serious," that's some understatement! This was the time when it was too cold for hard rock climbing, and too early for snow and ice work, or skiing. A time for getting venison. And lazy bothy nights.

One early December, Jackson and I overnighted in a railway bothy in the Cranach Woods, on the edge of Rannoch Moor. We spent a contented night, each taking turns at putting the world to right. In the morning, we made our way over the river Tulla, onto the Moor of Rannoch. We were working our way back to the

Glencoe road at The Ba Lochs, and, on the way over, we got a nice hind. The weather had been very bad since we left the bothy. Rannoch can be a soulless *pig of a place*. A north westerly was blowing cold freezing sleet. Surprisingly these are good stalking conditions. The beasts have their heads down and their back ends up. Another advantage being that the stalkers have a lot less chance of being out and about. We were seven miles out and face to the weather when the wind went crazy. As luck would have it, there was a ridge of rock standing close by, around 15 feet high. We got in behind it. Here it was a different world. It was like standing inside a windless bubble. Here was nature showing how fickle it can be, murder one moment, safe the next. How much more dangerous the hills can be without a slice of luck. Behind the ridge it was so calm we had our primus stoves going. We had a good meal of fresh liver. In the safety of our bubble, we were mesmerised by the awesome power of the passing storm.

As the wind dropped to a half gale, we got on our way. We were walking in a flat calm. Some climate! The Rannoch can be a captivating experience. Jackson and I had just had such an experience. But walking over the Rannoch when its sleeting and raining can be a Bastard! Once again, it was head up, ass down, and on your way. With the fresh liver inside us, and with the now flat calm, the weight of the packs seemed to lighten. We arrived at Loch Ba with our heads up. We read that British soldiers during the Falklands war were carrying 150 pound packs, plus weapons and ammunition. Falklands ground underfoot is similar to the Rannoch, as is the weather, so I think you could take that with a good pinch of salt. We had driven up the night before on a motorbike. This was hidden under a very low bridge on the main road. That way the gamekeepers would not know we were there. Leaving your bike out in the open was as good as leaving a calling card.

Before we leave the Rannoch, here is a story of stupid stubbornness, possibly a by product of a long bad day on the Moor. The Purveses and a Jake Galbraith were coming off the Rannoch near to the motorbike bridge. They had a long hard day out on the moor, and had troubles getting a beast. Being persistent kind of people, they kept going till they got the hind they were after. In the heat of the hunt, food had gone by the board. Jake could eat two men into the ground. He was short on temper, and patience was not his strong suit. He was good at making up his mind. He decided to eat. He stopped, got food out of his pack, sat down and started to eat. The bus lights could be seen coming down off the Black Mount. Try as they may, Jake would not be moved until he had eaten. They waited on Jake, and missed the bus. What are friends for? The others could have caught the bus easily. Here was a case of great determination and awkwardness. Jake was the salt of the earth. He also helped hold the absent landowner over the fire on Loch Lomondside. They say you love your friends because of their faults, not in spite of them. The boys had to sleep under one of the bridges that night, and they had fresh liver for supper! Jake ended up working on high steel in America. He was one of most obliging men, and one of the kindest. If a little wilful!

61

6. The Green Years

Before starting writing the previous pages, my work plan was to simply talk of how I got through life from the age of around twelve years up to and becoming an adult and of the people who helped me through that formative period of my living and growing up. I was full of trepidation as to whether I could continue an interesting narrative in what I thought was a complicated part of my life. As to its interest, that will be up to the reader to decide. As to its complication, I found this not to be the case. On reflection, this was the simple part of what has been a more than exciting journey through life. After what I've just written, I now know this next part will be much more complicated. There are a number of reasons for this. The main difference was the amount of people involved. The diversity of their backgrounds. The geographic spread of where they lived. In particular, their cultural makeups. Among them were people who would stand tall in any society. For good or bad, it is because of these people that British skiing is set up and organised as it is today. Club activities, racing at National and club levels, plastic slopes, and ski teaching.

Skiing, like the climbing world, had no class barriers, it was skiers that mattered. I am sure it is because the two sports take place on mountains that this insidious disease has no foothold in the Kingshouse Hotel. We first learned that the Scottish Ski Club were erecting a ski lift on Meall a' Bhuiridh. It is one of the oldest licensed premises in Scotland. It lies approximately two miles between the Buachaille and Meall a' Bhuiridh. This is the pub climbers and skiers use. It was from the three engineering fitters who were in charge of the work that we learned about the great event, as it certainly was, even though we never knew that then. Our curiosity took us up the hill the next day to see what this was all about. We never thought too much about it. Little did we know how much it would mean to us in the immediate future and indeed, for me, in all the years to follow. The fitters complained bitterly of the walk up *Thrombosis Slope*. It must have been a bind for them. Between the rain and the midges, and a natural aversion to that steep slog every morning, it would have made a mountain goat sick. I know, I walked it every day for five months for two seasons, and I was armed with the burning desire to go skiing. Conditions on our mountains leave you with two choices, you hate them or you love them. Even if you love them, you have to learn to live with them. How they ever got that first lift up and onto the hill still amazes me, considering all the problems. I'm sure it was "thrawn" with many painful and unforeseen events.

It was that winter most of us saw, for the first time, a proper ski lift in operation. I had never seen any kind of ski lift. This was an important occasion in my life. Getting to use it was another matter. It cost two and sixpence per run. Wages were about twelve pounds a week gross. However, providence is full of possibilities. By a lucky chance the Poma type tow bars, because of a faulty design, kept falling off the overhead towing cable. We started to ski down with the defunct bars. We got a free run for this. The following weekend one of the fitters from the company who built the lift could see the Ski Club would have great trouble operating the lift. It was most probably the fitter who suggested that we could run and maintain the lift. From this situation the "Work Party" was formed.

The Work Party's duties were to run and maintain the lift. Members were Willie Smith, Johnnie McLennan and myself, and this was enlarged to include Harry McKay, Jimmy Hamilton, Bob Clyde and Tommy Paul. From the Scottish Ski Club there were two leading lights, Philip Rankin and Robert Finlay. Philip was the ideas man. He was good at getting people going. He was managing director of the Glencoe skiing for some thirty years. Robert was a accountant and a lover of the Nordic Lands, where he spent much of his time. He lived in a ancient castle on the south shore of Loch Lomond. The castle was so beautiful, Sir Walter Scott could have used it as a background for any of his romantic Highland Tales. Robert looked right in *"Boturich."* That's what it is called - what a name for this splendid house, in a splendid place. On Loch Lomondside. Robert was so enthusiastic about the development of skiing, he purchased the first Dendix Plastic in Scotland. He laid it down in the castle grounds, and asked me to ski on it and give my opinion on its potential. As it turned out, I was right. Plastic became very important in "British" skiing .

Robert was a good listener. He would try any suggestion he thought would help the smooth running of the lift. His nickname was Davy Crockett. He wore a coon-skin hat. This name was given in fun and ended up as a badge of rank. Once the lift was up and running reasonably well, Robert seemed to drop out of skiing. Robert was an early corner-stone of uphill skiing in Scotland.

Lewis Drysdale, from Crieff. What can we say about Lewis that would do him justice? He was in the background, in low profile. Later he would come into full focus in all things to do with skiing, racing in particular. Though Lewis was not a Red Clydesider, he most certainly had all the humanity to be a "Clydesider." There's no doubt these three men were prime movers in getting the Scottish Ski Club up and going and leading this part of development in skiing in the UK in those early days.

Dundee Ski Club were in the process of doing things along the same lines in Glenshee. This club had some very strong willed, able men in charge of their affairs. As a result, Glenshee has, today, a well set up ski area. Something to be proud of. It should be understood at that time few skiers, if any, in the UK, knew of the coming explosion in skiing, world wide! The first benefits of the lift started to show immediately. All of our group started to ski at greater speed, and as a result, our skiing ability improved to cope with the problems of increased speed. These two events were in harmony and complemented our endeavours. Anyone who started their skiing by walking up to ski down, will understand how much effort this takes. The same effort converted into total commitment to downhill running changes the whole concept of skiing. It goes without saying that everybody who used the lift improved.

I've wondered over the years why this small group should have been different, and for the purpose of explaining to the readers, I'm sure what happened was the coming together of a lucky set of circumstances. Everything was in place for the results that took place. Here were a group who had unlimited access to "painless" skiing. This was a Pandora's Box of opportunity for each of us to test ourselves with a new and exciting challenge to any talents we may have had. At that time, none of us skied *very* well. In golf we would have been called *hackers*. So what was it that brought us on so quickly? Firstly, there was deep camaraderie engendered by the Doss. This gave all of us a collective strength. There was a mental toughness, we were *mountain-fit*. Best of all, they were all individuals, and, as such, there was no way they would let themselves down. Some by nature were very aggressive, in different ways. This produced a homogeneous result and bonded us even closer together. It was a rich time in our lives that I will never forget! And, as egalitarians, we had no illusions in life.

Another by-product of the lift, was the bringing together of two strong Scottish cultures. Even within their nativeness their cultures were different. Ours grew out of a background of what could be considered austerity, where luxuries had to be carefully sought after. It was only now, with the changing times, that we could be more expansive in our outlook to better opportunities to come. Because of this background, we had very strong views on how the world "worked." The other part of this new skiing equation was the established Scottish Ski Club members. All the things we thought were extras, they accepted as every day necessities. They had cars, they stayed in hotels, spoke differently, their demeanour and obvious confidence bespoke of a comfortable background. And like ourselves, most were nice folks. By pure chance of fate we were all together at the beginning of a new epoch in skiing in our own country. It would be up to us to contribute our share of solid fibre to what was happening, with whatever we were best at! Collectively between us, there was enough variety in our experience of life's problems to give it a good start.

In the years to come, it proved to be a successful and satisfying experience that made what at first appeared to be strange bed-fellows, into good and lasting friends. It moulded all the Scottish Clubs into a very productive Union, The Scottish National Ski Council. During the first winter of the lift, some of us became besotted with the exciting potential of the new kind of skiing. As none of us had skied anywhere but here, our experience was limited to that small compass, and, productive as it was, there was more about skiing to be seen. The only people we knew who had skied abroad were a small section of the Lomonds Club, known as the Wee Crowd. Jimmy Hamilton and his wife Pat returned from skiing in Grindelwald, Switzerland, raving about how wonderful Alpine skiing was. Plans were made for a trip to Grindelwald. This was not going to be easy, especially for the Finlaysons. At the end of the first season with the lift, I broke another leg.

With the season closed at Glencoe, it was decided to have a last weekend in the Cairngorms. It's to be remembered there were no lifts in the Gorms at that time. The famous Robert M Clyde, Bob, at that time lived and worked in Inverness. We camped in Glenmore, where Bob and Harry McKay would join us. There wasn't much snow. None of us were bothered. The Coe crowd were on a high after all the skiing we had taken off of Meall a' Bhuiridh that wonderful winter. However, it was still walkies from Glenmore in those days, through Windy Ridge into Coire Cas, where we stopped and drummed up in Jean's Hut. We trekked up to the top of the Head Wall of Corrie Cas and skied down. Bob, who had not skied with us for a long time, was amazed at how our skiing had changed. We never skied much that first day next day, Sunday, and we were treated to a Cairngorm winter's day in May. It was wild. We drummed up in the Jean's Hut in Coire Cas, wasting time kidding about breaking legs, a taboo subject. I'm not superstitious, but never make fun of how legs get broken. It's catching.

I should relate a warming memory, while we drummed up the day before in Jean's hut, with the usual gallon tea drum. In came one of the new people we had met in skiing. His name was Bill Watson, from Helensburgh, on the Clydeside, but he was not a Red Clydesider as such. He was invited to help himself to the hot, sweet, milky tea. After all he was *A Clydesider*. Next morning, back in Jean's, the tea drum was on. It was boiling away when we discovered, some *clown* had neglected to bring the tea! We had sugar and carnation milk. Not much good without the tea! Bill Watson, walked in to a wall of silence. "My contribution," said he. A quarter pound of "best tea," and two pounds Tate & Lyle sugar. Who said there's no Toffs in the world! We never found the clown who forgot the sugar. "None of our friends make *blunders!*" Bill went to a famous English public school. So much for our preconceived ideas and opinions.

As I said, the weather was terrible. Nevertheless, we walked up Coire na Ciste determined to get a run down what was then a famous ski run, and still is. Into the sleety rain and wind it was "under the arm." We were needing our heads looked at. After our run down, some clown of a friend decided we should have another run. Back up into it, with the sleet and rain in our faces. What you do to please friends! Which reminds me of a true axiom, "*a friend in need is a pest.*" Near the end of the run, there was a big hole in the snow. With the sleet, the rain and the thaw, the burn ran deep. You could ski down one side of the hole, on the left there was a gap. I, with all my new skills, took a run at it, and cleared it no bother. When I landed, the snow collapsed and I fell upside down into the burn. The left ski dug in. My leg was broken. *So much for fun making.* I ended up with my head in the "wee burn." No release bindings in those days. I was having trouble with the head in and out of the water, and the leg was giving me *gip!* Before the panic set in, strong hands grabbed me under the shoulders and lifted my head clear. I remember looking into Big Willie's face. He said, now I quote, "I think I've done a bad thing!" To this day, I'm sure there's many wonder, if he did the right thing! Willie, up to his knees in water, couldn't release me. The others eventually got me out. That was the last time any of us skied without release bindings.

Here we were the "The Cream Of The Mountain Men," and not one piece of first aid gear between us. We never even knew where a stretcher could be found. One of sorts was found 7 miles away at Coylumbridge. Lying on the steep side of Coire Ciste, soaked, freezing, the nervous system had the body shaking. However, the body did not know I was a "Hardcase." There is humour in all things. While I was lying there, a normal humanoid came by. He saw my predicament and poured out the last of his thermos of coffee and brandy, and gave it to Clyde for me. Bob downed it in one. *Some pal!.* He was good at that sort of thing. This poor ordinary person exclaimed, "the drink was for the injured man!" Bob's retort was that *his* need was greater than *mine*. On reflection, this was fair. But it seems to me, some superior power should *protect us* from our *"friends"!*

It was long hours before the my friends got back with the stretcher. The weather got worse and there was still a long carry through all the deep heather in the bottom of the Ciste to Glenmore and Peter's McGeogh's pick-up. They took me to Raigmore hospital in Inverness, where the leg was pinned the following Tuesday. For some reason, they kept me there for a month. All I needed, after a brilliant winter, was another broken leg! I had a long hard day that day. My friends had a longer one. They had a long drive back to Glasgow. Another memory. When they got me to bed, I started to feel better. I said to the wee, young night nurse, that I was starving. She said, "you think so?" and made scrambled eggs. I had a few mouthfuls and vomited on the bed. There was no way I could have stopped. She cleaned me and the bed up, and told me she knew I would not keep that down. My *Lady of the Lamp*.

When the plaster came off my leg, in three months, I went into Killearn Hospital, north of Glasgow, to have the pins removed from the first broken leg, as they had been moving and giving some trouble. The day after the operation for the pins, they let me out, and, instead of waiting for the ambulance, I hitch-hiked to Glasgow. Two bum legs not feeling too tricky. No wonder the ward sister was *not too chuffed*. I got a lift right away in a large black van. It was a van from a Glasgow asylum. There might be an accidental message there! When Jeanie found out, she thought I had been in the right means of transport. See, when you're down, they're never off your back! Not long after the asylum van incident, Jimmy Hamilton and Jimmy Thomson arrived at our house early one morning. They were having a day's climbing on the Cobbler. Would I like to come for the run? I could light a fire at the Shire Bridge, and spend a day out. A lot better than sitting in a Glasgow tenement. As they say in the vernacular, I was Joe-The-Toff.

It was a gem of a day driving up Loch Lomondside. The talk was of their day's climbing. Coming west from Tarbet, where the Vikings pulled their long boats up from Arrochar, the decision was made that I should have a go at getting up the Cobbler. We had forgotten the Greenroad. We had forgotten more than the Greenroad. My brain must have been back in the tenement. With the help of my two half-wit pals, I made it to the twin peaks. It's there we made the next blunder. I would have a go at the Recess Route. The brain was definitely not running *the full shilling*. The Recess is straight forward, but not with two bum legs. I got stuck for a long time. The midges nearly killed me. The temper was the real villain of the piece. I had to be more or less pulled up on the rope. I didn't like that. But beggars can't be choosers. Getting down to the car was *epic*. What some people will do for a day out! I was very thankful for my two pals. Without them, I'd never have made it down. Without the two Bums, I would never have been there! I suppose that's another *part of the learning curve*.

7. Learning the "Profession"

Not being able to work stops most of your income. Like most young couples, my wife worked. I was now on the sick. Getting to Grindelwald was now a monumental task, even though it was still possible. None of those going would be flush. There would be no fun money. What's new? We never had very much fun money We made our own fun. The first saving would be effected by driving out. I had just bought a Ford Ten van. It was a *horriblis* Glasgow Corporation green and was immediately called "The Green Vomit" by my friends. I painted it a nice powder blue, in an effort to eradicate this naughty name. Regardless of my efforts, the first name stuck. Which only goes to prove "you can't make silk purses out of pigs ears."

However, *the best laid schemes* don't always work out. We had the Suez crisis, with its petrol rationing. Driving across Europe was not on. We decided to drive to Dover, then boat and train. The Green Vomit had no heater. As a matter of fact, it was a fairly basic mode of transport. On the way back, the police stopped us. They were looking for dangerous, escaped prisoners They must have thought they'd got lucky. The police were quite amused when they heard where we'd been and what we had done. No wonder, when they looked at the Vomit!

Crossing the channel was something. Brits going skiing. A wonderment to behold! Most had their boots and ski pants on, and cloth anoraks. No quilted jackets in those days. Everyone displayed their British Ski Club badges, and why not! The duty free was getting hammered. Not by us, it wasn't that cheap, even at one pound five pence a bottle. We were not into drink much in those days. A few years later, we caught up in that department. How much different going skiing is today. You leave the airport at lunchtime, and have dinner in your resort in the evening. In those days, travel from Scotland took the best part of two days each way. I mentioned how big a kick you got when you saw the high Alps in summer for the first time. Well, for me, winter was just as sweet and just as exciting as the summer.

We had booked the cheapest chalet we could get. It turned out to be ideal, at two and six pence per night per person. We thought it might be a doss of some sort. The man of the house was a mountain farmer, and ski teacher. His wife was a gem. She took charge of our Iain. We had struck gold again. The group were Bob Clyde, Willie Smith, Harry McKay, Maggie Dunlop, Jim Kelman, and ourselves. We also had Peter McGeogh and family, and Bill McKenzie of the Scottish Mountaineering Club. We never really knew him very well, we did after it. He made a fine *pig's ear!* He's into his eighties now, and still gives the skis the full treatment. Bill has climbed in many of the big mountain ranges of the world. I'm proud to know him. Some time passed. On the hill, I said to Jimmy Smith, "that old bastard is nearly eighty!" as he skied by. Jimmy shook his head. He was tickled. I introduced them. Jimmy became a trainer to the British Team. He had to work to achieve what he became in British Skiing. I knew big Bill would enjoy hearing of Jimmy's success. Jimmy certainly enjoyed meeting big Bill. I was pleased to bring them together. Grindelwald was everything we dreamt it would be. We were first on the lifts and last off, at night. All were dressed in black. We became known as "the Black Blobs." We went for three weeks. It's the extra week that gets you leg fit, then you *really can* get the skis running well. The pound was good against the franc. Our son got skis and boots.

Jeanie had skis, ski pants and I had Molitor boots. Three weeks lifts tickets. Food, such as it was. All on sixty seven pounds, a tight budget for three weeks! This was our first Alpine ski holiday. The first of many.

By good luck, the Ski Club of Great Britain Rep in Grindelwald, at that time, was Leslie Thompson, from Helensburgh on Clydeside. She was ex British Team. This achievement she managed after starting skiing late in life. She was a most determined lady. She insisted we have lessons from some demigod of a ski teacher. It was explained that this was out of the question, because of our lack of funds. She insisted. She would put up the money, and we'd pay back later in spring, as we did. I spoke about breaking two legs at one time. Leslie, after winning her way into our Olympic Team, did just that, in training at Murren, and missed her Olympics and the "golden time in her life." *A shame.* She was the first of the great ladies I was to have the privilege to ski with in the coming years. She was a member of Kandahar Club of Murren, and the Scottish Ski Club, and the Ski Club of Great Britain.

After the build up she gave us about this teacher, we were looking for something special. We were not disappointed. He was all that he should have been, as a ski teacher at this level. I will expand on this later. His name was Werner Stager, from Lauterbrunnen, below Wengen. A mountain guide, and farmer. His hobby was horticulture. I found his love was a large greenhouse, where he grew flowers during the winter. Most of them went to friends. The heating bill must have cost a bomb, in that cold slot, in Lauterbrunnen valley. A place I would come to know very well. Werner and I became very close over the next number of years. He looked like what people think a ski teacher should look like, and most of them don't. Some of the finest don't even look sporty. And should they. What surprised me, was how he was feted by skiers who engaged him to teach them, even those who only *just* knew him. I found this strange. It went against my stringent background. In our world were many top people. There never was any chance of hero worship. Quiet admiration, certainly, and there it stopped. However, when we did develop a strata of *good* skiers at home, a number of these foolish people did emerge. Our heavy industrial background left little energy for such childish nonsense.

When I got to know Werner, I found a man of many talents, who possessed a kind and caring heart, which he tried to hide, like so many of his kind. He had a quick, bad temper and, considering all he had going for him in the world, it was his *Achilles'* heel. Six months in a Clydeside shipyard would have been a good "finishing school" for him. He would have learned to curb his temper, and possibly been more at peace with the world. This was another finishing school for me. There'd be a few more before I was "properly finished," if that would ever be possible. Smith, McKay, Bob Clyde and myself went for the lessons. None of us could be compared with good skiers of the day. We had a very long way to go. We had Werner for three half days. That was six hours. This was spent on a practice slope, doing turning and posture exercises. This, I learned later, was to help our awful body positions. That is still the cardinal fault of all unskilled skiers, and almost all good skiers. The three half days passed in a flash, yet, for me, I remember vividly the impact they had on me, and importantly, on my imagination. What I personally learned, was how little an idea I had of anything about skiing. This triggered a burning need to learn to ski correctly. This is a private need, you do not speak to *anyone* about it. This is a cross you place on your own back, and you carry it yourself!

With this new driving force, I could see a definite goal for me in to the future. This goal could only be achieved by total effort. Anything less, and the goal would have failed. I committed myself to its end. It was the most selfish total decision that I ever acted on in my life. And of all my many faults, selfishness was never one of them. What was the situation as to the possibility in my becoming a good skier. I was fully twenty six years old, and in reality was just learning to ski. There was the legacy of the two recently broken legs, that would cramp most people's style. Despite any natural ability, lack of time on skis, and I mean "thousands of hours," is the drawback to anyone's progress in any improvement they can achieve in the skiing, no matter how much talent they may have. I had a five year old son who had been on skis for three years. He was surrounded by enthusiastic activity in skiing, helpful "Aunties and Uncles." He also had the added advantage of not understanding how difficult learning to ski was, or getting to ski was, at that period of time. This may seem a bizarre statement to make, in the circumstances that prevail today. But it certainly was then, if money was limited.

Starting then, for the next six years, more or less, was a time of frustration for me. It was a constant nag in the back of my mind, that I could be injured again. The economic stress of such an event would have been the final obstacle in making any breakthrough in what I thought possible for me. It did happen the season before I was to go to *my* Olympics, as we'll see. After the lessons from Werner, our skiing, as a group, went from strength to strength in every way. Speed, difficult snow, through the poles, and, more importantly, for our own enjoyment. Our memories of the Jungfrau area were coloured by the value it added to the whole new adventure, and why not call it an adventure, as that is what it was. Those magnificent mountains the Mittelberg, Eiger, Mönch and Jungfrau that encompass that Walt Disney wonderland left the whole scene stamped indelibly in your mind's eye.

It was obvious I must get back to the Alps and, if possible, to a *fountainhead* of skiing, like Werner Stager, if I were to get what I needed out of skiing. It could not be done here, at that time. It can now. That possibility has been achieved, to get a real start to a skiing career here in Scotland, in my opinion. And those who helped to make this possible should be pleased with their part in it. And it was not only ski teachers who contributed! Time has shown, that much more has been achieved, as the needs of skiing has grown. The day of leaving Grindelwald came on us, as it had to. Staying for the rest of the winter would have been a fine dream. Dreams are invented for children. Part of my dream was waiting back in Glencoe. *The lift.* There's always a little sunshine round the corner! Before leaving the Grindelwald station, Harry McKay put his last ten cents in a vending machine, and got two dirty little Stogies for him and me. It was like smoking a couple of Havanas.

The other big effort that season was the serious début of our group into Scottish Ski Racing. You didn't need seed points, just as well. Lewis Drysdale would have been a prime mover in creating our points system. This was a period in Scottish skiing, when the opportunities to pick new skills *abounded.* I say that with a fondish humour, but it was true. Some of the "chancers," who took different opportunities, became prominent members of various sections of the British ski world. Some survive through to the present day. In the next four or five years, Jimmy Hamilton, Harry McKay, and Andy Scott, became Scottish

LEARNING THE "PROFESSION"

Champions, from that small, tight, unified group. They managed this with a limited skiing background, and certainly they had to learn to race as they went along.

All the racing in Scotland, up to that time, was pursued by the Dundee Ski Club and the Scottish. The Dundee went at it with a vengeance, and, as a result, led the indigenous competitors. But that would change. The previous year was the 1956 Cortina Olympics. Toni Sailer won three Gold Medals, Downhill, Giant Slalom and Slalom. He did the same again in the World Championships the following year. The world began to take a serious interest in skiing. This would be when our ski industry got started, as we see it today. When I worked with Toni Sailer, many years later, in a summer racing camp in British Columbia, we spoke of how unfortunate for him to have been at least five years too early with his medals, to become what Jean Claude Killy did later. Anyway, Toni did not end up skint!

Between the above happenings, the Glencoe lift, and the new freedom of thought that was abroad in the land, it left the way open for people, who a decade before, would never have dreamt of being ski racers, to become ski racers, to the enrichment of all concerned and of the participants themselves. As it turned out, I would not become a racer, as we'll see. We had the Coronation Cup that spring, in Glencoe. The British racers came that weekend. Allan Crompton and Leslie Thompson attended. It was like a gala, that seemed to bring a winter of many achievements to a pleasant and suitable conclusion.

Before we move on, it would be worth looking back to see what we had been about, after arriving at the end of our first full winter in a totally applied effort in our skiing. We had started with many advantages. We had the unlimited use of a ski lift. We were probably the fittest group of skiers in Scotland. We were mountain wise and hand found a tremendous challenge which we were well able to take up. The comfort and sanctuary of the Doss, the strength of the friendship contained therein. We were very fortunate to have coalesced, as a mixed group, in quite such a unique way.

Another anecdote. This one slays me. On the way up to the Doss, on the dark Friday nights, we used to stop at Crianlarich railway yard and stock up on good quality coal that fell off the wagons in the coal yards. Old habits die hard! It took us a long time to figure out, that it was less bother to buy coal than nicking it. We decided to buy it. Kingshouse Hotel had it delivered for the cost of two pounds each. This lasted the winter, with coal left over. Even we could afford that and it was legal! Years later, we were talking about how stupid *perking* (that's short for stealing) the coal had been. It turned out that a signalman in the signal box overlooking the yard, had been watching us pulling this stunt for some time. So much for being clever dicks! The signalman was the father-in-law of Neil Lafferty, one of the new, younger members of the group. It was his wife Frances who let us into this little morsel. Her father was the signalman! So ended our first full winter skiing. And the start of a future full of promise.

Since skiing became the driving force in my life, I had taken to working constant nightshifts, and Sundays, in the summer. This brought in extra money. It severely curtailed the climbing activities. There's a price to be paid for everything. In winter, I worked on Friday nights. With petrol rationing, we all used the Green Vomit, to save petrol coupons. The van users slept in my flat on

70

the Friday nights. I'd be off nightshift by 6 am. Willie would drive up to Meall a' Bhuiridh, where we would be skiing by nine am. I'd catnap in the back of the Green Vomit. When you hear some of the young Tigers saying they are tired after skiing, I smile. Skiing should not make you that kind of tired. What should concern you, is not getting enough personal skiing.

We went back to Grindelwald the following winter. And we drove out. This was more convenient. You load up at home, you unload at your chalet. There were no motorways, so driving was quite a bit more onerous than it is today. Back to the same chalet, which was pleasant. We now knew how to organise the whole deal better. The year before we had to put up with pretty basic food. This time we had the gift of two haunches of venison and a fourteen pound tin of Dutch ham. I had been skiing with a lady from a local shooting estate. When she heard of the coming trip, she insisted on the above contribution. She was the first woman I was to meet who had been born into the world where she had no understanding of the every day reality of how life was lived by most people. Her husband's estate was one that the Purves brothers and I had shot over, from time to time. I call her a lady, not because her husband owned a shooting estate, but because she behaved and looked like a lady should, in my opinion.

She would have been in her early forties, which to my tender twenty seven years, seemed quite old. She was beautiful, had obviously been so cossetted all her life, that the events of day to day life would impinge little on her freedom of thought. This made teaching her a simple chore. This I say as a compliment. I must have been quite a novelty to her, and I'm sure she never had a clue to what I was all about. I was to ski with her on a number of occasions in the future, and discovered her real charm was her complete naïvety. There are many women in the world, who are just as well placed, but who are anything but naïve. Here was me, a male chauvinist, who found this lady a source of tremendous interest.

One day, after skiing in wonderful weather and snow, conditions that bring out that bonhomie and a certain peace of mind such days produce, my lady pupil said, "Frith, skiing is a gregarious sport," and then explained the meaning of the word "gregarious." You know, I was almost stuck for words. I agreed with her. "But!." This was nearly a lesson in self control. It was likely one of the many sharp corners I was to lose in the coming years. Keep your ears open and your mouth shut, and you might learn something. Something I was better at than people gave me credit for. Mind you, if this had been some pain in the arse, I would have handled it differently.

An arrangement for me to collect the haunches the last weekend in January was made. The estate house was some six miles across the Rannoch from the Doss. The only good part of the track was where it passed over the main road. It was a *stotter* of a night, (that means, in Glaswegian, it's either marvellous, or horrific). The rain and the sleet were coming straight out of Glen Etive, and Glencoe, in horizontal screaming sheets. The Chindits had an easier time, on the Burma Road, during the war. The vacuum wipers were not very good in these conditions. The Green Vomit had done it again, it got there! It's great what a gentle hand on the wheel can achieve. It was terrible, I had visions of having to walk. The old house sits high on the edge of the Rannoch, overlooking the Ba Lochs, a truly remarkable location for a house. In weather like this, a wonderful haven. One of the sons let me in. You could smell the wood smoke in the hallway. In the living room, the large log fire lay on the firebricks of the hearth,

71

reeking and spewing a good feeling into the room. The January storm outside pressed hard on the old house, keeping in its soft comfort. Many's a night I've had the same sweet feeling, in less salubrious accommodations. There was another boy. Both were teenagers. They were dressed in estate tweeds that were too old in style for them. They did not speak my language, but we managed. They were mesmerised with my grossly exaggerated tales of the shipyards. I could have told them about shooting escapades that took place round that house!

Like all Highland houses, out came the whisky. I remember it well. It was called "Red Fox," and, of course, was a Malt. Domestic measures were served, the *imperial gill*, in a large heavy glass. What else. I say this with hand on heart. I was not a drinking man at that time. There was no offer of water, so, being a hardcase Clydesider, I persevered with the demon drink and drank it as it was served.

Between the *Water of Life*, and the heat of the roaring fire, the booze took the desired effect. The younger boy got me another *imperial* to go with the one I had not finished, so I downed what was left of the first. No bother for a Clydesider! The big boy brought in the two haunches, nicely wrapped up in greaseproof paper. I had never seen haunches so well presented. The eldest boy said he would put the venison in my car. It's when he left the room, I remembered there was a .300 US army carbine, under a raincoat, in the back of the Green Vomit. I wondered if the rough bumpy road had uncovered it. We would soon see. The big lad came back in. He didn't seem to be put out in any way. You can't beat luck! Between the pouring rain, and the pitch dark, he probably just lobbed the *loot* into the back of the van, and ran for the house. These little tests are sent to see what sort of metal your are made of. Bob Clyde used to say "its good spanner stuff." The end of that saying is not so polite! Between the pot holes in the dirt track of a road, the blinding rain and sleet, the bum wipers, and the drunken state of the driver, the drive back was not without its problems.

There was a grand welcome back to the Doss when they saw what I had brought back. I explained about the Red Fox and how I was forced to put my best foot forward to keep up our good name. They all took that with a pinch of salt. They were all interested to hear about the lodge. None of us spent a lot of time in these sort of places. The little slip with the carbine brought on a few laughs. I can't remember for the world of me, what that carbine was doing in the van. Anyway, you can't be perfect all the time. The storm was still doing its best outside and around the Doss, the ornamental cast iron stove was glowing red hot and keeping our lodge snuggie and comfy. Times like these cannot be bought.

We got back to Grindelwald. Some of the original group were added to, Jack Thompson from Glenmore Lodge, Helen Carmichael and Wee Tommy McKee. These people were to be very much a part of the future ski scene. In Grindelwald, we had three full day lessons with Werner Stager. In the class was a most impressive English lady, a Joan Shering. Joan had won the British Ladies Downhill Championship in 1956, at an age of around forty. Anyone would be proud of such a formidable achievement. She had trained with Werner over the course, for weeks before the race. There was another, Caroline Simms, an ex British Champion. We would become friends, and ski together many times in the future. Now, here were two ladies of comfortable background, with no naïvety.

After the first week, it started to rain. It rained all the way up to eight thousand feet. The skiing stopped. There is no more miserable place to be than an Alpine village in February when it's *peeing* down. This is a test of patience for the strongest willed. Then it started to snow. The village went crazy. Unfortunately, it snowed so much, that the upper hill was closed, because of avalanche danger. What skiing there was, was junk. Mountain weather makes no allowances for your personal desires. We, of all people, should have understood that. The three weeks *were not much cop*. We still had our skiing, on Meall a' Bhuiridh, to go back to.

The start of my life in ski teaching happened on the slopes of Kleine Scheidegg. This is the mountain railway station under the Eiger Wall. Werner asked me if anyone was teaching in my "station," (that's what the Swiss call a ski area), at home. I said there was no one. He said, "why don't you?" We discussed my limited experience, and background in skiing. His reply was, he understood I was the best technical skier back there. That may have been true, however, skiing was not yet at the stage at home where that sort of knowledge had developed to justify that statement. There was Gavin Ogilvy, from Angus County, who stood out amongst the rest of the pack as a skier. He stood up, shifted his feet in the direction he wanted to go, and turned his skis. It's still done that way, despite all the technical *bull* flying about today. If Gavin had been a full-time skier, he would have been a *good* skier by any standard.

The seeds about teaching were in my mind, but irresolution held me back, something I'm not guilty of. This was different. When I see some of the comedians who have come on the scene since, I know why I was hesitant. I carefully found out what my friends thought about the idea. The feedback gave me the final nudge. Brassie and bold, as I appear to be, I am not. My friends' opinions were most important to me. You know when you ask them a question, you get a straight answer.

When I got home, I told Lewis Drysdale what I was thinking about. To my personal gratification, he was very enthusiastic. Through his good offices, the Scottish Ski Club gave me their official approval. Doing things this way in the beginning most certainly helped ski teaching when we eventually got up and organised nationally. Philip Rankin, the boss of our "station," did everything possible to help our family on the Meall a' Bhuiridh, during this period. There were others on the sidelines, who were not so comfortable about my suitability for this undertaking. They were not my concern. What was the right and the wrong of it? The wrong of it was, if I *made a balls of it*, the future of indigenous, would be ski teachers, could have been very different today, from what it is. What was the right of it? If there was any right. Was I suitable? History has answered that!

Lewis Drysdale–RJB

I was introduced to the highest standards of professional skiing, by the highest standards of amateur skiing, which is the basis of all skiing. Lesley Thompson, who introduced Werner to me, had a late start in her skiing life and only missed her Olympics by bad luck. She was what's good about amateur skiing. I wanted to be a good skier. Unlike Lesley, I had no funds. Ski teaching might be a way through to this end. What it taught me, was to analyse the complexities of skiing. When I had to think for other people, that gave my own skiing a powerful base, which, in the natural chain of events, I built on. And still do.

73

Meeting Werner was important. What would have happened, if we had not met? The question is not relevant now. Some other way would have been found. I was lucky enough to have found this part of it. Skiing was rich in people of good heart. And I understood this at the time. There are people who try as hard as anyone I've known and don't make the cut in skiing, *That is how the cookie crumbles*. That is a sadness of life. Buddhists call it *"karma."*

What was the teaching situation in the Scottish mountains then? To tell the truth, I knew little about it at that time. I quickly made it my business to find out. The only teaching taking place full-time, was at Cairngorm. The only British ski teacher working on our hills was Jack Thompson. He has the honour to be teaching skiing longer than any other person in our not so short history in skiing. Jack started ski teaching at Glenmore Lodge, in the year 1950. His long distinguished career in teaching outdoor pursuits, has no equal. We will hear more of my old friend, as the story grows.

What is a ski teacher? I was just about to start a forty-odd year apprenticeship, to try and learn how to be one. I think I'll need another forty-odd to learn where I went wrong! I don't say that flippantly. I am just coming to grips with the problems of trying to improve people's skiing, and my understanding of the problems therein. All standards of skiers need help to improve their skills, if they are that way minded. There are several ways to do this. The use of a ski teacher is one. The other is to start as a child. Being born with talent is *the biggie!* So let's try and find out what a ski teacher should be. Firstly they must be personable, well turned out and punctual. Secondly, they must have more than a good knowledge of ski movements, and be able to break them down into their simple component parts. This is paramount, to enable the average part-time skier, from beginner to advanced, to be able to assimilate the information, without confusion, and consequently save unnecessary stress.

Thirdly, it's to be borne in mind that, because people, in their desire to learn to ski better, place themselves in your hands, does not make them any less able

to see through a poor teacher. Even more unforgivable, to find they are getting a bad lesson from a skilled teacher. You may find this hard to understand. But *it happens.* If this is the sum total of what I learned in all these years, I am satisfied. I've assimilated many things about the skills of skiing. I am sure that learning to teach has a much more varied demand on common sense than your ability to simply ski well. Skiing well is a *must.* This is how the ski teachers I respect feel about their chosen profession. We will extrapolate on this more fully, in the narrative, as time becomes ripe. The reader can then make a judgement on what has been said, on this specific and controversial subject.

Coming National Racers
Evelyn & Helen Carmichael with Iain Finlayson

Back at home that season, I started to introduce myself as a ski teacher. Unlike most debutants, in my first years teaching on Meall a' Bhuiridh, I only taught reasonably good to advanced pupils. The results from the lessons were very satisfying. Why not? Werner Stager did it. Hence the old adage, *have a good teacher*. The real trick is to have pupils like Glencoe produced. The better skiers of our group, because of their involvement in racing, spent a great deal of time practising through racing gates. Though I could not take part in racing as a "professional," I practised with them in the gates. This again was grist to the mill, and was put away in the memory bank, for future use.

New Ski School Boss
"Ski Maister Frith, one o' the Club's
hardest cases, he took the boys for
a week an' put them through the
paces."– CL

Having the complete run of the lift, we were allowed to open it as early as suited us, and that meant from dawn to dusk. In reasonable weather, we put in between us a *wheen* of downhill miles. All of us who were in that inner circle seemed to be living in a golden bubble. Nothing was too much trouble in pursuit of our skiing. This may seem like small beer in today's liberal climate of skiing for all. Everyone is entitled to find something they could only dream of. Some of us did.

Bob Clyde, who had been living in Inverness for some years, started coming down at the weekends, and joined the work party. Other new faces came and fitted in. No one was invited, it was natural selection. A sound and well tried way of keeping a healthy balance in a tight society. There was only one who lost their place in the scheme of things, and not without good reason. At the end of the 1957 season, the ski scene had not visually changed much. Under the surface, the roots of the future were deepening and spreading. Few of us would realise what was taking place, let alone what would transpire, in the world of skiing to be. The alpine resorts were only just awakening to the new increasing demands for more and better skiing facilities. It must be said the Scottish Ski Club's lift, on Meall a' Bhuiridh, fired the imagination of the Scots as to what *painless* skiing can do for those locked in the "walk up, ski down" syndrome. That could be how the state of play may have stood at the end of the lift's second season.

Back to Grindelwald and Wengen, at the end of January and beginning of February. This time, I arranged to ski with Werner Stager for most of the three weeks, as a private pupil. Joan Shearing joined us quite a number of times. This was good in two ways. It helped with the costs and the other advantage was being involved with, and watching, a skier like Joan. Under the Stager regime of direct and positive advanced ski teaching to a strong willed woman, she was an excellent pupil.

However, ingrained into the very fibre of her intellect was a method of unweighting her skis, which was used by some of the fine skiers of the same background she had been reared in. *I will try and come back to this subject.* The way she made her skis turn won her the British Ladies Downhill against all commonsense realities. To try and adjust her grooved and proved skiing, which worked in any conditions, was a tall order and achievement of *no small potatoes!* I'm delighted to say, years later, she still skied the same way. No teacher has the right to win all the time. That would leave little for imagination, and then where would we be? Speechless, maybe. I watched Werner stalking about and around this problem. She skied so well with her feet through the turn, it was hard to be insistent with her. The dreadful fault was her weight was fractionally back coming out of the turn. I know many skiers who would be pleased to be lumbered with Joan's dreadful fault!

Other fine skiers joined us from time to time. This, I was to realise later, had been a great opportunity for me, and was to stand me in good stead on many occasions to come. You can't buy experience. As the *time beast* ate into the shortness of my twenty one days, the tempo of the beat at which we skied, stepped up. During the last week, no one joined us. Werner was not always long on the mouth when he was working. As that last week drew on, he became progressively quieter. The speed, and the choice of terrain, became vicious. This was a test. We skied through places so rough, normal headcases would have avoided them. I had to prove I was up to it, or he was the master. This meant your brain and body had to be alert. When a good one is pulling out the stops, the one at the back has the disadvantage. Friends of mine reading this, will know what I am talking about. This lesson is burned indelibly in my mind.

The last day was "the Showdown at OK Corral!" All the way up from Lauterbrunnen to the Kleine Scheidegg on the mountain train, it was *no speakie.* It was a perfect skiing day. This would be *find out time.* We only had sweaters, no ski teachers bum bag round his waist, he was stripped down for action. And we both got it. We skied in places that had to be seen to be believed, where the snow was scarce and there were obstacles aplenty. From the top of Lauberhorn, down through the barricades, past the Wasser Station, through the trees, to top of the of the Hannig. There are many naughty places there. Every conceivable, awkward, unlikely place on that hill was our meat and drink.

The last run was Lauberhorn Race Course down to Mary's Café, now called Lang Ham's, an old ski teaching friend of mine. Now, there's not much you can do to the famous Lauberhorn Race Course, but skiing at speed, off the track, changes the ball game. That's what we did. He knew his way about the hill, and that makes a difference. To do what he was trying to do takes your best shot. He had a few in his bag. It took years of experience for me to understand how well he was doing his job! At no time during that last day, did I allow him to get up my nose. If I had done that, we would both have lost.

Another anecdote. The following winter, I had skied in Switzerland from the beginning of December to the first week in February. I met up with my family and the crowd from the Doss for the last three weeks in Zermatt. Werner came for a few days skiing. I had my first pair of free test skis from Authier. His Nibs called them *a bunch of shit,* They were excellent, brand new, and ready to go. This was to be our last day, until the following December. We were having a last run till next season. His skis were beat-up old bangers of Head Masters. We left the top of the Blauherd, to ski down the National Downhill Course. This is one of the old tracks not used any more. There had been no new snow for weeks. The snow was "firm," my edges were brand new, and his were shot. He was having trouble holding the turns correctly, with his bum edges. In those days, there were no piste machines. Half way down the run was a gully, where the lumps of the top of the bumps had been shovelled. I spotted my intrepid leader clocking the gully. In we went. The lumps were flying off the tails of his skis. He had a *shuftie* back to see how I was doing. That was his second mistake. His first was his beat up skis. As he jerked his head back, he caught a front inside edge and blew up! You can't win them all. I skied past down to Zermatt. Never take anything to do with "failures"! When he got down too, he was laughing, and full of it. I told him it was the old skis. "It was not the skis!" he replied. He knew he had blown it. Good skiers don't care about falls. He was pleased; I was pleased.

That last week in Wengen had *cut the custard* for me. This was skiing as it could be. At speed, where you wanted, how you wanted, when you wanted, in any kind of snow. I've tried to keep this thinking going ever since. I think it's called *positive thinking*. Back to Wengen, and the three weeks training. After we finished the run, and were going up the Allmend ski lift, to get back to Wengen, Werner put his arm round my shoulder, put a piece of chewing gum in my mouth, broke into a toothie smile, and then, using my local name, said, "Fritz, you are now a *good* skier!" Well, what can you say? If it had not been for those *no talkie* three weeks, the Zermatt *stunt*, as described, might have been longer in achieving. If ever. I'll be forever grateful for my *karma* being what it is. Later, before I left for home, Werner put it to me that I should come and attend the Skischulleiterkurs, or Ski Directors Course. The truth be told, I had no idea what he meant! Joan Shearing explained what it was.

This course is held the first week in December, all Swiss Ski School Directors, and aspiring directors, must attend. Here was something to wrap the grey matter round. I was given no indication as to the cost. We'd sort that little detail out later. I did ask how my skiing would stand up. This was more or less passed over. At that time, I still had no gauge as to where my skiing stood. Here I would be placed in a situation that may well be beyond me. Oh ye of little faith! Stager said the information would be sent to me. And the deed was done. However, the fates were not finished with me yet.

The season at home had a lighthearted atmosphere, the reason being we were all settling into the challenge of the future and learning to ski. That's how I felt about this new aspect of my life. The racers in our group were making their mark. Their endeavours were working, as were mine. I had taken my first professional class. They were ladies. Iris, Jenny and Suilven. I have always had soft a spot for lady pupils. This was an important occasion for me. I could not describe how excited I was, with my three ladies and my first "class ". Thank you, my ladies.

During that epic three weeks with Werner, while skiing on the Wengen Bumps, a stout lady skied into Werner and knocked him on his butt. While he was picking the lady and himself up, and dusting the snow off her, she was very embarrassed. When he finally got her language, which was Italian, he probably gave her a lot of ski teacher *bull*. As she skied off laughing, he gave me one of his few smiles of the week, and said, "always be nice to ladies, Fritz!" This was *me* getting the *bull!* During this period, the thinking and planning for the future development of Scottish Skiing was picking up momentum. Unsung heroes of the scenario were beavering away in the background. As we can all see, it turned out very well, despite the vagaries of our climate.

The rest of the season of 1959 at home, was a sort of anticlimax after what had transpired in Wengen. My head was full of broken bottles. It left me with much to think about. Here was me three months short of thirty years of age, married with a six year old son, living in what would be called poor circumstances today, having the temerity to be considering putting my head on the block. I could not even contemplate what would be required of me! Apart from what it might cost, it still may not come off. Werner may have been talking through the side of his head. What I needed was practice. Time was limited. Skiing in the early part of our season can be very iffy. I would need all the days that were left of our season, to cram in all the skiing possible It was catch-up time, which was impossible. But try you must.

Willie Smith had taken on the job of operating the lift full-time, for the last part of the season. We agreed to work together. I would hang up my *shingle* and teach *on spec*. Willie and I would combine our efforts and split all the "income." Making any income from teaching under the circumstances that prevailed at that time was doubtful. None in that group was skiing for money. There was no money in skiing anyway. There's a time in all of our lives when you don't expect monetary rewards for everything you undertake. If you do, you run the chance of missing something that could have been very dear to you. There are things that have no price tag. If you have found something that most can never have you should be thankful and you are due to leave something in the *kitty*.

This winter turned out to be all that I could have expected of it. The first taste of long, protracted skiing, where you could set a pattern of how you went about progressing what you thought you had to do in your own skiing. Not having to go back on the Sunday night, to spend the week in heavy engineering was almost as sweet as the freedom of the winter hills. At the end of that season, Willie and I had a wee bit of a drama, which neither of us enjoyed. As you'll see. Willie and I decided to stay up in the Ski Club's hut midweek, to save the daily grind up Thrombosis Slope. We were back in the Doss at weekends, for the partying. The Club Hut was a cold miserable place, compared with Our Doss, but grinding up that slope each day was like wearing cast iron breeks with barbed wire suspenders! This would be the most skiing any of us would have achieved in one season, and it was something bigger and better than our imagination.

There was one compensatory stimulant in learning this new trade. Any effort or sacrifice you may make only ends in pleasure. Most people have to work all their lifelong days in mundane boring jobs with no light in the tunnel. Those who are successful in life might remember there's sheep in the fold. When I hear some of the have-made-its speak disparagingly of others who live in meaner circumstances than themselves, I feel they should have more common charity. But expecting a free kick at the ball is not part of true life's tapestry.

It was around this period I met Luke O'Reilly. He was ten, small for his age, with a wee freckly face. We became friends straight off. Luke is one of the Lucky Ones, born to ski. Our friendship grew as he grew. He became a fine young man. We skied together into the sixties, when he won a scholarship to Dartmouth University in the States. He now lives in California, where he represents, of all things, Rock and Roll groups! Interesting, for an ex public school lad! I learned so much from Luke. What in particular would be hard to say. A better way to describe the process, was that I gleaned part of his skiing skills. When he was twelve, we were skiing in avalanche rubble, a difficult task for anyone, let alone a wee boy with no muscle power. He made up for his lack of muscle with his ingrained talent. A young man, who was to be in the British Team, skiing with us, at that age he could ski in the *crap*.

During the period he skied in Scotland, he set a very fine example to all our young emerging racers. In particular, to my son. He showed what could be achieved in racing, and, in so doing, contributed a great deal to our growing ski culture. More importantly, he became one of us, as he still is today. He became a British Team Member. He was highly thought of among the Scottish skiers of those days. There were other regulars who skied midweek. One was an outstanding character. A Pole from the War, Victor by name. Like out of Hollywood, accent and all. He was very Polish. A strong tough man. He used to bring us real, wonderful Polish sausage. His friend, Idris, was from Darlington. A doctor, they were a matched pair. And very much, opposites. Victor had been a political prisoner in Siberia. He told us a little about it. No one at that time knew anything of how frightful conditions had been in those camps. Here was one right out of the book, and as strange as fiction. Victor had a friend in the Gulag. People were dying around them. They decided to attempt an escape. They had to make for the Balkans. It doesn't bear thinking about the distance and the terrible terrain to be crossed or the hostility that they may have encountered there. Not long before they were ready to shoot the crow a rumour went through the camp that the Americans were arranging an exchange of prisoners for war materials. Victor decided to wait and see what transpired. The cross country route was no soft option. Victor was eventually exchanged. His friend did not wait. He made his escape in winter. Victor ended up in the UK, where he joined the Free Polish Forces. He went to Italy, where he met his friend. He had made it! There's a story for you. *Some Kid*, eh?

Big thaws are a feature of Scottish mountain winters. During the spring we had a big one, so much so, our main run was almost broken at Dead Man's Gulch. Willie and I decided to shovel it to make the run better. We did this at night under the light of the stars. It took hours. We woke in the morning to find a tremendous snowfall had buried the mountain. After all that work! Who cared, the starlight made it worth while. You can't buy nights like that with Yankee Dollars. The new snow turned our mountain into a skiing wonderland. I mentioned partying in the Doss. There developed solo and choir singing of a fine standard. We even made up our own songs which, in all modesty, I claim were very good. The weekends in the Doss became legend. As we grew and matured we got better. This was the beginning of a new era. Everything was in a groove, the snow on the hill stayed good, the sun burned us and made us look like real mountain men. This was the life!

We started the lift early. On such a morning, Willie went up to check the line. He seemed to be away a while. We were doing the breakfast. I went up to see all was well, and there was Willie, lying in the middle of the top basin. When I got over to him, he had just finished straightening his leg. I'm glad I missed that. His first remark was, I've joined the club. Some club. We were in a wee bit of bother now. Tommy Paul, and Tommy Laurie, Sunshine for short, were staying in the hut with us.

Now, we did have problem, how to get Willie down off the hill and run the lift, if people came to ski. Once again Lady Luck struck. A sixteen year old boy was hill walking, at that time in the morning on, of all places, Meall a' Bhuiridh.

He was pressed into service. Poor wee boy! That was some carry down to the road for three. It seems the wee boy was bushed. I'm not surprised. I was left to run the lift. It was the boy's lucky day, getting a chance to learn about mountain rescue from such skilled performers. A good experience for the boy? Sunshine came back up the hill to help with the lift. It seems they ran out of petrol and Tommy pushed the van into Bridge of Orchy. When things go wrong, they stink! I think it was Willie's van. They say it's downhill to Bridge of Orchy. Paul reckons its not. Tommy got Willie to Glasgow Western Infirmary, and got him booked in and bedded down. Next morning, Tommy Paul carried that heavy Nansen sledge back up the hill himself. That was another good carry.

A few days after that, I was forerunning the Downhill for the Junior Championships. I took a fall at very high speed. Not to be badly injured was the *rub of luck*. And more than I deserved. It was some time before I'd really find out what this left me with. At the time of it happening, it felt lousy! The following weekend, Tommy Paul said he noticed the fall had not affected the technique. He was not inside my head. Tommy was no stranger to bad mountain accidents. He's had his share. Reading this, you may feel it is cold blooded. In the doing of it, it was very *red blooded*. Several days after the fall, I limped in to see Willie in his infirmary bed. When I took my sunglasses off, and he saw my face, he almost laughed himself out of bed. Not bad with half a dozen pins in his leg. The pins should have been through his lip!

With the new demand for skiing in the world, the production of skis, and other equipment, started with a post war urgency. The standard of the new equipment started to improve dramatically. The introduction of release binding "safety" was an important step forward. This cut down the incidence of broken lower legs, which can become a pain in the butt. We were to find out that other types of injuries and mishaps can afflict you. The more you do it, the more the chance of injury. The Piper wants his pay!

Around this time, a tremendously important event happened. One of our new friends, a man larger than life, Fergus Sandeman, went out of his way to introduce me to the brothers Bill and Jim Greaves. They ran an old established family sports shop in Glasgow, and they were interested in enlarging the skiing side of their business. Fergie brought us together. As a result of this meeting, a long friendship over a third of a century was established, the cornerstone of which was complete trust. Something I personally believe to be one of life's rare possessions. As a result of the get together, we started a Dry Ski School. This comprised of introduction to skis, how to put them on, walking, changing direction, kick turning, falling down, getting up, and body position. There were also light exercises pertaining to skiing, ending with a talk on ski clubs, when to ski, where to ski and how to get there. There was a display of clothes and equipment that could be purchased from the Greaves shop in Gordon Street, Glasgow. This, believe it or not, was the highlight of the six nights. These dry lessons were good for people starting skiing. There were people who had skied before who came and thought they learned a lot. The Greaves made all the bookings from their shop, and, to our great satisfaction, all the sessions were fully booked. Jim and Bill left all the profit for me, even though they came every night and sat through the four long hours it took to complete the three groups. No work shyness with those two. All this ski teaching took place on a floor in a hall, in the "Christian Institute," Glasgow. I was working constant nightshift, so I was having long days and nights, six pm till eight thirty am.

We knew, with the starting of the Dry Ski School, that the Swiss Ski School Course was a reality. It would appear that all the pieces were falling into place. It looked as if the light was shining a little brighter at the end of our tunnel. I had the feeling Glencoe skiing was right behind us. As the time drew near for leaving sleep became difficult. The brain seemed as if it was on gimbals!

Looking back on the tail end of that year, and assessing all that had taken place, it was not finished yet. In the light of hindsight, there really had been some long Scotch Country Miles covered. The three weeks with Stager in Wengen. The invitation to the Swiss Course. The solid skiing on Meall a' Bhuiridh. The Bad Fall. Meeting the Greaves. The Dry Ski School. Is there any wonder that sleep was eluding me? One memory of those days is, some late evenings we would go back to Jim's house, where Helen, his lady, would give us a big Glasgow fry-up. Black pudding, potato scones, the lot. A big coal fire roaring up the lum. Jim and I would have our stocking clad feet resting on their fire guard. You couldn't take us anywhere! All in all, I was in good shape in every department. I had money earned through skiing. There was no way I could be physically fitter. Jim and Bill had supplied my first free skis and they made arrangements that, if I ran short, they would wire any amount I needed. They did not want me to be in anyway embarrassed. All possible needs were provided for. The lynch pin of this possibility in life's rich pageant was called Jeanie Finlayson. She would stay at home. There was a lot of family pride in what was happening.

The venue for the 1959 Swiss Ski School Directors Course, was the fabled ski town of Davos, Canton Graubunden (Grisons). Travel was by train. I even had sleepers booked. This journey, while it was exciting, was quiet and calm. Travelling alone was enjoyable. Contrary to what some may think, I'm quite comfortable being on my own. Naturally, I indulged myself in trying to figure out what the shape of this thing would be. How could I have any idea? In my mind, I settled down to wait and see how it might be. From Landquart up through Kublis, Klosters, Wolfgang, Dorf, and into Davos. Davos was as it should be. This was my second Alpine village. It could not have been more exciting or impressive. The high valley had been dressed in fresh snow the night before. Some presentation for a new boy. I was so wound up by the expectancy of the moment, I arrived in Davos without knowing it. Journey's end and the start of a new, unknown one!

Coming out of the station, I was almost in a flap. Davos was big in comparison with Wengen. I took a taxi to the hotel, another first. This was called the Europa, some place by any standards. It had a Casino. Out came a liveried doorman, and carried my gear into the *awesomeness* of my first hotel foyer. It was like a Hollywood movie. To my great relief, they were expecting me. Then I saw my first porter, who took my gear. They even had an elevator. As I was about to go into it, I was called back to the desk. The imposing fellow behind the desk said, "Mr Finlayson, there's a package for you." It was my gift of skis from Bill and Jim Greaves, that had been sent from the factory. Surely this was a good omen. I seemed to be early. A wee walk round the town let me see another facet of this small, extremely well run country. With the new snow, and the bright sunlight, the elegance and quality of that high old mountain town in that November morning is still fresh in my mind. Around midday, the others started to arrive. The big hotel started to fill and take life. Around then, Werner arrived with the Wengen group. He seemed take the fact that I was there for granted. As you can imagine, this was a momentous occasion for me. Looking around and taking sights, the first thing I noticed, was the shortage of sunbronzed faces.

Each year, new candidates turn up to take their place in the system of things so I did not stand out. There was big variation in the backgrounds of these men and where they were drawn from. In the years I attended these courses there were no ladies. Later, there were a few. What the situation is today, I have no idea. It must have changed, even in male chauvinist Switzerland. There were young mountain boys. These were quietly spoken and were similar to those from our remote glens and islands of the west coast. These young fellows lived in those high chalets, that their older folks were still eking a out a living from. The young men must have found the hotel just as strange as I did. I would imagine most of them have turned their chalets and ground into big money by now.

The day seemed to take forever to pass. The course was not due to start till next morning, and I was desperate to go skiing. What I didn't understand, at the time, was that these men had skied all their lives, and this was an annual get together. How could I understand how used you became to getting skiing when it suited you and that these men had thirty years of nationally organised ski teaching behind them. Consequently some very profound friendships had developed. This being their big get together there was a lot blethering to get on with. It was not difficult to spot my fellow *kindred spirits*. The new boys, the uncut loaves, were keeping low profiles. I was to find just how firm and parental the senior pecking order of this ski teaching society could be. Not a system I was in accord with. I'm not sure I am today. But I'm completely convinced, that, if the Swiss system had developed here, ski teaching would be of a much higher standard than it is. Real ski teachers would be properly paid for their efforts. More importantly, the clients would not have to put up with so much of the verbal crap that goes under the nonsense of "Superior British Ski Teaching Ability." I wonder where this horse manure came from. It normally emanates from self appointed experts of inferior skiing ability. Good British pros are no better than other good ski teachers. The assembly meeting was most impressive. The wide balance of age groups gave the assemblage an air of permanence. Speaking German or French would have been a luxury.

A famous French racer, James Couttet, was introduced to the gathering. We all stood and applauded the great man. He was wee and Frenchie looking. He had a hard face on him. Werner seemed to have left to me my own resources. I preferred it that way. I found later it was deliberate. A small bright eyed man sat down beside me. He was from Andermatt in Canton Uri. This village lies below the St Gottard pass. It has a long tradition of English climbing and skiing clients. He was the ski school director, and, in summer, a mountain guide and guardian of the Albertime Hut on the Gallenstock. His opening gambit was, "you are the Scotch One!" This was a politeness. Suddenly I felt important. The wee man's name was Kari Russi. He was to be one of the fine people I have met in my life. He asked me if I knew so and so from Edinburgh. It seemed they were a climbing family. A few years previously, a son of the family had been lost near Kari's hut. His body had never been found. Kari had promised the mother and father he would find the boy for them. This is another thing they have about people killed and lost on their hills. I've always thought the mountains would be a fine place to be left, if this unnatural event overtook a loved one.

That evening, another ski teacher introduced himself to me. He was Hans Graf, from Wengen, better known today as Lang Ham, the *mine host* of the restaurant at the bottom of the Lauberhorn Race Course. Hans and I have been good friends since. At this time, I knew few of the Wengen ski teachers. The coming week would change that. In the morning, I found a good number of Bernese Oberland teachers in my group. The first lesson was walking on the flat. This was new to me, and another first. My first impression was of disappointment, that was until the lesson progressed. Our teacher, a tall mountain guide. He was *good* and so said all of us. Before morning was over he introduced snow ploughs, snow plough turning, and stem-turns. The Maestro wore black ski clothes, and a white cap, and he was very old, maybe even fifty. How your thinking changes with time!

Before lunch, we went up the Brama Buel for a ski. The weather was poor, with windblown snow, and bad light. There were three groups skiing about. They skied on their own or in pairs. It was then I realised that the bad fall had left me gutless. I could not make a turn for thinking about getting hurt. No one can ski under those circumstances. The more you try, the worse it becomes. In the bad light, it might not have been spotted. But I knew. We eventually headed down for lunch. I sat in my room and felt terrible. No one deserved to feel this bad.

Sitting in that bedroom thinking, what got into my mind was, if I got hurt I'd go home like a *whipped cur*. Going home badly hurt would not look so bad. Thinking of my poor batting average in this part of skiing was not the best thing to be doing. *Filling Ma Breeks* would not in anyway cure *My Problem*. In the afternoon, I took the 215 centimetre stiff downhill skis, went back up the hill, and won the day. Not that I was too easy in my mind with my skiing. It would be a long time before the stress of that accident wore off, if ever. It did ease when my being injured had no effect on our income. That did not stop the bad falls.

In the bar, after skiing, Werner said, "you were good this afternoon, Fritz!" He said it must have been the good skis. He knew it was not the skis. At the end of the day it's up to yourself, how you face up to paying the cost of these upsets. You can't dodge, nor hide. That was a hard passage I had just gone through. The reason for it was ever present, and every time I skied, it could raise its ugly head. And the ugly head didn't know you were worried. On the bright side, for the rest of the week, I was never left without someone who seemed to be looking after me. Werner, Marcel Von Allmen, and I, shared a room. Marcel was one of three famous brothers from Wengen. One of whom, with an another guide, took a client up the North Face of the Eiger, for a fee. A hard town to turn Buck! Not many know of that event. Marcel ran a summer ski school at the Jungfraujoch, for over forty years. He was killed there, a few years ago, by lightning. What a way to go. He must have been knocking on three score and ten. Well done, Marcel, bad tempered an' all, as you were! Looking round the last number of years and seeing friends living, and so ill, given the chance, I'm sure I know what their choice would be.

In our group was a Walt Disney character by the name of Oskar Gertsch, director of Wengen ski school. Also a mountain guide. He could never resist trying it on with *the birds*. He was some kid! A mountain farmer with milk cows, which he loved. And he was as tough as old boot. He was as solid on his skis as a lump of mountain granite. Skiing for him was an extension of his zest for life. His brother was a founder of the Lauberhorn Race. That distinction would mark anyone above average. Ernst, like Oskar, was a wag. Werner, Marcel and Hans Graf were in the same class. The second morning we had a demonstration from other Alpine countries.

This was a damp squib, as the Austrians never turned up. They had been propounding that they had the best method of teaching that was said to be the *new way* to ski. A broad statement. Skiing moves on and improves. Whether it was a new way to ski was very debatable.

The Italians were the best, and in particular, a real old Geezer of forty odd. My Swiss friends, with their usual pragmatic approach to life, said their own team had not been very good. Which was correct. The rest of the morning was taken up by the new improved method, Wedlen and shortswings. Chief of our class was a George Felie, from Crans Montana. Werner was good at this. It suited his type of skiing. George treated us to a feast of ski teaching skill. Where Stager was forceful in his approach to his subject, George went at it softly, cajolingly, with a smooth voice and beguiling smile. He helped himself to your very best personal performance. In the excellence of his skiing you saw the tranquil dignity of the man's nature. After the lesson, Werner said to me, "you have just seen something there, Fritz!" I certainly had. There's not many of those in the dozen! What an opportunity, for someone like me at that time in my career. I'm sure I discovered George's thinking in that lesson. And it has stayed with me all these years.

In the afternoon, our teacher was Gottlieb Perren, a Zermatter. He looked like a ski teacher. He was very blond, the director of the Zermatt ski school and a mountain guide. He and his brother were well known racers. Up on the Brama Buel the sun was out, the snow was deep and very cold. Perfect for *good* skiing! I don't remember what the programme was. I do remember the drooling mouths! They were all off with their pals. I got stuck in behind Gottlieb. He stopped and said, "you've never skied in deep powder before!" He was right. I had skied in every possible junk, but here was the ultimate. In a handful of words, he explained the simplicity of the turn in deep powder. It was really no different, in essence, from average snow. There must have been a dozen groups who had abandoned the programme. An American ski teacher, a powder hound from Colorado, was *cutting the custard*. This was truly a memorable day. Here were dozens of skiers executing the "art" at a very high standard, in snow in the very best of all possible conditions. When you get it right, you know it's right and it is private, to yourself.

It was then I met John Clements, the American. He looked like an American. The crew cut, rimless glasses, and an open, smiling face. We became great friends. He had the gift of learning languages. He learned to understand the Glasgow way of speaking, with a good Glasgow accent. Not bad for a Yank! He had owned a ski shop in Alta, in the Rockies, which was sold because it was interfering with skiing. He was a skier of quality. He was one hell of a *Powder Hound*. Also my first American.

Before dinner, I was called to the course office, to report to the Director of the Swiss Ski School Association. What now! In the office there was "The Man." He looked old and unlike what I expected. A shortish thin man, with faded blue eyes that made you feel uneasy at first. His opening remark, "how are you enjoying "Our Course." I hear you are doing well, Frith!" He was the only one who called me by my given name. That was until his successor took over some years later. "The Man" was called Christian Rubi. He stood tall in skiing. He said, "we have decided to be nice to you and the American, we will charge you the same as the Swiss, eighteen franks per day!" I almost passed out. That was one fifty in today's money. This included hotel, lifts, and the classes. This was the generous hand of friendship being held out. A gift to be remembered.

In tandem with the directors course, they ran a parallel course for ski school classes, class one to class six. Pupils came from all over Europe, and many Americans from the forces in Germany, attended. Some of the class fives and sixes skied quite well. This was a colourful event with it running alongside of the Directors Course. Teachers from all over Switzerland took the classes. This gave the course a tremendous atmosphere, more like a Gala affair. Christian Rubi had been the first socialist MP in the Berne Parliament. I could see that kind of thinking in this man, as I got to know him. He was also one of the prime movers in establishing the Swiss Ski School Association. Had been a school teacher, a mountain guide and, of course, a ski teacher. His brother Adolf was a guide of high standing in the Swiss climbing world. He'd been on the Swiss attempt on the Kanchenjunja in the early fifties. We spoke about Kanchenjunja and how Joe Brown, the plumber from Manchester, had made the first successful ascent since the Swiss attempt. Adolf said, in his wee quiet voice, "Joe Brown must be a wonderful man to have climbed that terrible mountain!" Joe is just a wee man who happens to be a very good climber. More important he is a fine man. I said to Adolf, "you're not bad yourself!" and I quoted one of his achievements. He and some other hardman had climbed the Eiger ridge and summit, Monch Ridge and summit, Jungfraujoch, the Jungfrau summit down to Stechelberg in the Lauterbrunnen Valley. In sixteen hours. *Some trick!* When I pointed this out to him, his bland reply was, "I was young then." Another master of the understatement. These summits are four thousand metres. The two Rubi's had been on the rescue on the Eiger North Face in 1936, an early epic of the many Eiger epics, in the years to follow. Heinrich Harrier's book, The White Spider. He also wrote Seven Years in Tibet. Well worth the reading.

Davos laid on the dream Alpine weather and snow conditions. It snowed at night, and the days were clear and sunny. What a start to the coming new decade of the 1960s, in which skiing on Meall a' Bhuiridh would open up so much to the ever eager expectations of members of the Doss. I had made no plans for when the course was finished. Werner took me back to Lauterbrunnen to stay in the family hotel and ski with the DHO Club, so another door opened. The Downhill Only Club is a very old English club, set up in Wengen, where they are much respected. Over the Christmas holidays they ran junior race training. Here I would start and learn another very serious part of the teaching trade. With the greatest of good fortune I would learn it from fine Journeymen and, in the process, find out how very far we had to go at home to raise the standard of our skiing up to what could be called good. What was happening to me, made me consider for the first time the enormity of what we were undertaking at home, the difficulty of getting near to the established systems of the Alps, and *their skills*. The awful thing was, *we had no skills*.

During the previous week, I had been exposed to the top end of the teaching scale. In the following weeks I would see how different standards of emergent junior racers were handled. This was so different. Gone went clinical thinking and in came the skilful guile of experience. The *spectrum* of ski teaching is full of steps, and they are all extremely important. A number of years later, Christian Rubi said that the most critical stage in teaching skiing is in classes one to three, class one being a beginners, class six being the top class. How true his words still are. Here we were somewhere in the *spectrum*, Junior Race Training, a grossly abused figure of speech. Which we will get back to. As I observed the trainers go about their work, it did not take me long to realise how important understanding the mentality of your pupils was. Even more important was to get to them colloquially, in their own language, especially the very young ones. If you were capable. Having said that, Werner had excellent people contributing to the training. First thing I noticed was how at home Werner was with the kids. He was single. I personally never gave kids much thought until I became heavily involved later on, when I discovered deep satisfaction and a sense of purpose in what was taking place.

Wengen, having been English orientated since before the first World War, had ski teachers who seemed to have a good grip of how English folks liked things done. The trainers knew most of the parents. This made for a good collective effort from all concerned. Peter Hugelier, (excuse the spelling, Peter), from Lauterbrunnen, was an exceptional teacher at all levels. He was only twenty three. There is not many of them around. I kept a close eye on his work. He came to Scotland to visit some years later, where he fitted in with ease. I could write a good long tale about my times and experiences with these fine mountain people and how they treated me as one of them. At this, a vital time in my life, a memory I hold dear. The other trainers were Fritz Gertsch, and Alfred Ameiter. He was a mountain farmer. He and Fritz were mountain guides. This was peculiar to the old high mountain villages. The last trainer was from Interlaken, Rudi Gertsch. He was not of the mountains. He was from the Swiss Team. An entertainer, a magician. Some mixture! He was magic with the juniors. He never figured me out. He was one of the best I've seen, and he had a lovely touch in getting the trainees responding to his excellent gift in teaching.

The real Boss and *doyenne* of the DHO Training was Ros Hepworth. Ros was Matriarch of the DHO. Many a youngster of slender means was helped by Ros on their way to success in British Ski Racing. She told me once that she skied as a young girl with the long dress and the multiple petticoats under the dresses. She was truly *formidable*. Everyone walked carefully when dealing with her in pursuit of assistance for her beloved Juniors. Even the sharp business people of Wengen. When she did not want to hear something she'd turn off her hearing aid. When she brought her tribe to Cairngorm for the British Junior Championships, she had me running about like the proverbial *blue arsed fly* and I wasn't the only one. "She who must be obeyed." It was said she was a great beauty as a girl. She was a very handsome, dignified, old lady. Anyone who worked with her should feel privileged to have done so.

One of the strengths of the their system was the Coggins. These kids were coming into skiing. They were taken and skied all over the mountain and, when it was suitable, introduced to skiing through poles. Many a British Racer had a good start with the Coggins. All the trainers were ski teachers. Through them and Oskar, I was accepted by the ski school and afforded the dignities that went with it. As I write this, all the memories flood back, and rich they are.

Oberland Hotel was the home of the Family Stager. Werner's father was something else. He was a right winger of the old school, a self made man. Him and I *clicked!* The chemistry of friendship is strange. It would have been well nigh impossible to explain why someone who had more or less reared himself in the mean conditions of a Glasgow tenement could be anything other than a Red Clydesider. It might be compared with an Eton or Harrow boy being Commie. Very few Clydesiders were Communists. It was not in their natures to *eat dogma*, as it was not in their natures to be messed about.

"Herr Stager," that was always what I addressed him as. It suited him. I suppose he expected it. He spoke four languages and bit of Romanisch. He fancied himself as a story teller. Now that's right up a Glasgow man's street. I like to think this is a true one. As a youngster he was working as a boot boy in the Schweizer Hof hotel, Wengen, in the early 1900s. On a Christmas morning, an English gentleman came down

*Hotel Oberland, Lauterbrunnen,
home of the Stager Family* – RJB

to breakfast, dressed in a morning coat, a silk cravat with large diamond pin, smoking the Cuban cigar. He called young Ernst over, "come, boy!," as was their wont in those days. "I've had a good year in the market, boy!" With that, he put five golden sovereigns into young Ernst's grubby hand! The splendid gentleman said, "merry Christmas, boy. Make your fortune!" That Herr Stager did. He owned hotels and a good piece of the bottom land in the Lauterbrunnen Valley. I'm sure he knew fine well, that morning in the Schweizer Hof, what the "Market" was, young and all as he was. He never had a good word for Christian Rubi, Rubi being socialist. I had a firm handshake. His nickname for me, was "Old Shatter Hand." For some reason that tickled his fancy. As the years grew, our friendship prospered. He's been gone a long time now. I remember him fine and he left his mark on me. He told me that story "himself."

This is the sort of thing he'd come away with. He stood looking out the window of his bar. He announced, "Fritz, look how stupid the world is!" I looked out the window. There were women walking past. He continued, "look, they are desperate for it! So are we, and we are all too stupid to do anything about it, what waste!" Another train coming back from the Front Line, full of pregnant prostitutes. Written on the side of the train, "return when empty." Laughing was compulsory! Frau Stager, another Matriarch, the Grand Dame of the Oberland household. She'd taken to me. She was Werner's stepmother. There was a deep and warm relationship here. To my knowledge, she had no children of her own, so possibly Werner filled a niche there. Later I got the impression I was one of hers as well. When she was joshing me, she would say, "your as bad as the old one!" Not a bad compliment.

The young Stager used to say, "you do nicely here!" We were all doing well together. The place made me feel comfortable. In future, my wife and I would enjoy a happy Stager Christmas round the family tree, when we would all exchange gifts with each other. Jeanie and I always felt very privileged to be part of this private occasion. Teresa Follett, Werner's wife to be, and I met at this time. Teresa *had all her smarts*. She was the epitome of the upper class English lady. No nonsense, easy to get on with and did not suffer fools at all! Caroline Simms was her good friend, a staunch DHO member. A skier of quality, who skied as light as a feather. She was a favourite of Ros. She returned the favour, ten fold. Being Ros's assistant she helped in no mean way with the training. For some reason she gave me a DHO *solid golden* ski clip she had been awarded in 1952, for her skiing achievements. A nice memento. I still have the gold clip.

Trainees, for the most part, came out of public schools. Their behaviour was the same as other youngsters. There was the odd one or two who would have been "*bad backsides*" in any situation. What's new! Most of the trouble was the Mammies and Daddies. This was something where Scottish parents, at club level, would be even more difficult. The DHO welcomed into their training kids from the tenements, my son being the first of them. Thanks to dear Ros Hepworth. Ros was a great one for nicking as many good prospects as she could get her hands on. DHO seemed to be short of good boys. Ros always told me to keep a eye out for New Boys. This I was pleased to do.

left to right – Bob Clyde, Chris Lyons, Self, Toni French,
Charlie French – April 1961. – RJB

This winter of 1959/60 I'd meet my second Americans, Toni and Charlie French. From Southern California, Los Angeles, they were an all American couple. Toni was a tall woman, dark headed, well shaped. Said what she wanted, loud clear and in good crisp American English. This she did without being offensive. I thought she was terrific. With one proviso, she was spoiled rotten. Charlie was six foot slim and fair. When you knew Toni was there, you felt Charlie was *present*. They were, as is said in American, Good People. Charlie worked with the US rocket programme in the south of England. Toni was an

88

accomplished skier, and Charlie skied very well. Some time later he said to me that he was really sorry he had not taken a few years of full-time skiing, to work "the need" out of his system, like I had. Fortunately, or unfortunately, he was making such good money, he had no choice. Fortunately, I still have not got it out of my system.

We discovered them on Meall a' Bhuiridh where they stood out like *sore thumbs*. We took them into *the body of the Kirk*, where they were introduced to our way of enjoying our evenings. What greatly pleased them was the ease with they which moved about in our Tight Clique. Toni and Charlie came back that season, during our Championships. It was then Charlie decided to come to the Swiss Directors Course in Villars Canton Vaud. It was arranged he would join the same group as myself. This was done through the good offices of Christian Rubi.

One of the fine friendships skiing gave me started on Meall a' Bhuiridh in the spring of that season. Peter Todd, from near Darlington. He became a special friend to the Finlayson Family. Peter was a no nonsense northern English man who was unashamedly of the Old School. A spade was definitely not a shovel. Years later, in spring, when I had been hitting the booze, I said to him one morning, "I'll need to ease off the booze! I had been hitting hard all winter. He exercised his right as friend and said straight to me, "well, what are you going to do about it?" That was Peter. No crap with Peter. Some of the main players who were in at the beginning of the broaching of this new frontier, started to make their own particular talents show. As these individuals, and they *were* individuals, started to show their personal abilities for special tasks as they appeared, they would focus their attention on establishing all the different parts of the well serviced Ski Stations on our ski fields.

The second great step on the way forward, was quietly ramrodded by a Jimmy Hamilton. He designed and took charge of installing the first chairlift on our hills. He must have convinced White Corries that he could deliver a working chairlift in one summer's work despite having no experience in that field. A bold man. Boldness was the order of the day, and a very necessary ingredient, for what was afoot at the time. When Jimmy was done, Toni French could come to Meall a' Bhuiridh and join the rest of the happy throng gliding up and looking down at the path that used to be a big problem for most skiers who had to use it to get to their skiing. Thanks, in a big way, to James Hamilton Esq. Jimmy was a designer engineer in a Clydeside shipyard, where he held a senior position. How he managed to pull off the chairlift in his spare time speaks legions for the man. He even worked on it at weekends. I am sure that was the year he became Scottish Champion. A busy fellow. Jimmy was another who could have became a good skier if he'd had a couple of full seasons under his belt. Another who missed it.

Harry McKay came from a tenement not far from myself. A man small in stature, but big in every other way. He was one of the few people I know who got to ski during his army service, despite the *folksie* idea that people of our age group became fired up about skiing in the services. Harry was a climber who, at that period of time, was living in Fort William, some thirty odd miles from Meall a' Bhuiridh. A Scottish Champion. Like the rest of us he started skiing very late for these achievements. There's a fine ring to the title of having been your own National Champion. *I'm sure the grapes are sweet, that hang high.* He worked in the building and construction industry. Like Smith he had a capacity for doing things *right*. He worked full-time on installing the Hamilton Lift. He was "Top Gun," as they say in the modern parlance. He was responsible for all the on site work and this "First Chair" on our mountains. He'd do more, much more, in this field in the coming years. The work was completed in the summer and used with great joy in 1960. The start of a new decade. A decade which, for many skiers, was to be probably one of the most memorable in their lives. McKay, as he was known to his friends, was to stay in skiing for the rest of his working life, in a varied and substantial capacity. In the process, he justly earned the respect of all who had the good fortune to have worked with him. His knowledge of skiing, in all its aspects, is profound. His strength was the loyalty he gave to his work. Another trait he had in common with Big Smith. These are men you can *go to the wall with*, and be sure they would stand firm.

John McLennan also worked on the new chair at weekends. Known affectionately as Mac-the-Knife. Tommy Paul gave him that name. He was in charge of maintenance in one of Glasgow's largest hospitals. He and Jimmy were climbing partners and members of the Lomonds Club. And very close friends. He was a good hard rouster at our parties. When rendering some of his many songs, when deeply moved with the euphoria of the moment, he would close his eyes when his singing, or so it appeared, moved into a Wee World of his own, where we seemed to lose him for the duration of the song. He was the superb enthusiast. When anything new was afloat in the Doss that we wanted to do, he always cautioned those assembled that what ever we did we had to Think Big. Think Big. He was talking to the converted, We always thought Big. We were all too big headed, to think any other way. He had a brittle temper, which he seldom lost. He enjoyed life like a wee boy still growing up, which made him great company.

The last but not least of *the Bears* who worked the lift, Robert M. Clyde. One of the more significant personages who walked through the last three decades of our skiing. For those who know Bob, what can I say about him that will not be biased. The answer is quite a lot. If ever there was a Red Clydesider, it was Bob. He had a solution for most problems, till he lost his cool. One of the softest touches in the business. That was until he thought you had gone too far. Then you saw a temper. No open minded person who worked under Bob's management could say he had forgotten his roots on the Clyde. This tale could not be completed without constant remit to Robert's activities in the ebb and flow of the sometimes turbulent climate of what made the growth of skiing possible. Boab, that is what we his good friends call him, has not been well for a number of years. I speak for many when I say he is sadly missed on the hill. We lost a worthy opponent when Boab stopped turning up for work!

The last years of the decade of the sixties for me, apart from being productive, were certainly exciting. The three weeks training with Werner. Meeting John Clemments, Charlie and Toni French. Even the nonproductive fall which could have done more serious damage. The monumental event of attending the Swiss Directors Course. The Downhill Only Ski Club training. Becoming a welcome friend to the Wengen Ski School. Last but not least having been accepted into the Stager household for myself left me feeling replete, and ready for the next ten years.

8. Villars and Wengen

The Dry Ski School was once again a big success, giving me the financial kick off I needed to get started.

Toni and Charlie French and I drove out from their house in Lincolnshire to Villars in Canton Vaud where the Directors Course would be held. The mode of transport was a very up market Alfa Romeo with me in the back seat – my favoured way to travel if the driver is good. It poured with rain the whole way over, even though there were no motorways. Charlie drove the car at a average of a hundred miles an hour, *great.* I mentioned it was nice to sit in a good car with a good driver. Toni casually said that his driving should be good as he had raced cars with Phil Hill, a Grand Prix driver of the period. I asked him why he never carried on, and he said didn't think he could make it or something like that. I offered to spell him at the wheel, but he said he preferred to drive, and that suited me. Charlie never said much when he was driving, so Toni and I got on with the talk. After lunch we drove in silence for some time, then right out of the blue, "you guys are a bunch of Bastards!" then quiet for a while. Then she started again. "You can go out and get any Dame who's willing and have a great time whenever you want!" She was *going her duster!* She went on how "Dames" had to wait around, "till you Guys made your move." Then quiet again. I mentioned the way she was stacked! She would not need to hang around too much. That wasn't the point. Women should be able to go out and pick who they wanted. I must be thick, I thought that's how it worked.

She went on, "you Guys would be all right when the system changed!" Well, that was something to look forward to! I said to Charlie, "do you get much of this?" He said, "all the time, but usually in private." As he was saying that, we were driving down a lane of those giant poplar trees. It was then Charlie told me how they had been in Mexico, driving past big trees. Toni demanded he stop and find out how round the trees were. They ended up trying to link hands around the tree trunks. The trees were so big there was no way their hands could meet. So Toni never found out how round the tree was. Charlie had a tape measure in the car, but he thought he would leave the possibility open to conjecture. I never forgot that part of the drive. Nor how well Charlie could drive. Toni was no Bimbo, but I have noticed that people who have all the money they need can be quite simple. Not stupid, "guileless" would be a better word. Stupid is stupid, no matter what means you may have.

As my experience in life widened, I had to face up to the reality that not all of society was as practical and well balanced as the not so well to do people who work hard for their living, and often for little return. In the immediate coming years I would meet a variety of interesting folks, enough to keep the brain sharp and the "lip zipped," *sometimes!* We arrived in Villars late in the afternoon, that was some drive. How would our old Green Vomit have got on? First thing next morning Charlie and I hit the hill. It was snowy weather and a quiet hill made for ideal skiing for us. Getting onto the Chamossaire lift, we saw what was a skiing apparition for those days. It made you look twice. He had tight ski pants, a red scarlet three quarter length coat, with two very large white buttons and a tie belt. The whole rig was topped off with the classic Glasgow *bunnet*, white to match the buttons. He had a hard looking *kipper* that did not go with the rest of rig. Charlie and I decided he was one of the best skiers in the world, or the biggest *balloon* in the world. We never gave "It" much more thought then! We were too busy bumping the gums!

The top of the slope was steep. The snow was junkie, and deep with willow branches sticking through the snow. The Apparition peeled off the top of the lift, cut into the willow branches and junkie snow and performed a ballet down the hill then disappeared on his way to Villars. The apparition was Roland Blazie from Lenzerheide, who skied for the Swiss at Squaw Valley. We decided he could dress anyway he liked. Roland turned out to be as good at enjoying himself as he was at skiing. I was to teach him the correct words of *"Roll Me Over Lay Down And Do It Again."* His singing wasn't up to his skiing. He would never have made our Choir in the Doss!

That evening, at the opening gathering, Rubi made a thing about me returning to the course. This pleased the Wengen teachers, me being part of their team. It certainly made me feel more a part of these auspicious events. Werner had a class of directors for the first time. Naturally Charlie and I were put with him. Next morning, we turned up for our class to discover we would need to take a class of guests for one day. I had been given a group of Americans, likewise Charlie. My class was a top class six. Werner had given me quite a build up. As I left with the group he said, "now let's see what you can do!" and flashed one of his toothy smiles. Another first, a class at the top end of the profession in, of all places, Switzerland. No doubt the people in the class must have wondered what was going on. A special Swiss course and they get a Scots ski teacher!

There was one man in the class who I clocked straight off. He understood what movement was about. I'd need to watch my Ps and Qs. To his compliment, he only asked sensible questions. You can get *smart Alecks.* I could not make a move or say something he had not seen or heard, without careful explanation as to what was happening. I'm the one who got the most out of that lesson, that day! Years later, and countless lessons given, I made a profound statement, "never go easy when you can go *hard."* By that, I'm sure, I meant improvement in all fields of human endeavour. In particular ski teaching. This man wanted to know if he was getting the short end of a short stick. The class wanted to know how I came to be there. I told them the story of the Chairlift, but they wanted to know about me, so I told them a shortened version of what was taking place at home. To my surprise, they were delighted. When you think of human nature, what is ordinary for some is extraordinary for another. Natural curiosity can be very rewarding. I told them about Charlie and John Clemments, Americans teaching on the course. But that they had the luck of the Irish, they got Me! When they heard they would need to change teachers for the rest of the week, they asked if they could stay with me. However, the Swiss don't change their plans without good reason. Anyway, the reason for me being there was to learn for myself. In years to come I would teach in Switzerland many times.

Villars is not an old village, it is more of a quality residential area. There are many fine hotels of all sizes. The views across the Rhone Valley and to the Mont Blanc and Dents du Midi are quite something. There are beautifully designed modern chalets that look old and most impressive. It must look wonderful in spring and summer with all the flowers hanging from the balconies. Villars appealed to me a good place for a holiday. And here I would have a big success. It would have been easy for me to start matching this against the whole scene at home. But that's a poor, negative way to think, and not me. I was put in the Alpe

Fleuri hotel, a fine old five storey wooden building in the shape of the traditional Swiss music box. It stood on the edge of the escarpment overlooking Montreux and onto Lake Geneva. The nice thing about it was that my room faced out onto all this.

It was on the second day, while having lunch, I had my first bite at Villars Lucky Cherry. While eating lunch, a big fat man sat down beside me. His opening gambit "you are the Scotch One," This is now a title of note. We spoke for some time, then he asked how I liked the hotel. I said it was marvellous, then I qualified it by saying that the best thing about it was the food. *And that was an understatement.* His face lit up. He was Chef and owner, and I was now his Main Man. Before I went back out to work, I had been fortified by several large brandies. Oskar Gertsch and other ski school bosses were at dinner that night, when up came two bottles of the Chef's personal selection of wine. The waiter said, "for the Scotch One!" *You can't keep a good man down!*

Werner Stager, as class boss, was making his début in this particular part of the profession. I said there was a *pecking order* involved. Werner was the Lauterbrunnen ski school boss, and getting picked for the Directors Course as trainer might not have been a matter of straightforward ability. When I last attended the course, I had a trainer who was so bad, I had to fiddle a move to another group. The trainer was not too pleased. All is not perfect in the World. Watching Stager working at this level, and now understanding what was going on, was another important point in my learning and to my future knowledge.

Charlie and I being together in the class was good for us. He was impressed with Werner's powerhouse type of skiing. Charlie was a hermaphrodite styled skier, something between *power* and *ease*. With his tall, slim body, all his movements looked clear and smooth. He said he could see where I got my thinking for skiing from. He wasn't quite right. I am by nature a quick mover. Power skiing gives me the *buzz* and the challenge I need to turn me on. I can, at any time, cool it. Years later, my son broached this subject with me on occasions. He said "what will you do when you are older?" "Well I'll tell you, when we get to around the year 1985!" was my reply.

In Davos the previous December, I met a young ski teacher from Champery, who had been a bright hope for an Olympic medal in the Swiss Team. He had, unfortunately, broken both legs in training. As a result, his racing days were over. You could almost feel the sad regret in the man, or so I thought. The village of Champery seemed to produce mild mannered men of natural charm, their accented English put a lovely finishing touch to what the enthusiastic ski pupil thought an Alpine ski teacher should be. One of these young men was Michel Bochatay. What a name for a ski teacher! He had spent a winter in Deeside, teaching. As a result he had a Swiss-French-English accent, greatly improved with a lovely touch of the Scots tongue. His connection with the Auld Country gave us something in common. He kept asking if I knew this one or that one. So here was a good link in the new and coming ski world. He was always on about our Ner'erdays in the Highlands. They amazed him. They still surprise me.

Accents! One evening I was in a tobacco shop. Next to me was the beautiful Welsh actress Glynis Johns. Hearing her English brought to mind that English as spoken, with intonations of the Welsh or Scottish Westcoaster, cannot be matched. As you see, there were many accents abroad in Villars during that week, including Glaswegian. During this week, I renewed acquaintances made at Davos which was very enjoyable. Remember, at home we had no established ski teachers nor any culture in skiing to set any standards against. Here was a ready made high standard. A living working example of what was still to be done and there was so much be learned. I mentioned there was a change taking place in how skis should be turned and in the teaching of the same. Naturally there were many bones of contention among some long established quality teachers on what was taking place. This is another subject all on its own.

One night Christian Rubi button-holed me about the pros and cons of the *New Method* (?) He was not too keen on it. My contribution to the conversation was muttered "yes"s and "no"s. Who was I to differ with the great man? Me, with absolutely no mileage in skiing, far less teaching, stick in my two cents? Not likely! So *I bit my lip*.

This was something we would be cursed with when we started to establish training and grading here in the UK. Most of it was trivial garbage. We will find, as we come to a time in the story, that all self proclaimed experts in *ski technique*, have no real talent in skiing. When you hear someone laying off to learner skiers, in a situation other than on the snow, you've got a right one! Mouthing off is one thing, doing is another. I've never heard a *good* teacher mouthing off. Getting a class at the start of the week seemed to set me up for the rest of the course, especially a top class. That's what comes of having friends in high places. I noticed how the ski directors went about in these salubrious surroundings with comparative ease. Few of these men lived at this level. These were the conditions they worked in. The opulence of Swiss ski villages grew to what they are to be enjoyed by the guests. There are learner instructors here who are under the impression resorts were put here for their personal convenience. Some of them don't seem to know who *pays the Piper!* Alpe Fleuri hotel was a *hotspot* at night. This was my first ever experience of this sort of thing. Any fun we ever had in our lives was self-made and what took place in the Doss on those long winter nights took some beating.

Christian Rubi sent for me. He asked me to stay for the second week and take a class of guests. That was unexpected. But very good. I had arranged to go back to Lauterbrunnen and ski with the DHO. Werner told me to stay and have a good week, and he would see me when I got back to Lauterbrunnen. Back in those days, few ski schools opened before Christmas. Herr Rubi ran this course back to back with our first week and I have no doubt it turned the *proverbial buck!* These courses were so popular that there were over a thousand guests. Teachers came from all over Switzerland to take classes. Pupils were split into four smaller ski schools, one of which Oskar Gertsch ran. I was to work with Oskar. We would stay in the Alpe Fleuri. Not too much pain there.

There's a pecking order in all fields of human endeavour, and I was definitely at the bottom of this one, so I got the bottom class for the week. They were more or less starting. That was all right, the problem was the age mixture, with two kids under twelve, and one lady over sixty and very unfit, a young American couple just married, and two Swiss Air hostesses. They were trilingual and great fun. There was a kept woman. She was there with a middle-aged wealthy Swiss. She was very young, eighteen or so, and, considering her relationship with this man, she was quite plain. Though she did not speak English, she stayed in the top hotel, where English was the main language. I met the man one night. There wasn't much to him. I'm sure I felt hostility in him. There was no reason for it. It would have done him no good. I often wondered what became of that girl. It's not something I approve of, buying female flesh in that manner. The young girl seemed uneasy in his company. She had a fine talent for the skiing.

There was another like me, at the bottom of the pecking order. A French Swiss. He started skiing at the late age of eighteen. In those days that was an early age for Scotland. He was very dark and French mountain-looking. I explained to him that we were both *débutantes*. The French-ness in him found this most appropriate. This was when I found out what *born to ski* was all about. He was one of those.

The second day, I found out what a ski school boss was! I had my class on a wee slope. I thought I was doing great, then up came Oskar. He bawled out at me for having the class on too steep a slope. That was a confidence boost! I went through an uncomfortable day after that. In the Alpe Fleuri that night, Oskar put his arm round me and said "are we still speaking?" and laughed. He could be a bugger. He paid for the wine that night. That incident knocked some of the bullshit out of me, and was a lesson to be remembered.

Meall a' Bhuiridh was not producing many beginners at that time. As a matter of fact, Meall a' Bhuiridh, did not produce many pupils of any standards. So I just got on with it. The beginners slope was excellent, with a ski lift. This was an ideal place to introduce skiing at any level. In two days the class were skiing up and down, using the lift and moving well. Then we moved up the mountain. The kids took a bit of pushing at first, and the sixty year old needed a whole lot of encouragement. Near to the end of the week, Herr Rubi told me I had the best class of all Oskar's classes. *To the good be given the praise*. Its a change from "*a slagging.*"

Oskar organised an end of course party. We had to collect fifteen francs per pupil, for a entrance fee. Oskar got a hold of a hall in a hotel with a stage. He had the place all set out with tables for all our different classes. Many of the teachers did different turns. Rudi Gertsch, the DHO trainer, performed a magic show. He was as good as anything you would see on the TV. There were trampolines, Swiss folk singing, a general sing-song, and dancing. The night was a bang up roaring success. You can imagine the impression this left me with. Next morning, Oskar opened a cloth bag and said to me, "I've kept some for you, Fritz!," then emptied out small change Swiss money, five franc coins and ten franc notes. He said it was my share of the profits from the party. The wily old bastard! He then apologised for the small denominations of the money. It turned out to be a hundred and fifty odd franks! A private ski-teacher was earning sixty franks for four hours and that was good pay. I had learned a tremendous amount from that man about life in general in that last week. Some kid for a mountain farmer come mountain guide. Ali Ross, in years to come, would learn from the same man. Last but not least, my class of the week had made a collection, and presented me with bottle of Kings Ransom whisky, a box of Cuban cigars, and a hundred francs. The two kids had bought me a foot long presentation cigar! All in all, it was a most eventful week for me.

Oskar, Rudi Gertsch, Hans Gaf and I travelled back to the Oberland together by train. We were running for the train down at Bex station, when

Oskar, who had more than his share of booze the previous night, was sick on the platform as he ran. We got into the diner. Oskar insisted on paying for the lunch, to make up for his little mishap at the station. It surprised me how this little lapse upset the wee-man. There was me, sitting on a Swiss diner with colleagues, drinking Dole du Mont. A King wasn't fit to be my uncle! There was a lot more to come out Pandora's Box. It was not empty yet, as I had seven weeks in the area and three weeks in the famous Zermatt with my family to look forward to. Who says there's no justice! Back in Wengen I was to stay in the new chalet of Teresa,Werner's wife to be. This was called Chalet Tint, after her race horse. It had won the Lancaster Cup. I actually had the solid gold cup in my work hardened mitts, if I remember right. She had won it twice. Caroline Simms stayed there. They had lived in Wengen on and off for years. To hear them talking the local gossip let you see it was just a community like any other, where people live ordinary normal every day lives. I would stay here, then move down to hotel Oberland, Lauterbrunnen and into the tender heart of Frau Stager and the delights of her kitchen.

The DHO training was of much greater interest to me, for the simple reason of my increased confidence in my better understanding of skiing in general. Being accepted into the *body of the Kirk* by the trainers and teachers of the Wengen ski school, gave my ego another helpful boost. Fritz Gertsch, who had been the Oberland downhill champion, and Alfred Ameiter, were both mountain guides training with the DHO. Skiing down from Wengeralp to the slalom slope at the Hannegg, I got another shock. Fritz and Alfred, two big strong men in their prime, had big bundles of hazel slalom poles on their shoulders. These are very heavy, and they were going like scalded cats down throughout the Wengen Bumps, looking round and talking to each other. I was very impressed. I'd be doing the same thing shortly. Example is a fine thing! In this training, Ros Hepworth had gathered for the Club an outstanding team of trainers. Werner, the boss. Fritz, Rudi Gertsch, Alfred Ametier, Peter Houglier, and Caroline Simms, plus a very good back up of very able helpers. To my surprise, many of the older trainees did not seem to understand how lucky they were to be there. To some of them it all seemed such a bore. They were there because they were sent, not because they wanted to be! This formula has never produced anything, anywhere, at anytime. It was not because these youngsters came from well to do backgrounds. It was because they were drawn from a very narrow base. If all the places available had not been up for grabs and they had to be competed for, this situation would not have prevailed.

When training started in Scotland, this problem would manifest itself if not exactly in the same way the root cause was the same. Not enough people chasing too many places. However, the system did produce Gina Hathorn, Divina Galicia, and Caroline Tomkinson. There was John Rigby, a part-time skier, who was sixteenth in the first Innsbruck Olympics Downhill. We cover this very important part of skiing in more detail. I knew then, if I ever had anything to do with training in skiing, there would be certain requirements that would be mandatory, particularly at the higher levels. As it turned out, I was privileged to be involved in training skiers at a high level. The British Junior Championships were being held up in Wengen. This was to be the first of many to come, and something that would give me extreme satisfaction over a long number of years.

9. Lauterbrunnen to Zermatt

During these championships, the juniors who put their hearts into the training got the most enjoyment out of it and the fine people who put so much effort in making it work had their reward. At this time at home, we had nothing like this. It's a historical fact, we had almost no junior racers, apart from the children of ourselves and a few others. So here was another timely opportunity to garner more know-how for times to come. Strong in my mind was the downhill event and where it was held. The starting gate was just below the Hundschopf, on the famous Lauberhorn course, ending at the bottom of the Hannegg Shuss. I doubt if it could be held there today, with the pressures of modern skiing's demands on ski runs being what they are.

It was here I saw another side of Werner Stager. He was very clever at getting people to do things necessary for the smooth running of the championships. His local *clout* was considerable. His deep concern for the youngsters' needs and wellbeing was something that struck me most, with him being a bachelor. He and I waxed large numbers of skis each evening. Another important part of our work. Watching and working with all these different events, from the inner circle, you could say, let me look through a window not open to most people. Hearing the blunt discourses about the many difficult Mammies, Daddies, trainers, and other personalities was entertaining and very educational. This is a hidden part of junior racing, not understood by people not involved. Racing, as seen on television, would not be possible without the above mentioned players! Their contribution directly impinges on all full-time skiers and most definitely if they work in skiing. This became clear to me in the ensuing years, as I worked full-time in skiing and found out the ABC of how the skiing cookie crumbles, and in so learning, became enriched with new friends from within the ski world. The championships were over almost without me knowing it. Once again it would be a considerable time before the benefit of what was learned would be assimilated, and clearly understood, by myself.

The day after the championships, it was back to ski teaching in the Lauterbrunnen Ski School. This was to be a baptism of fire to be remembered. Werner had arranged for a group from London of unknown numbers. The meeting place was under the famous waterfalls that drop down into the picturesque village of Lauterbrunnen. Werner was up above working in Wengen, so I was on my own. Like a good wee up and coming ski teacher, I was standing there very early, waiting for the leader to bring my "class" up to me. As I looked along the winding road, I clocked the intrepid leader in front of a hoard of what was obviously first day skiers. My intrepid leader was my first Australian skier. He was the organiser of these students from London. I think "Hustler" would have been a more accurate job description for the fellow! As it turned out, the horde were all, for yours truly, not a bad start.

Now I knew, even then, my ability to handle difficult skiing situations was away above the average. The only other talent I possessed that was better was my natural modesty! I was fresh and ready for the fray, or affray. I was in desperate need of the experience and in more need of the money, but talk about starting at the bottom of the ladder! Here was one for the book! The class Oskar gave me in Villars, was starting to look good. The Austro-Asian said he was lucky, a lot more people had turned up for his "deal" than he had expected.

"Deal" was the *in word* at the time. What he meant was, *he made a balls of the deal!* The Hustler turned out to be great fun. Anyway, batting the breeze with him would not get the show on the road. The Hustler gave a *spiel* about how he would fix this little mix-up by tomorrow morning. I told him *I would fix it* for the morning.

1958 Top of the Lauberhorn
Self, Margrit Gertsch, Werner Stager

Here was me, with at least fifty students ready to be introduced to the pleasures of skiing, and I mean there was *fifty*. Like all students, they were very adaptable, The Mother of Invention clocked on. I got them sorted out in four lines, put my mouth in top gear, lit my back burner, and got stuck in. Anyone of the four lines would have made a big class. When the morning was over, I didn't remember much about it, and, unbelievably, they all enjoyed themselves. Back in the Oberland, over a much needed refreshment, I was telling Herr Stager about the size of my group, and how difficult my morning had been. He thought it was great, and that it would do me no harm. Frau Stager said Werner should have been there to see that things were right. My friend, the self made man, said, "see you get all the money for the lesson!" That was the last thing on my mind. Somehow, we got through the afternoon. What amazed me was that I had most of them all snowplough turning by the end of the afternoon. When Werner, the boss, heard how my day went, he wasn't too pleased with the Hustler. Anyway, we got the whole thing sorted out by having two Swiss girl teachers to help me. We still had classes that were too big. Stager said "you are now a Swiss school boss!" Joke!

There were a few more the next day, and the Swiss girls were great to work with. Another first. I took all the least able of the group, including the new ones. Even in bad there is good. A girl who just started, called Olivia, could not even stand up on her skis. When I'd get her standing on her skis, then let go of her, she would simply melt down onto the snow. Each time I stood her up, she would slip back down onto the snow. Lifting her up and down was no hardship! She was, without a doubt, a truly lovely creature, of raven black hair, peaches and cream complexion, a figure to match, and a soft husky way of speaking that completed the picture. No matter how hard we both tried, between us, we could make absolutely no progress. It was only her humour that matched the rest of her excellence, that kept us trying. I eventually suggested that, possibly, skiing was not for her. She was delighted. Off came the skis, and she spent the rest of the days watching all her friends getting on with their learning to ski. That was my first, and only, encounter with complete failure in ski teaching. That was one I could live with. After all, it's not everyone who gets to teach the Perfect English Rose. The old karma was still batting in the hundreds. I wonder what became of "Olivia."

The next class were two Canadian college racers. Werner said, "you better be on your toes," or words to that effect. Quite a difference, from Olivia, to college racers *from over the pond*. Just the job for a Clydesider, who had not been a racer. I had the new pair of Kastle Downhill 215s, with Marker bindings with longthong turntable heels. At least I had the skis, thanks to the Greaves brothers. The weather was so bad we got off the train at Wengneralp. The College-Racers must have wondered what they were getting. A Scots teacher in Switzerland! As we were getting the skis on, I noticed they were greatly taken with my long, heavy skis. When I saw their skis, I should have clocked them, and known their racing must have been limited. I took off *like a scalded cat*, along the long narrow track that is called Brooklands. Halfway along, my two toe-irons released. I did my usual. I ended up fifty feet down in the gully on the left. Some start, and quite an ego boost! Old friends of mine will know that this is one of my usual stunts. After I climbed up through the waist deep snow, and readjusted the expertly fitted bindings, we set off again, and I endeavoured to establish that I was not the local Scottish clown. Werner had instructed me to ski these two young men at speed. A big change of standards from a horde of beginners, to a class six. The two young men were typical, unassuming Canadians. This was to be my first exposure to the tendency of some folks to overestimate their abilities. I was used to people who had no illusions as to as to their ability, in general. In this Directors course, everyone knew exactly how they skied. As the years brought experience I never understood why so many people fool themselves as to their personal skiing standard There are many in the instructional world who should know better, who are pathetically the worst offenders. The fact that they are prepared to do this, shows how little they know of skiing. To fall foul of this unnecessary nonsense is stupid. They have to be seen skiing sooner or later, where their ability can be judged for what it's worth.

The Stagers held their Christmas a week earlier than the traditional one. It's called St Nicholas night. There was a long dinner table, with family and friends. This was a tremendous novelty for me. The great family gathering was something I had never experienced. It was a special feeling!. The main dish was Kid, as in goat. The way it was cooked, it could have been anything. The nearest we have ever got at home to something exotic was a wee bit of chicken if we were lucky! The Frau served a deadly brew of Gluwein. It was spiced with all sorts of bits and pieces. The aroma was sensational and it went down a treat. The Great Lady kept filling the man sized glasses from enormous jugs. The more you drank, the more you wanted. You couldn't take a Clydesider anywhere. I'm sure the firewater was 25% schnapps. Next morning, skiing at speed on the top of the Lauberhorn, all the starch was long gone from my tail!

Another facet of peoples' needs and traits in skiing came to my attention during this fertile period in skiing. I was finding out just how much human nature impinged on the culture of skiing, and, in so doing, made it a way of life for full-time skiers and part of a way of life for many recreational skiers. It was Teresa, Werner's wife, who brought this to my notice. One morning, when I had no class, Werner said, "you take Teresa skiing." Then he told me quietly that she liked to ski behind a good skier. Well, that's something we all like to do. She insisted she'd have a schnapps before she went on the hill. She said it relaxed her, and set her up for the morning. I found out later that, when she never got her schnapps, her skiing was not up to her standard, which was a good class five. A drink for needy, nervous pupils would be put to good use in the future.

A few days before I left, Werner was paying me out for my teaching. I had never asked him how much I would be paid. I left that up to him. I said that I hoped there would be enough for a new pair of Molitor boots, and he laughed, saying that I could buy more than one pair. He started counting out hundred frank notes onto a table in the bar room. It was so much more that I had expected. Frau Stager said "you have too much money, for just skiing!" Werner said, "Fritz worked very hard for that!" He wanted me to stay, and teach full-time, and he would fix it all up with the local powers that be. He said he and I would be good together. I've no doubt we would have been, but it was not to be, for several good reasons. The time for leaving Lauterbrunnen to join my family in Zermatt arrived at just about the right time. I must admit, I was getting weary *for my Ain Folk*. I also discovered, to my horror, I was tired! I could hardly believe it. How could I be tired, when I'd only been skiing! Before leaving home, I'd worked six nightshifts a week. I also had the dry-ski-school before work each four nights, eight straight weeks skiing in Switzerland, with no days off. Sure I was tired.

On the train from Lauterbrunnen to Zermatt, I sat thinking of what had happened in these last long, eventful weeks. As I turned it over in my mind and I meditated on the importance of the events, it slowly came to me the amount of ground that had been covered. Firstly, the unplanned opportunities seemed to come at me, as if by order...

> *Being given a top class in the Swiss Ski School in Villars.*
> *Skiing with the fine skiers in the Directors Course came to me with more ease and comfort than it had on the first course.*
> *Having the company of Charlie French and John Clemments, with the ever growing friendship between us.*
> *Making a success of my week's class in Villars.*
> *The experience of the Junior Championships at Wengen.*
> *The cementing the relationship with Werner's parents was a joy to me and was to last from then on into the future, when it became even stronger.*

If some deity had been asked to plan a chain of events which would be of immeasurable value and importance for our family's future, it could not have worked out as perfectly.

When knowledge and strength, in the formative years in BASI, were needed it was then I dipped into what I started to learn during those weeks. As far I was concerned, what the Swiss were doing was of a very high standard, and good enough to gauge what we had to do, in our beginning, until we learned, by trial and error, what suited our needs best. We will cover this in full at the appropriate time. If truth be admitted, I had become lonely, even amidst all the excitement and newness of this utopic world. Anyway, my "unlonely" world was waiting for me in, of all places, the fabled mountain village of Zermatt. For the skier-come-climber, Zermatt was as I expected it to be. The village is a delight, constantly dominated by the ever present Matterhorn.

Walking up through the Village to find the place where our group from Glencoe were staying I was so heavily loaded with luggage my wee legs were giving me trouble. Not far from where they were staying, I saw my son, Iain, running towards me. Jeanie was with him. I smarted up. Two of our menfolks turned up and became porters to *the conquering hero*. All was well, I was back in the land of the living! This trip was the end product of the dreamie talks that took place in the Doss, one stormy weekend the winter before. The dreaming became reality. A mighty effort went into this enterprise.

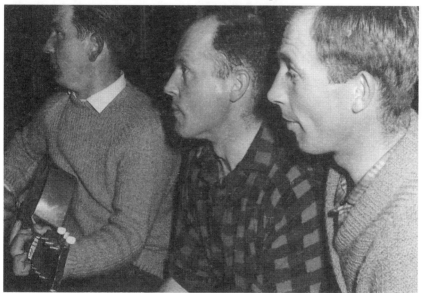

"The Balladiers"
left to right – Dougie McLean. Harrold Thomson, Johnnie McLellan – RJB

Just Alky and me and Dougie makes three
  we're happy in one three-way loader,
Now we're heading south but not to Portsmouth
  we'll end up in Dover.
Across the sea to Gay Paree
  and in our flat in old Zermatt we'll dump our gear
Then after skiing all we'll hit the Town
  to let them know the Boys are here,
  On our holiday in Zermatt.

To the tune of "My Blue Heaven"

101

Jeanie and I had converted a large, two ton van, into what would be called a camper today. It was known as the Three-Way-Loader, and would be our family's skiing headquarters at Meall a' Bhuiridh for the next few years. The Three-Way-Loader was to be used to transport a crowd of the Doss dwellers to Zermatt but the numbers grew so much that two minibuses were used instead. The Balladiers even made a up a song about the Three-Way-Loader and its drive to Zermatt, and what took place there even before they had been there. This song became quite famous. It told a story of people's dreams, their determination, their simplistic outlook on life, which made it possible for them to achieve goals that the unwritten rules of the day said were not for them. Not trying was something they never understood. Confidence they were never short of, but, having said that, "where fools rush in, brave men fear to tread!" We were *first!* Fourteen adults and four kids made up this group. We booked two apartments that could be used as one. These turned out to be just what we needed. When you look back on the different and complex personalities that went to make up that bunch, and how well they got on together, it shows just how much they had learned about the workings of the world. What we had discovered was that you could make a great deal out of very little, if you were prepared to use your brain, and get up and move yourself. So, this was the happy environs I arrived in, where the skiing would become personal, for me, by me. The skiing time could be used to suit any whim that took my fancy, for good or bad. This is something good ski teachers cannot indulge in, when they are working.

Amongst this happy band, there were two kinds of skiers. There were the racers, Harry McKay, Andy Scott and Willie Smith. And there were the rest, who were average. On the first day of Zermatt skiing, I went with the average skiers up onto Sunnegga Blauherd, where we had a lesson. This turned out very well, remembering these were very close friends. It was most satisfying. And it was the first and only time I remember teaching my wife. It may seem strange, but it was during these three weeks that I first skied with our son, who would have been eight, even though he'd skied for five years. My time was my own, so this made the whole thing a natural enjoyable way of dealing with a wee boy who, at the time, had no skiing companions of his own age. It so happened he could ski down most slopes at speed. Despite my involvement in ski teaching, I have never believed in hammering lessons into children. Our Iain had been extremely lucky in having many "uncles," who took a serious interest in him, without making a big deal out of it. He had been the only boy about, at that time, skiing with our group. Luckily, other youngsters were appearing. There were two sisters with our group who had just started skiing, Helen and Evelyn Carmichael, and, like Iain, would, in time, move into the British Ski Teams.

In the near future, when training started on our hills, the response and results were quite remarkable. The youngsters seemed to produce results as if by magic. It may be that we were *wearing the rose tinted spectacles*. The efforts of all the adults, not only parents, was a living thing. With the exciting certainty, the youngsters could only get better at their skiing and racing. During the growth of British skiing, I would enjoy many, many times of exciting skiing with Iain, my son. It would be true to say that I matured, and he grew up, within the growth of British Skiing. As the years advanced, it became more difficult for me to hold my end up, in the skiing department. Iain had only been skiing a few years less than myself. He was, by nature, a good skier. A unique situation. Werner and

Teresa, his future wife, and Caroline Simms, came to visit me in Zermatt. Werner took Iain for a day's skiing. Of course, Iain thought this was terrific. In particular, the cokes, and the fact he was called the "Little Fritz." It was at the end of Werner's stay, when we had the no holds barred run, from the top of the National Blauherd run, when he blew it. I knew I was on my way!

1957 Tennant Trophy Team from "The Doss"
left to right – Denis Barclay, Andy Scott, Tommy Paul, Johnny McLellan
Jimmy Hamilton, Iris Barclay, Willie Smith – Front June Lawley – RJB

The RAF used to have their championships in Zermatt. Andy Scott, who had been skiing for the Army during his National Service, was well known to them. I'm sure Andy had been the Army Champion, and various· other prestigious Interservice titles. The RAF let Willie, Harry and Andy race Hors de Concours in their Downhill and Giant Slalom. Harry was first in the Giant Slalom and second in the Downhill. Andy was first in Downhill and second in the Giant Slalom. Willie was close to the first places. The RAF were very good about this turn up for the book, but, in understandable hindsight, they scrubbed these three *bandits* out of the Slalom event and thereby protected their combined result. The RAF invited us to their presentation party. The Air Vice Marshall was apologetic to me about not letting these three race in the Slalom. I explained that their first mistake was letting these three *bandits* near their races! Included in this wonderful group was Bob Clyde, his wife, and his son Fraser. Also there were Helen and Alex Carmichael, mother and father of the racing Carmichaels. When I think back on who made up this group, and how many of them became hallmarks in British Skiing! Others in the group, who were not so prominent, but certainly just as important in skiing's wide tapestry, were Peter Ferguson, known

103

as Wee Fergie, Peter Simpson, and June Lawley. June was later to become Mrs William Smith. Yes, these were indeed memorable people. The visit of Werner, Teresa and Caroline, seemed to bring two other long established parts of the ski world into our new growing and, eventually, very influential part of British Skiing.

Even though all these things were taking place, I clearly remember being unsettled during those three Zermatt weeks. I was troubled in my mind as to how the rest of the season would go, when we got back home. How easy it was to envy Werner and Oscar's set-up, and their way of life. Of course, their well ordered lives did not come to them out of thin air, overnight! At that time, back home, we were still light years away from what we have in skiing facilities today. There were no ski lifts on Cairngorm. In Glenshee there was a shortish Dundee Ski Club homemade T-Bar. Glencoe had a T-Bar in the top basin and a partial access chairlift. There was the ever present certainty of our bad weather, which had a direct effect on obtaining pupils to teach. And many other problems. These thoughts came to me soon after I arrived in Zermatt and got stronger as the holiday wore on.

Charlie French and John Clemments had spoken to me about moving to the Rockies, in the States. They reckoned that I would have fitted into the scene as it then was. Skiing development was taking off. With the usual open mindedness of the Americans of that period, teachers of my *type* from Europe, could do very well in their industry at that time. I had plenty of good connections. There was the terrible bind at the end of each season, of coming back to Glasgow to work in a factory. The reality of the situation was that, after my season so far, and what my two American friends had suggested to me, plus the desire to obtain the best possible opportunities for our family and at the same time take my skiing as far as it would go, would have tested the wisdom of Solomon.

We were well into our three weeks of skiing, so the more skilled skiers were moving very fast, fast being the big object of the whole enterprise. The Wild Bunch had reached the stage that every possible skiing minute was a prisoner. We used to all ski in a bunch. On a morning when we were all going at it we left the Gornergrat railway station at three thousand metres. About two hundred yards below the station, I was behind the current Scottish Champion, Harry McKay, when, as we all do from time to time, he blew it. Unfortunately, when he landed, his hip bone made contact with a bit of the Gornergrat bedrock. When we got Harry sorted out, it was obvious he was past skiing for that day at least. So it was the bloodwagon for him, and down to Riffelberg station. While he was lying waiting for the train to Zermatt, he was not feeling *the full shilling*, and he gave me money to get him a wee miniature of brandy. When I got it back to him, he didn't seem to be able to get it down his neck. Remembering Bob Clyde, in Corrie na Ciste, drinking the brandy coffee meant for me, when I was mortally wounded, I just downed the wee brandy, to save it going to waste. *Waste not, want not.* Injured Scottish Champions don't need strong drink, it's bad for them! The doctor in Zermatt diagnosed severe bruising. As it turned out, when Harry got home, his pelvis and femur were found to be cracked. That was Harry's first bump. Four years later, he did his ankle in on the Cairngorm, while training in a group of mine. He, of course, blamed me for his accident. Nothing to do with careless skiing! Wee Fergie put his shoulder out, so his skiing was finished for the rest of the trip. Considering the pace of the skiing, and the numbers involved, I'm surprised that's all the injuries we had between us.

Two of the *sheep of the fold*, were Alex Cairns and Dougie McLean. Dougie got Alex and himself escorted home, one night, by a local gendarme. The nice police officer had the pistol out, when he delivered them to our door. He very politely asked us to keep them off the street for the rest of the night. I wonder how he knew where they were staying. Dougie would have got you into trouble in an empty house. These two could entertain any crowd. In a society of extroverts, they stood out. They had discovered the low paid workers' pub, the Café de La Plas. It had the cheapest booze in town. After skiing, we used to hold concerts in the place. All the snow shovelers, and street sweepers, joined in on the act. They'd set up bottles of wine for us. They must have wondered what kind of English ski guests we were. We eventually got it over to them where we came from. "Sheep of the fold?" Some sheep! Zermatt is without a doubt an outstanding mountain village. I've been back over the years. Despite the pressure of the increasing numbers of skiers, I believe the village that gave us so much pleasure and left us with memories we all hold dear still retains its charm and is certainly *a mighty place to ski.*

Back in Glencoe for the remainder of the season, we all seemed to settle in, and adjust ourselves to the perversity of the weather. This was one of the main concerns in my mind, when I was giving all the thought to coming back, after the twelve weeks of more or less ideal conditions of the Alps. Being back in the fertile newness of the level and growing playing field that was skiing at that time seemed to give the necessary stimulus to make up for the vagaries of the weather. There where so many new and interesting people, from all the different strata of society, most of whom were contributing to the common purpose of making skiing more comfortable and available to all. Skiing, like climbing, apart from being a mountain activity, was available to anyone who made the effort to get started.

There was, in this new, virgin field, a *new animal* being bred, the indigenous, native born skier, who started their skiing on Scottish ski hills, some of whom had not yet started their schooling. The first of these to make the British Team, and ski in the 1968 Olympics, was Helen Jamieson, youngest daughter of the Dundee Ski Club's famous skiing family. The head of this delightful wee clan, is a tough, *doughty* competitor, called David. A man of kindly understanding of the needs of others. He was one of the founders, and leading lights of the present Glenshee ski lift system, and contributed in no mean way to Scottish Skiing as it is today. The season before, he had engaged me to take Helen and tidy up her skiing. What he did give me was a wee girl who had been brought up like her sisters, to be able to walk up and down slalom courses where and when asked. He also, possibly without knowing it, gave me a vote of public confidence in Scottish skiing at that time.

This would be the year another dear friend, one of these tough no nonsense men the north of England produces, by the name of Peter Todd, asked me if I could arrange for his son to get training with the DHO. This was easy, as Ros Hepworth was always short of boys in her training. The boy's name was Ian. It so happened, he went to a public school, as most of the youngsters from the south, who skied, did. Ian was, and is, a lovable rascal. He became a member of the British Team. After he finished racing, he qualified as a lawyer. For long years now, he has been Mark McCormack's Vice President in charge of operations in Europe, this in itself a considerable achievement. Young Toddie would have been three years older than our Iain. They had been skiing together, even though they differed very much in size. Peter Todd asked me why I did not send our son to the training. Suggesting sending him to the moon would have been just as possible!

Later that day, in conversation, he put it to me in such way that I could not refuse. He would arrange for our Iain to accompany his son on the DHO training. These County Durham men can be *as thrawn* as any Scotsman! He handled me like a wee boy, so much so that any argument against his offer would have made me look churlish. A number of years later, Jeannie and I were privileged to be able to return the friendship to him in a situation he could not refuse. Peter was one of the *big persons* in my life. When Peter went to buy his first full season's pensioner's pass for Cairngorm, Bob Clyde issued him the first ever, No. 1! The going rate was five pounds. Bob said that, as it was the first, there would be no charge. Peter, with that pass, was the cat that stole the cream! I always told him he skied about two hours per day longer than was good for him. He never listened to a word I said. He'd be bushed at the end of each day, so much so, his tongue used to hang out. But that was "our Peter." For some unknown reason, it took twenty five years for us to get to ski together in Europe. We eventually made it early one December, above Tignes, with two other good friends. Sod's Law, the weather was terrible. We lost Peter some years back. That's the price you pay for all your experience, and the green years of good times. With age comes the *Grim Reaper*, for *the Piper must be paid!*

David Jamieson and Peter Todd were similar in many ways. They were of very reasonable means, bluntly honest, and very business like, in their way of doing things. They both spoke with accents which betold of their origins. In common with strong men, they were generous, both with their knowledge and their friendship. Not gifts that are handed around readily by most. This is how I saw these men. When you look back and think, that Helen Jamieson, Luke O'Reilly and the rascally Ian Todd, were all very young skiers at a time when ski lifts were still quite primitive and few in number, here in the Highlands, it leaves a nice taste in my mouth, that they all skied in the 1968 Olympics. I'm sure this gave the new up and coming young Scottish skiers a fine example to follow, and, as the record shows, many did follow in their footsteps.

What I have spoken about was not the only new happenings taking place in the new emerging and vibrant thing that skiing had became. Therefore, any misgivings I had entertained in Zermatt about adjusting back to our local difficulties slipped into the background, and were buried by the excitement of all that was taking place. Racing was taking up a large slice of the total energy of many of the better skiers and not-so-better skiers. This was bound to happen, as the type of people who were involved were of that breed. I've often wondered how they would have turned out as racers had they started skiing as children. If it was possible to have a regret amidst all of what was going on, for me it might have been not being allowed take part in the racing with rest of the crowd. At that time ski teachers, as professionals, could not race with club racers. In retrospect, where they were breaking new ground in their skiing, I most certainly was doing the same in my skiing.

Andy Scott was to win the Scottish Championship by the end of season. That would be three times in a row our *Neat Wee Crowd* had pulled that one off. It must have been what we were eating! I mentioned earlier that Jeanie and I had converted a large van into what would be called a caravanette. We had made a good job of it. Its best feature was the green enamel coal fired stove, this *wee gem* kept the place like an oven, and it was private for the family, so this made a tremendous improvement for the three of us. Iain and Jeanie came up at weekends and holidays. On Sunday nights, when all the weekend skiers were leaving, Peter Ferguson and I would be sitting at the green enamel stove with the tea brewing on the hob, waiting for the Sunday night play coming on the wireless. He would be listening to the van and car doors closing in the cold winter nights. This was the "townies" driving back, to spend their coming week in the *big smoke* of Glasgow and Edinburgh. As the sound of the last door closing faded away into the night, and onto the Rannoch Moor, he'd sigh a sigh of relief and say "that's those weekend bastards away back to the Big Smoke, this was too good for them." Fergie was a supercilious loner, who liked the big outdoors all to himself, but of course, with selected company! Quite a number of these townies were our dear friends. Two of them were my wife and son! This was all part of the patter. One of the great attractions of our group was their capacity to be extremely controversial, just for the hell of it. Fergie was a past master of the critique.

Looking back on the two winters of 1961 and 62, and having to *post-mortem* them in depth as to what happened, I've come to the conclusion that, apart from being *skint* all the time, these two winters were to be the least stressful I would have for some number of years to come. Stress was not a word being bandied about in those times. Getting messed about *went with the territory!* The "slings and arrows of good fortune" were easy to live with. *The Piper must be paid.* So called stress I could live with. Yes, the season of 1960/61 had been a Pandora's Box that most people never get the chance to live through.

10. This and That

*Climbing Comeback –
Fractured Route, Glencoe
Frith with Harry
above*

In summer 1961 Harry McKay and myself made a wee comeback in rock climbing. If you are going to climb at a reasonable standard you must climb regularly. With me having to work weekends to support skiing, regular climbing was not possible. Harry had not been climbing very much. For some reason we ended up on Buachaille one weekend roped and ready to go. Unlike most people, we warmed up by climbing a 280 feet *severe* to *very severe* route, called Bottleneck Chimney and Hangman's Crack. The reasoning for this thinking was that I had climbed these before. Alex Carmichael, who had not climbed, was being broken in at, very nearly, the deep end. He was doing very well. Mind you, he was in the very best hands! Flushed with the ease of our successful comeback, we nipped down Shackle Route and decided to test our reawakened skills a little farther by doing one of John Cunningham's routes, Shattered Crack, of some 120 feet. The crux of this is near the top. It so happened I arrived there first, which meant I should have climbed through. I went up onto the crux to take a look. Harry reminded me I had the pleasure of this crux, so I came back down and let him have The Cherry. I'm sure he would have pulled me off if I had moved on up! I'm also a very fair fellow! We did a few other routes that weekend. Not a bad wee comeback. This would come under the philosophy of *"never go easy when you can go hard."*

Around this period we fell in with one of the Creag Dhu's good climbers from Clydebank, Patsy Walsh. I first climbed with Patsy when he was about seventeen, and I was an old ex-serviceman of twenty one. We were camping down at Clachaig. The sleet was coming down at us as if it was fired out of a cannon. The crowd from the club bus were standing round a big fire with no enthusiasm to move. Patsy and I made our move and we ended up on Stob Coire nam Beith. You might find this hard to believe, but we never even knew what mountain we were on! The old "philosophy" again. We had one ice axe, mine, one pair of thin woollen gloves, mine, trousers tucked inside our socks, and crap boots. To say we were ill equipped would be a statement of fact! I never criticise young climbers, or their inexperience.

*Climbing Comeback –
Fractured Route, Glencoe
Harry*

Their right to come and go as they please is sacrosanct and the spice and spirit of the great outdoors. We climbed a very steep gully. We had to short pitch it. Patsy's rope was only about 50 feet. Nothing but the best of gear! That was my first Glencoe gully. It could have been my last.

108

But I digress. Back to 1961. Patsy was taking Harry and my good self on one of his first ascents on the Buachaille, called Revelation, on the North Buttress West Wall. I found out why it was called "Revelation." You make your way up a very steep face of easy climbing without roping, then you belay. I must take time to describe this big tough mountain man. He was the same height as wee Harry, about five four in his high heels. Where Harry was broad shouldered, Patsy had normal shoulders for a man of his height. Patsy's trademark was his glasses. They were like the bottom of old fashioned milk bottles. And, like Harry, he was as tough as the sole of an old boot. You can never tell what's inside the book's cover! After roping, Patsy started off to lead. He moved out to the right. Round a corner out of sight he started to climb vertically giving instructions as to how I played out the rope. After a fair period of time he let me know he was making a belay to bring me up. Harry and I were sitting on a nice big ledge on the cliff face and were very comfy. But when I made my move round the corner, the reason for name of the climb became obvious. The wee man with milk bottle bottom specs has used a nice touch of humour when he named the climb! The moment you moved round the corner the footholds and fingergrips became very, very thin. In other words, small.

The docker's son had named the route well. On these sparse footholds when you looked down all you saw was the bed of Great Gully and it seemed to be a long way down.

This is what climbers call "exposure." I've never thought much about it until now, but I suppose this is part of the *buzz* that climbing offers those who are lucky enough to get into it. However, with being top-roped the exposure does not come into play.

But I had a little problem that had nothing to do with the "exposure." My tummy was upset. When I arrived up to the belay, Patsy had left a sling, which I clipped onto. The belay stance was very small, not like the one I'd left, but we were well tied on. Patsy and Harry were out of sight. Just as Harry was about to climb up, Mother Nature called, so I shouted down to Harry to hold on before I brought him up. I then took down my breeks and did the business. When I was finished, I started to bring Harry up without thinking. When he discovered he had to climb up through the residue of Mother Nature he was far from pleased! I climbed up and explained to Patsy what all the shouting was about. He thought it was good crack, and anyway, being on the end of the rope took away any difficulty the extra technical problems Mother Nature may have added to this splendid route. Of course, Harry still had to face all the crowd when he got down to Jacksonville. He took a lot of stick!

A story about "chasing the wild deer," to quote Robert Louis Stevenson. One weekend the Lomond Climbing Club ran a bus to Cairngorm. A big bunch of the Creag Dhu Club and friends made it an occasion for a *jolly*. Now, most of these men had not been at the beasts, as the deer are affectionately known. Patsy was one of those, and, to get his share of meat, he had to come out on the hill to carry the meat back. Harry and I, being *hunters*, did not carry.

I had been out early and had got a nice hind. Harry caught up with me and, some time later, he got two nice beasts. Not long after, Patsy and another non-hunter came up. As there was a large number wanting meat, Harry and I went farther out to add to the bag. In our stupidity, we left the two clowns to dress out the beasts. When we got back, the beasts had not been gralloched, or quartered. Instead, the two clowns had cut off patches off the odd patch of skin and hair here and there, and left the beasts looking like poodle dogs! Just as well they were good at the climbing.

Harry was still on the rifle when we stalked a nice bunch of stags. We were in close, about fifty yards. Harry got one, and the rest were up and off! Now, like all animals, they are creatures of habit. After a shot, they run a distance, then stop and take a look back. This is when you can take another one. Being an ex-infantryman, I naturally took command. Harry had only been a medic in the army. I ordered him to up sights to two hundred yards. He then got another one. The beasts were off as usual. They were going to go a long way, and, being a good commander, I used my initiative. I gave loud sharp whistle. This stopped them. I barked out the order, "up sights four hundred yards!" Harry said it was too far because the rifle barrel was so badly worn. I told him to have go. Wonder of wonders, he got it! Some shot! Some commander! Big Jim Purves was divvying out the meat. We found we had rather more that we needed. Hugh Currie, a reporter on a well known Glasgow tabloid who had never been out at the beasts, was greatly taken with the novelty of the whole thing, particularly the venison. I spoke earlier about carrying heavy packs. Well, I'm sure Shuggie's pack was well over a hundred pounds and we had long walk out. But he had the bit between his teeth. He told us some time later he had difficulty with his mother about how he happened to have all the meat. She would have been a straight laced church going lady of the old school. Glasgow abounded with ladies like those then, and still does. I'm quite sure that Shuggie, with his smooth slippery oily reporter's lip, would coast through that little problem with consummate skill. I would never have had any trouble from Jeanie about the amount of venison I brought back for the pot!

Another wee shortie on climbing and John Cunningham. In the summer of 1958, Johnnie was climbing probably as well as he ever climbed during his distinguished time on the mountains. He had been out on the hills full-time all the season and was moving well. For some reason I'll never remember, I ended up tied onto his rope on the North Buttress on Buachaille. He wanted to look at a possible route between the start of Bottleneck and Gallows. The wee look became a very long epic. Johnnie had climbed up for about thirty feet when he called down that the climbing was quite thin and, with that, he dropped a single Scotch Bluebell with root down on my head. And that is how this famous route became Bluebell Groove. The bluebell had been growing in a niche that John needed to use as a hand and foot hold. He then moved up into the belay of Bottleneck Chimney and tied on. Then I climbed up. John then traversed out back onto the vertical wall that was Bluebell, where he hammered in a piton and clipped on a running belay. As he started to climb straight up, he found the climbing very difficult. As I watched him working out the moves, I knew it was thin. I also knew I would find it even thinner, which I did! After a long time he worked his way up and away out of my sight. Another long wait during which Harry, Willie and Jeanie, who were out for a scramble, passed by under the wall. Harry looked up and asked what the hell I was doing stuck in that wee damp wet miserable belay. I told him I was cold as I had no jacket, starving, and no grub! After all, I came up for a scramble.

A Man and a Boy – Iain aged 6 over Rannoch Moor & Loch Laidon, with John Cunningham, holder of the Polar Star and Pery Medal for Antarctic Exploration. Photo by John Cullen

What started out as "just holding the end of the rope for a pal" had become hours. In the *lingua franca, the crack was off!* And to coin an old saying, "a friend in need is a pest!" Johnnie had run up against a real tough bit of climbing and, with his enormous capacity for safety, he would not push it. After a long time he got a very small spade piton in for a running belay, which justified the move he had to make to finish the climb. I never saw any of this, as John was well above me. It's normal for the leader to give their second a running commentary as to as to what is taking place. This keeps the second on their toes in event of the leader coming off.

For example, once I was top-roping John on a thing called the Horrible Hook. This is so difficult it had never been climbed bottom-roped at that time. The hard bit was about 40 feet up. It's here everyone comes off. It was a hot, sunny day, so I was stripped to the waist. Without any warning, he came off. As a result the slack in the rope left me with a big rope burn over my shoulder and down my back. The old maxim again, "a friend in need is a pest." I don't know if the Hook has ever been climbed free. I hope not. It's nice to leave a little for the imagination.

I never completed Bluebell. I was too cold, too hungry and not good enough a climber. I got up to the very hard bit where I found I would have needed top rope to make *the hard move*. Before I would do that I had Johnnie let me down on the rope. I was fifteen feet clear of the wall when my feet touched the bottom. In the years to come, when I had a lot to do in training John in becoming a National Ski Teacher, I took every opportunity to see he got *no quarter* and that he made reparations for his ill use of me in the climbing! And in the doing, we had special times together. During some of these special times together over light refreshments, he told me that it took fifteen years to repeat Bluebell. This he said with his tongue in his cheek. He was good at that sort of thing. He must have been proud of that achievement. But hard men do not speak of such things. It is unseemly. On this same face is Gallows Route. It was the hard one, until that day. Gallows was another of John's first ascents. So, as you see, other good things were taking place in tandem with the new challenges, even if they were not available to me each and every weekend of the summer, with my overtime working. Few people get to pursue all the good things of life at the one time. There's usually a price to pay for the good things of life, and there is nothing wrong with that.

Where the previous season of 1960/61 was one of almost unbounded opportunity and was certainly a comprehensive look at the established ski world of the Alps, the experience set me up for the new coming season. Jeanie would go with me to the Swiss course, which was being held in Arosa, in the first week of November 1961. She fitted into the *camaraderie* and the spirit of this unique and exclusive event. To my personal delight, she was treated as part of the ongoing scene and, with her natural dignity and common sense, made her own way in this particularly male dominated world. I booked Jeanie into the open course for ski school pupils. She was staying in a very fine old hotel and by chance so was Joan Shearing of the DHO. Jeanie skied in a class of five, with Americans. Jeanie had every right to be at her course. She had worked hard to make this possible. Without her understanding of the reason and the purpose of the whole endeavour, I would never have been there in the first place.

I was staying in the Valsana. There was a Swiss song about this old hotel. This was the headquarters for the Directors Course, and all the High Heid Yins stayed there. Inner Arosa at 5710 to Arosa at 6200 feet. The skiing is of a straightforward nature, and the area has a good sunshine record. It has many good hotels. When we arrived they were short of snow and high on sunshine. We had a few days skiing before the course started. During this I met two local lady ski teachers. As I was running a ski clinic for two teachers who were with me, the Swiss were working on their skiing close to us. It was obvious they were more than interested in us. They knew that we were in the same profession as themselves. It was the language. They could not *clock* its source. With my usual reserve and backwardness, I made the first overtures and struck up a conversation. The ladies would have been a credit to any ski resort. They were taken by the presentation of how I was introducing the improvement of parallel turns and the square stance. With their native charm, they asked if they could join in on our teachers clinic. Their contribution made what we were doing seem more important. We had everything in common. Their boss was a big beast of a man. He was the co-director of the local ski school. His name was Werner Knoll. I knew him well through Werner Stager. The two ladies were on the Directors Course.

There was something strange afoot in the "State of Denmark," or was it the first whisperings of the "Wind of Change" that was starting to blow across the mountains of the Grisons. Women on the Directors Course. What were things coming to! These two ladies could teach in four languages. During the course, when we passed on the hill or met in a place of refreshment, we would have little reunions. This is another pleasant memory. I wonder how the ladies are faring after all these years.

A few years after this, Werner Knoll blotted his copybook in the village of Arosa. At the age of fifty he managed to get the mayor's 19 year old daughter in the family way. When he told us that he couldn't believe it, at his age, I wondered what he expected. Kittens? He did the right thing and married the girl. In a place like Arosa, it must have been Hobson's Choice. At least it never became a one parent family!

I said the snow was poor when we arrived. The night before we started, it snowed and kept snowing nicely through the next day. This gave the course a fine start. June Lawley went into a class of six. When I met her that night, I asked who she got as a teacher for that day. She was very pleased as she had skied with Roger Staub and he had said she was a good skier. Roger was the current holder of the Giant Slalom Gold Medal. He was from Arosa. Some years later he was killed hang gliding in America.

During this week Werner suggested I move in with a class of Canton Valais teachers. It was accepted that this particular class skied well, among about ten classes who all skied well. After he made the arrangement for the next day, he said, in fun, "don't stay up too late tonight, Fritz!" Jeanie asked what he meant. I had no idea. Next day, I got a very salutary and practical demonstration of how a group of a dozen or so good skiers can wind each other up. Now, what I'm going to say may seem a contradiction in terms, but some of these skiers were not all that good technically. But good, or not so good, they all skied with complete abandonment and impetuosity. The word "elan" comes to mind. They could ski in *any* conditions. It was like one-upmanship, and none of them gave a damn as to their style. A bad description of what is meant by *good* skiing. In fun skiing they hacked about as a wild bunch. You had to look out for yourself. Having said all that, they were good to ski with. And another lump of experience for future use.

The man in charge was from Canton Vaud. Arni Mueller. He skied in a flippant manner and with a skill that was a delight to witness. He was his own, and like all good skiers, skied like themselves! François Carron, from Verbier, was in the class. He was the same, but different. Yes, when skiing with these people, early to bed could be advantageous. All of these men came from French-speaking Wallis and Vaud, with the exception of myself and my friend Jean Pierre Zuber from Canton St Gallen, near Lake Constance, which was German-speaking. Anyway, Jean Pierre talked and behaved like a Frenchman. He was multilingual, sophisticated, and kind hearted. He was also a wild, unpredictable, loveable rascal.

On the last day before we all went our own ways, the class stopped early. They had arranged to have Hornli hut opened specially for us. It was a beautiful old summer hut. The white wine was going great guns. Arni was a squeezebox man. It was at this moment I really noticed how much respect he carried and the dignity with which he carried it. There was wonderful mountain singing. They insisted that I sing. I gave them my Glasgow rendition of *Alouette*, with all the rude and lewd gesticulations that go with it. This went down a treat. On the boozy run down I had my first whack at skiing the breakable crust. Under the crust was deep powdery snow. If you didn't already stand square on your skis, you would have needed to have tidied your stance on the spot, or you were in trouble.

During the week, I'd been sharing a room with a teacher who was working with clients in the open classes, by the name of Guy Reber. In summer he worked as a head doorman in one of the international hotels in Geneva, top hat and all. It was a big money job. He taught skiing privately out of St Moritz in the season. He must have been a *Cool Cat*, sniffing round the rich pickings of that wonderful ski station. He was another larger than life man-of-the-world. We got on well. He described his work to me. The things he told me about the international *High Rollers* and their goings on! Well, you just had to believe him!

Jeanie's hotel was at the other end of Arosa from the Valsana, so I only used my room in the early morning and before dinner. On the last day my room mate asked me if I would be coming back that night, as he needed the room for himself. Being a man of the world, my answer put a smile on his face. The *hanky panky* was on! Robert Burns, in one of his tales, called it "*houghmagandie*," a much rounder turn of phrase, meaning you're not supposed "to get it."

During that evening I took a raging flu. I went back to my own bed in the Valsana. In the wee hours of the morning I heard the door being boldly opened, amidst sniggering of *great expectations* that were to be short lived. I think I got the slagging in all of his many languages before they skulked off with their dignity in tatters. When he saw the state I was in when he got back in the morning, we were still pals! When I explained to Jeanie, sometime later, how I had let my new friend down so badly, she was very sympathetic towards this poor deprived opener of doors. I bet he's got his own hotel now, as he said he would. I told Jeanie, after we left Arosa, how I used to *tip the wink* at the two desk men as I left her hotel each morning at around six a.m. They'd be wondering how big a *bung* was coming their way. No *hanky panky*, no *bung*. Jeanie did not see the humour in the telling of the story.

Earlier on in the week I was summoned to the office to see the boss, Christian Rubi. He said I should have let him know my wife was coming to the course. Next year she would be staying with me in the same hotel as the rest of the Directors. He presumed I would be attending the course, as it would be held in Wengen. Jeanie ended up paying twelve Swiss francs per day for the course. Herr Rubi was a good housekeeper and, as it turned out, a good friend. It's touches like this that make it seem there's a comforting arm around your shoulder. Arosa was a very comfortable experience for both Jeanie and myself. For some perverse reason, attending the course in Wengen seemed to have some heightened attraction. As it turned out, it certainly had. Christmas in the Stager's family home in Lauterbrunnen turned out to be an excitingly moving way of starting the 1961/62 season.

While we were having our first high quality holiday, our son Iain had been staying with my sister. It was from here that he would leave for the DHO training in Wengen. As we were not yet back from Switzerland, my wonderful sister, Carol, had mixed Iain in with her deeply loved two girls and boys. She would see to it that Iain would be posted off to London, where Peter Todd, his sponsor, would take over. However, he was going to have a rather grand departure. Iain was barely ten and was travelling down to London with a sixteen-year-old, who I had arranged to train with the DHO. The boy's father had sent a chauffeur driven Rolls Royce! Not a bad way to leave a Glasgow Corporation housing scheme, to go on an event of a lifetime! It seems all the street urchins, and in Glasgow *they are street urchins*, were out in strength, looking at this wondrous thing, in silence. And it's not often you shut *them* up! But they are cute enough, and respectful enough, to recognise something different. It gave my sister quite a kick! When the boy, Chris Smith, and Iain arrived in London, they were to stay overnight with another boy, Ian Todd, at his Gran Ma's, who was Lady Tait, and it seems she was the Grand Dame, Matron of the *old school*, who treasured all the accepted values. I'd like to have met her. Young Toddie told me later that this formidable personage caught young Smith smoking and gave him the benefit of the two barrels of her indignant wrath. Full marks too! Toddie also told me she looked around for another victim and spotted Iain, who, at ten, would hardly be smoking. So, not to let him out of it, she barked the order, "stand up boy, stand up!" What a woman! I asked Toddie what she said to him. His answer was that he was "always in it, anyway," which was very easy to understand.

Iain was only ten, which would seem young to be away from home on his own. When the arrangements were made, it was understood that our Toddie would be his *minder*. Behind Toddie's rascally fun-making was a very clear thinking mind. There were ladies in charge of the chalets where they stayed who seemed to handle the kids satisfactorily. Most of these kids went to boarding schools, so they were used to being away from home. Iain was well able to look after himself, with all his weekending behind him. As for the training, he had been racing since he was six, but, in truth, there was no one at home of his own age for him to race against, at that time. This situation was quietly and naturally evolving itself forward without any unnecessary panic or ballyhoo.

115

The new season of 1962 started off for us, who were deeply involved in full-time skiing in Glencoe, in an atmosphere of confidence and assurance for the immediate future in skiing. Our family's start to the season boded well for things to come. Willie Smith and Harry McKay were established in a very comfortable hut they had built the season before. This had become the hub for entertainment at weekends and holidays. There was a feeling of oneness shared by us all. Harry and Willie would be running the ski lifts for the coming season. Peter Simpson and Andy Scott had been taken into *the body of the Kirk* for a full winter, and had a place in the Big Hut. I was nicely tucked away in my Three-Way-Loader. I should explain the three-way-loader was a former bread van with loading doors both sides and back. Wee Fergie had the Big Doss to himself midweek, which suited him just fine. Besides The Hut and our place, John McLennan had a wee tottie caravan, and Tommy Paul had an equally small, hand knitted hut. Between us we had a lovely cosy community, which would be the birth place of many important ideas that had a constructive influence in many parts of skiing in Scotland as it grew and matured. And indeed, as it turned out, in the UK.

The New Year of 1962 was to be for us, who were deeply involved in skiing, a time to find out if a full life in Scottish skiing could be supported. As if by an act of fate, the first Cairngorm chairlift started to operate, and in so doing became the linchpin as to whether we stayed in Scotland or moved to other mountains to fulfil our need to find our possibility in skiing. There were those among us (as there still are in today's society), those who were bloody minded enough to see the thing out to the bitter end, or to *the win*.

In the first year of The Hut, in 1961, we ended up with a bar. This would be illegal! How it started must be attributed to Robert Clyde. On Saturday nights we all used to go down to a local hotel for a few drinks, after which we would buy a *carryout* and borrow glasses from the hotel. For some reason, we never helped ourselves to them. The glasses were always returned the next day. One night the manageress refused us the loan of glasses. It would be true to say she had been *a supping of the barley wine*. Angry words were exchanged. Robert, who'd been absent when the row started, turned up and asked me what the trouble was. Bob made the following statement. "You lot have not handled it correctly!" However, "the woman was not for turning." Bob ended up telling her what to do with the glasses. Even I thought he put it rather crudely. The result was we all got barred from the place *Sine Die*.

What a to do! Most of the winter to go and precluded from the watering hole! Bob Clyde, to his credit, did something to repair the damage. He would buy drink in the liquor store in Inverness, where he lived, and bring it down on the Friday night, and, according to his thinking, we would all save a fortune. *Believe that if you're daft!* We got a lot more booze for our dough, but, if anything, we spent more. And in the process started two memorable winters never to be forgotten. Bob ran the bar. There was a big table in The Hut, where he sat and dispensed the bevy to order. Whisky at one shilling and three pence a nip, and ten pence for dumpy bottle of beer. As a favour to the ladies, he supplied lemonade for their whisky at no charge. Every so often he'd call glasses to the centre, for the barman's round. In our inept stupidity we would toast his health as a great fellah! Bob told the story of how, when he was buying the booze on the Friday nights, after three or four weeks the man in the off-licence asked Bob, in the most discreet way, if he didn't think he was damaging his health, drinking so much at the weekends. Bob, with his usual glib lip, told the man it was alright, as he never touched a drop during the week. That was another lie.

At the end of the 1961 season, Bob got the job as manager of the of the new Cairngorm Chairlift Company. As a result we had to get a replacement barman. We got a wee cracker by the name of Tommy McGinnis, and in the tradition established by that fine barman Bob Clyde, he would stand his hand every so often during the rumbustious evenings in our *illegal shebeen*. At the end of the 1962 season we organised a weekend at Cairngorm to visit Bob. To our pleasant surprise, our Braw Wee Barman, Tommy, picked up the bill for the meal and the booze for the night. When asked where the money came from, he said it was out of the profit of the bar. That left a question to be answered by Bob! How had Tommy managed to wine and dine 20 odd people? Bob, with a grin as big as the Cairngorm, said it was simple. Instead of saving the profit, he just drank twice as much as the rest of us. Not a bad swallow! Fair play to him. Bob had style when it came to milking situations like these. This he did without malice aforethought. He was a well known soft touch!

During that last season of 1961 that Bob spent in the Coe, he told the whole crowd about a dream he had the night before. He was a dreamer. Most of us are. The scenario was that all the crowd, Mammies, Daddies and kids, were staying at the ski club hut above The Plateau. Bob woke up early one morning to find the dreaded Atomic War had taken place during the night unbeknown to us. How they managed that I never figured out. Anyway, the world around us was flooded and only the mountain tops were clear of flood-water. Bob looked about and took stock of the situation and its possibilities. He lifted his trusty .303 (it's always a 303) and blew my head off. Big Smith took exception to this line of action, grabbed the rifle and demanded an explanation. Bob very carefully, in his own special brand of philosophy, pointed out that those that were left would need to repopulate the world! He wanted to give it a fair chance. Who needs friends! But Bob forgot one very important part of that equation. I was always up in the morning before him, and much more tricky in the corners than himself. The story is typical of Bob and one I'm very proud to know.

The season of 1962 was when the Glencoe Ski Club got under way, and, of all places, it got itself started round the big bar-room table. Like all things they did, they did it with great gusto, drive and efficiency. As would be expected, it became a force to be reckoned with in Scottish skiing. With their main drive to raise funds for juniors to enable them to race on equal terms with better-off kids. 1962 was a mixed up sort of heady cocktail, which was sweet in the drinking. Jeanie with me at Arosa and our son skiing with the DHO.

Early on in February, at the end of a weekend of terrible rain in Glencoe, when skiing was out of the question, Bill Greaves was driving from The Coe to spend a few days at Cairngorm. He invited me to keep him company. This was good chance to see Bob and his new chairlift. The drive up through Fort William and Loch Laggan-side was like driving in a monsoon. As we got closer to Newtonmore the rain gave up. We headed for the Carrbridge hotel where, on Sunday nights, the weekend skiers had tea dances before heading home. This is something Glencoe never had. We noticed all the skiers were in their ski clothes and they were still dry. When we asked about their weather on the hill, they said they had snow showers. Now, we know the climate has a penchant to vary from the western mountains to Cairngorm, but this seemed a tremendous variation. Experience over the coming years would justify this foible of nature.

11. A Wonderful World

The tea dance had a big effect on me. The atmosphere all these skiers created was a side of skiing that had not been in Glencoe at that time. To the best of my knowledge, it never ever did. We met Bob Clyde who introduced us around. What took me by surprise was the atmosphere of aprés-ski. Better still, it seemed as if it had been established for a long time past. Which it had not. There was feeling of permanence and growth. This would be because locals were involved. As I said, Bob introduced us about and, to my very pleasant surprise, people seemed to know me. A nice wee *ego boost*. Like all would-be, big-time, big-headed ski teachers, we saw ourselves through magnified rose-tinted specs! We stayed with Bob that night. Breakfast was the first I ever had in a house before going skiing in Scotland. I put my ski boots on in the same place where I had slept. It stands out in my mind.

Bill Greaves drove us up into the Cairngorm car park, where we could step out onto the snow. This was novel, there was a caravan selling hot drinks. It was Monday and there were people skiing all over the place. And, most striking, there were *other people teaching skiing*, here in Scotland! There were people other than me doing *it!* Bill introduced me to Frank Davis, who was a well known climbing shop owner from Ambleside. Frank and I became good friends. He introduced me to the famous climber, Joe Brown. With Joe was a man called Eric Langmuir. Eric and I would work together in the future in the development of ski teacher training. This we would do without ever having one cross word. Quite an achievement, considering the temperature of the climate in which we had to work. This over long years. Of course, strong men are not jealous of other men. Eric was the principal of Whitehall Outdoor Pursuits Centre, in England, at that time. He had two of his colleagues with him. Frank engaged me to take the group for a lesson. Joe was a beginner. He was wearing a suit before ski suits were the in thing. It was the worst suit I have ever seen, and I've seen some beauties. Jeanie had made one for me ten years before Bogner and Head started to design ski clothes. I asked Joe where he got the suit. He gave Frank the blame. It was something he had "flung together." Joe was to help market it. Bogner and Head had nothing to worry about future competition! Joe had a natural talent for skiing. He was also one of nature's nice people. The unique smallness of the UK's mountain world would ensure all our paths would cross in the future as the mountain activities increased.

It was interesting. A first visit to see the first chairlift in what was to become a major ski station in the UK, and I end up teaching three people who were, or would be, very important in our outdoor life! Karma again. This would illustrate the compactness of our mountain world and the possible reason for some of its weaknesses and very definitely, its strengths. We stayed over as Bill had some business at Glenmore Lodge. Fresh snow overnight had turned the area into a Fairy Winter Land. The chair was not working, so skiing was not really practical. The reason for this was that the bottom station was buried under a substantial snow drift. In their enthusiastic zeal, the people who had the guts to take the bull by the horns and make a start, had put the bottom station in the wrong place. That, however, is a story on its own. It's worth commenting on the fact that some of the strongest driving forces in the development of Cairngorm skiing were not skiers. *The Unsung Heroes.*

I left the hill early and skied off down the roadside. In the woods short of Glenmore were the remains of a woodsman's fire. I stopped, sat down, and lit up a Swiss Stumpem, "a cigar as smoked by Mountain Men." Bill Greaves was still up the hill, so here was a good place to wait for him. It was a place for thinking. A place to think of what to do for the future, and of what was best for our family. For a long time past my mind had been constantly preoccupied on the best way forward into the years coming, and on what to do to establish a good future and a better home and standard of life for the three of us. With the comfortable warmth and the smoke's aroma of man's old friend the fire, the snow, the skiers gift, came gently down through the Pines of the ancient Forest of Caledon. Watching it settle where it would, and in the quietness of the place, that's when I decided to move from Glencoe to Cairngorm.

Since then more than thirty years have gone. During that time I have, when I was on my own, stopped and looked about. The mark of the woodman's fire is long gone, but the memory of sitting there will stay forever. It's at times like these, when you are moving into a new way of life, and interesting happenings are taking place all the time, that day to day life is fresher and brighter than it otherwise would be. On looking back, opportunities were constantly presenting themselves for anyone with half a brain, and the sense to learn from the whole thing.

Not long after, I was back on the Cairngorms, this time with two clients. One was Peter McGeogh who I have spoken of in the opening pages as being a real Clydesider. Peter, with a friend, engaged my services on a Sunday night to "go The Gorms" as we are wont to call them, just as we call Glencoe "The Coe." We stayed in the Lynwilg Hotel outside Aviemore. Peter thought it would be interesting to travel up to the hill on the local bus. This turned out be a hoot! Considering Peter had one of the latest Rovers, the bus was something else. Unlike Peter's car, the bus was not the latest model. The driver wore an old torn tweed coat that went down to his ankles, and he got into the cab through a window that had been removed inside the bus. It would appear the driver's door did not open. The heating system was a open gas fire, with the gas bottle standing next to the fire. Even back in 1962, I'm sure the access to the driver's seat and the heating arrangements would have failed to pass the then rudimentary requirements of the law. But, as they say in the parlance of today, it was good crack!

The bus stopped outside the Cairngorm Hotel in Aviemore to pick up skiers. It seems we were waiting for the Swiss ski teacher. Peter remarked that it was unlike the Swiss. After a long time, this apparition came onto the bus. He had a full length raincoat, and he had a week's shaving to catch up on. His ski boots would have been more suitable for shovelling manure. But his crowning glory must have been his headgear! It was an old first world war flying helmet. There were cries of welcome from his adoring students. I would have given gold to have seen Christian Rubi's reaction if he had been there to see what was purporting to be a Swiss ski teacher! Peter said to me, "I see you don't have much competition coming from this Swiss Ski School!" with his tongue in his cheek. What got up my nose was people coming from Alpine countries and taking on the right to call themselves a national ski school of the country they had come from. I took no comfort from witnessing this charade. This is something I'll cover as fairly as I can when we come to it. We never got to ski because the chairlift station was buried under snow again, so we drove back to the Coe, where the wind had the lifts off.

That was my first professional engagement away from Meall a' Bhuiridh. The next one would be in Switzerland, in a few weeks time. Five Scottish skiers arranged for me to go and teach them in, of all places, Verbier and then to my old stamping ground Wengen. Another first. The party was made up of two different standards of skiers. Connie Wilson and Ian McNicol were, by the standards of the day here in Scotland, good skiers. Ian was a big strong climber who had learned to use what talent he had with great skill. In those days his main fault was impatience, a fault that has cost me, over the years, more accidents than I thought was fair. Connie was by nature an excellent mover on skis. Her big drawback was self denigration. There was not, at that time, a female part-time skier in Scotland who skied technically as well as she! Indeed, there were only a few men in Scotland, who stood as well on skis as Connie. But she was a bitch for bitching about how poorly she skied. I cured her of that! I've often wondered how far her skiing might have improved if she had managed to ski full-time for some seasons. Mind you, if we all got whatever we wanted all the time, I'm sure we would lose the interest and zest of the unknown, which is very necessary for most us.

In the second group were Peter Ferguson, "Wee Fergie," and Peter Simpson. These two became ski teachers. The third was Dr Donald Urquhart. Without a doubt one of the most colourful characters I have ever skied with, or been with. But I must add a rider to that broad statement. If Donald lived a thousand years, he would never learn to ski any better than he already did. Podge, that's what his friends called him, was one of the nice persons the world throws up from time to time. There was another, a Dr Thomson, a friend of Podge's. He was a wee bit straight laced! He never skied with us, but he loved the company.

Donald's father and mother were doctors and had been missionaries. His brother was also a Doctor and a practising missionary. How this family produced Donald is *beyond the ken*. It is possible he was a missionary of sorts. He certainly left his mark on me. A considerable achievement, in more ways than one. Podge was the unelected organiser of transport. In other words he had to get me out to Verbier. He was to pick me up at my house in Glasgow at midday, and then we'd drive over in Dr Thomson's car with the two Peters. He arrived at my place a couple of hours early. A good start. When I opened the door, there he was, dressed as for Ascot, with grey topper and silver shoe spats. To top off the rigout, he had skis on his shoulder. Donald was five feet zero in his bare feet, a bit bald in the front, and had a super walrus moustache. He actually walked up the slummy street we lived in, surrounded by a hoard of noisy Glasgow children. A formidable act of bravery. Lesser men would have paled at the thought. Not our Donald. "Where fools fear to tread." Mind you, Donald practised his medicine in a much rougher part of Glasgow than Agnes Street, Maryhill. I knew him to be an excellent general practitioner. Knowing the man, this was very understandable.

Dr Donald, with his wonderful captivating smile, explained to Jeanie and me that he had forgotten he had a wedding to go to. That would account for the garb! Little did I know this was only the start of what was to be the most complicated journey I was ever involved in. The skis on his shoulder he'd pick up when he came back for me at around six pm. He explained that Dr Thomson

120

had been told that we'd catch up and meet in Dover at 6 am the following morning, I suggested that this was leaving it a big tight. The irrepressible Podge laughed it off, "we'll catch up with those Bums easily!" These Bums were our friends. He was right. Twelve hours to Dover should be alright, even though there were no motorways. I was about to make my first mistake. I listened to Podge! But, from mistakes comes learning. What I learned was never to let Dr Urquhart organise anything. With one exception. Put him in charge of feeding you. Here he was king, as his wee rolly polly body showed!

However, back to the epic about to begin. Six pm, the hour of departure, came and went, and no sign of the good doctor. Now, anyone who knows me, will know that late coming is a heinous crime. It's almost as bad as a friend conning the last glass of whisky from the bottle and not sharing it. He turned up at about ten pm, with a long tale about why he was late, etc. He was still in the monkey suit. He still had to go and get his ski rack for the car. Back he came only half an hour later. Things were improving. We had to go up to his house in the north part of Glasgow for his ski gear. On the way up he stopped at a chemist to get medical supplies for our trip, in the event they might be needed. He'd be needing them sooner rather than later, if he kept this up! When we arrived in his folks' big house, he decided to have a feed. Around the time when one day moves to the new day, we headed south, another improvement. This was my first close involvement with Donald, and he had already mesmerised me. Never in all my life had I seen, or have seen since, anyone so *spaced out* as Donald. He grew on you. He was so full of the excitement of being alive, but so divorced from the realities of life, you never knew what he would do next!

Once, when we had been driving for some time, I mentioned that we could not hope to make Dover in six hours. He agreed, but he had arranged to phone Dr Thomson at some phone box down south and let him know, to coordinate our progress. Progress! We had nothing to report in the way of progress! The two doctors agreed to phone each other at the A.A. Dover office, at six thirty in the morning. This was duly done and it was agreed we carry on and meet in Verbier. That took pressure off the situation. Donald took a new lease of life. Not long after the phone call, he said, "we'll go to Lydd and fly to Le Touquet. We'll catch the Bums up!" Well, you can't beat a trier! So we duly turned left and headed east. As we drew up to this old beat up wartime airstrip, with my now over-worked eye for trouble, I clocked a wee queue of cars. I suggested that it may have been necessary to be booked, to be sure of a flight time. After all, the Bums had a six hour start and they were already across the channel. All the flights were booked. What a surprise! Donald's chin had dropped a little, but he assured me that the old Urquhart luck would come through as usual. We were put on the waiting list. As sure as Christ, over the tannoy the voice of the traveller's friend called for Dr Urquhart to start loading! This put Donald's smile back on the front burner.

When we got to the other side, Donald decided that we deserved a good meal. As a consequence, we ended up in Ostende, in a restaurant next to a sailing club in a grubby part of dockland. Now, in those days, it was not within my means to eat in such places, so I left the ordering of the food to our gourmet. We were in his country now, and he came up trumps. Two hours later we resumed our journey, replete with the best meal I had ever had the good fortune to sit down to. I thought it would have been bullish of me to mention that we were now about ten hours behinds the Bums! It was now dark and Donald was driving. I slipped into my sleeping bag, and, when I woke, Donald asked me to take the wheel. The first thing I noticed was that we were not on the main road. No motorways then, but this was not even the main road. Donald assured me it was a shortcut. He had worked it out on the map.

I should have smelled the rat. The meal must have dulled my brain. Mind you, my normally organised way of doing things had just taking a pounding. Donald slipped into my warm sleeping bag. His snoring was almost as good as his eating ability. The first thing I noticed was the gas was nearly gone. He allayed my fears. Not to worry, we had tons of gas! Not long after, the tons of gas went done. It was three in the morning, on a wee twisty road in northern France. It was freezing, and the little Jekyll and Hyde was in the only sleeping bag, as the great leader had forgotten to bring one. He was very close to death! But, being an employee on payroll, I took a walk with a half gallon can About a couple miles down the road I found a village, closed up as tight as Fort Knox. There was a petrol pump, a bit of luck.

When I got back to the car Donald was doing his Rip Van Winkle in my sleeping bag. I just left him. That part of France can be a miserable place at that time of the year. I walked, keeping warm. As it got light, Rip Van woke up. He was lucky I had left him breathing. He said he'd make me a cup of coffee. Out of the boot the car came a stove. He said, "I 'll fix you up in a minute." Being smart with the lip, I said, "you'll need water!" Quick as a flash, he whipped out a bottle of Glasgow water. Things were looking up! I mentioned that the stove looked a bit queer. Proudly he told me it was a special. It was petrol, a handy thing when you drive a car. The alarm bells were going crazy. He gave the stove a wee shake, it was nearly empty. My good humour evaporated. He lit the useless little piece of crap. It turned the water nearly tepid and spluttered out. If that wee man had not had all the travellers cheques, he would have been dead. We got over that crisis. I said I'd go for the petrol. He was so unreliable, if he'd needed to go to the toilet, I would have gone for him!

The French had cheap petrol vouchers for tourists in those days. With one in my now grubby hand, and with the feeling that I now had the Doctor under control, I went back to the pump. To my delight it was open. I filled the can. It held about a pint. I indicated to the man that I would be back to fill up. Back we came to do the business. Donald only put what was left on the voucher in the tank, and was off. Nosily, I asked him what the tricky move was. He casually said that we'd fill up at the next big station. The voucher was only for two litres. I thought to myself, "*if he runs out of petrol I'll kill him, to Hell with the travellers cheques!*" The wee needle on the petrol gauge was bending against the empty when we spotted a petrol station round this corner. He was Urquhart the lucky, and luck was still running for him. When I got him on the ski slopes, his luck would definitely run out.

Later, when he got his head together, he said to me in his usual good humour that he was amazed how well I was taking all the little hiccups. Another masterpiece of understatement! I pointed out to him that I was *on the payroll*, but the ones we were going to meet and ski with were paymasters, and might be a little less tolerant about wasting a resource, as expensive as "I." This turned out to be true. The rest of the trip passed without any drama or crisis. I got bored. I had nothing to worry about. On the drive up from Martigny to Verbier, it was snowing, and his front wheel drive car's tyres were dodgy. I had to sit on the bonnet all the way up! It was murder, I was freezing. There's an old Scottish saying..."*Ne'er cast a cloot till May is oot.*" If the drive out had been full of unforeseen events, the rest of the enterprise turned out to be just what all of us hoped it would be. This was indeed an enterprise. This was a first, and, as can be easily understood, was of great importance to me.

When you see the activity of British ski teachers abroad today, you can see the giant steps that have come about. Many do not approve of some of them. But the good ones are excellent! I will go into this in detail as caustically as I feel is necessary, and as subjectively as possible.

It was arranged that Donald, the naughty doctor, would ski with Peter and Wee Fergie for two days, followed by two days with Connie and Ian. The reason was that the less skilled and experienced would benefit by starting first. We would keep to this arrangement for the two weeks that Connie and Ian were out. Fergie was a Clydeside engineer from Alexandra, a town between Loch Lomond and the ancient town of Dumbarton. He was a Creag Dhu Club member. He wanted to learn to ski well, otherwise he would not have involved himself in this venture. He was about ten years older than me, so he was certainly late in being serious about "good" skiing. He was not short on balls, or determination. One of his legs had a plate in it from a motorbike accident. He had been with us at Zermatt, where he did in his shoulder. A droll wee man, with a caustic tongue. And definitely a Red Clydesider. Peter Simpson was a joiner from Bannockburn, and a number of years younger. Another Zermatt hand, Peter found his way into skiing through climbing. Like Fergie, he would give himself a good number of full seasons to see if they could become good skiers. I understood this, and it gave me quite a lift to know that these people wanted me to help them to achieve this elusive goal.

People like Connie, Fergie, Ian and Peter don't give their trust easily. What a fine opportunity to prove what can be done in three weeks of ski teaching. Here were two small classes, one of which had been skiing for a good number of years, and, for part-time skiers, skied well. The other class were about two standards lower but were skiing full-time, the golden ingredient. What they all had in common was that they were mountain-wise and strong-bloody-minded! Ski teachers reading this will understand that these opportunities are few and far between. Dr Donald, (no, I have not forgotten Donald), skiing with the two Peters, would be a constant challenge to our forbearance, but at all times a stimulant to our good nature.

The first day of skiing gave us perfect conditions. Verbier was Switzerland's first custom built ski station. That would be the correct name for it. Custom built. Teaching skiing to good running classes, with the weather and terrain as excellent as this, gave us instant progress from the two Peters. We had skied many times together before. This is always a plus in ski teaching. As I said, Donald did not ski anyway like the two Peters, but he was a constant spur to whatever teaching abilities I may have possessed. The big plus was Donald. He was a laugh a minute. The fact that he was overweight, overfed and most certainly under skilled, and really didn't give a toss about his skiing helped, if anything, to defuse the one hundred percent effort Fergie and Peter were putting in. Teaching at this level, with two skiers in pursuit of the goals that the Peters had in mind, is a good test of any ski teacher's ability to supply the needs of this type of pupil. Podge was a blessing. A Jolly Jester is worth a ton of gold in releasing some of the tensions, if there were any.

Skiing with Connie and Ian was another experience. Connie, as I have said, was a free moving skier by nature. This was the first time I had skied with her and I had the opportunity to find out how she went about her skiing, and, more importantly, what she thought of her own skiing. For a mover of her capability, it's necessary for her to have a clear idea of just how well she did ski. In knowing that, she would understand what she had to do to make the next big step forward into "good" skiing. A step not open to most people. Ian, like many men who are capable in most things physical, take good performance for granted. It has to be remembered that the standard of the better Scottish skiers had improved dramatically since the coming of the ski lifts. Like all Scots male chauvinists, he wanted his share. Fair enough, but there is a price to pay. You must be prepared to start from the beginning again.

Ian and Connie, unlike the two Peters, had skied well for years, and, in so doing, became very polished in perfecting the fine little mistakes that are the barrier to better skiing. It takes a tremendous effort to escape from being in this state of limbo. Whereas the two Peters were in the position where there were lots of easily learned parts of skiing that made you quickly better and more comfortable, Ian had to learn to undo many things he was good at. Undoing them made him feel uncomfortable and foolish for a time. That is part of the price! All Connie had to do, was find out how well she really could be as a skier. All I had to do, was to learn to be a better ski teacher!

Most of us stayed in a dormitory room in a hotel called the Casanova. The owner was the chef, always a good sign. The food was a memorable experience. In fourteen days we had twenty eight meals with only four repeats. The chef had words with Peter Simpson for putting tomato ketchup on his food. You can't take some people anywhere!

Our days started at 8.30 each morning. We skied till noon, and then from 2 pm till 6 pm. This would be a long day in a ski school, but this was not a ski school activity. As the lessons settled down, and we all became adjusted to each other, we struck up a rhythm to what we were about. I'm sure it's not often you teach friends to ski at such a serious level with total professional commitment. It had crossed my mind that this might have been a difficulty but it was no problem. The Peters quickly improved their body position and their stances, and this allowed them to pick up running speed, which in turn made their turning ability stronger. All that was needed was another 100,000 more skiing miles to be going on with. Which they eventually got.

I had a lot of trouble with Connie and her constant self denigration. This puts a halt to possible progress. She had the luck to be able to learn by copying her teacher. But only if she stopped slagging herself. This came about almost by accident. We were skiing in deep powder, and, to my mind, we were all skiing well. That was just as it should be. Skiing like Connie's is suited to deep powder. I had set a line down a steep slope, and Ian had skied down first. For where he was that day, in his learning curve, I left him alone. I had asked Connie to try and follow the line I had set. She skied down. For performance, I scored her 110 out of a 100. Before I could present her with the accolade, she started to bitch about how about badly she had skied the slope. The moment of truth had arrived. In

Clydeside language which is not in the ski teaching manual, I told her what I thought of her opinion and of her skiing. I asked her to look up and pick the best of the two ski tracks. This she did. I then told her to follow the track she was standing in back up the slope. It was the best of the two tracks! As they say in Glasgow "*her face was shut!*"

Now for Ian. He would be a harder nut to crack. There's a certain stage when a potentially good skier is a step nearer to improving and they run into a stone wall. The reason why they come against the wall is simple. The last few steps to good skiing for some can be a heartbreak. This, I'm sure, is a filter that keeps the number of good skiers down to what it is. In skiing there are some who are born to it. If they start when they are young, and ski a lot, they will progress to their possibility comfortably and painlessly. Ian was not in this lucky situation. To get farther he would have to *graft* under the stern rules of advanced tuition. Not an easy undertaking. Ian had become very good at skiing in the most difficult of places, and in most snow conditions. This he managed, with the age old curse that his weight was, almost always, slightly *back*, coming out of the turn. Great patience is needed to chip away at downhill skiing's biggest problem!

After looking at Connie's ski track, we looked at Ian's. There it was, the tell-tale skid-mark of coming out of each turn with his weight slightly back. A mistake we all make. Skiers like Ian were just being discovered as the knowledge in ski teaching started to improve with giant strides. With my blood up, and flushed with Connie's success, the immediate task to hand was to cure Ian's "little fault." After all, I had six days, or more, to fix it. Oh, foolish fellow! He agreed to go through all the rigmarole of the running exercises which lead up to eradicating the weight being back. It was purgatory for most of the coming time. He had only ever skied the way he wanted, and now he was going up and down the scale like a beginner. He had to try and do it the way I wanted it. Connie loved it. With her fine stance on skis, her turns got even better.

We met an Austrian ski teacher who was skiing privately with a Dutchman. We quickly became friendly. He and I went skiing one afternoon, and, of course, it was him and me for it! During that afternoon we found out about each other. In summer he was a mountain guide in the Stubi Alps, where he was building a mountain guesthouse. What a wonderful future he had to look forward to. He was a good skier. At that time, the Austrian ski schools were, for some reason, teaching a traversing position of leading with their uphill shoulder well in front of the other. Something I did not subscribe to. Our group wanted to know why Walter did not ski like that. I told them to ask him, which they did. He told them that *good* skiers did not ski like that, and that I would explain to them, next day, when they were on the snow, as I was their teacher. Walter Hass was his full name. He travelled around major resorts where he would ski with prearranged clients. He was very Aryan looking and his English was excellent. He became a constant evening companion to us. He became one of us, and, not surprisingly, was intrigued with Dr Donald. So was I. One evening, the men went back to our dormitory room. Connie always went to bed early. She was a wee bit of a Dormouse. Back in the dormitory our tame gourmet took charge of dispensing wine, cheese, bread, salami and other titillating little morsels. *This he was good at.* The dormitory did not sport much fancy furniture, and it was, if anything, over heated. So, like feasting Romans, we reclined on our iron bedsteads. Walter was on the next bed to me. I was, as usual, in my undervest and longjohns, and

125

so was Donald, but not as pretty a sight. In fact, his wee podgie body was more than comical.

The party was going great, but nobody was paying much attention to Donald. I remember it as clear as day. He was slicing up a chunk of salami with his Bowie knife, another piece of useless equipment, like his wee petrol stove. He was trying to get people's attention. I could see him out of the corner of my eye coming over to me and saying, "Frith!" As he said it, he stuck his hand out to attract my attention, and the point of the knife went into the side of my knee. He had my attention then! A fountain of blood shot out, and a roar went up. Only Walter and I really saw what happened. The other doctor was a nice man. He was a wee bit straight laced. He was also well mannered and was not, however, used to dossing about. Probably not used to seeing people getting stabbed. I wasn't used to that myself. Dr Thompson started remonstrating with Podge. He pointed out how his father and mother had been missionaries, his brother was a practising missionary, and here he was behaving like a hooligan. I thought that was putting it a bit strong.

Wee Fergie quietly pointed out that, while the two good doctors were discussing the merits of good and bad behaviour, the most expensive person in the crowd was bleeding profusely. So, would one of them move their ass, and administer first aid. I wondered if his concern was more for his investment in my ability to teach, rather than my general well being. I'll never know. First Aid was duly rendered and I was fighting fit and ready for duty with Mr Donald Hyde in the morning. I owe Mr Donald Hyde for one the great stories I have of the good life in skiing.

This one about Podge Hyde is a must. One night in the *dorm*, Podge was pushing his luck. He wanted to play rough. Now, from what I've told you about him, you'll realise he was not really cut out for playing rough. Too much salami and wine got him going. We were dressed in our *aprés ski* clothes of longjohns, etc. Podge was all fired up, and he started throwing things about. A glass of wine, if I remember right, hit Peter Simpson. He told him, "any more of your nonsense, and you're out the window!" But Podge was up and going and stern measures had to be used. The *dorm* was on the first floor. We opened a window, and down below was a handy, deep snowdrift. We lobbed him right out down into the snowdrift in his underwear! He was a bonnie sight when he surfaced. He started to verbally abuse us, and somebody threw a bucket of water down on him. Revenge is sweet! It was around ten degrees centigrade below. When he was finally allowed back in, his mouth was shut! His walrus moustache was frozen like walrus tusks. He looked terrific, and justice was done.

Walter Hass didn't know whether to laugh or what to do! I personally thought the bucket of water was a bit over the top. To his great compliment, when he could finally open his mouth, he was laughing. Some kid! Like all good things in life, they don't go on forever. The two Peters made steady progress. Podge continued to amaze us with his unfailing talent for screwing up. His efforts to draw out the very liberal two hour lunch and rest period never ceased to amaze me. Peter Simpson kept a tight rope on him.

The last two days in Verbier were kept for Connie and Ian, as they were going home. Connie was coasting along like a beautiful sailing clipper. Ian was deep in the cesspit of total effort and getting nowhere. I had almost lost my way in finding a key to his blockage. Maybe I did not know enough. It's interesting. I still don't know if I knew enough at that time, or not. Ian complained about his poor edges. His skis were brand new, state of the art. I changed his for mine. Mine were shot and that made him worse. In the last hour of the last afternoon, he *cut the custard*. He was through! It was time he was needing. Time to make the change. He skied well for the rest of the afternoon. That was most certainly the first time I understood that I could do something in ski teaching. Yes, there is a price for all of us to pay for everything that's good. I would meet Walter Hass later in St. Moritz, where he worked as a private teacher with a family for the season. He seemed to come and go as he pleased but he had to be there when they turned up. It would not have suited me.

One of those days in Verbier I heard a girl calling me from a ski lift. She was too far away to recognise. She skied up to me later. It was Margrit Gertsch from Wengen, the Olympic medallist. I asked her how she knew it was me from all that distance. Her reply was she saw Werner Stager's skiing in me. Praise indeed! Connie and Ian left for home. The rest of us drove on to Lauterbrunnen, to the Oberland Hotel. The Stagers got a shock when I walked in. What a pleasant feeling, seeing the family so soon again, in the same winter. We had another week skiing above Wengen. It was here I first discovered boot trouble, something that has given many well known people in skiing a load of fun ever since.

Never would I have thought that I would be skiing with private pupils from Scotland in Wengen. You never know what is coming your way! Reflecting back as I write this, what a wonderful lesson on life I had just experienced in these three weeks. In the quiet moments during the long drive home, I mulled over all these thoughts in my mind. It gave me much to think about not forgetting the coming move to the Cairngorms before the year would be out.

However, we were not finished with this episode. I was to drive back with the good Dr Thompson, along with Fergie. Peter would drive back with Donald. I forget why we changed cars. Anyway, as we sat in a lovely old coffee shop in Bern, I asked Fergie for my three weeks' wages. That would let me buy a wee pressie for Jeanie Finlayson. Fergie knew nothing about wages, the Bad Doctor must have them. Beautiful! the *spectre* had made his escape an hour ago. Well, you must admit he was consistent. It was about four weeks before I got my wages. Peter Simpson had another story to tell of his drive with the Mighty Podge, but that's another tale. Two strong memories remain from those three weeks. Donald Urquhart gave me a lesson on how to get through life breaking the everyday rules of general behaviour and, in the process infuriating, at times all those around him. It was most certainly because he is a wonderful person. In his practice in that northern district of Glasgow, he was known as Dr Donald and was greatly loved. Maybe he was a missionary of sorts. He got through to me. A few more Donalds in the world might not be a bad thing.

The second memory is of having the opportunity of teaching these two good small classes over a long enough period of time in ideal conditions that enabled me to see the results. This was an unknown possibility in those days. In the years to come, the luxury of teaching good skiers over long protracted periods of time would be a gift to remember. Full-time up and coming ski teachers and young budding racers, would pass through my hands. And leave me sweet memories.

Ian Todd, the boy who accompanied my son to the DHO training, stayed with me for three weeks. During this time he worked very hard at his skiing. His progress was remarkable. This was helped by the fact that he was skiing constantly with a bunch of hard, no give, no take, competitors in life's tough road. In the midweek he stayed in my converted van. He was so useless round the cooker I made him stay in bed in the morning, for breakfast. I never even let him wash the dishes. At weekends Peter, his dad, came up and took him to a hotel. This was a public schoolboy, and he was great to have in our tight wee enclave, where he was treated as an equal. From here he went on and into the British Ski Team. He became a lawyer and has, for many years, been Mark McCormick's Vice President in Europe. A fine achievement for anyone.

Ian and I went through to the Cairngorms just before the Junior Championships. He stood out because of his skiing. At that time, our good young skiers were still in the making and had not yet shown what their own skills were to be. In Speyside, I was to meet my first young Cairngorm skier, Arthur McLean, a good friend ever since. Arthur, in the ensuing years, has became an outstanding figure in Scottish skiing. In his own special way he has enriched our skiing culture. Being in his company is always a trip into funnyland. He and I have entertained many skiers on Cairngorm, over the years, just by having *the crack!* Arthur will crop up later, as the tale unfolds.

This last season in the Coe, was one of exceptional snowfalls, so much so that, when we returned to the Coe after our week in the Cairngorms, the steep slope under the access chairlift had deep cover of snow. This is something that seldom happens. The snow was so deep it was skiable. While waiting for Toddie, early in the morning, I made some runs down under the lift. The tracks that were left were good ones. That slope takes mighty snowfalls to leave it skiable. As for this being our last season in the Coe, it seemed that "The Hill of the Roaring Stags" had laid on one the most wonderful of all parting gifts in all of my skiing seasons on our Scottish mountains.

The Greaves Cup – Glencoe Club 1962
left to right – President Peter Ferguson, Harry McKay, Alex Cairns, Iain Finlayson.
"Wee Harry n'at! Aye cheery an' friskie,
who trained on a diet of Capstan an' Whisky!"– CL

One of the highlights was of Harry McKay winning his last race as an amateur. It was the first Greaves Cup and the Puddock Wright Cup. He did this in fine style. I set one of the courses down under the Wall of Death. It started to snow again during the race. We never got the poles back until the spring thaw. Staying in Glencoe was not possible for our family. Having seen the vitality of what was taking place in Cairngorm, the Rocky Mountains were put on hold. I get to wonder how the Rockies would have worked out if we'd made the move out there!

The achievements of Glencoe skiers during the 1962 season were considerable. The new Glencoe Ski Club put their hands firmly on most of the skiing activity on that hill. After all these years we still look back with pride that all the very fine people who made it possible are good friends to our small family. It's also worth reflecting that all of these fine people were mostly Clydesiders, whether they were of the Red or Blue persuasion. The regret of leaving was tinged by losing the vital stimulation of the company of our dear friends. As it turned out, I later became very involved in the Club's junior training programme, which gave me some of my most exciting memories in skiing. What the richness of the Glencoe ski scene afforded to me personally, was the opportunity to practice the physical skills of skiing in the most uninhibited way. Because of the lack of pupils in those days, I got unlimited amounts of skiing for myself. Besides which, I was skiing each day with some of the best skiers in Scotland. They were fit, tough, and extremely competitive. This created a fertile field in which the strong could only prosper. It must have been a unique happening in any time. When something so important is taking place, great changes are in the grist mill. The right people, by luck, are in place and it seems to follow, how consistent and lasting the results can be. Many of the people above did move to the Gorms, and became a vital part of what is now skiing history. That was how I remember the *energetic beast* that was Glencoe Skiing at that time. I was about learn what The Cairngorm Beast would be like.

12. The Birth of British Professional Skiing

As a family, our first problem before moving into Aviemore, was accommodation. Like all places in Scotland, it was at a premium. An impossible situation, unless you had the means to buy. Jack Thompson had a large house in Aviemore. With his usual open handedness he invited us to locate a residential caravan in his large wooded garden. The caravan as a house was far superior to the flat we lived in. And it goes without saying, the wooded garden in the shadow of the Cairngorms was a lovely place to stay after the Glasgow tenement. Our lifestyle was about to take a very big change as far as our living conditions were concerned.

Chris Lyons recorded the event in one of his epic poems–

> For the year '63 had barely got started
> When Frith, Ian 'n Jeanie had us awe doonhearted
> To the Ski School D'Ecosse in the 'Gorms they departed
> Along with them, Big Wullie, Peter n' Geordie they carted
> Wee Peter Ferguson joined in this trudge
> To do Mine Host in a ski doss at Carrbridge.

At that time skiing was only organised at club level, and well organised. There was in place the Scottish Council of Physical Recreation. This government body took serious interest in all outdoor pursuits. Its function was to promote and help to bring all outdoor activities within reach of all sections of the population. This they have been doing with great success over long years. A meeting was called to be held in Pitlochry. The purpose was to discuss the need for setting up a system to be responsible for the conduct and eventual training and grading of ski teachers for our mountains. This was later changed to include all of the UK. The date was November of 1962. It was one of their senior members of staff, a Jock Kerr Hunter, who called this meeting. Jock was one of the early pioneers who brought skiing within the reach of many who otherwise may never have found their way into skiing. Jock was responsible for bringing many other outdoor pursuits to the populace in general. Jack Thompson and I attended on our own initiative, and out of curiosity to see how the wind was blowing.

The Scottish Ski Club were represented by my old friend Lewis Drysdale. It was a small attendance. There were less than ten people there. If such an open meeting were held today, a large hall would be needed to contain those interested. As it was, a small cosy room in one of Pitlochry's old hotels made a comfortable venue for what was, until now, an all but forgotten very important event in the background of our skiing past. It was certainly a most congenial skiing meeting. This would not last. Later on, when different bodies started to shift about and manoeuvre for their own ends, meetings would be much more acrimonious. And, at times, very disagreeable. Another meeting would be called when the new season 1962/63 got under way. By that time I was staying in Aviemore. As Jack and I drove back up the road, we were caught in a early winter snow storm. Did it portend well for the future? We would find out as we moved forward into what that was to be! In the car we mulled over what we thought of the loose ends, and where and what was blowing in the wind. It was obvious the Scottish Ski Club and the Scottish Council of Physical Recreation would be wanting a big say in how ski teaching would be run and organised. Jack and I made an *ad hoc* resolve on behalf of BASI-to-be, that only recognised ski teachers would be responsible for how their business would be run and controlled. That's the way it's been ever since, for good or bad. I'm sure, on reflection, that it was on that drive back up, through that good omen of a snowstorm that the seeds of BASI were set and took root. What surprised me was how quickly the roots grew and produced fruit. Jack Thompson and myself would be the only two BASI people who knew that this is part of how BASI got its first *breath of life*. And so took place the first ski business meeting! Another first!

In the summer of 1962, our own fortunes, as far as the Cairngorms were concerned, took a turn which made our setting up much easier to get off the ground. This was brought about by the death of the man who had been responsible for running the Scottish Swiss Ski School. This was only a name, it had nothing to with the Swiss Ski School. Jock Kerr Hunter was responsible to the SCPR, which is now the Sports Council. It was part of their remit to help the development of all outdoor pursuits. Jock wanted me to set up and run a new Ski School to take place of the one that had been. This was a most fortuitous opportunity for me. The fact that I had such strong connections with Swiss skiing could have had something to do with the offer. This timely event allowed me to work out of the Cairngorm Hotel in Aviemore. A tremendous start for us. Karma again.

All ski schools at that time were somehow or other attached to hotels. This meant the hoteliers had a great deal to say in how they were run. Jock arranged for me to meet the hoteliers involved. This turned out to be an enlightening experience for me! As happens in small country type communities, people had preconceived ideas of outsiders. As they still do. There was a crazy notion that men from Glasgow were wild and difficult to get on with. Glasgow's no different from any other big industrial city. No doubt I was on display. Like most developing Highland holiday places, the bulk of the developers were incomers. The dreaded *white settlers*. This humorous, if inaccurate, pseudonym is still in use, sometimes snidely. The meeting was a revelation to a simple wee Glasgow man. I was amazed how few local people were involved. Two of the hoteliers' men seemed to think they were being cajoled into some quick manoeuvre. They became almost hysterical for no reason. Even if something was going on, their behaviour was unbelievable. In the outside world, they would have lost. The death that caused the problem had only just happened. Jock, in his effort to keep things running had done what he thought best under the circumstances. He and I had not known each other until this time. The meeting ended with total agreement, and new friendships resulted from what transpired in the future.

Before the winter of 1962/63, I personally was wound up as tight as a halfpenny watch. We had just had the meeting at Pitlochry that left the brain and the imagination working away. Little did I know what an adventurous feast was just about to begin. Bill and Jim Greaves, Jeanie and I had formed a company called D'Ecosse Ski and Sports. We had a letterhead on which it stated that I was Managing Director (printed by another good friend Bob Benzies at Culross printworks in Coupar Angus). Oh, how we come up in the world! I even had wee cards with my name printed on, declaring my new and lofty station in the world! This new company was financed by Bill and Jim Greaves. We did not have a written contract in the beginning. I don't think we had shaken hands on the deal!

A rich memory to have. I'm sure we never thought about it much at the time. I even had a new Mini car!

There was another interesting happening, before that first season that D'Ecosse got started. In the middle of July, we ran a D'Ecosse Ski School Clinic on snow. This took place on the northeast side of Cairngorm. This would be the first of very many to come. Those attending included Bobbie Birnie, Eric Leiper and John Milne. This was also an early meeting with the 16 year old Ian Baxter. Bobbie and Ian are still very much an important part of my ski world. And good skiers, too. Between them they gave a fair share to what is Scottish skiing today. Ian Baxter fell and stuck a steel spike into his backside, which left a hole in his butt. He wanted to go see a doctor, but I made him finish skiing. He still whines about it. I did explain that it was character building.

Once the season of 1962/63 got started, it became a roller coaster. So many things of major importance took place they seemed to be everyday events. We were still running the Dry Ski School which helped to pay for the cost of going to the Swiss School Directors Course. This year the course was to be held in Wengen, of all places. This I looked forward to so very much. Wengen was always special to me. Before going to Wengen, we had made arrangements to spend some time in Andermatt, to visit my friend Kari Russi, the Ski School Director of Andermatt.

We drove out in Jim Greaves' new big shooting brake. Peter Simpson, June Lawley and Jeanie all came along. This turned out to be a drive full of excitement. The roof rack had a dozen pairs of skis, bound for the Kastle factory in Austria. Yes, we were busy little bees. Of course, we were picking up some *goodies* for our own use. We had just left an autobahn resthaus when we got side swiped by a German car. There were two young couples in the car. They'd been clowning about. The outcome was Jim's car was bounced off the central barrier, and ended up on its side, buffing up the auto bahn. Off came the roofrack, skis and all. It had a slide along the road just like the car. The whole side of the car was wrecked but it was driveable. Finding the wee rubber pads for the roof-rack was a bit of good luck. When I was calling for Peter to find the pads, he and June thought I had finally flipped my lid. We had to stay over in a local hotel. Jeanie and June were very upset, and so was Peter. I wasn't too chuffed myself.

After dropping the skis at the Kastle factory, we headed for Andermatt. Driving up onto the pass to Andermatt it got very snowy. I had discovered the previous day that the tyres on the car were not what they could have been. Peter mentioned something about a sign saying the road was closed. I brushed this aside, pointing out that if the road was closed there would be a barrier across it. Anyway, there was a set of tyre marks on the road, so it must be alright. I did notice the road had became very narrow. It was a hellish job getting the car up it. However, we got up and onto a long, easy, flat stretch. The snow was very deep. It was here we saw the Land Rover that made the tracks. A local! Worse was to come. As we dropped down to Andermatt, it was frightening. It seemed as if you could drop off the road down onto Andermatt. Looking back, I noticed the passengers had their doors opened, as if ready to abandon ship! Peter had his brand new suit under his arm, traveller's cheque book in hand. Not a great vote of confidence in the driver. I slipped my door open!

Later on that day, Peter came and told me that June, Jeanie and he had decided that if I was driving out that way they would be taking the train. I told

Peter that if some headcase thought of taking the car out that way I'd be on the train myself! It seemed the girl in the bank told him that the road had been closed for more than four weeks. The road we had driven over was the Oberalp Pass, at 2044 meters. The things you do in pursuit of pleasure!

We found Andermatt to be a super village, small and compact. And Kari Russi, that wonderful wee man, the Mountain Guide, the Ski Teacher, the Everything that a person can be proud of, was there to be enjoyed. I was to learn quite a lot more about this man during the next two weeks. For some reason he asked me to give him a ski lesson. I was quietly embarrassed. Was there something else here for me to learn? There was. Here was a man without illusions, and of open honesty. And at peace with the world.

Kari's sister had a typical Swiss mountain hotel, where we stayed. Needless to say we were made more than welcome. Kari had a lady friend. She will be nameless. A most handsome sophisticated citizen of the world, a bundle of laughs. She was a lady of means, if that's of any value. During the lesson I had one of my usual bad falls which left me a bit groggy. The lady was the first to fetch me some first aid, a large brandy to calm my nerves. You can't hide quality! Peter Simpson's first remark was, "you asked for that!" I hope he meant the brandy.

Lydia held a dinner party for us on our last night. She laid it on as only a lady would. (There, the name slipped out!) The meal was a meat fondue. I can't spell it the French way. Each place was set out on a linen tea towel, which portrayed how a fondue was served. This was a keepsake. Kari told me quietly that Lydia kept her own vintage in the cellar. Just the thing for an up-and-coming ski school boss with his own wee embossed card! Festivities lasted into the wee hours. Kari's sister had many daughters, and one of them served the table during the meal.

During the pleasantries later, the daughter Desiree and mother were having quite a serious row. From what I heard, I took it for granted she was wanting to marry a non-believer. The family were devout Roman Catholics. Many had taken the cloth. I asked Lydia if she was marrying a Protestant. Lydia said, "no, a Japanese!" All of a sudden, my liberal outlook took a jolt, and I said that I could see the mother's point of view. The nice wee man, Kari, said, "Fritz, what is wrong with that? In 50 years, we'll be coffee coloured!" Desirée was a beautiful blond Nordic looking creature. You could have taken her home to your Mammy.

Some years later Jeanie was back in Andermatt for the British Junior Championships. Desirée was married with coffee coloured children. The Japanese father was chef in the family hotel. The wee Japanese man must have been a hardcase. He had *made the cut* in that old fashioned mountain village, in old fashioned Switzerland! We drove up through the Swiss Lakes to Lucerne where Kari treated us to lunch in a beautiful hotel. We stopped off in Lauterbrunnen and saw the Stagers. There Kari gave Frau Stager the full Swiss bull! Like the previous December in Arosa, the snow was poor. There were many long faces. Like Arosa, it snowed during the night. Sods Law! In years to come we who worked in Scotland would learn to live with this. With the new snow the atmosphere was just correct. Wengen, like Arosa, was a nice compact station for the course.

Peter Simpson joined one of the good class sixes. He fell in with evil companions in the evenings. Good evil companions. Jean Pierre Zuber and the Olympic skier Roland Blazzy, (I hope I've got the spelling right.) Between them, they seemed to have some sort of bother most nights. What a mixed bag they were. There was another big animal who made up the four. What a mixture, an Olympic skier, a mountain farmer, and apprentice ski teacher from Bannockburn, and a sophisticated headcase from the south shore of the historical Lake Constance. What a motley bunch of bandits! Still, the world was the better for them being part of it.

While we're on about animals, the nice wee Kari Russi had a pal, the ski school director from Flims, Hinnie Kaduff. This man was ten times larger than life. He looked like an escapee from the working class district in any big city. He was priceless! After drinks, after skiing, they retired to their room in the Silberhorn Hotel, started running a bath and fell asleep. Their room was above the entrance hall. The water coming through the ceiling was not welcome in the hotel's entrance hall! Such was their popularity they were forgiven. They had the decency to look sheepish from time to time! I skied with Werner's group where I met many new people. This was another plus.

During this week I saw a piece of survival skiing that has stayed with me. Near the end of our week our class met up with the class of Gottlieb Perren of Zermatt. It was obvious we were going to have a *bang off* down to Grund, not quite a race. There would be around 28 of us and it was every man for himself. We stopped just below the Mannlichen cable car station to wait for a very fine skier from Engelberg. He must have gone for a wee-wee! The two groups had stopped short round a corner under what was a very steep wall of 50 feet. Willow bushes and boulders stuck out of "The Face." That's what it was. As we looked up, we saw Fredy leave the top. He took *the wall*. Those of us who knew the place let out a cry, but too late, he was going like the proverbial "*off the shovel.*" He appeared above us, saw where he was, and, in mid-flight, he changed his stance and his attention to the task in hand. He abandoned himself to the slope, and found a way down. In the process, he trimmed out a few willows and bit of bed rock. A spectacular performance of skiing! And life saving too. He took wee bit of stick about his route finding! A *good* skier. The run down by the two groups was terrific. Everyone arrived in Grund as a group. On the run there's a long poling section near the bottom. August Julian, from Zermatt, was poling alongside me. He looked over and said, "I'm too old for this." This to me sounded daft. Of course, I was only 33. How your thinking changes with the passing of time. During this run I discovered the speed did not bother me any more. This was probably all the work and the skiing time I put in paying off.

Before leaving for home to start the second part of our what would be a new life I would gain my Swiss Ski School Directors Licence. What a time for this to happen and in, of all places, Wengen. That night, in a bar crowded with ski school bosses, in a state of euphoric stupidity I ordered drinks for the whole bar. I was with another drunken French Swiss ski teaching fool like myself. It seems I collapsed before paying for the *bevvy*. Peter had to take me back to the hotel on one of those nice wee electric carts. Next morning in the dining room, I gave a hearty good morning to this big air hostess. Jeanie mentioned that I had a cheek to be talking to the lassie. It seems the French Swiss drunken ski teacher and my good self had been trying to put our naughty grimy hands down the front of her elegant topless evening gown. Some people you can't take anywhere! I pointed out she must have enjoyed it as she was all smiles. You might not be able to take some people anywhere but *natural charm* cannot be suppressed! On enquiring of Peter Simpson who I owed for the crazy gesture of "drinks all round", he said he didn't know. I never found out who picked up that tab. It must have been a cracker! Who says the Swiss are tight? That's another fallacy about national traits.

Driving home in Jim Greaves beat up newish car, I once again pondered on this long run of great good fortune. I was up and running. To say I had a *gut warming feeling* inside of me would be putting it mildly. However, we are not finished with Jim's beat up car yet. I say that with tongue in cheek. I was still using Jim's banger to transport twenty cartons of hire skis up to Aviemore. Peter was with me. The car looked terrible. We were stopped for speeding going past the Perth ice rink at 38 miles an hour. The big Highland copper asked me to step out of the car. I could see he wasn't too chuffed with its appearance. Neither was Jim Greaves. I was driving with climbing breeches, long Harris wool stockings, no shoes, and smoking a Swiss Stogie.

To say he was impressed would stretch even my imagination. It was pouring with rain. He looked down at my stockinged feet, and then had a look at the car. The tailboard was hanging down with the ski cartons sticking out over the back. I'm sure for the sheer need to say something, his opening gambit was, "what's the number of that car, because I can't read it!" Neither could I! The skis were covering the number plate, and I didn't know the number, as it was not my car. The rain was lashing down. He took the odd look down at the stockinged feet. Eventually, after he heard a brief resume of the autobahn incident, he let me know that he would not stand for speeding on *his roads*, but because of the special circumstances he'd let me off this time. Who said the Polis are pigs? Before I left I gave him a big bundle of ski school brochures, admonishing him to see that they were well distributed round the Fair City of Perth. Peter suggested I was pushing my luck. The luck would be pushed rather a lot in the next few years!

In preparation for the new Ski School, Jeanie had made red white and blue nylon uniform jackets. Nylon was only just coming into use in sports clothes. As mentioned in part one, there was a lot of non-ski-like garments being used by skiers teaching skiing on Cairngorm. Our jackets raised a few eyebrows. It would take a few more seasons before other ski schools followed suit. One of the first things that marked our small team of six fulltime teachers out from others, apart from the uniforms, was the morning ski clinic group practice sessions. All of our team were mountain type people. They were in instructing mostly to farther their own personal skiing. People who say they prefer teaching to skiing for themselves are shooting the bull. And none of them are ever reasonably good skiers.

People ski instructing do so to gain more access to the higher goals of skiing. And in so doing gain certain perks. This will be covered later. There are, of course, many, many very fine people who have been part-time teaching for long years. These well known people would be assets in any ski school, then they would be *Professionals*. You ask anyone if they'd rather ski for themselves, or go teaching. The answer begs the question. Of all those who were racers, very few became ski teachers. Those who do, always make *good* ski teachers. In my opinion, it's because they understand how skis *work*.

135

The clinics in our team bound us together in a common purpose, in which we learned a great deal about each other. For the first time British ski teachers had the opportunity to work together to investigate the possibilities of what was needed to establish a base of cooperation for the future. The standard of skiing amongst the indigenous skiers was, on average, not up to the standard of qualified European teachers. How could it be? There were two Austrians, Karl Fuchs and Hans Kuwall, who had skied since childhood. They had settled in the village of Carrbridge, where they fitted in very well.

Most of the better Scottish skiers were club racers and all had skied abroad, not a common achievement in those days. What was needed was a serious charge of adrenaline into the general thinking of the *home brewed* ski teacher. Little did we know that the Pitlochry meeting had been the catalyst that would process and supply this need. And in doing so, it caused Cain for quite some time. Seeing some of the scruff that passed as ski teachers took a lot of believing. The weekend skiers took pride in looking their best. We still have some scruffy looking articles, females included.

1963 First British Staffed Full-time Ski School
left to right – Self, Eric Leiper, Peter Simpson, Willie Smith,
Bobbie Birnie, George Shields

D'Écosse had straightforward standards. You were clean shaved or bearded, boots polished, ski shirts or polo necks, ski pants pressed. Late coming was not tolerated. *One minute* was late. The agreed rules were applied right across the

136

board. I don't remember too many having to be fired for being late. Now this could not take place without it being obvious. The stories that went about of the "hard-nose Frith" were unbelievable. All the people in our team wanted to be part of it. It goes without saying, that none of our team took crap from anyone. Including me.

The snow on the hill before that Christmas became very thin. The night the guests arrived we had a foot of snow in the village. Ski School D'Écosse's first lessons were held on the lawn of the old Aviemore Hotel. This is where the first organised instruction was run by Jock Kerr Hunter on behalf of The Scottish Council of Physical Recreation at the same time of year in 1947. Jock told me they went to bed with the hills black, and woke up to a winter landscape!

Connie Wilson, from Verbier, taught for us over the Christmas and the New Year holiday. She had a natural bent for ski teaching and she certainly looked the part. The marvellous snow that started the season for us, was the herald of a long Alpine mountain winter. What a start! However, trouble was just round the corner.

Between the colourful uniforms and the morning clinics, our ski school stood out. It did not take long for the petty squabbling to start. The pros and cons of which national ski technique was best. Who skied best. We had less than a handful of good skiers, native or otherwise, in all of Scotland at the time. Yet we were surrounded by unskilled self appointed experts. It was painful listening to them. It was purgatory watching them skiing. Oh how self destructive a *little knowledge* can be! The stark fact was that most of those involved in this vacuous verbiage were playing at what we were trying so hard to establish. As for national ski schools, we had none of these. What we did have was small ski schools calling themselves national ski schools. As a matter of fact, putting the total skills and experience of all of us who were teaching on Cairngorm, it would not have come to much. That includes everyone. The Scots ones an' all. We had young "Men" in the their late teens and early twenties, with little skiing behind them, *shooting the bull* about teaching and advanced skiing. Put a ski teacher jacket on most young men and it seems to imbue them with a wisdom and knowledge beyond their ken. As Robert Burns said, "*O wad some Pow'r the giftie gie us To see oursels as others see us.*" But this nonsense would cause very serious trouble in the near future. Trouble that was so unnecessary.

In the meantime, we in our group spent every moment we could skiing together, exchanging and discussing all the aspects of skiing as they came to us. This was the first time a group of native born skiers had the opportunity to work at skiing for a whole season. On looking back, I know we made the best of the opportunity. With hindsight, and the benefit of long years of work in the trade, I'm sure the backgrounds we all had made the whole thing gel. As a result of the Pitlochry meeting, another was convened. This took place in the Cairngorm Hotel, Aviemore, on the 16th January, 1963. Jock Kerr Hunter organised the event. All those who may have had an interest in the business had the right to attend. All hoteliers who were involved seemed to be there.

Those teaching seriously were in attendance. It was very obvious from the kick off that the hoteliers thought it was trade-unionism raising its ugly head. How they ever got that into their heads was beyond my comprehension. Before anyone could form an opinion as to what the reason for the meeting was for, we

137

had to assure the meeting that there were no alternate motives in what may be under way. How little did any of us know at the time just how conservative average ski teachers would turn out to be as they grew in number. Here it was again, this unjustified aversion to something they probably knew nothing about. I myself knew nothing about "unionism." The meeting turned out to be very successful. Even better, it was most amicable.

The chairman of the Chairlift Company, Archie Scott, a true blue conservative of the old school, supported strongly the need for what we were advocating for the future training and grading of ski teachers. He and Bob Clyde from that day forward were staunch friends to ski teachers. There were many who should have known better who never seemed to take cognisance of this fact of life. Both Archie and Bob gave BASI solid support during the time I was so much involved with running BASI. The meeting gave us a mandate to form a body to train and grade ski teachers. No one said how wide our remit should be, but, in the event, we made it national. Because we were first in the field, we had a clear run at it. The British Association of Professional Ski Instructors, became the first national skiing body in the UK. Being part of this was one of the things I have been ever proud of. Jock Kerr Hunter talked us into changing the name to BASI in the hope of getting finance from what is now the Sports Council. We never got a farthing. I will come back and explain the pros and cons of the political comings and goings of the *scramble for power* as I saw it. If we had called it the Scottish Association, instead of BAPSI, the abbreviation would have been SAPSI. I've always regretted not having called it SAPSI. Just for the hell of it! Imagine having to admit you are a SAPSI member!

On looking back it is very clear that ski teachers never managed to coalesce with each other. A fault that would do them no good. This has not changed. The possible cause is their natural tendency towards conservatism. In my opinion, they pay the price for this shortcoming to the present day. Another wee anecdote concerning Archie Scott and professor Sir Robert Grieve. I spoke of Bob Grieve in the early pages as being one of the real Clydesiders. A tenement boy who became the first Chairman of the Highlands and Islands Development Board, in which capacity he became friendly with Archie Scott. They were so different in backgrounds, one being a Red Clydesider, the other a True Blue, from Edinburgh.

A number of years later, on a November day, I found myself walking on Cairngorm. The weather was wicked, with high wind and pouring rain. What I was doing up there in those conditions I'll never know. We men are not inclined to commonsense. I noticed a fire was going well in the top station of the chairlift. It sure was. The big pot-bellied coke burner was red hot and round it stood some of the hardcases who worked on the outside squad. The steam was rising up off their clothes. I joined and added my steam to the production line. There were other headcases about in the hills. The door opened and in stepped the High Heid Yins. Robert Clyde, the general manager. Archie Scott, chairman of the Board. And a Knight of the realm, Bob Grieve. An imposing trio anywhere. Unlike Clydesiders, the local men were a wee bit chary of people the likes of these. Bob Clyde put them at their ease about being in the bothy and not out at their work. Out at their work in that weather it was horrendous. Anyway, the conversation turned to men working and living in the world's bad weather climates, such as what was taking place outside. Sir Robert, the new Knight of the Realm, was a famous teller-of-tales. There was nothing he liked better than a new audience. He had one here.

*1963 New Racers –
The Team who beat the
Big People in the
Tennant Trophy
left to right – Rutherford,
Fraser Clyde, David
McDonald, Arthur
McLean, Iain Finlayson,
Jack McLean, ?,
Sherrie Sutton –* RJB

He started to relate the story of how Brian Barru had to shack up for a month or more in an Alaskan winter. It so happened that there was an Eskimo woman stormbound in the same shack. Brian was a lucky man, a careful man. To cut a long story short he produced a home made French Letter, or, in the modern parlance, a condom. He had quite a comfortable four or five weeks. As he heard the ice breaking up on the river, he knew it was leaving time. There was one thing he wasn't too happy about, so, on the last night, he made it clear to his lady of the evening, "it's hairy side out tonight, dear, hairy side out to night!" There was a stony silence. I looked at Bob Clyde. Then, in harmony, we burst out laughing. I told the chairlift men they could laugh, as Sir Bob was only a man. I can't remember if Archie Scott laughed. I don't know if he approved, he had a very reserved outlook on life. Or so I thought. He was very good for skiing on Cairngorm. Now to say Sir Bob was a storyteller of the highest calibre would nearly cover the possibility. Bob Clyde and I knew the Knight of the Realm was capable of the odd bawdy tale. I got the impression that Archie and the other chairlift staff did not expect Sir Robert would tell such stories. Never judge a book by its covers.

To go back to the ski teaching monster-to-be that was in the process of raising its hoary head... From the above meeting, a committee a Founders Members was formed. To qualify as a Founder Member you had to be a ski school manager or a ski school owner. This was a first time, once only, expedient arrangement that enabled us to organise the first training and grading course. The committee had 10 members. One of these was Karl Fuchs, an Austrian who had an hotel in Carrbridge. He was appointed chairman. Of the 10 members five were born outside of the UK. Also in Carrbridge was the Austrian, Hans Kuwall. Both these men had skied since their childhood. Jack Thompson had been teaching skiing since 1950. He was the longest practising ski teacher in the UK. Quite a distinction. These three men would the be the most experienced in British ski teaching.

The first work we would carry out was to run a ski clinic. This is the name given for an on-snow exchange of ski technique and teaching methods. It was apparent from the word go that the total skills and skiing ability of many of the founder members was rudimentary. I say this as a matter of fact, not as a criticism. That was how it was. Nothing starts as well as it *should* finish. The fact that there was such a big disparity in the skiing abilities created many difficulties. What's new? We were very fortunate to have waiting in the wings, a few good skiers who would be qualified as full members in their own right by the end of that season. They would be the first ever qualified in the UK. And they would have qualified under a system instituted by working British ski teachers whom they had appointed themselves. You can't get fairer than that! After a few short years, they would take complete command of how their day to day affairs and future would be shaped. There was without a doubt *a coterie* of some of the founder members who became anti to what BAPSI started to develop. The reasons for this attitude have always escaped me.

While reading this, it should be borne in mind that what was taking place was the very rapid growth of a set of hard and fast working rules and regulations. The speed was only possible because of the excellent examples that were working very well in European countries. I'm sure "the antis" read things into this that were certainly not there. BAPSI's work since its inception, has never ever impinged on any ski school's operations. It goes without saying that the good work done by British ski teachers in those early days, in their National endeavours to make this new body, BAPSI, work, was not arrived at without trials or tribulations. BAPSI had its first serious trouble. And this brief account of what happened should be told.

Not long after we got the show on the road, in the middle of February, on our second committee meeting, and before we got the meeting properly started, our newly appointed chairman started off on what was an attack on myself and Jack Thompson. Unfortunately, Karl's English was at times difficult to get a grip of. Neither Jack or myself had any idea of what had triggered this outburst, and outburst it was. The outcome was that Karl left the meeting, and resigned from our wee, embryonic, hardly breathing national ski teachers body. Jack Thompson asked me what it had been all about. He was as wise as me. Next day, I found out that one of *our* team of six had been criticising the quality of Karl's ski school to one of Karl's old pupils. Despite overtures to placate Karl, he would have none of it.

There was a chastening lesson to be learned here. BAPSI would have many more difficulties before they became fully established. The one that caused all this bother ended up working in Karl Fuchs' ski school. How he managed to equate what he had said about Karl's school, far less his conscience, went over my head. How Jack Thompson was lumped in with this stupidity I never ever understood. Jack had nothing whatever to do with our ski school and he was so straight-laced and tight-lipped, he would never be involved in upsetting anyone. Unless he wanted to. Then it would have been very clear and right out in front.

The snow conditions continued to be excellent throughout the season. As did the Bull about what ski technique was the best, and this, it must be said, came from those who had the least talents and experience. You never hear clear thinkers being involved in these arcane arguments. The great thing about skiing is, if you want to enjoy it, just get on with it!

With the big snows came the blocked ski road. The road was narrow and the snowplough most inadequate. It was a wartime snow-blower meant for airstrips. By the middle of February the Cairngorm seemed to be buried. There was a long period of windless, sunlight days. The young up and coming skier's paradise and the road to it was completely closed. The wee ex-war-department snowplough could make nothing of it! The only lift we had, the top chair, had to be dug out. When the you see the provision for snow clearing and snow drifting fencing, and we still get trouble with the road to the ski lifts drifting in today, you can maybe understand how the road was closed for the best part of two weeks. One of the memories was teaching parallel skiing in the trees, walking up and down. You have to be very inventive to keep the interest of pupils going. What it does do for yourself, is that it teaches you a great deal about the *art* of ski teaching. Even more, it teaches you a great deal about yourself! Jack Thompson did it for 12 years and never lost the quality of his work.

The ski clinics on behalf of the new BASI dropped off. They were going nowhere. We in D'Écosse worked away every moment we could after lessons were over and, when possible, before lessons in the mornings. As a result, the overall standard of our group got physically and visibly better.

In the opening pages I spoke of a John Young, one of the Red Clydesiders. John was one of the very special persons in my life. His skiing left a lot to be desired, like many others I've had the privilege to work with. He could still give *wonderful* ski lessons. That first Easter, he was helping in the school, when a local lady of much importance phoned me and asked if she could have private lessons for her son and a school friend, who were home from a famous English public school. We were so busy, private lessons were almost impossible. But there are those with clout, and there is *She Who Must Be Obeyed*. We met as

John Young, The Hanging Judge's Teacher with Frith

arranged next morning, and John was appointed to the task. Now, I did say that John was a declared communist and I thought it would be a nice touch putting the two extremes of political and social backgrounds on a level playing field, so to speak. Not *quite* true, as very few people were on a level playing field with John. He was a humanist with a diamond sharp brain. John knew the background of the lady. I had pointed out to her that John was on holiday and this was a special favour to me. A lie. But then I've always been good at milking a good situation. At the meeting place, I called John over to meet his class. The bastard overplayed his hand. When introduced, he pulled off his stocking cap, bowed like a knight of old and, using his magic mouth, charmed this lady who was as sharp as a tack! I thought he was going to lift her hand and kiss her fingers. You could put nothing past him.

John's nickname was Toadles. I never knew the reason for the nickname. Sometimes not knowing the reason for certain things leaves a nice wee touch of mystery for your imagination to work on. Most of us don't need such stimulants. Our brains just keep soldiering on, dreaming dreams, as surely we were meant to do! John used to stay regularly on winter weekends with us at a time when I needed some private company that I did not work with each and every day.

After he left with the two young men, the Lady asked me if it would be alright for her to watch how the class got on. For the sake of something to say, I cautioned her not to disturb John when he was working. At that time great emphasis was placed on how you planted the pole. The lady wanted a private lesson with John, in which she only wanted to learn "that delightful little trick with the stick!" During the lesson, I'm sure John had to go some, to hold his own with this lady.

Another day he had a very difficult middle-aged man from the north of England in his group giving John earache. Hire skis had painted soles in those days and these soles did not run well in many snow conditions. They were the bain of struggling ski teachers' lives. This strong willed gentleman was having a great deal of bother with snow sticking to his skis. So the skis got the blame.

Like many things in those days, everything was far from *kosher*. The classes were large, making teaching difficult. The man disappeared for some time, reappeared, confronting John with the declaration that a young Austrian expert ski instructor had waxed his skis perfectly. After putting them on, he launched off to show John, and got stuck! The best skier in the world could not have made those skis run. John grabbed the skis, rubbed on a big lump of Silver Wax and launched his favourite pupil off down the hill. According to John, he never saw his star pupil for some time. The wax job was a friendship clincher, as John and the man became good friends. Once they were on speaking terms, the man told John that he was a circuit judge. John's snappy retort, was, "I bet your an expert at putting on the Wee Black Hat!" Well, the judge was tickled to death. He then became known as the Hanging Judge, and the judge loved it. John used to keep me going late of an evening with such anecdotes. He was one of the most philosophical smart arses I've ever had the privilege to call a friend. A few seasons later, the Hanging Judge came back and asked if he could go skiing with John. I had to tell him that John had died. The man was shocked. John was young when we lost him. I've often wondered how much richer my world would be if he was still here?

That first season I had a class of the great unwashed from Glencoe. There was Harry McKay, our already ageing ski champion, but far from finished in leaving his mark on British skiing. And Alex Carmichael, whose family became prominent in British ski racing. And also Glen Perry, who became known as the Purple Plook, because of the jacket he was foolish enough to wear that week. He's still called the Purple Plook, and he's proud of it. He's also easy pleased! We had a new face in the class, a Willie McKenna. He was to stay skiing and contribute his fair share to what Cairngorm skiing is today. This class went under the misnomer of Race Training.

It became a self propagating week of hard graft of no-give and no-take total effort. They were of mixed standards, and all were Clydesiders. Most of the week we had to walk up because the lift was buried under our old friend, the snow. We did a lot of our slalom in the Sugarbowl. Part of that slope is now covered by the new part of the road. When I think back on how many days we skied in the Sugarbowl that season, I shudder.

When I used the word "misnomer" to describe the training of that week, that was not quite true. Most of the serious skiers of that time raced, even though most were far from young. And very competitive racers they were, because that was the kind of people they were. We were only just then starting to breed, and I mean *breed*, most of those who would be our first racers, who started skiing before going to school. We did have a small number of very young racers. Now, these ones above were tough, and the harder you pushed them, the tougher they got. Harry McKay kept saying that I would end up doing him an injury. Well he should have been used to it. After all he cracked his arse in Zermatt! We had a fine week of days and the nights were not too bad. Harry got his wish, during the last half hour of the last day on a slalom course near the Shieling. He did his knee in. As a result, I got the rough edge of his tongue. Just the same as that day on the rock climb in Glencoe, when my stomach was on the blink. But, *he's no a bad wee man*, if a bit short on tolerance! So many happenings took place, they seemed to pile on top of each other. It was an Aladdin's cave of adventure. You never would have thought, that hard-nosed types the likes of us, would call every day living an adventure, but it certainly was then. Mind you, it was not all sweet and smelling of roses. The sweet smelling roses were things like our big caravan, where our son had a wee bedroom to himself, with its spare bed. And like the

Three-Way-Loader, a wee green coal burning stove. The electric heating was an extra. The caravan sitting under the Scots Pines in the big garden, completing the picture. Yes, this was our *bolt hole*.

Working collectively each day with other ski teachers and not being isolated was very productive. There was a feeling of growth and, more important, you were part of it. There was a *hole in the wall* you saw through, to something that could grow and prosper. So this was how things had panned out as we drew near to the end of the season of 1962/63.

Not much had been done in pursuit of BASI's affairs. Few clinics had taken place. They did not seem to be of interest to most founder members but, despite this, it was agreed to run our first training and grading course. I was appointed director of training, with the clear understanding that I had complete control. With that proviso under my belt, I set up a two week training and grading programme. Jack Thomson set up the examination policy. This policy lasted for some 15 years. From some idiotic brain, or more than one idiot, it was suggested we should get "some expert" from abroad to help us set up and run the course, to give more credibility. I clearly remember what Jack Thompson and I had to say about that. The defeatism of them also defeats the imagination. They had to be reminded that the rest of the ski teachers working on our hills had entrusted us with this responsibility. It was also pointed out that I held a Swiss Ski School Director's Licence. This was most certainly the reason I was in charge of the work.

This was the open sign of the Anti Lobby. The following season it manifested itself. The above idea was no way to start what had to be accomplished. I have never, ever, had any respect for the "Anti's." I personally held them responsible for the completely unnecessary resistance to the aims and objects of working ski teachers on our hills. The success of BASI's fine work over the years put paid to their mean crassness.

Hans Kuwall and I had to work on this first course, and, to the very best of my memory, the two of us had no troubles all the way through what could have been a *dog's mess*. We never made a deal. It seemed that we must have realised the graveness of our combined responsibility to the many people in skiing who gave us their trust in getting this job done. We did it. Hans has always been a BASI person. There was, however, a serious problem which would impinge on the outcome of the course. I've mentioned this before. It was to do with the shoulder position in one part of the technique. Here Hans and I differed, and there was nothing we could do about it as far as the coming to terms with it before the course was concerned. Years passed before this sorted itself out. The most important thing on the agenda was creating our *own* first Qualified Members, who in turn would have the *full rights* to how they would teach. And thereafter, look after *their* affairs, in *their* own way.

13. Looking at the Future

We had 22 candidates. Most of them came from the Scottish ski fields. We had two colourful candidates. One was Joe Hohl, a fully qualified Swiss ski teacher from, of all places, Andermatt. Joe worked for Liliwhites in London running dry ski schools and their ski department. When I asked him what he was doing here, I was delighted with his reply. He said he wanted to be part of what we were doing.

The other was a wee man called Guy Chilver-Stainer. Guy was right out of *the book*. The epitome of the Englishman who had been a professional soldier pre-war and through the war. And a holder of the Military Cross, no less. Guy later became the secretary of the Scottish National Ski Council-to-be. He was a foxy, loveable, wee rascal. He had raced in the Arlberg Kandahar in the middle of the nineteen thirties. Guy was Scot-o-Phile. There's one for you! "He spoke with marbles in his mouth."

The standard of skiing among the course was only what it could be, not very good. The bulk of the skiers had not been skiing very long. Most had only skied at home and, to crown it all, had not had any extensive use of lifts. But that's what we had. What we did have was people who could be worked hard and I would venture to say there was a sense of adventure in the atmosphere of the course. If I may be old fashioned enough to say so. The first two days were used to sharpen up and relax everyone's skiing. This would be the first time most of these people would have been under such close scrutiny as far as their personal skiing was concerned. That in itself was a big step forward in setting a example of the self discipline involved in being responsible for teaching skiing.

There was supposed to be a lecture programme. We really had no skills in lecturing, nor, indeed, had anything to lecture about. What I did do was have discussion each night on the day's events. Here we found out what we needed to know and, in knowing, we could do something about it. Each group quickly became close-knit. Better still, the whole course became a homogeneous entity. This gave us common ground on which to manoeuvre. Before breakfast we had outside exercises, with a wee run thrown in as an extra. The second day a male and female turned up for the wee run a couple of minutes late. I pointed out the importance of exact timekeeping, which had been agreed by all at the pre-course briefing. They agreed this was so, and I cautioned them not to be late again. They had worked in our ski school. They kept proper time after that. Naturally, the rest of the course knew this occurred. We never had any indolent timekeeping after that.

Teaching teachers has never been troublesome to me. It could be because I started by teaching friends and what were more or less the better skiers on our Midden-Heid at the time. Also, skiing with the Swiss School Directors had left me with no illusions when it came to being forthright and the need for bluntness when extrapolating all the facets of how this side of skiing works. Confidence is the keynote in this approach. The justification for assuming that this is right, must be the recognition by your peers of your ability and your right to the responsibility. We have so many these days doing it who, in my opinion, do not come up to the above requirements. This is how many respected trainers see the present situation. Even worse, up and coming ski teachers can see the situation clearly for what it is. It is to be hoped that this shortcoming is being seen for what it is, and is being sorted out.

Hans did not seem to have any difficulty with his class and the course progressed steadily with no complaining mutterings let alone any trauma which, on later courses, became common. How confusing a little knowledge can be. During the next spring course we would get our first bellyful of this. The communal evening debriefs were a great source of new information to me. I'm sure it helped to keep at bay much of the self inflicted anguish that became part of these courses and still is.

In the start of the second week the course started to ask what form the examination would take. Luckily, Jack Thompson had his examination policy ready. The night before the big event Jack gave a marvellous diagrammatic layout of what would take place. I was delighted and it took a lot of the stress off me. This was Jack's twelve years of working experience in Glenmore Lodge manifesting itself.

The examination panel was made up of five of the founder members. Jack had produced a system of marking, and there would be two parts to the

Jack Thomson, Britain's First Full-time Ski Teacher

examination. Jack was the head examiner. There would be two grades:- Associate Member and Full Member. Skiing Technique split into 10 parts, with 10 possible points for each part. The parts were from walking on the flat, to advanced skiing. Teaching marks were set up the same as above. To pass as a Full Member, a candidate had to achieve a technical mark of 80 from a possible of 100. And it was the same for teaching, at least 80 from a possible 100. To pass as an Associate Member, a candidate had to score at least 60 marks in the two sections. The top mark would be dropped, as would the low mark. Jack had examination papers printed in Glenmore. As head examiner he instructed the panel on how he wanted the procedure to work.

Jack was very well placed to be in charge of this. Firstly because of his background in Glenmore Lodge, but more importantly as he had no connection with any commercial ski school, ski shop or hotel in the ski business anywhere. This made him unique amongst the rest of us. There was, however, a problem over the difference of the shoulder position in one part of the technique, where, as I've already said, Hans and I differed. Of the candidates, taking into account the mixture of their skills and experience, their followings would be divided about fifty/fifty for one side or the other. Unfortunately, in the examination panel, only Jack had leanings towards how *we of our opinion* felt. And, as I have already said, it was not possible to do something concrete to equalise the situation. I discussed this with Hans. He, of course, agreed there was a problem. I decided to divide the two classes into equal numbers from the two camps. That's the way they would be trained, more or less. In mixed groups, this might balance out the different views. Hans and I had nothing to do with the examination. Trainers have never been involved in examining their own trainees.

So, *the die was cast*. The first ever British ski teacher's qualification examination was up and running! Kuwall and Finlayson had to stew in their own juice for two days, while the second part of this *Great Adventure* ran its course. The weather had been bad all through the two weeks this persisted. I spent most of the two days observing how the course was panning out. I got the firm impression I was an outsider looking in. And I kept well away from Mr Jack Thompson during those two days.

Waiting for the results seemed to take forever. The candidates hung about the Shieling, some sitting in small groups, some in twos and some alone. They seemed to cocoon themselves in a bubble of silence, as if waiting for the Four Horsemen of The Apocalypse to bring them personally the Shroud of Failure! They seemed to distance themselves from reality. With the experience of the coming years, this is something which would continue. No matter how sophisticated the quality of the running of the courses, nor how high the personal standard of the skiing became, this did not change. Human emotions are deep and complex. In this part of my life I have learned to be very careful with people's feelings when you hold dominion over them! When the results of the examination were known, my forebodings were justified.

Candidates who performed their skiing in the "My Style" had definitely been marked on their style and not on their skiing ability. Those who were so treated and are still in skiing remember well how they were treated, but that's in the past. This thing called style, is still erroneously confused with good technique. The goal of most candidates was, of course, to achieve Full Membership. Getting an Associate was like not passing. There was no need for this stupidity. A cosy blanket could have been thrown over the two trains of opinion. After all, we had to do this with the *founder members!*

This accident caused by inexperience should never happen again? The next examination would have a very strong input from those who had experienced the pain of being examined. Mind you, I had not walked gently through the troubled waters of the debates on standards of ski teacher skiing in professional skiing in this country in the buildup to this first course. Only Jack on the panel was of the same opinion as me about the "shoulder position."

But there was another piece of gross stupidity, in my opinion, that came out of this examination. Joe Hohl, the fully qualified Swiss ski teacher, who came here to be part of our *new possibility*, had not passed as a Full Member. This staggered me much more than the "shoulder position." Joe stood high in the eyes and good will of the Ski Club of Great Britain. He had been qualified for many years. He also knew that he and I were the only qualified people there. The examiners had no qualifications.

His shortcoming was he did not ski like most of the examiners. I'd said nothing about how I felt about our teachers who had not passed as Full Members. Before we left the hill I had serious words with Jack Thompson about the possible outcome of this act of absolute gross stupidity. And it was completely unjustified. I could see Jack was tired. I was bushed myself. I also understood he carried a heavy responsibility. It still surprised me how much trouble I had getting Jack to see how much unnecessary bother this might give us in the future. Jack finally agreed to talk to the rest of the examiners. We managed to stop all of them at Loch Morlich. In the road, there was pain-in-the-arse argument about the pros and cons of the expediency of not failing this man, etc. etc. Out of the corner of my eye I kept seeing Jack, checking all the marking papers. Then right out of the blue, he made this clear statement. "This candidate has the highest marks in all the examiners' papers for teaching in the course!" Jack was a cunning fox when necessary. I often wondered what those marks would have been like if I had got a wee shuffty at them!

Agreement to revise their thinking on their marking was made. No examination will please or suit everyone. I never heard anyone who passed at the level they had aimed at cribbing about the examination. I'm afraid some of the people with whom we were forced to cooperate, if that be the word, left me with a poor opinion of them.

If that be the price for getting BAPSI, now BASI, a good start, with members who had won their spurs in the field, so be it. Getting BASI started left me with a gut-rich feeling that was easy to live with.

The telling of this story will explain part of the birth and growing pains that gave BASI the platform from which it started to grow and mature. In telling this version of how our Association got started I'm sure it will be of great interest to young ski teachers and also to the public in general. During the following summer, no work spoiled my pleasures. However, the S.C.G.B. with imaginative skill, organised a ski meet at Pontin's Holiday Camp, Torquay, Devon. The Ski Club have great skill at organising these sorts of meets. Bob Denton and I went down to take part. The camp comprises of nice chalets in a bonny wee dell close to the beach. The occasion was to mark the opening of their plastic slope, which may have been the first one in England. The weekend turned out to be a big success and much fruitful, good thinking and understanding came out of it. New friendships began. Being with Bob Denton was always an adventure!

Maria Goldberg, manager of the British Ladies Ski Team, attended. She added quite a flair to the scene. People from all different parts of skiing found it very interesting speaking to Maria. At that time the Ladies Team was very strong. It included Gina Hawthorn, who just missed the Bronze Medal by three hundredths of a second. Also, there was Divina Galica. I once fitted bindings on two pairs of Kneissl skis at three in the morning in Lauterbrunnen for her to race in the British Junior Championships. And there was Bunny Field, another good downhill racer, and Caroline Tomkinson.

A Norwegian, Arni Palm from Geilo, had been invited by the powers-that-be. He was a gentleman. It was from him that we learned that ski school owners in the Cairngorms were organising a ski training week the coming winter. This came under the guise of a get-together. That was not how we saw it. Arni said he had been invited to run this get-together.

Dougie Godlington, a very well known ski teacher, and I explained to Arni that he should have nothing to do with it. He could lose good friends in ski teaching in the UK if he came and interfered with the internal affairs of the young and what, at that time, could have been fragile stability of something that was very dear to some extremely strong minded individuals. Despite what Dougie and I had said, he did turn up the following winter and ran a week of skiing. The only two ski school owners who did not attend were Hans Kuwall and myself and of course Jack Thompson. I don't know what this event, a charade in my opinion, was meant to prove. What did come out of it was that Arni Palm lost a great deal of the respect he had hitherto enjoyed. In particular, Jack Thompson's. Jack was not a man who forgave easily. I told Arni in no uncertain terms what I thought of his part in this nonsense. Anyway, young British ski teachers should find this of interest. Also, that their "course" made no stir whatsoever on the Cairngorm. I'm sure Arni knew he had been badly used when he left for home.

It was here at Torquay I witnessed one of the finest ski lessons I have ever seen being taught on snow or plastic. The teacher of the lesson was an amateur. He took a class of children from walking on the flat to starting parallel. He never put a foot wrong. The man's name was Mark Heller. He's written many books about skiing, and excellent they are. I had the privilege of sitting at a BASI dinner with him. He was being presented with an Honorary Membership back in 1988. I recalled him giving the lesson and how much I admired his skill. He told me he was terrified when he saw it was me looking on. I don't know why. You can't hide quality as he displayed that day.

Round that table were many notable new Honorary Members, such as Bing Crosby and Terrence Kitcat, and those were their real names! This presentation dinner was for around ten people who had worked in skiing since the Year Dot. Most of them had been contributing to skiing in their own time and free of charge for years. A night to be remembered, and one BASI can be proud of. There were two ski teachers at the dinner, Elif Moen a Norwegian ski teacher for almost thirty years at that time, part of our ski clique. He runs the Norwegian school. I'm sure he thinks like a Scot. Tommy McKee a dear life long friend of mine was the other ski teacher.

Tommy McKee,
Boilermaker to the Queen

At the backend of that summer, in the month of October, Ewan Cameron, of Lochearnhead, gave me the opportunity to learn water skiing. Ewan owned the famous hotel from which the water skiing was run. I would drive the boats for the skiers. In return I'd live in the hotel, and have complete use of the boats. The most important thing about this wonderful chance is that I would be taught by some of the best water skiers in the country. I had Luke O' Reilly, a junior champion. Another champion, Sue Mason. And Ewan's wife, who was reckoned to be a first class coach. Many of the water skiers were also snow skiers, so I fitted in, having a wonderful time. With the unrivalled tutoring and the unbridled use of the boats, my progress was rapid. In the month I managed to learn five tricks, get over the jump, and get through the slalom.

At the time I was asked how I felt water skiing compared to snow skiing in how it is performed. I don't think it does compare. On snow you stand up, and on the water you definitely keep your weight back. I would say that most competitive water skiers don't continue their skiing after they give up competition. Whereas snow skiers seem to carry on till they bury them. Not many people get the opportunity to start in a sport like I did here in water skiing, and to be treated with such clinical exactitude. Ann Cameron and Sue Mason will remember putting me *through the wringer* behind that big Chrisscraft of Ann's. I stand in debt to these two considerable ladies and of course, Luke!

1963 Frith with Karl Schranz at Greaves Sports.
One of the great racers from 1956 to 1972

In November of that year, the first ever Winter Sports Show was run in the Alexandra Palace in London. It was amazing with how big an effort the small business people in Speyside rallied together and, with short notice, produced what turned out to be the best stand in the show. The small hotel and boarding house owners, at their own expense, stayed in London and staffed the Scottish stand. The ladies wore tartan. Some men were kilted. Our stand was very heavily attended. The whisky distilleries of Speyside supplied copious amounts of "The Water of Life", so that, when we had our Scottish day, we literally got all the rest of the stand-holders drunk! As a matter of fact, *some were blazing!* There was a reasonable plastic slope which was the centrepiece of the show. We had short slalom races. Hans Kuwall beat Charles Bozon, a French Gold Medallist. Not

150

LOOKING AT THE FUTURE

bad for the wee Austrian from Carrbridge! There was a style formation competition. Our Cairngorm team won this. Another *not bad* effort.

A young American couple came to our stand. The wife was Beverly Anderson, an ex-national team member. Racing on the slope, she won a Cairngorm holiday for two. Most of the week they were here they had to walk up, because of the strong wind keeping the chairlift off. It never seemed to bother them. They were hard cases. Beverly knew Margit Gertsch and Roland Blazzy from the Olympics in Squaw Valley. We gave them a real Speyside welcome when they were here. This was a very exciting affair for all of us who were putting so much of our life into the future of British skiing.

There was only one unpleasant incident, so childish as to beggar the imagination. The Scottish Tourist Board, who were paying for the stand and other bits and pieces, had organised a lunch. Angus Ogilvy, the then new husband of Princess Alexander, was the guest of honour. The invitations were up to the Speyside Hoteliers who, with Jock Kerr-Hunter of the Sports Council, had made Scotland being there possible. Two well known small hotel owners, one from Boat of Garten, George Cameron, and Wilma Reilly came to Hans Kuwall and myself about the lunch. We knew nothing about it. Why should we? They were to invite a ski teacher as a guest. In their wisdom they had invited a teacher who worked privately, and was more or less unattached to a ski school. The man involved was a Scot by the name of Walter Hay. By pure luck, Walter was one of those who qualified that spring. In a manner of speaking *he had gained his spurs in combat.*

Hans Kuwall and I thought this to be the ideal choice. We were wrong. Some ski school owners created Cain. They seemed to think they should have been consulted. They ranted and raved. You would have thought they were kids who'd had their sweeties nicked. Wilma Reilly, not famous for suffering fools, gave them the rough edge of her considerable vocabulary, learned, I may say, in years of handling halfwitted bar-room drunks. Before I say this, we all understand that behaviour like this is not confined to countries other than Scotland. But, unfortunately, none of those involved were native born. I'm sorry to end on such a shallow note. But you must have very Bad before you have Good.

14. A Steep Learning 'Curve'

Having got through all the possible pitfalls of last season we ended up better equipped to look to the future and start to improve on the work and advancement that had been won the previous season. The equipment we had acquired would settle down and make it possible to be *good* skiers, to give our profession credence which was obvious to knowledgeable skiers who really knew how the skis work. That "equipment" was the freshly qualified members of BASI, whither they be Full or Associate members. For among them was a nucleus from which it might be able to stabilise what had been gained. This would give us a breathing space until the young and the very young talent we had waiting in the wings were ready to make their mark. Little did we know it would be sooner, rather than later. With this in the back of my mind, and patience being something that I *did* possess, despite some opinions, I was like the cat who had nicked the cream and looked forward with Great Expectations!

The Swiss Directors' Course was in St. Moritz This was another mouth-watering goodie to look forward to. From our ski school we'd made up a group comprising Peter Simpson, Bobbie Birnie, Eric Leiper and Hilary Best. They had all qualified on the BASI course. Aged 18, Hilary had become the youngest ever BASI Full Member, by now known as Grade I. Bobbie was one of those lucky skiers who had been born with the gift to ski well. And he still can, to this day. This would be a very interesting experience for us all. Here was a group of newly qualified ski teachers who, with the exception of Peter, had not seen the Top End of the Professional skiing in a clinical situation, en masse. Seeing their reactions and opinions to the scope and scale of this very large operation and how it affected their thinking would be very interesting. We arrived five days before the course was due to start having driven out. On the way over the pass from Chur it started snowing, and with our non-snow-tyres we just made it over to St Moritz.

John Clemments my American friend was already there, so we had a nice wee group. Bobby, Eric and Hilary were very impressed with John and how he skied in the very deep snow. As I have mentioned John in no way looked like an athlete, but by the Christ he could swing his skis in any snow. John was delighted to meet the up-and-coming ski teachers of the future of Britain's professional Ski Teaching. They in turn found John's knowledge of the international ski business something they'd not possibly thought about. I took pleasure in watching this interchange. When they went back home it was for sure they would talk to others about what they had seen and heard in St Moritz. I wonder if they remember that part of their start in skiing?

The snow we drove through in coming over from Chur kept falling. It went on and on and turned St Moritz into what it should be. To describe this fable of a place where people ski is beyond my ken. It is everything that is said about it and I mean everything. Its skiing will stand up proud with any other "Ski Station" in Europe. It is not only where the very rich ski, it's a Swiss ski resort, where ordinary people ski. Jeanie and I looked into a wee shop window. There was a three-quarter length man's jacket, with tie-belt. No buttons, fawn in colour. It was *twelve hundred quid!* If it had been navy blue it might have passed for a Wimpey donkey jacket! That's also St Moritz. Wee fat middle-aged men walking about with ankle length mink coats with hats to match, closely followed by tall slinky burds, they too having big long mink coats and hats.

We were given free use of the lifts for five days. This was a good start and it gave the group a nice wee lift! Between us had we had memorable skiing before the course started. This was some time before there were such machines as Snow Tracks. At the end of the day before the course started we were all button holed to sidestep all the way down from Corviglia to St Moritz. In two feet of powder, it was *murder* and a dreadful waste of powder. The head ski patroller said ski teachers who skied all week free should be good at side-stepping downhill. There's no free lunches! The side-stepping down through the deep powder was a mental torture. I thought I was leg-fit, but later on that night my legs were *leaden*.

I had explained to the powers-that-be about our group and where they stood in skiing. So I was very pleased to find their teacher was *"a cracker."* Joan Shearing was in their class, and I wondered how she would get on with Bobby's and Eric's Dundee accent. She was impressed with their skiing, as they were with her's. Joan was great at mixing. When you saw that group skiing, it was *crisp*. On the last day I skied with them, the teacher was indeed out of the top drawer. A mechanic in summer in St Moritz, and he knew how to teach skiing and had captured the group's imaginations. Joan was very impressed with the group. She had skied with good skiers most of her life. I was back in Werner's group. We would never ski together again after this. None of us knew this at the time.

The skin-tight elastic-sided ski pants were just in. Bill Greaves bought me a pair at the Trade Fair in Salzburg in April. They were so way out in those days you had to be brave to wear them. On the first morning Marcel Von Allmen from Wengen shouted, "look Fritz is wearing racing pants!" Then he said, and I quote, "he would not wear them to the Shit House!" He had a pair the next season. He probably got his free!

Rolland Blazzy was in our group. He was great fun to ski with. A powerhouse who skied with aggression, and, as usual with skiers of this quality, his talent rubbed off on those lucky enough to be skiing in his company. I mentioned earlier that he and I gelled well together. I was to find that he and Werner never saw eye to eye with each other on skiing. To his credit, and knowing my relationship with Werner, he kept his feelings to himself. He was too big a person for cheap behaviour. There have been many here over the years who, had they had been more honest with themselves as to their own skiing ability, would have saved a lot of time and in the process, left the Profession a stronger "Beast" than it is today. This relationship between Rolland and Werner produced two events, as follows.

On one of our days we went up onto the Diavolezza near to the Bernina Pass. The weather was duff. Flat light, falling snow, so the group sat in the restaurant. We tried to ski on the top T-bar, at near ten thousand feet, but it was a waste of time. After a long time we all set off for the bottom. Diavolezza Cablecar was a new installation, and in the group there was no local knowledge of the run down. We set off and it was a *needle match* from the start. The speed Werner set off at was out of order, Blazzy was up his backside and I was not left dragging my tail. It was in no way fun, it was more like survival. There were men in this class who were very Swiss and serious about their position in skiing. While we were waiting for the bus some of these men were complaining most strenuously about the carry on. Hans Graff from Wengen went on about broken legs at the start of the season, he had a *moot point*.

Next day, skiing on the Suvretta in glorious sunshine, everyone was having a ball when it started again. Before I knew it we were going like the proverbial off the shovel! It was a vicious no give, no take, thing. How I kept up, I don't know. I remember being comfortable at the bottom and very pleased with myself. None of the rest of the group tried to follow. When we met up you could feel the hostility of our fellows! Later that night Christian Rubi got a grip of me. Herr Rubi had been a school master. After he was done with me, I was like a wee school boy. He had also dealt with the other two. There was no use me telling him I was only following the leader, he was not for listening. And my mouth was *shut!* This was one of the times when I got my skiing going good. So a bit of *slagging* wasn't too much to pay.

The difficulty Stager and Blazzy had with each other must have been a straight personality clash. I'm sure it had nothing to do with skiing because when I followed them down that long, long slope, they both skied more or less the same. This was Christian Rubi's Swan Song. He was retiring. He'd run this organisation since its inception, and I had been more than fortunate to have been taken under his wing. Kari Gamma from Andermatt would take over and run their affairs for most of the next thirty years. He would become prominent in the international ski teacher's body, where he would bring a wise firm hand to those affairs for many long years.

On to a lighter vein. Jeanie my wife was in a good class of five. She had a local ski teacher who was also a mountain guide, always a good combination. The rest of our group with their St Moritz teacher were having a great time. What they were seeing here could only help them in their outlook to any future they'd have in skiing. It was a long way from the Red Clyde to St Moritz. Karma would bring me back to this marvellous Ski Station on a number of occasions.

Like all experiences good or bad, they do end, then you move on. We had parked our cars in an open car park and more or less abandoned them for the two weeks. They were frozen solid. Bobbie's was starting to be towed away, and for some reason he got out just as the mechanic started to tow. If you had seen Bobbie getting back into that motor, it was like something out of the Keystone Cops! We had to wait some hours for the cars to thaw out in the garage. These were the days before the motorways. The drive back was horrendous, with ice and fog all the way through France. It would be years before I would drive back out at that time of the year.

Back home the season got under way. Harry McKay my climbing partner on the "Naughty Rock Climb" became our ski school manager that season. As Harry and I were old friends with many solid good times behind us, we became a good team. Harry was good at managing things, very responsible and loyal all the way to the wall. Loyalty was something we from our narrow background of the Red Clyde took for granted. Over the next few years we would learn that it's not to be taken for granted. Loyalty is not a ball and chain round your ankle, it's a pattern of behaviour in your conduct with those who you are very close to. Harry was another one of these who lived by these standards. Harry would stay in skiing for the rest of his working life and in so doing become a well loved pillar of strength to all who worked with him.

It would be around this time that *new* people started coming in to our lives through skiing. Unlike most of our long established friends they did not have

154

industrial or climbing backgrounds. This in itself made the relationships all the richer. In those first ten years or so when skiing in the Cairngorms was setting down roots, it was like living on a new frontier. Energy seemed to be boundless. Each day was fresh and exciting, and there was so much to do. Most people enjoyed being part of the growth of the Great Enterprise. There was a *feel* about it.

Like all New Frontiers, the pageant had a downside. Everything did not come out trumps! There developed a "them and us" syndrome between the foreign would-be-ski-teachers and the home-brewed would-be-ski-teachers. This was started, as I saw it, by those would-be-instructors whether they were native born or otherwise. It's always the poorer performers in their own skiing who become involved in this nonsense. The good skiers, *do* it, they don't *talk* about it. How often have you heard in the nineteenth hole on golf courses high handicappers talking about fading and drawing the ball onto the green? Many skiers are just as daft. Climbers never seemed to get into shooting the breeze about how good they were. The price of most mistakes in climbing usually result in much more than a broken leg, it's usually in a rubber bag. We even had non skiers who were involved in skiing contributing to this diatribe. Everybody was an expert. I seldom got any of this crap. There were two words that people like me used for *daft blethers* such as these!

If this account had been written closer to its happening, I'm sure I would have used more explicit language to describe just how I felt at the time. However, with age comes dignity! What took place was a course run by ski school proprietors with Arni Palm. It took place and having done so, it left no mark apart from a bad taste in some of our mouths. There was so much work to be accomplished, we did not need any of this childish side-tracking of work which had just been successfully and officially carried out by the newly mandated BASI.

During this winter we produced our first Ski Teachers Licence. I copied this right off the Swiss Skischulleiter Patent. All I did was change the words from German and French to English and alter some words. This substantial well presented rather handsome booklet was very well received by our enthusiastic members. It was tangible. Something they could feel and touch, something you could be proud of. I have always carried mine with pride.

So where did BASI stand in the middle of the 1964 season? Physically their collective skiing was much the same. The big steps in this department were not too far distant. About half of those who became members through our first examination would be on their way to other pursuits by the end of this season. They'd be replaced by a new breed of Ski Teacher and as I said, it was sooner than it appeared possible when we first started. Skiing in ski schools all over the world was in a state of flux as far as what and how they taught. To be honest *technique* was just really being looked at and starting to be understood. This part of skiing is the realm of very few skiers. Few people had that depth of knowledge at that time. It's still much the same today.

Very many people in skiing used words that did not relate to what was really happening. Nomenclature in use in the technique was often wrong. It sounded impressive, but in the important areas it was describing what was taking place wrongly. This does no good in disseminating the means of teaching skiing, in any shape or form. This is still going on and I'm afraid it will continue, for the simple reason that some people think fancy-sounding words give what they are saying more impact.

During this time we had became members of the International Ski Instructors Association. Kari Kamma, the new boss of the Swiss Association, arranged for our membership. That May a meeting of this Association was called to be held in Italy. We were accordingly invited to send delegates. Easier said than done, as we had *no dough!* Funds had not yet been accumulated. How to take eleven out of ten, was always a *nippy sweetie.*

We had fifteen candidates for the spring course. I suggested that I take the fifteen candidates and make one class. We'd save a trainer's wage. This helped us raise the money and we sent two members on the Italian trip. This took place during the first week of our course. This was a mighty step for us considering there was almost no money. We ran a few dances and raffles, no doubt illegal! The delegates did without pay. Hans Kuwall went because of experience and a full member, Walter Hay, who had qualified on our first course. He had been elected onto the committee by the new members so it seemed proper to send him. Association fees were three guineas, £3.15, Grade twos, were one pound fifty. We did well getting those two to Italy.

Even out of this wonderful step into our future we got serious trouble. On the Monday of the second week of our course a candidate complained that one of the delegates to Interski had told her that, when they had been at Interski, they learned what we in Scotland were teaching was wrong. It was certainly was not Hans. It had been the newly qualified Grade One who had been to Italy. As I said earlier a little knowledge is dangerous. A little more is a disaster. You'd have wondered if his head was buttoned up in the back in any half decent way. The rest of the course heard this.

Now the girl who complained to me was one of our better skiers who at that time fortunately knew about skiing. That night I made a straight-from-the-shoulder no-nonsense statement that what was being taught was what they would be examined on. I also in no uncertain manner gave the "Fountain of Knowledge" a directive to keep away from my class. Some time after the season was over, I told him what would have happened to him if he had pulled that crap in Switzerland with Christian Rubi. And as far as he was concerned, I was the British Christian Rubi for the time being! When I think back, I was in the middle of two weeks work, with nearly double the size of class it should be, and the weather was once again awful. With the top chairlift not operating all the time, we had a lot of walking. My mind was made up that no matter who was to be the director of training it should be made impossible for this to happen again. Despite our teething problems, we were getting along our road quite nicely.

We had our first professional lecture on that course. Eric Langmuir, the new Principal of Glenmore Lodge gave a lecture on map and compass. But it was more than just lecture. It was an illuminating and interesting story of moving about over mountain terrain. Eric was very much a mountain person, a climber of skill. He came into BASI's future very soon after that, much to my satisfaction.

Jack Thomson was now the elected Chairman of BASI. He was also the Head Examiner for all BASI's Courses. Ambiguity and loose ends would be cleared away, made tight, ship shape and Bristol fashion. The examiners for this course had all qualified on the first course. Once again this seemed appropriate and apparent for all to see. The candidates who failed to get their Grade One the first year, became Full Members this time. And came into the "body of the Kirk." Where did we stand as to having produced more good skiers? Not all that well. But a *firm base* had been established. The new crop was in the making. At the end of this course my big class presented me with a suitably inscribed tankard, which I keep well displayed to this day.

In our effort to clarify, neutralise and bring together different opinions we adopted the new Official American Teaching Technique Manual for immediate use. This had been written in an English speaking nation and written very well. It would tide us over till such times as we were in a position to produce our own Manual. Through the good offices of Eric Langmuir we made arrangements to run the next spring course out of Glenmore Lodge. Jack Thomson and I had a nice wee smug feeling about how BASI was going about its business. Glenmore Lodge even then held a most prestigious place in the UK's outdoor world and only associated itself with enterprises deemed worthy. So all in all, despite people doing daft things, our batting average was coming on.

Jeanie and I went for an Alpine spring holiday, where we stopped off in Lauterbrunnen. The reason why Werner and I would never ski together again was waiting for us. Werner was on a kidney machine. This was the result of having been buried in an avalanche when he was young, working as a mountain guide. I had a brand new car and was feeling on top of the world, looking fit. And here was Werner, a shell of the man I had known. At the same time his father was in an Interlaken nursing home, and was far from well. Frau Stager and I made a night visit.

This magnificent old bull entertained me with his usual rumbustious behaviour which suited both of us. We reminisced about our good times, me of course being the butt of the humour. Frau Stager had been spending her nights in his room. On leaving, I bade them good night, and old Ernst said "Fritz, God willing we'll meet again!" God was not willing. I never saw the Old Bull nor the Young Bull, again. This Karma we speak of, has two sides to it! There was a fifteen year gap before I would enjoy Wengen again. Commitments to Alpine skiing took another track. Several years later when our son Iain was racing at Murren, Werner came up to him and asked him, are you the little Fritz. Iain told me he did not look well. So ended our intercourse with the male Stagers.

Jeanie and I drove East through Europe, in a golden spring. The promise of the holiday seemed to have lost some of its gloss. With the new car, and the best part of eight hundred pounds to spend in anyway we wished, for the first time in our life, we could indulge ourselves. This was much money then! Memory takes me back through life where certain events stand out. Driving East Jeanie told me how she felt somewhat guilty, when she saw how ill Werner looked and how fit and well I looked. Knowing the man so well and seeing how poorly he looked, I had said to him, "you'd be better out of it!" His reply was, "I want to live." He was in no way angry with me. So much for us *macho* men.

That same winter, in our ski school we had a piper of the Black Watch Regiment who had played at the funeral of John F. Kennedy in Arlington cemetery. I asked him what it was like and he said it was very deeply moving and that they played the Flowers Of The Forest. That seemed to me very suitable for a U.S. President who had died in such a way.

A thought to close the chapter on. We had intended to spend our first weekend skiing on the Zugspitze at Garmisch-Partenkirchen. At the time we could have been there, a tremendous avalanche took place and swept over the sun terrace, down the ski slope. Some 20-odd people died. On thinking about this disaster, if we had gone directly to Garmisch-Partenkirchen, we could have well been involved in that tragedy.

15. A Little Bad, A Lot of Good

In October 1964 the new Coylumbridge Hotel with its ice rink was opened. This was set in natural woodlands by the side of the river Druie two miles up the ski road to Cairngorm. It was designed to fit its surroundings, even better it was run to very high standards. Another long step forward.

John Clemments, my American friend, passing through on his way to Switzerland, made the remark, "your area is well on its way now!" Even better the "Old Faithful" Corrie Cas T-bar opened. How that hand-made, work-in-any-weather-machine has served Cairngorms in the most outrageous weather conditions never fails to amaze us, the locals who have been blessed with it being there over the long years.

BASI ran its first Grade Three course. This was of one week in December. It was run out of the little Alt Na Craig Hotel in Aviemore. This was meant to prepare future members for grades One and Two. Experience gained with this one week illustrated to us that more time would be needed for the job, for the following reason. The skiing standard of candidates coming forward at that time was not up to what was needed. If the truth be bluntly told, we had gutted all the suitable skiers in our first two courses. Most of the fine people coming forward then were weekend skiers. Almost all of them were mountain users. This is what linked them to skiing, producing the interest and desire to learn anything to do with skiing, This course was the first available with the stamp of officialdom open to them. Naturally this was attractive to them. But clearly the root need of any candidate in ski teaching training must be to have an above average ability in skiing.

Luckily we had a small number of fulltime mountain people who were fortunate enough to ski during the week. They could be utilised. You can help make a reasonable skier start to become a instructor much easier than you can with a poor skier. That truth stands good nine times out of ten. The Grade Three was really started as a selection course. People could find where their personal skiing stood. In our efforts to make this more attainable for the candidates we changed the course to two weeks. We made it extremely clear on the application form, that *good parallel skiing* was mandatory. Even this was misunderstood. We were forced to include the proviso in the application form that skiers found not to be up to this standard would be excluded from the course. On many occasions I had the task of expelling some of these misguided folks. I would cherish a very low golf handicap. *But?*

Experience has shown you must start the way you mean to finish! If you do not go down this road, it's at your peril. There is skiing proof of this in our profession today. And that was how BASI Grade Three got its beginning. I was never in accord with having a Grade Three. Two grades are enough.

Another significant event of this new season, was the opening of our shop. This was built by ourselves in the middle of the village. Harry McKay, who was what you can only describe as a master builder, was in complete charge of all the building. Work started in May 1964, and we had it open for the middle of December. Harry was the Straw Boss and as such, carried the can. That went with the territory! There were never more than five fulltime workers on the job at one time. Jeanie and I left for the Swiss Director's Course in the last week in

November, and came back in the second week of December. When we left, the shop windows were still to be fitted. We were opened in time for Christmas. All the local pundits were left shaking their heads.

The snow was good for that first early December course. We had the use of Old Faithful, the Corrie Cas T-Bar. What an asset this was, in running a worry-free, pleasurable course. Eric Langmuir and his wife Mo were in my group. I remember finding this very interesting, him being the big Chieftain of the Lodge. With him and I having to work together in the spring this would be a reasonable way to baptise each other, with each other. Eric and I would work for about ten seasons during BASI's build up. We never once had a cross word. Eric was a no-nonsense Hard-Nose. He contributed very much invisible input into BASI in those early days that most people knew nothing about. I don't know if I ever thanked him. I thank you now, Eric. Also for the many tumblers of sherry in your living room before the evening lectures! How those helped to lubricate my tender vocal chords! Apart from it being *most potable*. Cooperation. We in BASI would step a mile in pursuit of this. At the "Lodge" with Eric this was forthcoming in the most unobtrusive and most welcome way.

A Group of BASI Grade I
left to right – John Angella, Neil Lafferty, Ali Ross, John Hynes, ?, Trainer Bobby Birnie,
Clive Freshwater, Lift Attendant Pat Stewart

At the Lodge at this time a new profession was "giving birth to itself" because of the variety of their work, and different skills that would be needed in the years to come. Such as the following. Climbing in all its many facets, sailing and skiing. Those hoping to become fulltime professionals would need to apply themselves in a very big way. To the great credit of the management of the Lodge it was made as easy as possible for their staff to improve their skills and attain these goals. It was in these environs that BASI found a base from where we could do our thing. This gave what we were doing an almost "having arrived" look, which at that time we certainly did not have. I knew that, as director of National Training, the road BASI had to travel was still a long Scotch Country Mile. And I fully understood that being linked to the activities of Glenmore Lodge could only be good for us.

In the spring of 1965 BASI ran its first course out of Glenmore. This was a time of proud satisfaction for Jack Thomson and myself, realising another bridge had been crossed. The Lodge sat close under the ski grounds, and the public rooms looked up into where the skiing happened. What better place to house such a course? This was *the* right place to be having our course! Coming off the hill each afternoon down to the Lodge for tea was a clincher to the day's activities on the snow. Candidates could wind down together. They could also talk to the other trainers. This made everyone feel much more part of what was taking place. They'd sit in private conclaves, possibly discussing the rights and wrongs of how we were doing our work. Which to my mind was a good thing. We were now using trainers who had been through the training and grading process. This again was correct and gave me satisfaction.

Out of the results of this particular examination, from six passes at Grade One, there was John Angella, Neil Lafferty, and none other than Alasdair Ross. They all had very high marks in the two disciplines, teaching and technical. Their marks were identical, from the possible of 200 in each discipline, they each had achieved 190. That was a remarkable coincidence. Even more coincidental, they were ski teachers in my ski school. And that comes straight out of my memory, crisp and clear! These results would show how BASI was starting to bring out good results from within its *own self*. The coming seasons would also be very fruitful.

We had our first end-of-course dinner. This was held at Carrbridge in the Rowanlea Hotel. Mine Host was Jimmy Ross, friend to climbers and skiers alike, a friend to all. A man truly larger than life. He was blessed with a golden heart with a free roving spirit. We lost him some years past. I'm sure there's many like me who miss him dearly and remember him with much more than affection. It was a long fine night. Many of those who were there would stay in skiing for a long time. Many are still contributing to the sport. Writing these pages have stimulated some very fond memories.

This season had been very productive for all who had taken part in it. Probably things were settling down. People may have been getting used to what was happening and contributing to the collective work, which was for the general good. For those of us in the middle, it had seemed a bother-free course. Maybe the bothersome ones could now see "*how the cookie crumbled.*" If I've given the impression that this was primarily a ski teachers' society, this was not intended. It's true to say however that skiing came to the attention of the hoteliers in Speyside through the early efforts of Jock Kerr Hunter running his first courses in skiing and climbing from the Aviemore Hotel. The Lord Douglas-Hamilton was Commandant. Now there's a fine title for such a simple task!

1965 First BASI End of Course Dinner
Clockwise – John Hynes, FF, Bobby Birnie, John Angella

Anyway, a start is a start. That was in 1947. As I mentioned earlier these were the first organised ski courses. 120 people took part during the two separate weeks of these first two week's of organised ski teaching on Cairngorm. There was an immediate demand for a repeat course in 1948. Hugh Ross, the manager of the Aviemore Hotel, was delighted to have them back. That could have been when the Smith's Hammer striking the first blow onto the anvil started off what we have on our Scottish hills that serves today's skiers. If so, ski teaching was a very important part of the catalyst that started the endeavours that brought us to where we are today.

From these simple and unobserved activities in 1948 to our third spring course almost two decades later in 1965, skiing was starting to move forward, and with it came other people who started to bring their different skills and influence to bear on what was taking place. While we were getting on with establishing our image in the public's eye on the hills – a difficult chore by any occupational comparison. These others were the hoteliers, boarding house, bed and breakfast operators, many of whom had been working quietly away in skiing for many years. In a previous chapter I spoke about how successful the Scottish stand had been at the Ski Show in Alexandra Palace, These were the people who made those six days the success they were.

To name a few there were George Cameron of Boat of Garten, Jimmy Ross of Carrbridge, Cameron Ormiston of Newtonmore, Wilma Riley of Nethybridge, and Colin Sutton of Granton on Spey. These were all so completely different, I'm sure that's what made their collective input to what was taking place in Speyside the success it was very quickly becoming. These folk stride their paths through life at different speeds, with their own shades of patience, arriving at where they want to be in their own time. That gave this communal enterprise its strength and more varied and better balanced. Old Alpine villages stand witness to this so delightfully today. This becomes possible when many small businesses work toward a common goal. This situation prevailed at the time of Speyside's commercial beginning in skiing. This is how it stands today for the most part. There are many younger people working in many of the outdoor pursuits in Speyside who should find this of important interest. There may well be people reading this who remember all or some of these events in their making. If you're one of those, you have been privileged. In matters of great importance, a beginning only happens once!

December 1967 Grade III Course Trainers
right to left – Bobbie Birnie, Joe Docherty, Ali Ross, FF, George Shields, Ian McPhee
Competition to spot Tim Whittome

When a new thing starts to grow, becoming part of people's way of life, it brings out certain personalities. They come in all different shapes and sizes, male and female. Males have been mentioned mostly so far. After three full seasons of ski teaching being dealt with in a serious manner the strong characters started to stand out and, all things being even, among them were the Ladies. Wilma Riley of Heather Brae Hotel Nethybridge, not a ski teacher, she had no need of the use of a ski teacher's jacket to make her mark. She lived in her own jacket. She held her own corner and still does to this day. There was Hilary Best, a Ski Teacher. She had already had struck her own coin. She was the youngest ever qualified

Grade One. Not bad in what was a male chauvinist world. She didn't need ski teaching as a vehicle to gain attention. She was her "own person."

There was Hazel Bain! No one who has been in British Ski Teaching since the mid fifties up to 1992, could help but know Hazel. In the second year of my teaching on Cairngorm Hazel was a pupil with me for a week. I remember little of the week. It seldom fell to me to teach intermediate skiers. At best, at that time, that's what Hazel would have been. Many years later she related how I, at the end of that week, privately advised her to give up trying to learn to ski "as she'd never make it!." I was serious. She had no talent, poor balance and weak legs. How wrong I was, and it was Hazel who made me wrong. In the process of making me wrong she became what she was in our part of the skiing the world. She was one of the most respected of all the successful people I've known during my long career in skiing. And here is how she arrived at where she did. After getting the Ski Bug, she worked in ticket offices on Cairngorm, at nights in odd jobs, anything to help maintain her presence in the ski grounds. It was during this period that Hazel became part of our group, and in time became a special friend to our family.

I invited Hazel to come into our school as an apprentice ski teacher, this gave her the opportunity to ski in our ski clinics. From this, after a number of seasons, she won her Olympic Medal. She passed her BASI Grade Three. Success is relative. She became a first class ski teacher. A specialist with children and a friend to all the Mammies and Daddies. But she could never cross the Rubicon and become a Good Skier. She was trying for about her third time for her Grade Two. I remember clearly the morning of her exam, in Glenmore talking to Hans Kuwall, who was in charge of the examination. I looked at Hans straight in the eye knowing he was a stiff backed bastard like myself, and I broke every rule in the book. I said "you bring me back a new Grade Two" , I did not mention any name. In his wee tight Carrbridge accented English he answered me, saying "I'll try the best I can, Frith." Hazel was his dear friend also. I was the Director of National Training, and I was now passing the buck! Almost. To make a pun, I had left it in good Hands!

I never went near the examination that day, as was my wont. It was a long day's waiting. Hans came back to the Lodge from the hill late. He did not have to tell me the result. He explained that he held the Short-Swing part of the examination on the Headwall of Corrie Cas. Before I could say anything, he said, "I had to, because it was Hazel." To Short-Swing the Headwall you've got to be a *good* skier, which Hazel wasn't. Hans did what was right. BASI Two, was not in our "Gift" to give.

Hazel became the secretary of BASI in the early 1970s, then full time administrator. During the period she worked for BASI up to the end of the eighties, the scale of the work grew by possibly fifty fold. For a lot of the time she seemed to be left to get on with it. Near the end of the 1980's. she parted from BASI for reasons which were far from clear. Many members and other interested onlookers thought she had been poorly treated and badly dealt with. We who were close to Hazel knew how deeply grieved she was by how her long service ended. When will people ever learn?

Alastair Ross is a famous part of our skiing past and he came into it early on. He was not like Hans, Jack Thomson or me. He was of a new generation of skiers who had started differently from us. Alastair and I first skied on Cairngorm in the season of 1963. This skinny teenager came and asked if he could ski with us. He was so keen he was more than welcome. Any young skier would have been. Speaking later, he explained that he wanted to learn to ski well and become a ski teacher. He always stuck to straight ski teaching. He's the most successful all round British ski teacher in Europe. That will set the cat among the pigeons. I doubt if any other has earned as much in tuition fees. For any teacher, that's what it's all about. It happens that Alastair is, "by the way", good at *the caper!* So here we were at the threshold of something good. Something that was bound to happen, as sure as day follows night! I use Alastair as a fine example. Many have followed Ali in Europe, as we'll see.

Before 1965 was out, we as a family would attend the Swiss Ski School Director's Course. I say "as a family" because our 13 year old son accompanied us. Wilma Riley also accompanied us. She had her son Martin with her and this made for a cosy wee group. The course would be held in Crans Montana. This, sadly, would be my last attendance at this premier event which had been so good for me. With BASI growing so quickly my total involvement seemed to bring these exciting happy days to an end.

It was here for the first time that something was brought to my attention. Our son had been placed in the top class open to the public. We found the class was well below his standard of skiing. It seems I had not been paying attention to what was going on around about me. This was the first time my son Iain and I skied together in a serious way. On the last day in Crans we had a day to ourselves. Kari Gamma had brought the Swiss Ski Team to demonstrate for our course. Iain being a wee boy was excited about going skiing with his dad. I got him going about getting to watch Swiss racers. The Swiss team put on a terrific show. Iain was starry eyed. It had been snowing very heavily during the demonstration. As Iain and I set off skiing the sun came out. It was then I discovered, the boy could ski. Even at 13 years of age he could ski in deep snow and anywhere we went. From then on I'd keep my eye on him.

At the start of that week I learned something which shook me stiff. I ended up in a class of Ski School Directors with a trainer who was a dumpling of a skier. I was devastated how this could happen. I was shattered, disillusioned, and angry. My skiing went for a Burton. I managed to swing a move to John Clemments and Jean Pierre Zuber's class. Their trainer from Arosa, Peter, could ski. He was a Technique Freak, but, being a good skier, made that bearable. So all was well. How could this happen? It seems the poor trainer was well connected. He was from Klosters. I promised this would never happen in BASI. Naïvely, I never thought I'd suffer from that. I was wrong to take things for granted.

BASI had been invited to send an observer to a pre-season course in Norway. I had to attend on BASI's behalf. I would leave Crans and fly from Geneva to Oslo. But there's a wee story to be told before we get to Geilo in Norway. I would drive down out of Crans Montana with John Clemments and nip on the train at Brigg for Geneva. Easier said than done. Before I left Crans it seems I emptied Jeanie's purse of all loose change. That left her skint! It's a hard town to turn a buck. Anyway when needs must, the Devil rides. There was a horrific snow storm when we were leaving Crans. John's wee VW's wipers really couldn't handle the snow. Getting along to Brig, was murder. Luckily John was used to the Big Snows of the Rocky mountains. We'd have been better off with good wipers.

We met Zuber in Brigg. Flower Power was a big thing, and Zuber had dug two American birds from the course. They were wearing wonderful Flower-Power-Hats, things of great beauty. Jean Pierre had nipped one and would not take it off his head. It suited him. He could have worn any old thing and made it look good. We met other ski school bosses and then the fun began. How we were not arrested, I'll never know! We had a wee International Ski Teacher party. The bar owners just laughed at us. They also looked after us.

I'll never know how I got to Geneva. I remember waking in the morning at around six. I found a Bistro somewhere, had coffee, and a few "straighteners." I got myself to Oslo and into the Viking Hotel. There I took a well needed rest. Not bad for a Red Clydesider! That evening in the hotel bar I witnessed the rapid fire drinking of the Norsemen. They were business men and stood without talking, throwing drink down their throats as if the Grim Reaper was after them. Never have I seen men spoiling the pleasures of drink. They've a saying in Glasgow, "It was piggery."

Oslo's railway station around 7 am was moving with cross-country skiers. Family groups of wee tots, skiers of all ages, shapes and sizes. Outside, the streets were moving with them. I thought this a terrific sight. Here was a whole city on a Sunday morning, up and moving in pursuit of a real participator's sport. Some were still eating their breakfasts as they ran for the train. Maybe they had slept in.

The train was like a Swiss train of a very high standard. I was excited and looking forward to the fabled land of the Viking. The slow train travelled through forests held in the grip of a true *northern winter*. This was something new to me and I was in no way disappointed. The forest seemed to run forever and like the West Coast of Scotland there were very few people. Passing through the steep landscape, looking up and seeing terrain that would have been ideal for skiing but no facilities surprised me. The train was slow moving. The dining car was like we all think a train diner should be. The food and service matched the ambience, and I enjoyed a high quality meal. Just as well, as I'd find out.

Geilo lay in a flattish sort of landscape that was timbered differently from what I had been travelling through. The weather had been snowy. Geilo, in contrast, was smothered in a clear Arctic sky. Getting off the train I was dressed in my best Bib and Tucker:- collar and tie, blazer, thin soled dress shoes. You must look tricky, after all I was representing our country! All my cold weather gear was packed away in my case. I stood down onto the platform into the blazing sunlight, 25 degrees below. The 25 degrees shot right up through my thin soled shoes straight up into me. By the time I got a taxi to where I was staying, I was a Frozen Snot! As an ex Boy Scout I should have "been prepared!"

It was with where I was to stay that any Gilt went off the Ginger Bread. It was a Youth Hostel. Four persons to a very small room, in bunks. The food was at best, poor. I'm a man who had lived rougher than the average who would be there. So these circumstances were not novel to me. I had just left Crans Montana. It was night and day. It was the middle of the day and there was no skiing. No lifts were running. It turned out there was a very short T-bar down low in the village. Arni Palm turned up after dinner, made me welcome and introduced me around. The bulk of the people on the course were forty plus. There were a fair number of English outdoor types who were obviously very Norwegian oriented. So much so, some lived there, this being a common thing in certain parts of Continental Europe.

I mentioned this earlier that there is a tendency among some Brits in climbing and skiing to place what they consider "Top Performers" on pedestals. Arni Palm was placed in this category. The candidates had him on a pedestal like a Messiah. I thought a lot of Arni as a man. But? The skiing standard was like ski party leaders and artificial slope instructors. And that's me equating it to present day standards. There was a younger group of better skiers. They had this attitude towards Arni. I found this incomprehensible. The Swiss and certainly the Scots would not in anyway indulge themselves in such frivolous behaviour. Now I say this in no mean way. Arni Palm was a run-of-the-mill ski professional. What I now say, I say with deep-seated conviction.

When the people near the top of any pile start to polarise the top of *their* pile, they are on the slippery slope to being less than their total potential. British snow skiing suffers from it today. And has done for years. Climbing and Water Skiing do not and never have. They stand equal with their peers all over the world. A fact! *There goes the cat, running loose again!*

The content of the course was simple. It dealt with the fundamentals of introducing the early turning manoeuvres. It was very repetitive and drawn out. They were employing this extreme reverse leading shoulder. This was being used by some people of the same mind on Cairngorm, nothing new to be picked up there. Here we were in a country which had been skiing back into the dawn of history, with their shoulders square to the right angle of their skis in the Telemark turn, the first turn. As is executed today. And for some reason *beyond* reason, they were teaching an extra piece of crap into their teaching system. A *dogma*. Where it came from does not matter; the fact that they were doing it, did. Arni was covering the parallel turns in the same way. There was no reason for me to spend any more time there.

The snow conditions were superb, deep snow everywhere. The hill above Geilo was there waiting to be used. I asked Arni when the hill would open. His reply left me speechless. He said they were waiting for the weekend skiers to come up and track it. We had ski teachers skiing and we needed weekend skiers to track the slope! That was my cue for home. I told Arni that I had to go home as business was pressing. Once again I'd learned a lot. What we were doing in BASI was what was needed. I knew in myself we were right. I made that report verbally to the committee. I saw no reason for putting my opinions on paper. Not that I had any qualms in stating my findings. But why upset the nice people who had strong ties with Norway? There would be no grist to the mill from beating the drum. I got on especially well with the young good skiers, who "by the way" did not ski with one shoulder way in front of the other.

There was one from this group who gave a lecture on waxing for cross-country. It was excellent! He had Wee Donald Duck slides showing how the wax worked in conjunction with snow and the skis. Pure Genius! He gave the lecture in English! There was another evening when a man in his sixties came to give to give a talk. It was more a talk than a lecture. When he entered the large room, the assembly stood and gave this man a standing ovation. His subject was cross country. He spoke away in a mixture of English and Norwegian. I took the trouble to find out who he was. He had been a ski jumper. A very famous one. A most impressive man. Arni Palm came to see me off on the train. Despite the unhappy affair of him coming to Cairngorm and running that "daft" course which could have soured any relationship there was a healthy respect between us. And we parted friends.

I had to stay over night in the Viking Hotel. After the Spartan conditions of the Geilo Youth Hostel I treated myself to the rooftop dining room in the Viking. I had a private Baronial Feast. It cost the best part of sixteen pounds. Heavy money in those days. That included wine and brandy. After the Geilo hostel, I was due a breakout! (Or was it a "blowout?") Paid for by myself, not BASI! The flight from Copenhagen to Glasgow was on the New York Clipper. The plane was an old fashioned turbo-prop, stopping at Prestwick for Glasgow. The plane was near to empty. The "room service" was that good, I felt like staying on. But no dough, you cannot go!

On the train back to Aviemore Hans Kuwall got on at Perth. I explained to him he would need to pay for the drinks. No bother to Hans. Clive Freshwater, a member of staff at Glenmore Lodge, was on the train. He was tickled with Hans buying the booze. I gave him his chance! Clive would become a *main player* in the outdoor life in Speyside from those early days and up to the present. So here we were on the threshold of the coming season of 1966. A lot of ground had been covered.

The new hotel at Coylumbridge had started its own ski school. There were 8 young Swiss brought over to work in it. They had a few good skiers. To their credit they fitted into a difficult situation that existed here at that time. They had a smart ski teacher from St Moritz in charge of them. He was Mario Veradari who had a string of languages and was as smart as a whip. He and I got on very well. We had friends in common in Switzerland which was pleasant. Mario and I would have pleasure together in his home town of St Moritz in the future.

Before we go forward into the season 1966 here is something that happened near the end of 1965. In my first season on Cairngorm Bob Clyde asked Hans Kuwall and myself that, if the Chairlift paid the two of us, would we work together and train the local juniors at weekends? Hans and I were delighted, and we worked together until Hans went to take charge of the Hillend ski slope in Edinburgh. I kept the training going, the numbers of juniors grew and the training settled down. It became very successful. In its first season of 1963 our children beat all the adult teams in the eliminating team race, the Tennent Trophy, beating the favourites, the Dundee Ski Club Team. Oh how I liked that!

The Scottish National Ski Council was formed in May 1964. In its effort to promote Junior Training nationally, it decided to run National Junior Training. In their "wisdom" they wrote to all the known trainees informing them to turn up for National Junior Training during the Easter holidays. They seemed to forget to write to and inform the people in charge of our training, principally, *me!* When I made enquiries I was more or less told that it was all organised. So much for good relations! The powers that be had appointed one of the Swiss teachers from the Coylumbridge Hotel to run the this National Junior Training.

I had Luke O'Reilly, Emily Worrall from the British B Team, Ali Ross and some others working with our usual spring training. All our Cairngorm Trainees and the Glencoe kids turned up and reported to me. That was by far the bulk of kids involved in training at that time. The ironical twist to this completely unnecessary stupidity was that Walter Brugger, the Swiss boy, reported to me presuming that I was chief of training. I tried to explain what the situation was. He found it impossible that things could be so screwed up. He said he wanted to be part of our training. I wasn't thinking too straight and wasn't for it. Dear little 18 year old Emily Worrall nipped me and said to take Walter with us. The impasse was over. Walter was excellent with the Juniors. He was lovely young man. We produced between us a most impressive ten days training. Walter's boss, Mario, said later that I'd handled the crazy situation well. It was Emily who had handled Frith well!

On the day of the Downhill Luke and I were waxing the skis for our Juniors. At that time waxing did not have the high profile it has today. The race was being run down the Corrie na Ciste. We were waxing in the workshop of the top station of the Chairlift. We had mixed a concoction of wax we thought suitable for the snow. This in a gallon pot. Luke had skied on it, and declared it suitable. Not only did we wax for *our* kids, most of the kids had their skis waxed by us. We waxed around sixty sets of skis that morning. That is some chore. We sure needed the gallon pot of wax.

The story does not end there. That night at the prize-giving in Carrbridge Hotel, one of those responsible for the balls-up that almost wrecked the training, had the effrontery to say that "the training worked out well." That stuck in my craw! But he was not finished, as he topped it off with "don't you think you got some of the wax wrong." That was enough. I was tired, and none too chuffed with this one and some of his side-kicks. I asked him very bluntly what he could possibly know about ****ing waxing skis. He was shocked. I was sick of these weekend experts. My lady wife overheard this unpleasant exchange. She does not always agree with my behaviour. On this occasion, she said, "he deserved what he got!" No matter how bad the wax might have been, all the skis we waxed were waxed with the *same* wax. So all were equal!

This part of the narrative has got to be told, for the very reason that it's part of how some training became what it is today. The same kind people are still making decisions about how racing and training is run and controlled today. I don't use the names of those involved - there's no need. People who took part in the many different facets of this story, from which ever point of view they held, know what happened. In these last pages I've been forthright and downright blunt. I had to be. In my opinion its the only way to describe how the training was approached by the people who seemed to presume they were the ones who should be in charge. You would wonder if that way of thinking has changed much at National level.

16. Trouble in Racing, Success in BASI

Learning time was on me again. Before 1966 season got started, prior to a meeting of teachers in our school, two of them approached me in a very formal manner. They announced that they were resigning from the ski school. I was more than surprised. What amused me later, was the use of the word resignation. There was nothing to resign from. And that's not being smart arsed. There was something said about they didn't like how things were being run, then they were off. Not much room there for any kind of dialogue! I had been responsible for obtaining a house for one of them, when houses were almost impossible to get hold of in Aviemore.

The previous winter was so poor, there was little teaching work. I had kept these teachers on wages straight through the season. I'd learn as time went on that this sort of thing happens. You must never let these things annoy you too much. By the time the meeting with the other ski teachers took place I had my head straightened out. That was lesson one. I met the other teachers later and explained what had happened. They seemed to be surprised with what had taken place. There was no discussion about what had happened, nor would I have had any. We fixed the money for the coming season. Before the meeting came to an end I made it very clear now that everyone had agreed on how we'd work together for the coming season. And the matter was closed.

Jeanie and I were still in the caravan. We were just leaving for dinner, when one of those who had not long left the meeting we'd had, turned up wanting to talk. Before he started I said that I hoped he was not wanting to talk about what we just concluded. I was mistaken. He wanted more money. I'm sure he said something about him being better than the others in the school. I don't know where he got that idea. Anyway the deal had been made, the die was cast. And the new deal was now off, as far as he was concerned. Opinions and actions where two parties are involved are natural. It's also natural for either of the parties to react to any decisions that may effect them. And I had just reacted as far as the above person was concerned. The use of personal power can be a two edged sword. If we all went through life without odd contretemps and mistakes, we would have little of importance to yarn on about.

Anyway, as the ancient pageant of life constantly shows, there is no person or groups of persons irreplaceable. The school was still well staffed, and there were new younger ones. Ali Ross, Emily Worrall, a new one; John Lumpton, a Londoner and ex soldier. He was also an excellent skier. Harry McKay, Neil Lafferty and others. Some Kick Off for the Season 1966. Anyway, life goes on. A dream had arrived, the new bottom chairlift. This turned a big corner for Cairngorm skiing.

Before the end of the decade BASI would gather into its ranks a New Breed of indigenous skiers. There'd be a proportion of women, who, apart from skiing well, gave us a balanced look. This new blood brought the quality of their skiing which had been garnered in the young part of their lives, where skiing was something they'd taken for granted. This must have forged an inbred confidence in their outlook to skiing and their right to be there. As one year came on top of the other, the visual part of professional skiing became much more professional to look at. That was very important.

Like every other skiing country in the world we developed Ski Bums. This was an American manifestation, which unfortunately came to most Alpine countries. The Swiss didn't suffer from it. We had it. They've tapered off to almost nothing in the last ten years or so. They were obvious, they were Bums and must be mentioned because they were part of the scene and should be included in the narrative. Many of them came forward as candidates for BASI qualification. Not many were successful in passing at the level they aimed at. They seemed to treat what we were doing in BASI as part of the Fun.

Paul Turner was one of them, he was being examined by John Angella and myself at Grade Two level. At the same time an Eric Morrison was in the same group. Paul had been working as an instructor. He had no idea what he was doing, his performance had nothing to do with teaching skiing in any way. Eric Morrison was taking his Grade Two, he had a big problem. He was a personal friend of mine, and as such he'd need to be put through the hoop! Eric came on after Paul had been doing his teaching practice. Now John and I had given Paul a lot of extra time in his teaching practice to help him try and draw back some marks. His eventual marks were appalling. Eric was not the skier that Paul eventually became. He gave a demonstration on that day of high quality ski teaching, I was carried away watching his performance so much so that I forgot to stop him. John Angella quietly asked me if I had something against this guy. When I looked at Eric sweat was dripping off him. Poor bastard!

I tell this story to illustrate that passing our examination was a serious undertaking. I never knew Paul very well at that time. He came and asked where he went so wrong. I explained about the difference between Ski Bumming and professional skiing. A couple of years later he passed, with flying colours. We had been working together. He was a tall Irishman, and a good natured rascal of great charm. He and Ali Ross stayed in Coylumbridge Hotel. The manager at that time was nobody's fool, a man of the world, yet he gave them the run of the place including the A la Carte menu. They stayed there for free. Ski Bosses cannot get enough ski teachers of this calibre; it was so even back in those days. They are still hard to find.

BASI would in the next two years make big inroads in establishing itself. People came from outdoor pursuit centres. Eric Langmuir was a great help. This was important to us. All the staff from The Lodge became solid members. All of these people reached the top of their profession. I'm proud to have worked with all of them. In those early years we had some great end-of-course parties in the Lodge. Lifelong mountain based friendships had their beginnings from these courses. This in itself started a camaraderie which we all enjoy to this day. We had our first Austrian candidate, Ludwig Langreiter. He worked as a ski teacher on Cairngorm. He was a good skier. I remember asking him the reason for coming to our Course. He said he wanted to see how well he could do in the results. He was above average. At that time we still had Austrians working in ski schools on the Cairngorm who had no qualifications whatsoever. When we started out to establish BASI these young men stood back and naturally looked at "what we were about" with what was nothing but scepticism. Well, the days for sceptics were past.

Jack Thomson and I worked out an arrangement whereby foreign ski teachers who had been working in Britain since BASI's inception, would be offered a special Transitional Course of two weeks. This was a once only offer,

171

never to be repeated. Native born were not to be included, as it was agreed they should have taken the same road as so many of their peers had done. We made sure that the few who fitted in this special arrangement knew about it. If at any later date they needed our qualification it would mean going through the full training and grading. One came and went through the whole gamut. Karl Luttenburger. A rascal. All this was done with the approval of the full committee. There was never any chance of any decisions being made in pursuit of BASI's business without the committee's agreement.

We did have at that time an arrangement where fully qualified teachers from other countries working here would be offered a one week adjustment course and become Full Members. The Americans had started this system because of the influx of European teachers. Something similar had to be used some years later for a problem on English plastic slopes. By pure luck this was when a national body which had been planned for some time was on stream and working. It was called the British Ski Instruction Council. This had been established by all the national skiing bodies. Its function was to mediate in any extraneous matters concerning the general good of skiing and ski teaching in UK. All the above matters for the rationalisation of BASI's affairs into the future had been welcomed and approved by BSIC. BSIC was first mooted by the Scottish National Ski Council in 1964 and was formed in January 1965. Jack Thomson and I represented BASI during the period of its fine work. This work consisted of maintaining as high a standard in all aspects of British Ski Instruction as possible. BSIC during its life had an independent chairman by the name of Peter McGeoch. Peter is one of those in the list of honour at the beginning of this narrative. By pure chance a dear friend of mine and one of the Red Clydesiders. Peter was one shrewd son-of-a-bitch. He could keep the peace when tempers were running amok.

There were 12 members on the this very national body. There was one man on the board who was memorable. He was a full General in the British army. General Sir Roderick McLeod, Roddy to friends. He looked like a Hollywood General. He and I *cut the custard*. He spoke with a quiet modulated voice which was backed by a clear-thinking head. He represented the N.S.F.G.B. They were very lucky to have such a man on their side. Oh yes, there were sides!

One of my very strong memories of a very strong man was as follows. We in BASI wanted a clear answer to a direct question about something that we thought the Federation had done which was wrong, but important. Roddy had really horsed me about for two or three meetings until I nailed him. I had him dead to rights! He had to admit what I had said was right. It was the first time he lost his cool. The meeting was being held in Edinburgh. At the end of the meetings it was our habit to retire to one of Edinburgh's Conservative Clubs. And very nice it was. Roddy had established the habit of buying the first round, always a large malt of his choosing. When we settled down he said that I had nearly made him lose his temper. I explained that would not have helped his *lost cause*. What a shame a man of his calibre was carrying a Slippery Baton. Jokingly I said that ex NCOs from the British Army are hard to screw. He saw great humour in this. Not many like him come along every day that you're lucky enough to meet.

While BSIC. was in place the standards of all parts of instruction in the UK were reasonably maintained. Unfortunately the manoeuvring of the politicals got up and going. The outcome of this was that at a BSIC meeting held in Carlisle on the 11th June 1973 it was announced that the following parties had decided to discontinue their support of BSIC. They were:-

Scottish National Ski Council
National Ski Federation of GB
Association of Ski Schools in GB.

It seemed to be all cut and dried. The Chairman, Peter McGeogh knew nothing of what had been obviously arranged between these parties. BASI certainly had no inclination as to what was afoot. Why did they not bring it up on the Agenda and have it carried properly and honestly? They would have had their way. BSIC could not exist without their complete cooperation. Poor honest Lewis Drysdale was very embarrassed. We who knew him understood it was done despite any influence he may have had. I made so bold as to say so to the meeting. I apologised on behalf of BASI to the chairman for the shameful treatment he'd received. He was grateful for the sentiment. I think he said he was not used to affairs being run in such a manner. They could not look Jack or me straight in the face. I told them calmly what I thought of their unprincipled behaviour. Wasted breath! This would be one of the most disgraceful acts I can remember in my whole life in skiing. It was all the worse for being a completely unnecessary blunder. Going through the minutes of the meeting and other correspondence on the events, it is very pleasing to remember the only organisations who made any objections to what was taking place. There was the Principal of Glenmore Lodge, Fred Harper, who wrote a letter to that effect. Also Barbara James and Roger Orgill. Roger was Deputy Principal of the National Outdoor Centre at Capel Curig, North Wales. They were writing on behalf of the Ski Council Of Wales. It's even more important to note that they were all involved at National level in training British Mountain Guides. Here is an extract of a letter from BASI's secretary Clive Freshwater to the Hon. Sec. of BSIC, Guy Chilver-Stainer:-

BASI   *17th October 1973*

Dear Guy,

With reference to the last meeting held in Carlisle and the suggestion that BSIC should be dissolved.

BASI intend to discuss this at their next meeting in October. For the time being though, it is felt that this would be a retrograde step, not in the interest of promoting ski instruction standards. We are already appalled at the suggestion that ASSIs (Artificial Slope Ski Instructors) should be regarded as suitable teachers for mountain areas on condition they don't leave the pisted areas. It is well known that in many resorts, lifts take people to pisted slopes that are totally unsuitable and positively dangerous to students even in the best of weather, and almost all of us have at some time been overtaken by mist and cloud on unfamiliar terrain and it demands a high standard of not only skiing but mountain knowledge to lead pupils safely down in these conditions. How is it possible for sensible Educationalists to justify taking four weeks of training to make a "Winter Leader" in mountaineering and only a weekend course to make a "Winter Ski Leader."

BASI feel that standards are being lowered dangerously to accommodate the enthusiastic educationalists anxious to show how many children it can push through a ski programme, but without paying due regard to technical ability, teaching ability and above all, safety.

It is only by the retention of BSIC. that standards can be maintained at a really safe level for the student, through the training and experience required of the present ski instruction syllabus, and BASI will fight to see that this is done.

The above is part of a longer letter to the Hon. Sec. of BSIC. Little good it did. They did disband this essential controlling national body. There have been many tragedies before and since involving children while being looked after by people well short of the minimum skills required for such a responsibility. What Clive Freshwater foresaw happens today. The situation has not been improved in any way. If anything, it's more diluted. This makes salutary reading if you have any reasonable standards in ski teaching.

For all you young aspiring BASI candidates, I have this to say to you. If the people who disbanded BSIC had been left to set their standards for becoming a "National Ski Teacher," it would be less onerous than it is, under the democratic management who control the National Ski Teacher Training as it is set up today! It certainly would be a much more *shallow achievement.* As Clive said, disbanding the British Ski Instruction Council did no favours to the future of British Ski Teaching. This was our first experience of something that can only be called what it was. Back Stabbing! In a less polite society that is what they would call it. Mind you, in less polite society you don't get any of this sort of unmanly behaviour.

Back to the middle sixties and the closing of that decade brought to BASI new skiers and they carried with them skills more plentiful than we started with. They also brought their own notions and personal idiosyncratic ideas of how to ski. This is a normal healthy result of collective progress. All ski teacher societies from their ranks produce ski technique "wizards." Ours was no exception.

My first experience of these pain-in-the-arse individuals, and individuals they are, was at the Swiss Ski School Director's Course. They had one by the name of Manfried. If you were a "new boy" the Old Boys would set Manfried on you. Fair do's. I went through it, as did my two American friends. In the large scale of the Swiss set-up this was easily absorbed. In our wee tight narrow ski world this was impossible. The one we had seemed to make a bigger impact on our affairs than his skills would have justified. If our Profession had been established and more mature this would not have happened. In this case he was given enough rope, and the cure sorted itself out. We don't seem to have them any more. Maybe there are so many skiers skiing well that they are not noticed.

If you think I'm avoiding putting names to some of the players in the narrative through the text, I'm not really. Those who lived and enjoyed these days will know the character involved. There's nothing being said that's disparaging about anyone. What's being described is my memory of what we all did together, coloured by my opinions. As for readers without any knowledge of the events, the names will make little difference to the story.

Before the end of the 1970s there would be around 70 new Grade Ones, most of them working on Cairngorm. Human nature being what it is, from this number about half a dozen emerged with strong views and opinions on how BASI's affairs should be handled. From this developed what is popularly called the "politics." With this inevitable happening, BASI ended up with what every other organisation has. The burden of petty politics. These politics were mainly about the method of the skiing we would pursue, or to be more accurate one or two Fine Points. One is not sorted out yet. At least that shows a wee bit of good old fashioned stubbornness. The other was, of course, how BASI would be run. Fair enough. Unfortunately I think we allowed too much energy to be wasted on this kind of childish nonsense, to the great detriment of BASI.

Now I'm going to describe things as I remember them and I make no apologies for doing so. There were the odd individuals who seemingly adopted a particular Alpine country's skiing technique. Some of them actually copied what they thought were the habits and style of ski teachers of the country to which their alliance had been given. One of these misguided halfwits was observed teaching in an English Austrian accent on the White Lady run on Cairngorm. This man ended up on our committee. Democracy is expensive.

What I'm about to say is meant to sound the way it sounds. With the exception of two of these people, they had very limited Alpine skiing experience. Worse, their personal skiing was poor. It took a deal of forbearance to listen to them. Unfortunately they caused more bother than was obvious at the time. It is a fact of life that perverse behaviour is typical of these types. They've been gone a long time now and in their passing only the grey beards like myself remember them.

During the period 1965 up to about 1972 there was a large influx of good skiers into BASI. The written records show that this has not been repeated since. In the spring of 1969 I had a class of Grade Threes. Most had been in British Team training. Arthur McLean, Andrew Fitzsimmons, Richard Berry, his wife Sue, Ingie Christophersen, Ginny Cox, and Bridget Newall, now Mrs Fraser Clyde. This was an exciting class, if at times wearisome. They were so serious it was almost impossible to extract humour.

Arthur McLean, a local man, was expert in this department. Eventually he got them going. I had the distinct impression, that behind my back, he was in charge of that class. When I accused him, he denied it. When teaching these people you had to have the answers to the many commonsense questions on all aspects pertaining to skiing they constantly asked you. They were without a doubt the most nervous class I ever worked with. Their taut nerves were caused by their concerns of how they'd get by their teaching exam. Many others on the course presumed they would walk through the examination. This proved not to be the case. For some reason I could never understand, nor could I ever agree with, BASI examiners deliberately marked Team Members low. You could see why this could happen in teaching practices, but not in the turning of skis.

This reached a head in the spring examination of 1970. Ali Ross had a class of Grade Twos. They were almost the group as I mentioned above. In those days there was a separate mark for a free run. Iain, my son who'd been ninth in the French National Championships that season, was in the class.

A Fine Mixed Group – Ski School D'Ecosse 1970

Three "Pros"
left to right – Harry McKay, Self, Ali Ross

TROUBLE IN RACING, SUCCESS IN BASI

The free run was held down the White Lady which was a field of rolling bumps. Most of that class could ski as well as anyone in the UK. They gave a collective demonstration of bump skiing that up to that time had not been seen on any of our ski slopes. I remember thinking how far skiing in the BASI courses had come on. I was standing next to Jack Thomson as the last of the candidates skied by, and I made some remark about the excellence of the skiing and how good the marks would be. Jack showed me his marks. I was amazed. All of them had only made enough marks to pass. The rest of the examiners were the same. Now as Director of Training I had no say in the examination. That's as it should be. But I had a healthy and legitimate say about the results and I asked what was the possibility of getting near full marks. That's when Clive spoke out. He said "if you have a scale of marking, it should be seen to be used from its top end to its bottom end." I said to Jack I could not understand how after the exhibition of skiing we had just witnessed, the marks could be so low. He said you must be careful how you mark a class like this. They were being marked tightly in every other discipline. The marking here should have reflected their special skills in the end-form of skiing that had just been demonstrated. The marks certainly had not!

Another wee anecdote. Ingie Christophersen was taking her Grade One the following spring. She was a bag of nerves. Why I don't know. She skied like she could not put her foot wrong! But she did put a foot wrong. She was given the teaching practice of introducing snowplough turns. In all the teaching practices the choice of terrain can make or break a pass mark. Now, in total fairness to our examination policy, you were given half an hour's notice of what you were going to teach. More than enough time to get your brain in gear.

Ingie, with her loveable impetuosity, took her class on a steep part of the White Lady. This was a blunder beyond belief for someone of her ability. The slope she picked was so steep she could not get the class moving. They gave her time to rescue herself but she had gone too far. Even during the questions she never recovered. They failed her. They should have stopped her at the offset, sent her away to think and get her brain back in gear. It had been done before in 1968. But that had been with a Grade Three. With the young racer Allan Thomas. Ingie and I had been working together for two seasons so it fell to me to be nice to her, when I felt like putting my boot in a certain place.

She could teach the Baw Bees out of a Scotsmans Sporran and she managed to get herself failed. She was as close to the Fountain Head of BASI as you can get. So whenever I've been told, it's who you know that makes the difference to pass, it is then I feel like putting my boot in that "certain place." As I've mentioned before, Ingie is one of our very fine ski teachers. Like all true professionals, she came back and romped her Grade One.

I take the trouble trying to take the readers back into these happenings so that, by hearing how they took place, it may give an idea of how serious the responsibility vested in the examiners by BASI was taken. This was a two-fold trust. One to the candidates, the other to skiing in general. In the middle of this there was the Devil's Advocate, the Director of Training. He was solely responsible for getting everything to come together as a cohesive entity. And that included keeping the many very nervous candidates assured that they were all very special. I know that their trainers would in no way have allowed any of their class members interests to be impinged on, in any way. If anything, they would take any liberty possible to advantage their pupils. And they did.

After hearing how the most stringent treatment was applied to candidates, it may come as a surprise that it was possible for someone who was completely unsuitable to slip through the barrier. The barrier being an invisible thing that we hope experience should build in as we went about learning how to create a solid workable reliable set of rules to work by.

To make an analogy, the rules of golf have taken hundreds of years to form and grow. But they are based on undisputed performance. To gain your position in the order of things, your "handicap," it is necessary to *score* your way into becoming a first class golfer. This can only be done through the rules. A first class golfer is from about a three handicap down to scratch. You must score your way to this standard. Ski racers have to win their way into teams by racing against the clock. Climbers must climb their way to the top standard. To become a BASI trainer or examiner is in the gift of human judgement. Such judgement is cursed by human frailty, and therefore suspect. Another good comparison is the driving test. Now how to overcome this difficulty would test the wisdom of Solomon.

We have people who slipped through. As I mentioned I had a trainer in the Swiss Ski School Director's Course, who was way under par. But at least I was not under examination at that time. If you end up with one these lemons, as trainer you must be able enough to keep a weather eye on them. In my day as director of training we ended up with a few of these. One in particular was so wrapped in the vagaries of ski-technique, he could not come to terms with the simple every day act of skiing. Through his political influence on the committee he had to be given an opportunity to train a BASI Grade Three class. Political influence meant one or two on the committee supported him. If I had just bombed him out it would have been called "personal."

This man had been in my class during his Grade Three. For the first two days he tried to blind the whole class with ski-technique. I let him go on and on, then finally had to deal with him in no uncertain manner. This was done simply by good skiing, of which he was not capable. After this he was told to confine himself to the course programme. Two of the class, Jack Maxwell, a well respected local PE teacher, and John Cunningham, told me they were sick of him and he should have been stopped at the outset. I pointed out that if I had done that, I would have been accused of picking on him. He went on to become a Grade One. And that is how he finally got a Grade Three class. Straight off there were complaints from his class. So bad were the complaints that some of the class were ready to leave the course. By pure luck I managed to shift him and use him in another capacity. What a situation to be in when it goes against the grain, and all you believe in, to be lumbered with the likes of that. The other candidates in that class, knew exactly how bad he was.

17. Olympics 1972 and the Haute Route

The Junior training Hans Kuwall and I started became very successful and was growing. We who were involved got terrific satisfaction in working in it. Many of our juniors went forward into National Racing. Harry McKay, who had been so successful in Scottish Racing, despite his late start, was now helping with the training. This was something he was good at. His power of communication turned out to be very special.

Around this time I became involved with junior training back in Glencoe. This meant driving down on the Friday night or early Saturday mornings. This was the bind of the commitment, after a long hill day on Cairngorm the drive of 90 odd miles to Bridge of Orchy. West down past Loch Laggan, through Fort William, and at times driving round Loch Leven when the Ballachulish ferry was off when it was dark. Up through Glencoe. Snow tyres were not the big thing they are today, and the road was of pre-war vintage. It was a long haul at times. The welcome waiting made up for the drive. Glencoe Ski Club which would have maybe fifty members. Adults and children had built an impressive three level club residence which became known as "The Lodge." They raised the money and did all of the work themselves. When you saw the titanic effort of its members, you felt proud to have been a Founder Member.

No matter how wild the drive down had been, the welcome waiting in the lodge made the drive seem like a mere bagatelle. I had known most of these folks all of my adult life, but even though, I was treated very specially. Any help that was needed with the training, forward would step some of the most able mountain people to be found anywhere. There was no competition for position, something that was becoming more voracious at Cairngorm. This merry band of friends used all of their energies for the general good of *all* the members. What made this possible was that they were very practical. None of them had any commercial interests in the use of the mountains. Only in skiing. To try and describe all these individuals would be futile, so I'll take one of the group who will very much personify all of them.

In all societies leaders come to the fore. When this happens by a natural non-selection process, the leader is usually a person of the highest order. The Glencoe Ski Club had one of these by the name of Christopher MacGregor Lyons. In the start of this narrative Chris has his place in the Roll of Honour of Red Clydesiders. In the Lodge he held the exalted but unenviable task of being the "Doss Fuehrer." He made sure everyone behaved and enjoyed themselves, whether they liked it or not. This took a mighty talent amongst all those Clydesiders, not given to behaving like lambs. So when you arrived here, no matter how bad the drive had been, it was comforting to be back among your "Ain Folk."

The training was not too long started when it needed two of us to handle the work. Bridget Newall, now Mrs Fraser Clyde, who had skied with the National Team was the first of this group to come forward to this new part of ski teaching in UK. I know she was impressed with how these folks could work so efficiently together. I'm sure it was their personal kindness to her she enjoyed the most. Ali Ross was another who left a mark here. There is close by me at this time and in other parts of the world young mature adults who I'm sure will remember with deep respect and fondness the names I will be mentioning now.

179

In return I know that the teachers who worked in the body and close to the heart of Glencoe Ski Club's wee-tight-big-world must be the richer in memory for having been part of those early days. Others who followed them as trainers were all treated by the Club with the same care and attention. And despite their youth, as adults. There was Ginny Cox, who worked down there with Iain Finlayson. It seemed fitting that Iain, who started his skiing on Meall a' Bhuiridh, should be putting back a little into something that had been so good to him. Ginny and Iain did a great job for the Club.

Stan Watt and a French Canadian girl had a season down in the Coe. The girl spoke English with an accent you couldn't put a name to. Her name was McKenna. At the end of the season there was a thank you party for Stan and Annie McKenna. Chris Lyon our rhymer of rhymes had written a thank you. "The Ode to Annie," a tale of Annie's blunders and her very many successes. Chris wrote this in the Scots way of speaking, that is, according to "Lyons." He made a ceremony of reading it out in front of the assembled Club. Annie was dumbfounded and of course deeply moved. Chris had written this out beautifully, on a vellum type paper. She asked me to tell her carefully and in detail what it really said and meant. When I'd finished she was deeply moved. I suggested that it be framed and kept for her children. She told me she had every intention of doing that. I wonder if Annie has "The Ode to Annie" hanging somewhere in a homely, loving living room.

Of all the wonderful days of skiing that Meall a' Bhuiridh gave to me personally one stands out and this came from the Club Training. It would be more accurate to say, one of the most memorable of all of my best days of skiing anywhere, anytime. On a day that only the mountains of the West Coast of Scotland in winter can give you, I had my day. I was skiing with the young girls

1968 Young Ladies Training
left to right – Jeanette Watt, Evelyn Carmichael, Charlotte Horrocks, Carol Blackwood,
Jane, Self, Helen Carmichael, Jane Fowler, Anne Sandeman, Stella Shields
plus Girl in Helmet

of the Club. It was around the time in young girls lives when they were becoming young ladies. It so happened that at the time the girls of the Club were much better skiers than the boys. And pulling my rank, I was skiing with them. We'd been skiing all day "cutting the custard," as they say. We ended up at the top of the Spring Run. It was the gloaming time of day, the sun was Westering. On Meall a' Bhuiridh's summit ridge the view was staggering. You felt touched as by the hand of silence, and in the silence was the sense of freedom. Mountain life on occasions lets you have one of these days, but not too often to leave you blasé. I wonder what the girls were thinking in their youth and inexperience. They were not saying too much anyway. I remember saying, "let's see what you've learned!"

The run to the car park, something not often on the menu, can be made into a fair "bang off." I picked a line as rough and difficult as that terrain could produce. Above the car park it's steep and rougher, and, knowing their legs tired, I stepped the pace up. The skiers in the car park had been watching the girls, the speed of their skiing and places they were skiing through. None of the them faltered nor fell. We stopped near to my car, as the skis were being taken off I said nothing; it was a pregnant moment. As I was putting my skis on the car they stood waiting to be given their leave. I quietly thanked them for their good skiing. And bade them goodbye, till next week. I should have put my arms round all of them. Another moment missed! They were Anne Sandeman, Carol Blackwood, Evelyn Carmichael and Jeanette Watt. I'm sorry girls I never thanked you properly! I do so now.

In that year of 1967 another marvellous memory became mine. The BASI course was finished. It was the middle of May. One night late in our home, Frank Davies, a well known climbing shop proprietor from the Lake District, mentioned he was going to try the High Level Route the following week. Casually I said that I always fancied that. Jeanie said, "why don't you go?" A week later I was in Frank's old farm house in the Lakes ready to leave for Chamonix. The High Level Route is one of those goodies, like the Cuillin Ridge in Skye. This undertaking could be called a small expedition. It consists of climbing and skiing over a distance of 85 miles through the Hinterland of the high Alps, between Chamonix in France and Saas Fee in Switzerland. We started in Chamonix. Given the weather and reasonable party you should cover the Route in six days. We lost a full day after being storm bound for two nights in a mountain cabin, and as a result we stopped at Zermatt, a good place to stop or start any enterprise.

At Frank's I was informed that Helen Jamieson, one of my first young trainees, had been included in the party. Christian Bonnington who had been added to the group had arranged to have Helen along. This was to give the outing a wee touch of glamour. Chris had arranged to write an article for the Daily Telegraph Colour Supplement. Helen was by now a member of the British Ladies Alpine Team. When Chris got in touch with Maria Goldberger, the manager of the Team, Maria was not for allowing one of *her* girls to go unescorted, even if it was the High Route. Mountain users pronounce

Haute Route
Support Team Member
Jeanie Finlayson

it the French way, "Haute Route". When Maria heard I was going, all was well. I suppose I was to look after Helen. Helen was well used to roughing it. David, her father, did not rear her to be soft.

In the rest of the party was Neil Mather. Neil had climbed with Joe Brown on the first ascent of Kangchenjunga. John Wilkinson was another climber of no mean timber. Bob Brigham, a climbing shop proprietor, was a strong capable climber, well able to handle what was to come our way. Helen and Frank were the only two who were known to me. Meeting new people always makes for fresh interests and good fun.

Chris, Frank and I were to drive out to Chamonix in Frank's hot-shot rally car. But before we made the journey's end there would be a few bits and pieces of bother. Our first hiccup was when Chris turned up some hours late for the departure time! That was all right but Chris was to give a lecture in Lincoln, if I remember right. So rally car or not, the lecture would be starting late. In the world I lived in, ten minutes early and you were late! What the hell! I'd just finished nearly three weeks of being in charge of BASI's timekeeping. So I was just coasting.

When we arrived in Lincoln, to my amazement there were execution-like crowds all waiting to get seats in the theatre. The lecture, was "The Eiger North Wall in Winter." Christian and his slides were terrific. I could have listened to it twice through but we were running late. The organisers were so pleased we were taken for an excellent Indian meal. We were to drive straight to Dover. Problem number two! The car had been burgled! The skis were off. Chris's special camera case was gone. It was full of photographic goodies. There were passports and travellers cheques, all offski. My money was pinned in my shirt pocket. Old habits die hard! We had the all the gear back within the hour. The toe-rag thieves had been seen and nobbled.

In Paris next day while having coffee in one of those charming pavement cafés, we were informed we would need to wait until sometime in the afternoon while our travelling celebrity consulted with his French publisher. Without prior agreement with Frank, I told Chris he'd be better on the night sleeper. He could catch us in Chamonix next morning. This was agreed without discussion.

Before we got away from Paris Frank was not too pleased with the car. We messed about with it in a leafy side street. Having finished our hands were grimy, but as luck would have it, water was running down the gutter. Just the job for ablutions! As we were kneeling down washing our hands, a shadow came over us, and looking up we beheld a French Polis. He had the wee shoulder cape, a gun, a baton, and one of those wee queer Foreign Legion hats. He was giving us the beady eye. He shrugged his shoulders in that indifferent Gallic way and slouched off. I bet he was muttering to himself, "the mad English!" So I kept my Scots mouth shut! Mind you, the water in the gutter was definitely from a burst toilet. As a wee boy in Glasgow, I was used to playing in broken toilet drains.

Frank, like Charlie French, my American racing driver friend, could drive. We had a smooth run down into the high mountains. Life was good! Lunch in an old French Inn with its inimitable house wine topped off a most enjoyable drive. Chamonix is much like Zermatt in location and its historical past, as a sister-like village. This was the first time here in spring. Like all these high places, spring comes slowly. We have the same climatic conditions at around 1,000 feet. This is more noticeable if you live in these places and are concerned in outdoor activities. After the long winters it is more apparent to us. This I had learned in the immediate foregoing years. And here in the narrow confines of Chamonix's valley it was very obvious.

During the course of that first day the stalwarts of our wee expedition gathered together. This I was looking forward to. Neil and John were very pleasantly what I had expected. Good solid mountain men, with long years of classical climbing behind them. Bob Brigham seemed quite content to let things set their own pace. Helen and Chris were still to arrive. John, Neil and Bob were being filled in by Frank about the final details. As I remember there was a an objection about a "bird" being in the group.

A guide had been added. This was for insurance purposes now that Helen was included. Paid for by the Telegraph. We did not need a guide. Neil and John were a bit peeved. They had a good point. I assured them Helen would in no way hold the party up. She walked through it as most Scottish hill padders would. She had the odd wee bit of bitching. What could you expect, she was more less dragooned into this marvellous trip? She added a nice touch to what was for sure a male chauvinist cabal of Northern Brits. That in no way would fash Helen. She grew up in a society stuffed with them! Frank told me later the idea of the route was Neil's and John's. I explained to them that Frank let me invite myself. They were very pleased to have me. The three of us were good together. Before we get to the end I can tell you the whole thing was a roaring success. And certainly everything you would have wanted it to be.

These little memories of the in and outs of any enterprise are worth relating. They give the effort a fair bit of body. How sterile life's path would be if our affairs were all cut and dried, organised and run by rote. It was a wonderful treat to walk around Chamonix relishing the memory of my first trip in 1950. It was still the old Chamonix, with the strengthening sun of the coming summer adding new life to the expectancy of the new season. This gave me a feel for the place. It made me feel almost smug, knowing I was about to get another *big bite* of what was not up for grabs for most people. This was worth remembering.

Another wee anecdote. In one of the rooms Bob and Frank were sorting out their gear. To make a pun, they had a mountain of it! Good, that meant there was enough for all of us. They got me to worrying as, for the most part, they had soft kind of boots. They then made a point of telling me my "normal" boots would cripple me. Well, that would sort itself out. We'd two spare days. This turned out to be a good thing. These were super days. We got to run the famous Vallee Blanche. The skiing is nothing of consequence. Any weekend skier can manage it provided they are in a party with reasonable leadership. It's not worth doing in poor weather. Take a camera. The scenery is very special. Our second day was skiing on the Grand Montet. A cable car takes you quickly up onto this steepish peak. The views get anyone's adrenalin going. The skiing is steep. On our day the spring sun had the snow in a dangerous condition. What we found out was the group's overall skiing ability. Christian could more or less only run straight. Ambition is a heady nectar.

We met the guide on the morning we left. He was a member of a famous family of mountain guides and skiers, the Bozons. We had Francis. His cousin was a Gold Medal Alpine skier, Charlach, who had at one time skied on

Cairngorm. He died on the mountains. Not a bad way to go. Francis was the epitome of what the mountain guide should be. And looked the business. His demeanour bespoke the cool approach he took with his work. He and I got on fine. He worked fulltime training mountain guides in summer and ski teachers in Winter. This at the top national standards. This man was at the top of his profession. I'm sure Chris had given him a fair run down on the skills and the kind of people in our party. There's only one way you find out about people on mountains. That's by living with them, on mountains.

Bonnington, Jamieson, Finlayson

You can start the Route by short-cutting it up the cable car on the Aiguille de Montet. This would have suited me. We preferred to find the strength of the party by climbing directly up to the Albert Premiere Hut. This was a good idea. From the small hamlet of Le Tour up to the Albert Premiere Hut is 4000 feet of very steep climbing. When you move off the road you're onto the steepness rapidly. There's no slow adjustment. We were late in getting started. Helen and I were traversing across a very steep broken section when I heard it coming from above. A rake of loosened stones of assorted shapes and sizes. If you've been through this you know there is little to do. I pulled Helen close to a small outcrop of rock. She wondered what all the violence was about till the stones started bursting around us. As they exploded off the outcrops above, they left that evil smell of sulphur. I'm glad she never really knew how close this display of nature's power had been to a serious accident. No crash hats then. They'd have made no difference. Sweet innocence can be a staunch friend at times. Helen wanted to know how these things happened. I pointed out why we should not have been there at that time of day. And explained how and why the stones come down in the heat of the sun.

As we got out from under this naughty bit of mountain and stopped to draw our breath by the snout of the glacier, there was Alphonse Supersaxso from Saas Fee, a ski teacher friend of mine. The world is a small place, even on a mountain! Alphonse was a Saas Fee guide bringing a party through from Saas Fee to Chamonix. His hair was pure blond, his eyes were a pale blue, so much so they were startling. When he smiled the world seemed to smile with him. He was the epitome of the mountains, the way he apparently enjoyed just being there. We had the heat of the day for the short but steep and not so sweet 4000 feet ascent up to the Albert Premier Hut. There is only one way to handle that with rucksacks and skis. Head down, arse up. Shut down the brain (if you've got one), slow down and have done with it. If you for one moment let it get to you, it grows in size. It's big enough without giving it an extra advantage. Hurrying will only slow you. Helen did me proud. Her tough old dad whom I've told you about would be proud of her. But then it was he who helped make her able to handle such things. That grind up was good for anyone who may have been a mite concerned about their durability. "If you try i'ts nae bother!" It was also good for the group, being flung in at the deep end.

The Albert Premier Hut was named after the prince of the Belgians. Whatever for, I never found out. It was a new big handsome affair. There was an old stone beauty next to it. Anyway, ours had a weekend Guardian who had good tough steaks, chips and a fine house red wine. The French do get their priorities right, in the important essentials! The next day was the easy one of the trip. We put skins on the skis. With these you can walk up hill on the snow without sliding back. This makes a tremendous difference to the weight you carry. I don't know what a computer would say about that. It does make the carrying less onerous.

On the way up the first Col, Fenetre du Tour, it was just like home. We could not see a thing. We must have brought the Highland Mist along, or so it was suggested. The skin up to the lip of the Col Fenetre du Tour was comfortable and short. We dropped over a wee ridge to the north side. The ski down was a simple descent over the Plateau du Treint to the ice fall that led to Col du Ecandies. Here there were crevasses and seracs, deep slots and great blocks of ice. The guide made his way through this on his skis. That was all right, he was a fulltime skier, and I

Helen Jamieson

185

was the only other one there apart from himself. Helen had no trouble, but the others had fair bit of bother. If we had taken the skis off and walked in it would have taken a lot less time and less wear and tear on the others in the group. I would find this was the French way of doing things. It's part of their psyche. It in no way detracted from the man's excellence.

Once everyone was gathered at the bottom of the icefall, we then had a short climb up to a narrow gap to the lip of Col du Ecandies. Being at a much lower altitude the air was muggy and warm. Once again a bit like home. Even looking down from the Col's lip, it appeared like looking down a snow gully at home. The slope was steep and full of Gurram Goo. That means "real crap snow." After a rest we were faced with a slope steep enough to give some of our party more ski problems. The slope eased off in a distance of 150 yards. Some of the group had a bad time getting down. Walking would have been much better. With packs and skis skilled climbers could have slid down on their backsides in minutes. It would have been a brave leader who would insult the ability of skiers-come-climbers in this group to suggest they should walk when they could ski. *Hobson's choice*. An impasse. The snow was beyond the capability of recreational skiers. The guide, Francis, made light of it. Helen skied it well, as you'd expect. She bitched about the snow. When I skied down, Francis gave the Gallic shrug that said "professional."

From there down, the narrow valley became timbered, and there were great long end-of-winter snow slides coming down across our path. We skied straight over the top of these, and skied into a lovely wee Alpine meadow, the sort of dream campsite. The sun started to warm the dampness out of the morning air. We settled down to have a snack. The snow was melting round us as we sat there. I'm sure the Alpine flowers were pushing their way through into the new day as we sat. This is what I hoped the High Level Route would be all about. Dreams coming true. You've seen it all before, but it never loses its surprise. In the walk down through this gem of a place in the delicate morning air, we passed some beautifully sited holiday homes, sitting there as if by the hand of nature amid the pines and the young leafed birch. It was delightful. As you turned right into the flat of the main valley, Champex, a picture of an Alpine habitation, seemed to be there as if in welcome to this lovely Swiss place. It sat beside its own wee Lochan.

In a traditional Swiss timbered restaurant, run by the Swiss Alpine Club, we fed grandly on simple mountain fare, which, as ever, was blessed with fine Valais Fendant. A wine from Canton Valais. What a way to slow down near the end of our second chapter of this gift that nature makes possible. And the party were still going well, as a group.

From here we had to take two taxis to that high village Bourg St Pierre, near to the top of the Grand St Bernard Pass. The drive up from Champex was when we were in the most danger during the whole route. The driving was desperate. Frank Davis, a rally driver, was not impressed. I wasn't too impressed myself! Bourg St Pierre was almost still asleep from its hemmed-in winter. I am sure it must have changed since then. Most of these places have. The place was quietly still. It was physical. The old village creaked with it. This made a serious impression on me. At the time, my days along the Kelvin, the roving around Milngavie and adventuring in Loch Lomond country all came back to me. This was without a doubt, a wondrous extension of these good things.

186

We overnighted in a very old pension run by a stout classy lady. She was far from young. In the dark hours before dawn she saw to it that you were filled with fresh bread, coffee to match the bread, and strong cheese that I'd like to presume came off the mountain. Even the house had class. It was called Pension au Beau Valais. The name suited the house. In the pre-dawn light, madam fussily saw us on our way. She would probably do this as a habit. If she had had the Glasgow tongue, or I the French, we could have told each other daft stories. Anyway, you can't win them all! With the party settled down and now used to each other, we set off on the third chapter of what, for the average person, would be an adventure of considerable importance and enough to last them a lifetime.

The start of the route was more or less behind the back door of the Beau Valais. It led from the start up and onto a stony treeless corrie. The ascent rose steadily and slowly. This made the early morning adjustment to stiffness and the toil to come sneak up on you. Unlike the first day's 4000 feet up to the Albert Premier Cabin, when we had to buckle down from the word go, here we had a chance to build up slowly. About an hour up we found the Swiss Army on manoeuvres. They'd have had an early start. We had a bit of crack in passing. Not long after, we came onto a flattish basin. There were a number of substantial well built stone cow byres. What surprised me was the number of these byres. The available grazing looked a wee bitty sparse. Maybe a Red Clydesider is not the best authority on Alpine dairy farming.

We passed through these summer settlements up through a narrow rocky gorge into a world of Himalayan proportions, still wrapped in the depth of winter. A place that people like us dream of. This was one of the ways onto the Haute Route that takes you up onto the Grand Combin. It was considered to be one of the most challenging of the several ways to take in the Route. It turned out to be just that! We stopped and rested in a great amphitheatre, which seemed to finish the easy part of the approach onto the Combin. We started up the path leading to the Cabin de Valsorey. This is another Gem that the Alps are so liberally endowed with. The Cabin sits at the top of the way leading to the western flank of the Grand Combin, and "Grand" it is. I later found out a nickname "Grand Combien" noting that it was often those who could afford it who travelled the Haute Route. This mountain carries a reputation for bad weather. And for *killing people*.

On the path, others on the Route started to appear. With them came what seemed to be out of the ordinary, a climber- skier with one leg. He wore a bizarre white face mask to protect his face from the naughty rays of the sun. I don't know why, he had a face like an old boot. Chris found out that he lost his leg skiing. I was personally of the opinion it went at Stalingrad. He was the right age. It turned out that he and his pals liked their own way in the huts, as we were to find out.

From the Valsorey the westerly views of the Mont Blanc Massif present themselves in a spectacular and breathtaking way. Moments like these, when mountain travellers' inner senses are aroused, don't keep happening. It's in special moments, when your senses are aroused, that they impact on you. When they do, it's in a most dramatic way. You don't have to be at 10,000 feet on a continental mountain range. It had been a fair grind up from the Beau Valais, about five or six hours. When I arrived in the Cabin one of the Alpinists was ready with a large steaming jug of highly sweetened lemon tea. He was a climber of the old school. It reminded me a bit of Bill Watson on the Cairngorm with the tea and sugar back in the 1950s.

We got into the Cabin early, so I nipped upstairs and booked the best place in the sleeping room. Francis was calling me the "Chef de Haute Route" by this time. We were getting on fine. Around noon the weather started to go on the blink. Sometime later a small group arrived, a young Chamonix guide and two girls. One of the girls had been hit on the head by a falling stone on the way up. There was a fair sized gash on her head. They had started late. The way up to Cabin is subject to stone falls after late morning. The modern helmet would have saved her injury. She was a Yugoslavian, working as a stripper in Paris. These girls were very poorly equipped. As things turned out this could have caused them big problems. With *my* track record I should zip my lip!

The weather broke down into a heavy snowstorm. Stormbound for two nights. A serious problem for our food, if we were to finish the route. I spent the time teaching some of our group to play shipyard solo whist. The snow was a worry, if it lasted too long we'd need to come down. As it was The Deil looks after his own. The snow stopped around 7am on the second morning. It was make-up-your-mind time. To go on, or come down.

Above the Valsory was a long steep slope. It could have been 1500 to 2000 feet in vertical height difference. There was now at least a metre of fresh snow lying on a very slippy old surface, making the whole slope at best unstable. Apart from make-up-your-mind time, it could have been *avalanche time!* I'm sure I was asked about going on. If I was, I am sure my answer was yes. I know we never learn, but I was not missing my chance to finish the Haute Route.

That hut was heaving with climbers, and not one made a move till we did. Francis and myself set off, and I had Helen with me. As I said, the snow was a metre deep. That meant it was up to our naughty bits. Francis was up in front, paid professional by courtesy of the Daily Telegraph. I'm sure I heard the ominous crack of the frost crystals. The harbinger of the avalanche. Normally you only hear what you want to hear. Was I getting it the wrong way round? Near the top, at about the last 500 feet, I roped Helen to Francis. I hooked Frank on, then moved up the broken rock that runs away up to the summit and made belay as fast as I could. It went through my twisted mind, "avalanche now you bastard!" A nice sentiment, with my new friends down there!

I brought Frank up. While he was taking a breather I was nipping a few photos. Almost immediately from away down below, in German, up came complaints about the "Stalingrad Team" being held up. I knew I had them clocked right! They could have tracked their own way up, but no, they were happy enough to use our track. And now they were bitching. I sent down salutations, in Glaswegian! They understood that all right! We had a traverse of 50 feet to the right, with long exposure below. A cornice bulging from the ridge added a nice touch to the finish of what was an arduous morning. Even if it was a bit *dicky*, it was good!

We were very high on the Combin now, on a shoulder where the wedge of the summit seemed to start from. The watershed to North and South divided here. This opened up tremendous vistas, from the south where we had came from, and to the North where we were going. The heavy snowfall, as if by magic,

188

had changed the ancient mountains back to the days of their youth. They looked as if they were newly made. Yes we had been gifted again. Another of those special moments.

To describe this new scene would be difficult. It could demean the beautiful memory of only two days past. And for no reason. Helen now was starting to notice. She seemed, for the first time, to realise where she was and what this was really all about. With youthful excitement she started to babble! She was pointing out all the wonders around us. This was her moment of awakening. She was hooked. It's not often you get to enjoy a moment such as this. I hope she *remembers*. Skiing and modern day high standard rock climbing is full of participants who do not see around them the physical world in which their activity takes place. How sad! The rest of the groups started to gather on this roomy shelf. Not a word of thanks for our uphill bashing from the Stalingrad mob. So what! The view made up for their churlishness and Helen's girlish pleasure at the wholeness of her achievement should have made heady wine, even for these Teutonic boors!

The way down to the Cabin de Chanrion was an easy long slide with a slight uphill traverse in the middle. The Cabin was a big stone built summer hut set in the middle of the confluence of what could be called high corries. It was just in the snowline. Here for the first time we had running water. It was stripped to the waist and a good scrub! That night I had trouble with the Stalingrad Mob. I had set our cooking pots on the stove. When I returned, I found one of the Mob moving our pots to the side. I let him know that if there was any more bother, his pots would be on the floor. That seemed to settle any misunderstanding. You can't beat the direct approach! The weather next morning was bad, with zero visibility. We were off before daylight on our sixth day of climbing. It was a shame. Here in the heart of the Pennine Alps and we were being denied the scenery. There are times of no justice. We were heading up this long easy slope on skins, once again breaking the trail. No sign of the Mob. My wee pal Frank Davis had altitude sickness. This is something you can well do without.

Later on, well up onto the Pigne d'Arolla, we had to move up and round a steep snow wall. The left hand side of the wall was very exposed, and we were on it before I realised we should have been roped, or at least have a hand line because of the exposure. As we were traversing diagonally up, Helen, who is not a climber, got into difficulties. She had *no idea* of the jeopardy she was in and was moving carelessly. I moved up under her, settled her down, and then we moved on to easier ground. I'm afraid this was an example of what I mentioned earlier. These excellent French pros have a spaced out approach to these situations. Helen and I had been in a bit of danger for a period of time! It was then that my past experience on the Scottish mountains came into play.

Some time later we got ourselves quite high on the Pigne d'Arolla. The light was impossible. In light as poor as this, only skiers of the highest order can hope to cope and it's *still* a struggle. The loss of contour creates the sensation of vertigo, and you end not knowing whether you are stopped or moving. This makes falling over easier. Skiing past Chris Bonnington who was on his back, I let him know about the situation with the vertigo. He was doing great for a non-skier. Climbers have a marvellous advantage when they take to skiing. They are at home in the mountains, it is their environment. And their legs are *mountain strong*.

Not far below where Chris had his wee touch of vertigo, the glacier was crevassed and broken. The groups drew to a halt. We were wandered. It seemed to be getting dark and I actually started digging a snow hole. Helen wanted to know what I was doing. She thought I was kidding when I explained she and I might have to overnight in that hole. I wasn't too keen at the prospect myself.

However, Francis gave me a shout and we were off. We were determined to beat the Stalingrad Mob for the best place. We didn't, but we got the best place. By the time the others arrived Francis and I had hammered a bottle of Marc d' Valais, a 100 proof of fortification! There was no altercation about the use of the stove. We had a Guardian who had a good pasta dinner. This was accompanied by Dole du Mont. Life was feeling good! So here were Francis and I, two men who take their living from mountains, sitting *half-smugged* in the beautiful Cabin de Vignettes high above the village of Arolla in Switzerland. Anyone will agree it certainly was much better accommodations than a snow hole in a glacier!

Cabin de Vignettes stood on a spur of rock between two glaciers. It was built of well cut stone. A fairy castle could not have been in a more beautiful situation. Nor could it look more beguiling. Like many of these wonderful refuges, the woodwork inside is often very decorative. I have always thought our mountains would be the better for having something along these lines.

The Guardian was up from Arolla. His teenage son, who was retarded, worked with him in the kitchen and at serving food. He was proud that the boy worked with him and rightly so. In those days the Guardians would have to carry all the food and essentials, like House Red, up on their backs. And also the wood for the controversial stoves. A worthy calling. Unfortunately this was a Saturday night, and weekend climbers filled the hut. The place was heaving.

The last day was the big one for us. There are three Cols to be crossed. The last one, Col de Valpelline above Zermatt. This was the Biggie! From de Vignettes the distance is around 20 kilometres. We left in the dark of night. 3-4 am. We skied down to the glacier. The lights of Arolla cheerily winked up at us. They seemed to sparkle and dance in the hazy light of their own private valley. These were startling moments. It made you want to ski down and discover how good it really was! While experiencing the wonder of the moments, we put skins on the skis, then we were off to start a day that would be a sensation, to be remembered, cherished and kept cosy forever. Our party were moving with confidence fired with the strength of how much fitter their skiing legs were. As we were breasting the first Col, the sky to the east was brightening in a crystal clear new day. Again we were being part of the birth of something, that would be a personal memory, to each of us in a different way. I'm sure of that.

The top of the Col was very high and there could be few better places to see a sunrise. We stopped to take in the world starting its new day. Of all those standing there, no one seemed to want to speak. It could have spoiled the Golden Moment. As the sun climbed, lighting the great peaks, we skied down into the bed of a high corrie. This place was completely snow covered, not a shade of black or green showed through the virgin whiteness of that high valley. We put the first unnatural marks in that unblemished cathedral-like place.

Easy poling took us to the part of the head wall that leads up onto the Col. We were now near to the centre of this great, glaciated part of the Pennine Alps. Once again seeing it at its best. Below the Col we had our first rest since we left the de Vignettes at 4 am. The morning was young. Before us stretched the long snow slope to the Col de Valpelline. The sun was burning in that hot crucible. No breath of air moved to ease the long slog to the Valpelline. Again a feast of Alpine giants were there to be seen. The wedge of the Dente Blanche. The sheer north face of the Dent de Herens. Standing proud among them was the Matterhorn. This was waiting for us at the Col de Vapelline. Even after all we had seen, this was *mighty!*

Zermatt sat below in its deep slot. Looking down, if you did not know the place, you would wonder how skiers found their way down into the pleasures of the village. Something I was looking forward to. There was hand shaking as the groups started arriving at the Col. The sign of camaraderie. Without it, endeavours like these would be lonely affairs. And for most people, pointless. Certainly very dangerous. There were mile wide smiles, as well there should have been. After all, most of these folks were part-time climbers and skiers. When you work full-time on the hills it's very obvious the effort needed by the average weekend skier or climber to be good at what you work at!

From the Col de Valpalline to Zermatt is a long way. A good part of it makes for good skiing. Near the bottom, at that time of year, you must be careful. Before we set off I did mention to Chris Bonnington he should not ski with cameras hanging from round his neck. There was one with a whopping great telephoto lens sticking out of the front. I suggested that falling might be the order of the day, especially near to the bottom. I'm sure Chris said the insurance was in order. Toffs are careless, and I mean "careless."

At the top I met another ski teacher guide I knew. He was from Canton Vaud. Snow at the top was very good, then, as nature ensures at that time of the year, snow conditions change the lower you go. Until Gurrum Goo raises its ugly head. Chris, despite his improved performance, had a few nose dives. At the bottom he took a cracker right in front of me! When he stood up I noticed the Big Whopper of a lens was missing, leaving a gaping hole in the body of the camera. What the hell, he was insured!

Skiing stopped below the Matterhorn's eastern flank. When we arrived, Neil Mather's lady wife Jill was browning herself in the sun. She had a bad knee at the time. That's why she was not on the Route. Her bad luck was our good luck as she had big bottles of beer buried in the snow! I've always said it's the ladies that's got the brains! I've always thought how she must have felt missing that particular crossing of the Haute Route. Anyway, she had the calibre of spirit to bring well earned *elixir of life* for us, the successful Haute Route traversers. How long she'd been there was anybody's guess. Neil and Jill now live close by in Speyside. During the beer drinking the usual photos were taken. It was still a good hike to Zermatt, two good *Scotch Country Miles*, by my calendar.

I said I'd meet the crowd in the Valaiser Kann, a local pub. Francis and I were off. To save a touch of walking we went over the Schwarzee Luftseilban. Francis kept going, as he had to meet his wife at Visp. I settled down out on the terrace with my first bottle of Fendant. I would sit in the sun and wait for the back markers to catch up with me. Not too bad for a waiting room! While waiting I did in a litre of excellent Fendant. When I finished that I made my move to Zermatt where I could have my next litre. No more walkies! Down in the cable car, free, with my Swiss Ski School Director's Licence. Life's simple.

It's either *good, bad*, or its *rotten!* What's in between is usually *dull*. From the bucket I looked down to see Frank and Chris. They had missed the short cut, which added a long *Scotch Country Mile*, at least.

We had a lovely afternoon party. It wasn't planned. It happened, you could say, as a celebration of *our success* on the Haute Route. All of us enjoyed the same satisfaction in completing the Route. How could we not? This route is not always completed. Weather regularly puts paid to the stoutest of efforts. We just made it, despite the bad weather most of the way through. The only damage was some badly blistered feet. Only Helen's, Francis's and mine were blister free. The reason was that the fulltime skiers use boots for six months or more.

Christian very kindly, on behalf of the Telegraph, laid on a handsome no-holds-barred dinner. And so said all of us! Christian (that was his Sunday name for "Chris") did us proud! Next morning we all went our separate ways. With our parting we were all the richer by the new friends we had gained. That was the real gain. Frank, Chris and I went back to Chamonix to collect the car. We had a farewell dinner with Francis, compliments of that fine newspaper.

A résumé of the generally important bits and pieces that made up Our Haute Route. Firstly I have Frank Davis to thank for stimulating me into making the effort to get up and go. I'm sure I have said thanks. This was the first time I had ever been involved in anything as serious as this, with people I did not know very well. An experience recommendable to anyone. It certainly was one of my rich memories. About the Route. It can be done by taking in some of the classic peaks like Grand Combin, Pigne d'Arolla, Matterhorn and others. You would need a strong party for this, plus time. It goes without saying this is worth trying. It must be said that this is a serious undertaking. These high mountains do not give up their gifts freely. Many people have died when attempting passage over this Route and indeed in the Alps in general.

Memories. As you read this, it can be seen that the people involved are as fresh in memory to me as if it were yesterday. It's interesting how well Francis Bozon and I got on, being so different in nature. He knew my son was maybe coming to Chamonix the following season. He invited him to stay in his home. A touching invitation. Francis was at the top of his pecking order, in both skiing and climbing. In is own quiet, mild mannered way, I'm sure he left his mark on all those he mixed with. I remember him well. And so the season of 1967 was topped off handsomely. By pure chance.

In the season of 1968 there would be an event that would change Scottish ski racing in a forward direction. Up until then the club racers led the field. As I mentioned earlier, ski teachers were now being allowed to race in club races. With the proviso that none of their results or activities be used in any way in promoting income for themselves. This was something I'd helped to bring about. This allowed fulltime skiers to participate in what was a very full racing calendar. The only fulltime skiers were teaching in Scottish ski schools. The best of these were made up of younger skiers many of whom were from Norway and Alpine countries who had been racing and skiing since their school days.

Kenny Dickson and Ian Baxter were two home grown racers who were already working in ski schools, much to my satisfaction. Others were standing in the sidelines. The immediate benefit of this was that the standard of skiing within the "Home Racers" improved in its efforts to meet the new challenge. The new circumstances meant that those who had been winners became losers. To their credit they enjoyed the excitement of the new competition. Better still, they enjoyed it and got stuck in about it, as was their wont! In particular, the Dundee Bunch. I'm sure they know who I mean. They will also remember all the great times we had together.

The technical side was in the excellent hands of Lewis Drysdale who saw to the all important race timing, and also to the training of those prepared to take on this thankless task. There was a warm wholesome feeling of common endeavour in skiing in all its facets. You felt, as you went about doing your wee bit, that all was well. That most of what you did was in concert with the general effort. Cooperation was the order of the day. This was something we enjoyed for a number of years. The social side of skiing was roaring away. It was small wonder as we all knew each other very well. The night before a race all those involved would be whooping it up till the wee hours of the morning, racers included. But not all of them!

In the season of 1968 the venue for the Scottish Championship was the Glen of Weeping, Glencoe. For some reason, during the weekend of the last two races, there had developed among some of the ski teachers who raced the idea that they could predict the winner. A foolish notion. In the hotel that night some of the forecasters had been nominating their preference for who would take the silver away. While they were doing this, some of them were having *a wee touch of the Water of Life*. Jeanie was standing next to me. I quietly asked her if any of these clowns knew or forgot that Luke O'Reilly was sleeping upstairs and had been since 9pm. Our son was sharing the room with Luke.

A Good Weekend's Work! – Luke O'Reilly and Iain Finlayson

Anyone who remembers those times and Luke especially, will know he was capable of outperforming, by a fair chunk, any of those standing at the bar. This was the year of the Grenoble Olympics, where Luke had skied for the UK. He was spending the rest of the season with us. On the Saturday, Luke blew out of the slalom. He blew out of the Giant Slalom on the Sunday as well. That's consistency for you. None of those who were fancied in the bar on the Friday night were in the running! Joey Gough, a Club skier, was winner one day and Iain Finlayson was second. Next day Iain won and, as a result, became Scottish Senior Champion. He also won the Junior Championship that season. He'd started skiing at 3, and had been racing since he was six. Ten years of racing experience. 13 years skiing experience.

This was the start of things to come. To win against people of this background you would need to be up to par. This could only be good for skiing. Helen Jamieson, who had been on the Haute Route, had been the first Scot of this background. Iain was the first male. Something that stands out in my memory is, when Helen had stopped racing in the National Team, how much the quality of skiing had improved. She started to race on our circuit. She set the cat amongst the pigeons as she consistently beat the men. This was not a giveaway as some of the men could move themselves. Clearly in my mind it was then that Helen went from being nearly a good skier, to being a good skier. It *pleasured* me seeing it and knowing she had *crossed over*. I even told her so.

Helen once worked with us on the spring Junior Training. Here we discovered she possessed a natural bent for training. She slipped into gear like an old pro. Her group was fortunate to have had Helen's experience so ably used for their benefit. It's not automatic that someone like Helen is suitable for the responsibilities involved at this level. She told me it was great to be so well paid for enjoying herself. She was not long married, and, near the end of the two weeks, she had been bitching about being "frustrated." Poor wee soul, lonely and missing her man!

This was the year BASI qualified its first members who started skiing as youngsters. Another milestone in BASI's progression in growing up. Kenny Dickson and Ian Baxter became Grade One members. They had raced and still raced with success. This they would do for some years to come. They would teach at the highest levels. Another nice step forward.

Iain Finlayson became a BASI Grade Three member that year. I was so proud. With his background this would seem to be an obvious road for him to travel. He would find that his situation in skiing would not make his passage through the different stages of qualification easy. Examiners kept marks tight, when dealing with candidates of this sort of background. Sometimes they carried it a bit too far at times.

At the end of the course party Iain mentioned to me how mean he thought his marks had been. I was pleased he was through considering the pillory he had been on. The examiners were making it apparent that being a champion and the son of the Director of National Training cut no ice. In years to come this nonsense stopped. I told Iain to look around and look at those who had failed, then to think how they would love to have his poor marks. I also pointed out that this would be their only and last shot at becoming a BASI member. To remember that he had only recently made history, becoming Senior and Junior Champion at 16 years of age. And to spare a thought for the "sheep of the fold." Iain never ever forgot that salutary wee lecture. Its more than likely I'd forgotten he was only sixteen. How we who have so much are guilty of taking the good things for granted! This has a habit of back-firing. When the penny eventually dropped that better skiers did come out of non-racers this unnecessary harshness ended.

Iain had in his BASI class a friend of ours, Gordon Bruce. Gordon was an experienced ski teacher. He kept his eye on Iain during the two weeks of the training. This was an advantage, like having a permanent tutor by your side on call so to speak. Their lifelong friendship would have started then. So here was BASI making its way forward, laying the foundations for the future, with the help of new members like these.

Sue Field, now Mrs Kenny Dickson, was another. Hugh Clark, a local farmer's son, would be another. They've stayed in skiing, working at the highest levels. There's a large lump of quality experience among these few names I've mentioned. The above mentioned would be the first of many whose early skiing was taken up in racing. They stayed in skiing, working at all levels and contributing to the sport in many different ways. Slowly we gathered other good trainers into our cadre. It was a fine crop. Things were looking good for the future.

Speaking of memories, here is honourable mention (or maybe described in some other way), to those who underwent the experience of being "apprenticed to myself" to learn the intricacies of the Ski Business. Their principal objective was to get as much skiing as possible with good skiers. And at the same time subsidise the undertaking. But there is always a cost. Our arrangement with these stalwarts were as follows. They would start early in the morning in the ski hire. That would be the equivalent of being galley slave under the Marquis de Sade! There were two reasons. Leather boots still dominated ski hire. These monstrosities had to be black polished. This was late night and early morning work . Pulling on a galley's oar could not have been much worse. And *then* they had to learn to ski! They in fact got much more quality skiing than the average ski teacher. In return they worked longer hours than ski teachers. I made it a personal chore, teaching the boot boys to ski.

They had another wee problem;– their boss in the ski hire was a doughty fellow by the name of Bruce Howe. Bruce kept a good distance from the average ski teacher. Like my wife he had seen among many of them a haughtiness that ill became them, but that is another story. Bruce was an Aviemore man who had spent 8 years in the U S. Air Force. Bruce ran a tight ship in which he brooked no nonsense. Instructors are guilty of taking severe liberties with workshops if you let them. Not with Bruce's work benches. However once you had passed muster, you were all right. If the ski school boss wanted to borrow one of Bruce's boys to help in the ski school, the boss had to go carefully about how he went arranging it. Bruce and his sidekick would be found after work each evening at the corner of the Winking Owl Bar standing as if in private conclave. They stood there among the posturing newly arrived would-be ski teachers. The two professional ski hire experts stood there with that "we know better," superior, smirky look written all over their faces. I always felt I was doing well when I bellied up to the bar to join them. Its a good thing to have bit of clout going for you if you hope to keep company with the elite! The first of these sidekicks would have been Liam Chalmers, a folk singer of earthy charm, who was by pure chance a Red Clydesider. He is to this day a family friend.

Peter Woollcome was the first ski teacher trainee that came to us. He is still in ski teaching. In the winter 1995 he's been teaching sailing in Murmansk University. This is his first love. In summer he sails on the four masted barque Sedov as shift bo's'n. This is the largest four-masted barque in the world. Some trick for a non-Russian. The people we meet in skiing! Peter had a public school background. My remit from his father, a Royal Navy Admiral, and another *wee goodie,* was to make a man of him. Peter made a man of himself. I worked his butt off. I gave him no quarter, and he asked for none. There was none to get. Peter had lived in Les Diablerets, Switzerland. He later had his own restaurant. He learned to move about in the high mountains and continued teaching skiing. All in all, a fair achievement for a Portsmouth man.

Andy Blair, A Home Grown Skier

Andy Blair followed Peter. At sixteen he was young, and this mattered because he had to be away from home on his own, to be our apprentice. This turned out to be no problem. Andy looked after himself very well. He was another Clydesider, and came to us through an old friend, Jimmy Watt, a Glencoe Ski Club member. Jimmy pointed Andy to me, saying he was a "good boy." Praise indeed! The reason for this accolade was that Jimmy had found him hitch-hiking one Friday night outside Glasgow in the dark. He was heading for the Cairngorms, complete with rucksack and skis. A terrific effort for anyone, far less a 16 year old. I cannot for the life of me, remember how Andy became our apprentice. He moved into an attic room above our shop. For some obscure reason the room was called the "Poop-Mizzen." Peter Woollcome could never connect the small room to a Tall Ship. So what's wrong with a touch of *artist's licence?* Andy has been in skiing ever since. During this time he became a very experienced ski teacher. He also learned all the other important parts of the business which most ski teachers know nothing about. As a result he is now running a large shop, and is also director of that company. He is a good skier which I'm sure pleases him greatly, because we do not have many good skiers. That could set the cat among the pigeons. Not for the first time!

Next one was another local boy. Willie McLennan. It was said he was a bit wild, but I never noticed that. If he was, what's new! He fitted in just fine. Gifted with first class hands for working on skis, we taught him to tune good skis to a high standard.

Now the next one was a *whopper* and, of course, from Clydeside. Gordon Kennedy, "Him of the Charmed Life." To describe him would beggar the pen of the author of the tales of Walter Mitty. So why bother! I first met Gordon walking through the Lairig Ghru. He was handyman at Glenmore Lodge. He was *handy* all right. Of all the villains and rascals I've run with, he's the one who got me into most trouble. To manage that with me, he had to be *some kid*, which he was! He would have been in his early twenties. There were two other strong hardy characters in that Lairig Ghru party. Gordon was going easy with his mouth as he was just finding his way into the establishment. But a mouth like that cannot be kept shut for long. We'd had stopped for a drum-up and a wee drinkie. By this time Gordon's mouth was running in full flow. He nipped round behind a boulder to answer a call of nature. His mouth was producing abuse from behind the boulder, so I lobbed a half can of beer over the boulder. Bingo! It caught him on the skull, with the result that he sat down quickly! There's many ways to *join the club*. He had just made membership.

Bruce and he were poles apart. To quote a smart modern cliché, "they were polarised in their natures." Still, they worked in tight harmony. Once a week Gordon would have dinner at Bruce's home. It takes two to tango! Naturally, each evening they would take their place at the Winking Owl bar. Where no doubt, in their smug superiority, they would quickly slag away the young stumble-bum struggling ski teachers-to-be. Mind you, if you had around ten years in ski teaching experience and skied well, they made a space at the bar for you. In lieu of that, a "letter from the Pope." They would make a special allowance for you. Getting a BASI Grade One was a doddle by comparison. Life can be full of wee problems.

These were the years in the Cairngorm area when all to do with skiing was changing. It was growing rapidly, and in its growth it attracted the kind of people who in the past pushed frontiers forward. Much of the energy these people had was used in the social *after ski* activities. We all played a full part of what was a self generated never-to-be-forgotten and never-to-be-repeated one-off experience in our lives. These were magical times! The stimulation came from the newness of what was taking place. This was a new entity. Everyone who was taking part knew each other. This produced a close-knit comradeship, which in turn gave skiing in Speyside a nice intimate feel. That is gone now. There is a price for everything; in this case, it was progress!

A definite Ski Culture was emerging and like us with our "ski apprentices," we were all apprentices who had to learn how to look after skiing guests. Skiers can give the impression of being very demanding. Well, you can't have skiing business without skiers. It took a while for this to be fully understood by many of those working in this new industry. An industry that has helped to dramatically change life in Speyside. If you wish to live and work in beautiful Speyside, there is a price to pay. Here, in the Highlands of Scotland, this lesson has been well learned. As a result we have communities working away for most of the year's twelve months. Whether we like it or not, big changes have taken place since the days of Bruce Howe and Gordon Kennedy standing at the Winking Owl Bar, disdainfully observing the stunts of up-and-coming ski teachers. What we do have now are young adults who have grown up in a ski culture, even if they have never skied themselves!

18. The Greener Years

By the end of the 1968 season progress in all of skiing's departments was steady. A sign that the varied interests were getting their acts together, by dint of learning from personal experiences, good, bad or indifferent. So we, who were deeply involved and proud to be active in our "ski world," were smugly pleased with ourselves at how clever we'd been getting so far in so short a period of time. Having said that, early in the season of 1969 I was to get a salutary lesson in not taking anything for granted.

This, and I'm sure I'm correct, was the first year two Scots went out to train with what we understood to be British Junior Training. Ian Blackwood and Iain Finlayson. Both were members of Glencoe Ski Club and the Scottish. The Glencoe club were delighted, as were their parents. Here was the ultimate. Two of our young members in National Training. Young Blackie was old enough to drive, Iain had just turned seventeen. Before they left it was clearly explained to them that they were to do what they were told and to keep their mouths shut. Blackie's father, like myself, could be blunt and to the point. We said how privileged they were to be skiing, racing and training all winter. There was no financial support from the National Ski Federation. Fair enough. For someone like myself to have a son in the National Training could only be a deep personal satisfaction. Here again, events were happening that justified all the years of effort.

In January the two Iain's phoned from the Alps. It seems the training was a mess and they were sick to the teeth with it. I was amazed! These were two hard noses. Upsetting them to this extent must have taken a bit of doing. I phoned them back after I had time to sort out their *beefs*. What I eventually heard decided me to go out and have look for myself. I severely cautioned them, that this *better be kosher* or they'd see the rough side of *me!* The last thing I needed was a non-skiing trip to the Alps. But even allowing for these two Clydesiders with their Bolshie, naturally aggressive approach to life, something was badly wrong for them to be looking for succour from the likes of me. I arranged to meet them in Geneva in two days time. When the phone call was over, Jeanie remarked that those two would be worried stiff wondering how I'd react to this mess. She said that they would presume I'd blame them for what had transpired.

I flew out, having to pay full fare, and rented a car to meet the two recalcitrants. We got off to a bad start. They were sitting on a bench in the station, heads down, like two whipped curs! I didn't take to this indifference. Through a tight mouth I told them to get on their feet when I spoke to them. Who did they think they were dealing with? And to get the car loaded. We then discovered the car was too small and the roof rack too flimsy. Two monster ski bags dwarfed the poor wee VW.

They had to meet the rest of the trainees in Briancon close to Serre Chevalier. Once we got on our way and the Boyos realised I was on their side they settled down. I let them ramble on and bitch until they ran out of steam. It was a lovely day and we stopped at an old French Inn where I dined and wined them. When we drove off, the vibrant resentment we'd had in the car was gone. I explained that I would be expecting a tremendous improvement in their skiing. They were too tricky to rise to that bait! We stopped at Rossignol and Dynamic. The boys got more skis. I picked up a nice pair myself. The boys at least had learned some useful skills. We stayed overnight in a small town where, surprisingly, the food was awful.

Next day we skied at the new Ski Station of L'Alpe d'Huez. I was pleased to see there had been a considerable improvement in their skiing. I'm sure they were waiting for a wee touch of praise. Unfortunately, before I got round to telling them, the only rock in the Dauphine Alps got under my skis, and the big compliment I was planning slipped out of my mind. I was disgusted! New competition 215cm Giant Slaloms! Trust my luck. I called off skiing for the day. The boys were not that keen. You could understand they might be under some pressure. They had no idea what I would do, or how I'd react after I'd seen the scenario being played out over the next few days.

There was a downhill and slalom to be run over the three days in Serre Chevalier. There would be no better way to see how the *ball of wax* got waxed! Then, and only then, could I make my mind up as to what the situation was. Then appraise it for what it was. I had explained this carefully to the boys. I asked that they ski as well as they could in the races. Afterwards we would decide together what to do, to resolve this mess without treading on too many toes! I reminded them of the many good people at home who had great faith and trust in them as their representatives here in the Alps.

When we arrived, I was introduced to the manager. Naturally there was a fair degree of tension. Not on my part. The reason for my being there was bigger than the opinions of two teenagers' about how things were being run. The issue was more important. The future training and how it should be organised was important. The gravity of the problem came to me when I met the manager. It was then that the fact that he was in his early twenties came home. His young wife appeared to be in charge of the junior girls. They were Richard and Sue Berry. Both had good backgrounds in skiing.

Now before I go any further, there is no one more in favour of young folks being given their head. Never in my experience up to then, or since, have I seen this function being achieved in a situation as complex as training juniors. It was tried here since by that type of administration. It never worked. Once again it was the trainees who suffered. The man's task was impossible. Firstly, the transport consisted of a grossly overloaded minibus. Two of the squad had to travel about by public transport. These were the two Iains.

As soon as I found the opportune moment, I explained to Richard why I was there. This I did as carefully as possible. In complete frankness he gave the whole sad pathetic old tale, that British skiing is cursed with literally no funding. I was sure Richard wasn't being paid expenses or a salary. How could any national body expect to keep a manager in the frame of mind to cope with the multiple problems that sort of economy must produce? The food was less than it should have been. When you're dealing with a mixed group of juniors who can be as smart as whips, this in itself would cause trouble even in a stable situation. Where there is discontentment, poor food would add to bad morale. Kids at this level are not short in the "Smarts Department." You must give them credit for this, or they might end up *kidding* you! The whole thing was a mess and, in my opinion, the fault of the organisers, whoever they may have been.

There were two young French trainers working with us. They did not appear interested in the task in hand. Once again, in my opinion they were too young, and consequently too inexperienced for work of this importance. On the hill I spoke to a French trainer with French juniors. He was around 40. His group moved about with a freedom of purpose which can only be inspired by total interest in what was taking place around them, completely different from what was happening with our juniors. This was not good enough for Blackwood or Finlayson. They could be taken home and looked after. What of the others?

Race Training – Richard Berry and Self

None of this was Richard's responsibility. The blame for that belonged to whoever lumbered him with an impossible undertaking. Richard loved the art of skiing, which he was good at. He got his place in the sun. He was manager of the men's team at the 1972 Olympics in Sapporo, Japan. I was very pleased for him. All this trouble may have been the reason Ian Blackwood's father never let Ian have a couple of years on the circuit. It may have been fortuitous luck that someone like me was involved when this happened. I would be listened to.

Many young racers were to come out of Scotland and into National Junior Training. Knowing the mentality of those who ran Scottish skiing, it was clear in my mind they would not tolerate poor organisation being involved in their juniors' future in skiing. The Ski Club of Great Britain had always looked after and run British international racing. I've already said how much I admired the

200

"Ski Club." But they were at that time just a wee bit monolithic in their outlook on the bludgeoning changes surging through world skiing at that time. The National Ski Federation of Great Britain were now responsible for National Training. It would be true to say the chiefs who ran the "Ski Club" heavily influenced the "Federation." This was understandable when skiing was in a state of flux and finding its way to how it is structured today. Which, I may say, is not to everybody's satisfaction. Once again, *that is another story!* So it could be expected that a fair amount of paternalism may have inadvertently become part of how things were done. Changes would be made, a new road would be found along which National Teams would be managed. This was find-out time. I have just said I had salutary lesson. What I learned was that, if you do not have enough funds, you have no chance of putting forward a team that has any hope of skiing to their potential! And that is all that can be said about that.

The following season our son had a car. He was properly funded by his parents. The two boys raced in Serre Chevalier. They did quite well in the slalom. The next race was in Italy, just over the hill. They had to make their own way over. That was the clincher! The boys were for home. We had a kind of epic trip home with a drive to Paris and train to London. All their skis went missing at Victoria station. Another rented car. After a stop at a motorway café, Blackie was taking a turn at the wheel. I jumped in the back and got the head down. By some stroke of luck I opened my eyes a minute later. We were driving down the motorway the wrong way. It so happened, just at that time there was a gap in the verge between the carriageways. Remember the motorways were quiet in those days!

Blackie came to Aviemore to spend the rest of the season. Iain and he would be *apprentices*. And for them the gloves were off. They would work under Peter Simpson, our ski school boss. They would be free to race at weekends. Peter had strict orders that they'd not be allowed above the beginners' slopes for a month. This was a wee touch of stick, for the bother and expense they'd caused me. It would also let interested spectators see that *a piper must be paid!*

The snow conditions over this part of the season were Alpine. Going up the lower chair one morning and looking down I saw the two bold boys teaching away like busy wee beavers. I asked Peter if they had been whining to get up the hill to teach running classes. Peter assured me they had not been near him. There was something rotten in the State of Denmark! Before we knew it the Wee Bit of Stick was over, so it was too late to allow some time off for good behaviour. So what, they were young! A few years later, in company one night, I reminded Iain how I'd worked it on him and Blackie on the beginners' slope. I'd put my foot in *it*, again! Iain said, smirking, "do you remember the groups we had?" I didn't. They had been a private school of teenage girls, Monday to Friday for the four weeks that fitted in with the four weeks "of stick." Four weeks of what Burns called "Houghmagandie." My mouth was shut!

Many historical events in the ensuing years seemed to come one after the other, as if by some prearranged plan. The British Ski Federation brought the British Championships to Cairngorm. I have no doubt Lewis Drysdale and Jim Currie had influence in bringing this most prestigious event to Scotland. Aviemore Centre had all the off-hill facilities in one place. All we needed was a freak weather window. A window that would last ten days. We were to run Ladies' and Men's events end to end. There is a Glaswegian word "gallus," meaning that you will take on anything. In other words you push your luck! Those who were heavily involved in skiing were immediately called to the Colours. No dodgers were tolerated. One of the benefits, as I remember, was the great excitement among our local kids. Very few of these had been to the Alps. It was amazing how much they knew about the ins and outs of skiing.

When the star racers arrived, the kids moved right in beside them. They were made welcome by the racers speaking to and mixing with the juniors. This made the scene exciting and visually colourful. The kids were all hyped up and you could feel their excitement. This stuff dreams are made of! Unbelievably, the weather held still for us. The races attracted, of all things, non-skiing spectators. Another surprising plus! We had Scottish country music playing through loudspeakers. There was a complaint from the village about the noise. Would you not believe it! So we turned the volume down. This was a festival of skiing. All of us who mustered to the colours and worked the long hours on the hill, played into the "wee hours" of the night. The whole event made all who worked in it much more skilful than when we started. And I'm sure we were richer in ourselves.

To mention the names of all who worked so creatively will mean little to most readers today. The people who did the work were ex-racers, ski teachers and ordinary skiers. They did unseen and uncounted hours work on Cairngorm, very early in the morning and late at night. All of those who helped will remember the camaraderie we had together. As chief of courses I thank you all once again!

To claim total success would be reasonable. Out of it came a burst of endeavour to produce Scottish Racers. Another story. Skiing seemed as if it were well planned at that time. And the growth of these good things appeared as if to order. But in fact, what we were seeing was the manifestation of years of work that was just coming to fruition. I mentioned earlier having a BASI class with a number of the British Team in it. This happened at the end of this same season. What a coincidence. For this to have happened in the same year as the British Championships were in Scotland would suggest a national cooperative effort was taking place. It really was spontaneous. The results *might,* in the future, become self propagating.

The snow conditions that were making the Championships so successful actually kept improving on to the end of the season. As a result, the Team Members on the course had plenty of snow on which to show their skiing prowess on the Free Run part of the examination. They did it with elegant flamboyance that was a delight to see. And in so doing, they showed the direction in which British Skiing could go. It would be 1979 before there would be so many Team Members on a BASI course.

When the BASI course was over in 1969, Sue Dickson was a full member. She is the longest working lady ski teacher in *our* ski world. Sorry Sue, I never made the years go so fast! They've been running for me also! But you have no complaints, you have worked at all possible levels of skiing. You also have the honour of being the first "Lady Trainer" in Great Britain. What a season, so much excitement, so much done, so much learned. How fortunate were we who took part in it.

The following season, 1970, was the end of the decade in which Scottish skiing started to blossom, giving many people an opportunity to change their way of life in a way that they could never have envisaged when they first started working in heavy industry. 1970 had none of the glamour of the one just gone by. It could have become an anticlimax. When writing this I came to the conclusion that this was not the case.

That season we had three young men from Speyside training with the British Men's Squad. Stewart McDonald from Carrbridge, Fraser Clyde son of Bob Clyde, and there was Iain Finlayson. As you would expect they were different in character. Stewart, born and bred in Speyside, a quiet and even tempered young man with a smile you are born with. Fraser quietly spoken, confident and a strong competitor. Iain was quick, fiery, aggressive and smart. These last two were the sons of their fathers. Stewart and Iain teamed up and drove off in Iain's Ford Anglia, his pride and joy. Proudly, as we watched them go, we realised they were now young men.

Somewhere in the Alps they met up with what was to be the rest of the team. Julian Vasey, Alex Mappelli Mozzi, who raced for England and Royston Varley who, for some reason or other, raced for Scotland. These three were Alpine based. There were others who came in and out, making up the numbers you need if you have any hope of making any kind of team. This set up a training squad and gave the powers-that-be some time to organise and train for the Olympics in Sapporo Japan, 1972. That was not so far away.

The BASI spring course was interesting, in particular some of the Grade Ones. These were a mixed group as far as their skiing went. Grade One candidates did not come as well balanced as we would have liked, but this would slowly improve. At that time Grade Ones and Twos were still using the same training programme. The difference being that, in the examination, Grade Ones had to achieve higher marks. It was around this time the system would change, and Grade Ones and Twos were separated.

On this course was Edward Pirie. Eddie worked in our school. A more motivated skier and ski teacher I have never encountered. He had walked through his Grade Three and Two. When I asked him how well he might do in his One, his reply was, "I'll get the best marks." For someone not long on words and quiet by nature, it was a definite statement. In teaching and technique his marks were close to maximum. Not bad for the quiet man. I'm delighted to say he still contributes to skiing in a big way. He trains juniors from the Aberdeen area, very successfully. Among them his own daughters, Tessa and Amanda. Looking back on his preparation that winter, he took no prisoners. The man was an example of how to go about giving yourself *a big shout* in being a winner at anything!

Another in this group was Jack Maxwell, a PE teacher at our local high school. Jack is a natural born athlete, a smart competitive man. This can be a formidable combination in the physical world we live and work in. Coupled with these attributes he had the gift to ski well, but unfortunately, skiing full time was not possible for him. "*Often in my musing my mind drifts and I think of people I knew who had the gift to ski well, but not the time. It tickles my fancy if I could see them ski to their potential.*" Such are dreams, and why no?

John Cunningham was another in this group. John I've already mentioned. One of Britain's top climbers. John's skiing was not what he would have liked it to be. Despite his legendary cat-like ability to move on vertical rock faces, he found good skiing hard to sustain. John failed his One on this occasion.

There was a girl in the group who skied in the Alps. Her name escapes me. A racer and a good skier, she passed her One with style. We never saw her again. If she ever got to teach, I'm sure she did us proud. We had three other characters who were more or less ski bums. They had been in the area all season learning to ski, instructing a bit and in general playing about. I've said before, this is not how you go about learning to be a ski teacher, let alone pass any serious examination. They never achieved Grade Ones. Their attitudes certainly precluded them from that standard.

There was another know-all in the group. He was an outdoor pursuits instructor from the South somewhere. It so happened he skied with less skill than any of the group. He possessed skills in sailing, canoeing, orienteering, climbing and of course skiing, or so he thought. I had been told on the grapevine he was not pleased with me or the course. He had gone so far that candidates complained to me officially about him. They were being put off their stride. It must have been very upsetting to be constantly told that the man in charge was a Stumble-Bum. I was far from pleased, not because of his opinion of me, but with the fact that he was undermining the work of the other candidates. It was intolerable. Plus, it was insulting the intelligence of the others, by presuming to think for them. A couple of the men in the class almost fixed him.

He was that used to signing wee bits of useless paper, paper that stated the holder was some sort of instructor or other in the multiple skills taught at whichever centre he worked in. Being an instructor in a Outdoor Centre can give some people an over-inflated opinion of their own abilities in the outdoor world. The hubris of this man was something that was only matched by his stupidity. After the candidates complained I had to tell him the facts of life.

I am writing this to illustrate how screwed up some people can get about how skiing works. It's almost always a male sickness. We have a few Grade Ones and trainers like this. All skiing societies have them, throughout the world.

Needless to say he failed his Grade One. After the examination was over, I told Jack Thomson of the trouble we had with this man. Jack was not pleased giving the impression that he should have been informed about his behaviour and that something more public should have been done with him. I never fathomed out what he had to beef about. After all, Bobbie Birnie was his trainer. Jack not knowing about the bother, could get on with running the whole examination. There was no question of this candidate being put under any extraneous influence when being examined, if Jack knew of his behaviour. Jack was above that. His below-par skiing would see to that. He never came back to resit his One. Most folks do.

Richard Berry and Iain Finlayson passed their Grade Twos. These two were a good gain for BASI. Before the year 1970 was over BASI had planned and arranged to run a training and grading course in Gotzens, Austria, in January 1971. Jack Thomson, our chairman, wasn't too keen on this. He made clear that the Grade Ones would always be held at home, a sentiment shared by all. This has gone by the board in recent years. I would imagine, for good reasons. Did I say 1970 may have been an anticlimax!

19. Trip to Torridon

1971 was the year before the Olympics were to be held in Japan. It was BASI's first excursion to the Alps. Between the possibility of our son going to compete in Japan and me with the responsibility of making the BASI Alpine Course work, there was a great deal of excitement to look forward to once again. In 1959 when I first arrived in Davos to attend the Swiss School Director's Course I was mesmerised. 12 years later, with all the wonderful things that had happened to me personally, new doors were about to open. Never in anyone's wildest dreams would the odds of life's glorious gamble throw me another possibility to compare with Davos. It did! Here was I in charge of organising and running the first British Professional Ski Teachers Alpine Course. Our son was in the British Alpine Training Squad for the coming Olympics. It was a long way from a Glasgow tenement and the adventuring along the banks of the River Kelvin. Not bad for two Clydesiders. By which I mean myself and Jeanie Irvine Finlayson.

Undertaking this first Alpine course was a giant step. It might look *small potatoes* in comparison with the extensive activities of today. The scope and volume of ski teaching in those days was fractional by today's requirements, therefore the demand was still an unknown quantity. We had to book so many places through a travel agency to ensure a certain price, when we did not *have* that many bookings. Anyway, the die was cast. It's worth pointing out this to BASI members of to day. With almost no cash reserves, (I doubt if we had a hundred pounds in the bank), I was frightened to tell Jack Thomson. What he didn't know could not give him cause for worry!

At the same time, we had our first demonstration team to the 9th International Ski Teachers Convention, "Interski." This was to be held close by in Garmisch-Partenkirchen. We had to fly out Hans Kuwall and Jack Thomson. Yes, we were once again pushing our luck. We must have been doing things right. British skiing seemed to like what we were doing. We managed to attract near to fifty people. Some who skied in Europe turned up hoping they could get on the course even though they had not booked a place. This was manna from above! With those extra bodies we had enough money to pay all the trainers. I felt like kissing the lovely extra bodies! The old karma was still running hard! Even more satisfying was that seventy-five percent of the candidates were English. The ripple was spreading, and we had a respectable looking course.

Gotzens was an excellent place for the course. We got a friendly welcome from the local ski school. Even though I found out from a young Austrian girl ski teacher that they had almost no work as we had filled the big hotel. There was not much I could say in our defence. I spoke to the ski school boss about it later. He was a man of the world. And as such he understood the vagaries of it. He and I had a few *slams of booze* late some evenings.

We had a Swiss woman on the course who lived in Dublin. She spoke English with a Swiss accent, tidied up with the Dublin way of speaking. She had the million dollar smile. She was Trudi Bishop. We had a big Irish man Michael. He was as Irish as the "Pigs of Docherty." He had the golden tongue, and he gave the world a rosie glow. The quiet gentle people were comfortable with him. He seemed to hold court and take laughter from people, people who were normally a bit mean at enjoying themselves. He was bigger than life. In later courses I would have the privilege to having them in my class, as we'll see.

205

On the middle Sunday of our course I arranged for a coach to go through to Garmisch-Partenkirchen to support our demonstration team which comprised Hans Kuwall, Kenny Dickson and Alasdair Ross. They were splendid. They skied their hearts out! When they were finished, Hans told me he did not remember being out on the slope. The Swiss delegates were very pleased to see our effort. Small is beautiful. Standing there with my class I felt ten feet tall. Sometimes the world *can* be your oyster!

But before we go farther, it was the quiet Jack Thomson who prepared the programme and took the responsibility for its presentation. It shows the power of the man who had limited Alpine skiing experience, when he was able to lock horns with the might and resources of the established ski nations. And produce, with his small team, a performance that left me with a hard lump in my throat. Jack also had to speak our team through their demonstration. I remember on the coach going back to Gotzen's feeling completely washed out. My brain was running as if on gimbals!

The rest of the course went on from strength to strength. I gave a slide and lecture show on the High Level Route. We had an end-of-course party. The talent that was waiting to be released was great. Some of the performances were most revealing, in as much as they gave you an insight into people who had throughout the course maintained *low profiles!*

This course seemed to bring forward a wee coterie of characters. They, somehow or other, seemed to filter into my class and became known as the Rubbish and Scrubbers. As elite a group as you'll find in Christendom! What it did achieve was to set aside the impression that BASI was a Scottish animal. As is very obvious in today's BASI, it is not! For the rest of the 1971 season our snow at home was very good. It seemed to snow all the time.

In the March it was arranged to bring the men's Team up to the Cairngorm to finish their season, prior to the Olympics. As our snow was so good, and with our local connections on the hill, we would have all the cooperation to get on with training at a very high level. There was also a tremendous saving in the costs of maintaining the team. This was arranged through Bob Clyde and myself. Royston Varley and Iain Finlayson had done very well in the French National Championships. They had been 8th and 9th in the Combined. This was a big result. Once again it would appear we were going forward.

I picked some of the team up off the London sleeper. It was then I met the new French trainer. He was young, but not so young. He was a fully qualified French Ski Teacher. This was a step in the right direction. He was a small man, built like the proverbial toilet. When first I met him I liked the "cut of his jib." His name was Michel Rudigoz. We got them fixed up in their accommodation and as it was snowing the skiing was not on. He said he'd to like work on some skis. When he saw our workshop he was delighted. We were careful with each other in the beginning. Rudigoz was a clever wee man. He broke the ice by quietly showing his skills. Bruce Howe, the boss of our ski hire, and I watched him working on the skis. He stripped the bindings off one pair, thoroughly cleaned them, did the soles, tuned them, and waxed them. This was a demonstration par-excellence. The ice was broken! That night he bellied up to the Winkie Owl Bar beside Bruce and Gordon, the ski hire gurus. I nipped in and joined the company myself.

During the month he was in Cairngorm it snowed so much that we could have had a good giant slalom down under the top chairlift, and that before all the extensive snow fencing that's there today. Michel fitted in well to our society. I arranged for him to take BASI members for a technique clinic. What he did was close enough to what we did to be more or less the same. What did stand out was his command of ski teaching English. There would be few in BASI who could match that in French.

As I said, it snowed most of that March. Bob Clyde suggested that, like him, I may be a wee bit sick of living in this white wilderness. Before I could answer he said we could take the wee Frenchman and show him a good part of Scotland. I thought Speyside was a good part of Scotland. But who was I to differ with the Lord of Cairngorm? The good part of Scotland was to be Torridon. He's right, Torridon is a fine part of Scotland. The following tale is well worth the telling.

Bob made the grand gesture of saying the Chairlift would pick up the tab for lunch and all that went with it! I would supply a car with a non-drinking driver, or if one of those "be not available," one who would stay off the bevy. I had just the man, Alasdair Ross. Ali and the wee Froggy, Rudigoz had struck up a fine friendship. We had nice comfortable car and Ali was a good driver. So that was the wheels fixed. Alasdair was delighted, a day off from the hill, with full pay, and out hob-knobbing with the two Lords of the Cairngorms, Bob and myself. Heady stuff for a young boy! How lucky can you get?

The then chairman of the Chairlift Company, the Earl of Leven, had made a reservation for our elite party to lunch at Torridon Lodge. Sandy Leven, that was his name, assured Bob that the food would be up to standard. Rudigoz had turned out to be quite a gourmet, very fond of the good things in life. Bob said to me, "I hope this is as good as the boss says it is." The wee Frenchman was delighted. The food was better than good! The weather on the day was wintery and dreich. A good time to escape. We had a stop at Inverness to take on refreshments to keep us going on the journey and we were off.

A stop at Beauly at a local pub for a midday quickie was inevitable. Ali Ross is kind of local to that area, so he met people in a hostelry that he knew. So that held us up for an hour or so. Clyde and I were a wee bit heavy handed with the large malt whiskies. Rudigoz was mesmerised with the performance of Clyde and myself. We got away from the pub and made *westing*, and, with that, the rain that had been hosing down eased off. This gentled the feel of the weather and brightened up the countryside. Even in weather like that, moving into Wester Ross with nature in the mood it was that day gave an eerie, haunting feeling to the countryside around us. There was no movement in the air. The stillness was almost a living thing. After five months in the constant winds of Cairngorm, you were more than aware of this phenomenon.

The whole scene was capped off by the enormous snow cover on the mountains. These became all the more spectacular the nearer you got down to sea level. Being on the west coast, another phenomenon manifested itself. The snowline at around 1500ft appeared as if it had been trimmed by some giant's knife. This brought about the capped off effect and that very whiteness brightened up the winter sky. The lack of people brought a great sadness and humbling to the severity of the surrounding beauty. It was as we approached Loch Torridon that Rudigoz asked, I quote, "where are all the people?" It must have been the malt whisky I'd taken, prompted by the surrounding evidence of empty glens, because I started to tell the story of the Highland Clearances. Between the drink and how I feel about our Highland Holocaust, I waxed on. Rudigoz, incredulously asked, how Scots could do that to Scots. I explained the Scots who did it "were the Scots land owners."

In all of Europe's Alps from the Sierra Nevada in southern Spain, from the Alps Provence, all the way through France, Switzerland, Italy, Austria, down through the Dinaric Alps of Yugoslavia, all the low and high valleys are peopled. This despite some of the most rapacious feudal systems the world has seen. It does not leave much for the few descendants of these wretched people to be proud of. There was some justice. The Flesh Pots of London, put paid to a number of these gentlemen. When they debauched themselves with their ill-gotten gains, some ended up in debt prisons and worse. Anyway, as my interpretation of this historical event was coming to a close, we arrived at the watering hole. Torridon Lodge. This was a handsome pile. Whoever owned it kept it in mint condition. The lodge lay at the head of Loch Torridon, a sea loch. Liathach, the 3456ft mountain, rises straight up out of the loch, adding that extra dimension to the scale of the scene. The loch was glass calm. It would have taxed a well travelled mountain person to have made a quick decision as to where they might have been at that moment.

The food was very Scottish. A game soup, rich and thick enough to have made a main course. Prawns like wee fat lobsters in a thick sauce that would have made a fair repast on their own. I'd dined well on less, and been thankful. I remember asking if it were possible to have more. Unlike Oliver Twist, up came another large steaming bowl to the centre of the table. It's marvellous when you've got the ball running for you. The sweets and cheese board complemented the excellence of the simple Highland Provender. We had coffee served in front of a lovely open fireplace. A fine brandy was served on a silver tray. We had more than one brandy.

Ali and Rudigoz went to play croquet on a lumpy lawn. Clyde and I moved outside, sat on cast iron chairs and had more fine brandy, while shouting encouragement to the croquet players. Bob Clyde was good at milking any situation, down to its final *drop*. Driving south down that magnificent West Coast, Rudigoz was singing the praises of the meal. Clyde said to me, in Glaswegian, "for a meal where the main course was less than a five pound per person, you've managed to work the bill up to fifty-odd quid!" Ali nearly ran the car off the road. Toffs can be careless! My reply to Bob was, "well, you let me order the wine and you would not have wanted me to make a poor impression on the wee Froggy!" Rudigoz was more than delighted with his Highland lunch. By the time the trip was over late that night, the most part of fifty quid was gone from my pocket. To put a cost on special events the likes of these would quickly turn you into a very dull fellow.

We made a few watering stops on the way home and I know for sure our young sober driver had a couple of *slugs* of the Water of Life! A memorable day's outing. "Gone, alas, are our joys forever." If you knew Michel Rudigoz, you at times called him by his given name. Bob Clyde was the same. But you had to earn the right. He was a clever observant man. His mentality suited ours. He did not need to be punted around the place, he made his own mark!

Near the end of his stay he approached me in a most circumspect way. I wondered what was afoot. He asked me if I thought Ali Ross might be interested in working with the team. He meant, of course, *our* team. This work would be in the capacity of an assistant. Smart arses use the metaphor gaffer or Go-For for this responsible job. It's not how I'd define the correct person who is capable of such difficult work. It needs someone who's smart enough to know when to bite their lip, and yet have a high degree of skill in skiing. There are those who presume they have these elusive special talents who would automatically deem this "simple task" beneath them. Alastair has proved he was above and beyond such futile thinking.

Rudigoz for some perverse reason thought I might be somehow put out about this. I let him know he could get no one better. And I suggested he speak directly with Ali. As a result Ali made a step I'm sure he's never regretted. This would be when Ali became a European Ski Teacher. That was not so simple an undertaking as it seems to be today. The night Rudigoz was leaving he had a nice champagne thank you party for the teachers in our ski school. And there he was, dressed in his suit and collar and tie.

In November, before the training started for the 1972 Olympics, he brought the team up to Cairngorm for some mountain running. We got them the use of the new gymnasium at Kingussie School. Jack Maxwell will remember this. It was a grand effort on Rudigoz's part. But with only half a dozen in the team, it was hard to generate competition. That has always been the UK's problem. Anyway we looked after Rudigoz. He warned me that if I ever came to Val-d'Isere that he would see that I was looked after *special!* And that he did the same year of 1971.

*Cabaret at SSC Decathlon 1971
"Alouette" by Glen Perry, FF,
Chris Lyons.* – RJB

209

20. Snots, Grots and Championships

For some reason or other I decided to go out and have a look at the training prior to New Year. It's not that I was in the least nosy. As far as I was concerned the training was in good hands. Rudigoz had more than proved his worth to me. The fact that all the team members believed in him made him all the more valuable. Ali being there was another plus. Richard Berry was back in charge. And for my money, *his spurs had been hard earned.* I'm sure if Richard reads this, he'll agree that he and I had a good rapport running between us by this time. This was the run up to the Olympics in Sapporo in Japan. Richard would be in charge of the men's team, so this trip would be an opportunity to see what happened to some of the juniors we had been helping to produce over these years. It was all the more attractive for the fact that all those involved were well known to each other.

Richard had agreed to take a young Edinburgh boy to tag along in the training. His name was Christopher Holigan. I made it very clear how tremendously fortunate he was to be given this gift. I warned him if he let me down, I'd *kill* him. Richard even met Chris and me off the night sleeper and we stayed in Richard's lovely farm house in Kent where we met up with Ali Ross. It's very much worth mentioning that Richard's father gave the team the gift of a very practical Humber shooting-brake, in which we all drove out to Val-d'Isere. Richard had a portable double-sided waxing bench specially made. This was another contribution. Wee Rudigoz was tickled pink with it when we arrived. You would have thought it was Christmas! Yes, wee Chris was a lucky boy. Unfortunately he broke his leg. I felt very much for him, but *that's how the cookie crumbles.*

Richard had somehow managed to procure a big Ford car which was lettered with the Team's motifs. While I was out there, Rudigoz managed to prang the Ford. His driving was terrible, even for a Frenchman! Richard was not best pleased. All the nice lettering didn't look very tricky down the one side

We also had got the services of Jack Pitte, a French trainer, who had worked with the previous men's Team. All in all, with two good trainers, and Ali and Richard in support, they appeared well organised. They were all well equipped. Along with the two team cars, Royston, Alex and Iain had their own cars. Rudigoz told me that the head trainer for the French had quizzed him about the size of the Brits' support team. Counting myself, who was skiing about with them, it did look impressive. There were only five in the team at the time and there appeared to be five staff working in support. There was, however, a big problem. The morale of the team was non existent.

Now how this should be was beyond me, after what I've described to you. It was difficult to understand where this trouble originated. It went right over my head that we could not get a hundred percent out of this bunch. I was to find out why. As there was no skiing in Val-d'Isere we were up at Val-Claret, in a small family hotel. There was some bitching about the food. We'd had some of this In Aviemore, in November. There had been nothing wrong with the food in Aviemore. The food in Val-Claret was excellent French cooking. Jack Pitte, Rudigoz, Richard and myself were very impressed. We had a full meal at midday and dinner at night. A wee bit of "short commons" would have sharpened up their appetite. Ali was eating with the boys and, like us, was delighted with the food. Of course, Ali, being brought up on a Highland croft, knocks off a lot of sharp unnecessary corners. Not all the boys were "at it." It doesn't take much to rock the boat.

Everyone in the team had complete sets of slalom, giant slalom and downhill skis. They also had training skis, handmade boots. Rudigoz got me a pair. Back at home, Ian Baxter nipped them off me. Anyway after a few days I learned that Jack Pitte was far from pleased about the team's fitness. Not all the team were unfit.

I was sharing a room with Richard, and it was difficult for me, being who I was and what I may, or may not, have known. While we were resting in our room with a nice malt I'd brought, Richard asked me what I thought was "making the fan stink." I put it straight to him that it was the two trainers who were the cause of the bother. They were not telling the team exactly what time they were to meet, and a few other bits and pieces. So it does not take much imagination to understand that young men, who can complain about high quality provender, can soon pick holes in something that was so wrong.

When the team appeared to be late because of poor instructions from their trainers and then be sworn at in French (which was the language used in the training, and no complaints about that), the team became very confused and resentful. Jack Pitte's temper would not have taken him far in my world. He would oscillate from non productive temper to long chunks of indignant anger. I explained to Richard carefully that he had a very bad situation on his hands. He asked me what I would advise and I explained that if my son had not been in the team I would have spoken to him about it earlier. As I said to Richard, the trainers compared our racers with the French product. Their biggest mistake. Firstly, the French had an enormous reservoir of established racers. This precluded any chance of us matching French talent.

Secondly, the mentality of the average Britisher in no way related to that of the average French person. Consequently the Brit could not, and would not, respond to that sort of regime. A group of six or so persons can never create a truly competitive "team spirit." In my opinion, as a team, they were slack. But Jack Pitte, who'd been in the French Team, had hold of the wrong end of the stick. Alex and Julian were, again in my opinion, needing a firmer hand. This may have seemed a difficult thing to do with so few skiers to choose from. Not so. I would *close the shop* before I'd be horsed about by unfair pressure of any kind. Having said that, calling the bluff is always worth a try. It is seldom those *calling the shots* that lose this one. As life proves.

I suggested to Richard that he make a clear arrangement with the trainers that he be told the meeting times and any other instructions needing to be passed on. This would let all concerned see that the arrangements were going to tidied up. This would soon establish proper time keeping. And straight off, eradicate this gap which was in fact the fault of the management. I did point out that Jack and Rudigoz would twig that both of us had been discussing this. So what. I said that he would need to take a firm hand with these two trainers. After all, he, Richard, was the *boss!* It worked. The training settled down.

A wee bit of historical humour. Rudigoz and Jack Pitte were called The Snot and The Grot. They both wore Val-d'Isere ski school jackets. The jackets were *minging* and wee Rudigoz constantly picked his nose. Mind you, these nicknames were kept a secret from the two they were bestowed on. Rudigoz, good to his word back in Aviemore, looked after me. I was introduced to the Mayor of Val-d'Isere. As I said, he got those hand-made boots. And from him I gleaned some of his skills in turning competition skis into personal skis. He saw to it that I had the use of some of the finest skis that was possible for anyone to ski on.

With my usual stupidity, one day I made a balls of it. There was a classy pair of Slaloms I wanted to try. I had skied with them all morning up on the Grand Motte in the bumps. I thought I was going great. On the way down I met the team. They had been up running wax tests. On the long straight above Val-Claret, they were taking it straight. I tucked in behind them. They were on downhill skis and I was on 207cm. This was another of my many skiing blunders. Trying to keep up with national racers using stiff slalom skis is not too clever. Actually it is impossible for a stumble-bum ski-teacher to keep up with racers even with downhill skis. Rudigoz had a fine rapport with all the team. Work started on the skis after dinner and it was often ten before we'd finish.

Until I started onto this part of these events, I'd never really given much thought as to what Ali was thinking about the scenario that was acting itself out. And I certainly was not going to discuss the trouble the Training went through in the beginning. He was going to be in the middle of it. Therefore he could well do without any of my opinions clouding his thinking. I had no intention of detracting from his own conclusions. Ali was good at keeping his own council. Something that stood him in good stead!

When I got home I was accused of setting Ali up as Team Trainer. This was completely untrue. To start with, Ali was not a trainer. His job was to assist the trainers. And it was Rudigoz and Richard Berry who thought up the idea of using Ali. And a very fine idea it turned out to be. What amazed me was that it was Kenny Dickson who came to me about this. He was incensed about a non-racer being involved at that level.

Years later, when Fraser Clyde was manager of a much bigger team, he took Jimmy Smith on as a trainer. Jimmy had only raced here at home. And Jimmy did a first class job. Fraser also took Jimmy to the Olympics in Sarajevo. Ali Ross never got to Sapporo in Japan, though plenty of hangers-on from the Federation etc. were on the plane. My son reckoned it was a two-to-one ratio of hangers-on to competitors. And we wonder why we have made no inroads into better results in Alpine skiing!

Fraser Clyde never got to the Olympics as a competitor. He broke his leg. I felt strongly for him. What he did achieve was that he managed the team in the way a team should be managed. If the British National Ski Federation had been using its brain-box they should have had Fraser on a ten year contract to manage both teams. We might by now be producing much better overall results. I am absolutely certain that Britain can do much better than they do currently. What did happen to Fraser was that he made a very fair comment about the Federation's Alpine Committee and a certain lady on the committee took the huff. For some reason Fraser was dropped after the Olympics. I remember talking to Bridget, Fraser's wife, about the awful waste of the excellent work he had established. I'm sure Bridget agreed with me. Dropping him was an act of spite.

Back to the team training. Richard must have had a word with The Snot and The Grot. After that things settled down. I would imagine he had a word with the team too. I was quite proud of Richard. We could now settle down before dinner and enjoy a good Cuban cigar and large domestic malt whisky. It was then I got to know the man.

Time for going home, and Rudigoz and Jack Pitte took me out for a French mountain farm-kitchen dinner. This was a memorable affair. Something else for the memory box. The following morning Ali drove me to Geneva and put me into the duty free. After what the French trainers did to me the night before I needed the duty free! And when I said goodbye to Alasdair Ross, little did I realise that Scotland was losing one of its finest ski teachers, *permanently.* Our loss was Europe's gain.

On the way home I had a good think of what I had seen and learned from the time with the team. I had not been allowed to spend any money on anything. The Snot and The Grot let me buy the odd bottle of wine or beer. Not a bad memory of a fine time in my life. And once again left me much richer in knowledge than when I had started.

I was speaking of how well off the team were in transport. Royston Varley, whose home was Murren in the Bernese Oberland had borrowed his father's *pride and joy,* a pristine classic Alvis. The team had an excess of motor transport by this time. When I saw Royston driving our Iain about in this big, pale green, completely unsuitable vehicle for young ski racers, I shook my head. I did mention to Iain that Royston's father was a bold man. Indeed he was, if not somewhat foolish. Some time after that, the young master Varley managed put this collector's item off the road onto its roof. Mind you, my own son managed to write off my Daimler Jaguar a year later. As I said before, toffs are careless!

The year moved on and ended. We took the BASI Course back to Gotzens. On the third day I came off the hill in real bother with the proverbial boot trouble. I had taken three pairs of test boots to try. Not one pair fitted me. I was skiing with a fast class, and the feet were pounding. This was in early January. I was sitting in the Altwirt hotel in my bare feet. They were "gouping." Around six in the afternoon Iain drove up in the wee yellow VW. He walked in and saw the red raw feet. I really was not in the mood for the slagging, but it was justified. I told him I was going out to buy new boots. Iain went out to the car, came back with the boots I'd left in Val-Claret in November. These were the boots I had jocularly discarded as having had it and had asked Iain to give them to some deserving "hardship case." Well I became the "hardship case!" Richard and some of the team arrived later and we all had a good night together. The course candidates were very pleased about this added attraction. After all this was part of their National Team.

The interest in our home was, of course, the coming Olympics. The team was picked and no sign of Iain Finlayson's name on the list. It could not be there were too many in the team to pick from. Fraser Clyde and Julian Vasey were out of it because of serious injury. Maybe the Finlayson mouth had been working. Iain was not slow in stating his case if he thought someone was putting it to him. I never ever found out what the "beef" was. But I do know that he was left out right up to the eleventh hour, before he was told he was getting on the plane.

The good thing that came out of it was that Iain got a twenty-third place in the slalom. Also, it was a wonderful experience, which was topped off by the slalom result. The experience was completed on the way home by racing in the Rocky Mountains where the Americans looked after him royally.

1972 had been full of what today may be called "high powered" events. For some of us a lot of very interesting events had transpired. And to finish off, it had been decided to run British National Championships inviting the best possible world class racers to compete. A most ambitious undertaking. All the more so since there were two events, the Ladies' and Men's. This meant we would need about ten days of "usable weather." The approximate kick-off date was the 13th April 1972. With the best will in the world, and with all the possible luck of all the Irish in the world, this was pushing our luck! The Scottish National Ski Council were running with a full head of steam at the time. They must have been to have taken such a gamble. Anyone having reasonable local knowledge of Cairngorm weather, in particular, would have given very long odds on losing many days that were needed to complete this momentous event. And they would have lost their bet. We did get all the competitions run and in good time and in better than average conditions. So there you are, wrong again! Not only were those bold personages who decided to run the Championships lucky with the weather. They were very clever in who they "selected" to be in charge of all the many different units it took *to **make** the cookie crumble.* They seemed to know who to pick to get the most impossible jobs done with what appeared to be no bother at all. I use myself as a good example. The job I was given was chief of the courses.

This job means you are responsible for preparing the slope and for course setting. And once the course is set you must see that all is in order to hand over to the Technical Delegate. We never had any real bother with TDs. We did have some unofficial experts who proffered their unsolicited useless advice. It was here we used the famous "doing words." *Where Halfwits did tread, Fools fear to tread!*

That statement may make it seem as if this was a simple job. Not so. This was in the days before we had piste machines on Cairngorm. In spring on any mountain, at the end of a day's skiing, the snow is left in a terrible condition. Without going into detail, it's like the wavy sea, only *frozen.* Impossible for most skiers to make their way down it. And it cannot be raced on. Eskimos call it sastrugl. It comes in different shapes and forms. A great deal of work must be done on it before the night frosts wreak havoc on it. Without piste machines, you need around forty to fifty reasonably skilled skiers. Among these you need good commanders. The long and the short of it is that you need these people early in the morning and certainly late at night. There is a great deal of skilled work to be handled throughout the day, to make a success of this thankless task.

As for me, I was ideal for this job. All the managers on the Hill were very close friends of mine. Also the working chairlift gaffers and I knew and held mutual respect over a long period of time. This meant I could almost get away with anything I needed to get the courses prepared and ready for the races. And I used everything I found necessary to make the Cairngorm courses worthy of our Ski Station. That was a tremendous advantage to have had.

What I'm about to tell is the untold story about the "commanders" I've mentioned above. They were from two distinct parts of skiing. There was Hilary

Best, who was BASI Grade One from our first 1963 course, Allan Bell, another Grade One from 1963, and Lyndsay Durno another BASI. These were particular friends. We'd all taught together and knew each others' moods. Despite their misgivings they "volunteered" to come as deputy commanders to help make work what looked like a hopeless undertaking. No pay, no glory. None had been racers, so their contributions were all the more commendable. They were there from 7am in the morning until very late most nights.

Now, for another four redoubtables from the Dundee Ski Club, who were a priceless part of this *volunteer force*. Hugh Scott, Ian Steven, Alan Christie and the one and only Jimmy Gellatly. These four *bears* had been more than enthusiastic racers, and very much a part of Scottish racing. They turned up and presented themselves for duty. With their experience and total commitment to skiing, things were looking better. Maybe I had better take this chance to thank these people. This was another wonderful time in my life finding out just how well people can behave for no reward. For without contributions such as these, ski racers would find it difficult to find any races to test their skills. There were many on the Hill who should have been standing to who never even gave a token gesture.

Walking down from the start of the Giant Slalom on the high shoulder on Cairngorm, late one evening, with about fifty ski teachers who were foot stamping the men's course, a very fine Austrian skier, Tony Wimmer, said to me, and I quote, "these nice ski teachers would make one good Cairngorm Ski School." And how right he was.

The local skiers took all these international racers in their stride. It's hard to make a mark on the Scots psyche just because convention says you are something special. The Scot is not dour. What the Scot is good at, is not being easily impressed! The Championships got going. We were on a roller coaster and we were all hooked!

People who impressed me. Firstly, the Swiss Technical Delegate, a Swiss National Racer, Odette Perret. As I said earlier we never had a cross word. She knew all there was to know about setting up races.

Then, Hugh Hunter Gordon, a Scot. He was Chief of Championships in charge of the whole shebang. He had an English public school type Scots accent. All the jury meetings were chaired by Hugh. This he did with skilful humour. At the final prize-giving he made one of the most impressive addresses on the importance of skiing for all, that I have ever heard, and in the process made all the visitors glad they had been part of our first International Ski Championships.

Next, Florence Steurer the famous French racer who did so well in the Championships. She was retiring from international racing and was presented with a Celtic silver brooch. Hugh explained this was a token given by the ancient Scottish Celts to young maidens starting out on a new journey in life. I don't know how accurate that lovely story may have been, but the French loved it, as did the rest of us. Who needs to be accurate when the story's good!

Then there was the indomitable Helen Tomkinson, who represented the National Ski Federation. Helen came from a long line of English skiers. At the jury meetings she stated her case clearly in French and in German. This lady knew the F.I.S. Rules from cover to cover. Trainers at jury meetings will try any lying subterfuge to get "their" racers' start numbers improved. With Helen they had to be more than right, with a covering letter from the Pope, or it was no go. A marvellous personality. There were many different colourful happenings that added to the overall impressiveness of this once-in-a-lifetime experience.

On a free day the French team went over to Deeside, where they managed to cross the River Dee and were found inspecting the grounds of Balmoral Castle. That would probably have had more serious repercussions today. Or, as an afterthought, be seen as "an offence."

To finish on a real high. Some of the French team had attended a football match in Glasgow. While they were standing watching play, a Glasgow man asked if they were skiing in the races on Cairngorm. It was Bernard Orcel and Alain Penz he spoke to. The Glasgow man was Davy Todd, a member of the Creag Dhu Climbing Club. Davy wanted to know if they knew all of us who worked up there. When Davy Todd told me that story, I asked him how he knew who these people were. He had spotted their French Team ski jackets. I'd like to see some Irishman beat that story!

With these pleasant anecdotes, we'll leave those long gone memories of a tremendous gamble that came off. We finished the season very late with the BASI Course. When it was over BASI had two new Grade One members, Bridget Newall Clyde and Willie McKenna. BASI was gaining strength.

21. A Special Trip

The season 1973 started well, having attended the start of the men's team training, and having had a son who competed in the Olympics in a country as interesting as Japan. Being part of that ten days of international racing on Cairngorm certainly set us up and left a good feeling in all of us who were deeply involved in skiing, in its totality. The Men's Team had changed. Konrad Bartelski and Peter Fuchs joined and it appeared that Julian Vasey had given up. As I said previously, Fraser Clyde had been injured. We had arranged for the team to have fitness training in Aberdovey Wales, for a period of four weeks. It was a tough course that had been specially prepared for them.

Even better, the Men's Team were to train with the Austrian National Squad. This was a tremendous opportunity. To my exact memory, almost straight off, the downhill performances of our squad improved dramatically. When the odd phone calls came from our son the conversations were spiked and vibrant with enthusiasm. You felt as if you were speaking to a different person.

Toni Sailer was the head of the Austrian Training. Toni had six Gold Medals. Here was our team being trained in the middle of one of world's top skiing nations. Just being part of the training was like being in actual competition. So everybody was very happy, or should have been.

Unfortunately a mistake had been made. Fraser Clyde, who'd broken his leg in the run up to the Sapporo Olympics, had not been invited to be part of the training. Golfing one day in November with Bob Clyde, Fraser's father, I casually mentioned if Fraser had gone off to Austria. It turned out that Fraser knew nothing about what was happening. I'd presumed that Fraser would have been invited. After his terrible luck at missing his chance of the Olympics, you would have thought the powers-that-be would have made some sort of gesture towards him. If they had considered him unfit they should have communicated this to him. Instead he hears of it through a family friend. What a way to find out you are considered not fit for something you have worked for all your young life! It's possible that you may be completely unfit. But you should be told the moment the decision has been taken. Even if you wore tartan knickers you could not blame this mismanagement on the National Ski Federation in London. Unless my memory is serving me wrong, the Scottish National Ski Council was in charge of the Men's Team at that time.

Without flogging a dead horse, this was a very poor effort in dealing with a very simple but very serious time in a young man's life. At the time this happened you got the impression that those in charge presumed that Fraser had quit. How little did they know the man! Because of the clout Bob Clyde carried, Fraser went out and joined the team. As it turned out, it did not matter. The training with the Austrians, for some reason, had come to an end. I never ever found the clear reason for this. But I would like to think it was finance and not some other kind of truncated reasoning.

Fraser would get his *time in the sun*. He would be manager of the teams. And in the opinion of most knowledgeable people I knew, they were in agreement that he had the right ideas and experience to establish a long term progressive system for the future of British ski racing. But, as I said earlier, he had the effrontery to criticise a part of the establishment, and therefore, had to go. All because of the small-mindedness of a particular part of the establishment

217

that he had the cheek to criticise. What a shame. We will never know how well he might have done with the teams. At home, skiing was settling in and starting to look as if it had been on the ground for a long time.

A bunch of good skiing friends got together and decided to have an early skiing holiday in the Alps. I'd go with my ski school minibus and a hand-picked group. It just so happened we all worked in skiing together. The fun started when we all met up in the fine city of Edinburgh. The time of the year was the end of November. We had arranged to meet Iain Finlayson in St Moritz. It is seldom that a trip you organise and have so much hope for its success turns out like that. But it turned out to be just exactly as we hoped it would be. We crossed over from Harwich to Rotterdam. The crossing is well known for the excellent food and the long sleep. We all got the dinner, but very little sleep. I had a private cabin booked, went to a party in a big cabin, got lost going back to the private cabin, couldn't find my way back to the party, and ended up sleeping in the urinal. So "the best laid schemes..."

Luckily, next morning we had in our group the first BASI lady trainer, Sue Dickson, an excellent driver. And, need I say, in better condition to drive than any of the men. We also had Carol, wife of Peter Simpson, and another good driver, but not a skier. The other two appointed drivers, Ian Baxter and myself, were in no condition to drive. Bless the ladies! When we got about a 100 miles into Germany, we got the Solo Whist gambling school going. Carol had never played Solo before, but it only took her about half an hour to play like a veteran Clydeside shipyard worker! Later on, under closer examination, she admitted to having some skill playing Bridge. A female hustler from the Western Islands of our West Coast.

As I remember, Sue did a big lump of the driving as the other fit good driver– come Bridge player was too busy taking advantage of ex-Red Clydesider's expert Solo players! I did mention to Tommy McKee that I hoped Carol would give us a break and not take up the skiing in any serious way, otherwise we'd all be in trouble!

We had another character in the group, the only one I never knew very well. He was a Brummy by the wonderful name of John Henry Morgan. He went by the name of Mugsie. Mugsie had a zest for other people; this in a society like ours, where this was common place. Of all of this group, when the holiday was over I'd would have said he got more out of it than any of us.

There was wee Tommy McKee a boilermaker from Clydeside. Tommy and I went back to my early days in the outdoor life. He was a bachelor, had the nicknames of the Millionaire Boilermaker, or Goodgear McKee. This would stem from him being a bachelor and having more spending money than most of us. He also, at one time, had a wee Pools Lift. In my opinion he was just a wee tidy man who would not go out of doors unless he looked "a treat." Well turned out.

Peter Simpson and I had overwintered a number of times. He had been our ski school boss for a number of years. You learn a lot about a person when you have to live and work in such close proximity over the years. Like Tommy, he was a very special family friend, as he is to this day.

I have also spoken of Ian Baxter, another of the merry travellers. Ian is one of our *good* skiers. He and I first skied in July 1962, in a ski teachers' clinic. Since then the two of us had maintained a good understanding of each other. Ian, like many of us, had been unfortunate in that he came into British skiing before fulltime skiing was possible for the likes of us. But, like many others, despite this he made his mark in the profession.

The last, but not least, of this mixed but well balanced group, was Hazel Bain. For readers who are not conversant with some basic knowledge of the history of British professional skiing, Hazel was what could be called a *doyenne* in British ski teaching. For years she has been the secretary and manager of BASI. Hazel was very much part of the bones of BASI. This is when ski teaching was still finding its feet in the growing strength and possibly of things to come. Almost all of the people in that van were deeply involved in fulltime skiing. It could be that this stimulated everyone's endeavours and in the process turned the trip into something to be remembered.

Our first Port of Call would be St Moritz. It was here we would meet Iain Finlayson. We drove from Chur early in the morning through Lenzerheide and over the Julier Pass. It was one of those brilliant Alpine mornings. Being so early in the season even we, who were no strangers in these high mountains, become spellbound. As we breasted the crest of the Julier Pass, there it was, the Engadine in all its early winter glory. That's the way it comes back to me. In all the time I've had the privilege of being in and around the natural world I've never became blasé, or taken occasions like this for granted. Nature in the mountains is never bland or dull. If you care to look about, even on the dreich days there is much to be seen. The run down to Upper Loch Torridon that early afternoon with Rudigoz, Bob and Ali Ross, was one such day, dreich an' all, as it was!

Out of the group it was John Henry "Mugsie" Morgan who stands out. When he saw that long slot of a valley that is the Engadine, he started to gitter in his quick Brummy way of speaking. He got so excited in trying to describe what he was seeing, he became tongue-tied. But there was more to come. We drove through Champer straight to the bottom station of Piz Corvatsch. When Mugsie saw where we were heading, his mouth was off again. His biggest mountain, up to that time, had been Cairngorm. He was not a mountain person, and there he was standing, looking at his first cable car that soared away up a steep mountainside.

When he reached the top station of Corvatsch, he was amazed when he saw the luxury of this newish way of catering to the new generation of skiers. A modern restaurant sitting at 3451m, with its commanding views. Today there are many great rotating restaurants. The first of these would be the Schilthorn above Murren. Another at Eginerjoch at Saas Fee. And many others. The tragedy of it all is that the Swiss franc against the pound exchange rate precludes the use of these wonderful ski areas to most skiers today. We had a super day, full of events which come sharply to memory when looking back. Later that day we met Iain Finlayson in the Hotel Steffani in St Moritz. This is a famous place where British and Scottish Ski Club members are always especially welcome. It was then we learned that training with the Austrian Team had come to an end. Anyway we all had a fine get-together that night.

Iain had a wee New Zealand racer with him. This wee young fellow was travelling around Europe trying to get into the odd race, and Iain had taken him under his wing. It's a long way from New Zealand to be on your own and trying to get into a decent race. Sure he had to have to money get by, but it shows a fair degree of spirit and enterprise. I called him the Dormouse. He was always sleeping.

Those who had not skied in St Moritz were naturally thrilled and Mugsie was set to gittering again. Carol Simpson, the non-skier in the party, was loving it. On the first day skiing on the Corviglia and Piz Nair, Carol Simpson came up to work on her sun tan. There is an area where non-skiers sit and sun themselves. Carol, dressed in her Marks and Spencer's jacket, found herself in among a big number of ladies and men doing the same thing. There was a dramatic difference in their dress. These others were attired in various fashion designed ankle-length mink coats, hats and snow boots of the same material. There was a distinct difference between the men and the ladies. The ladies, for the most part, were tall, slim and *helluva good looking*. The men, for the most part, were far from that. Rich men with their play things. That's life.

I skied down with Peter to see how Carol was getting on. We found her sitting between two of these long Slinky Burds. I'm sure she was purring, and rubbing herself up and down on the minks. As a matter of fact I accused her of doing it. Carol, never short of an answer, said, "it's the closest I'm going to get. It might rub off!" There's more than one way to enjoy the delights of St Moritz.

While we are on about these Slinky Burds, when we arrived at St Moritz we met a well known ski teacher from Cairngorm, called Plum Worrall. While Carol was doing the rubbing and purring, I found Plum trying to pick up this gorgeous, be-minked American lady, not quite a Burd. If truth be spoken, a helluva lot better looking than a mere Burd. She had a nice wee delicate touch of mileage on the clock! I'm sure the magic of St Moritz had gone to his head. Anyway, the lassie was lucky. I rescued her!

That day the whole group was going up to Piz Nair. Mugsie and I had to wait in what at that time was a nice small restaurant in the top station. Up came the waiter, black jacket, black tie and slick as silk. Like an old hand at the caper, I ordered a bottle of good Dole du Mont. Nothing but the best for Mugsie and friend. Back comes the waiter, silver tray, white towel over the arm, the gleaming glasses. He gives me a wee taste, I nods the head. Mugsie was most impressed. Needless to say, the Brummy's mouth was off again. Mugsie was going to go back and tell Bob Clyde how you should run a mountain restaurant. I did point out to him that the Swiss had been looking after mountain travellers since the turn of the century. And warned him to keep away from Clyde, about how he should run what Bob called "His Mountain." *Where fools fear to tread.*" Being with Mugsie was a breath of fresh air. The rest of the crowd arrived just in time to see us swallow the last of the Dole du Mont.

Unfortunately, being so early in the season we did not have enough snow to ski down the front of Piz Nair, so we skied down round the rat-run on the north side. This was icy and the rat-run path is cut across a very steep slope, which is terrific in deep snow. We'd all battered down, as is the wont in a group like this, and stopped at the bottom, where we noticed Hazel Bain was coming round the corner well above us. In her effort to catch up, she was going far too fast for her ability. She caught an edge, came right over and off the rat-run head first on her face, going like the stuff-off-the-shovel. Baxter was nearest, and, because he's fast on his feet, he managed to get to her and stop her. She was in no way damaged, but it goes without saying, she was in a state of shock. Which she of course tried her best to hide. Unfortunately you cannot hide shock. Or should I say, fortunately. Hazel had to put so much into her skiing that, when she stretched herself, she became vulnerable to making mistakes from which she had no ability to recover. This was one of those occasions. Once again, there's a price to pay for all things good. Some people have more to pay than others. And in skiing, Hazel was one of those.

It was later that day that we met a local ski teacher we knew. He had spent a winter in Cairngorm, and his name was Mario Veradari, a St Moritz man. He was well educated and spoke a number of languages. He even had the old mountain language of Romanisch. Mario could understand us when we spoke quickly. His own English was without accent and he greatly enjoyed our humour. I personally had a good rapport with him.

He had me home to his parents for dinner one evening. They had a flat in the centre of the village, which would indicate considerable means. Yet neither the mother nor the father spoke English. I found this strange. They were typical Swiss mountain people, strong and of quiet demeanour. The evening went exceedingly well. I seemed to have long conversations with the father, despite the lack of common language. This is another pleasant memory of the Swiss mountain people. Once they take to you, their natural mountain reserve seems quickly to slip away.

The week after we were leaving, the Swiss Ski School Director's Course was starting. I met one of directors of the Open Course that is run in tandem with the Director's Course. They were desperately short of English-speaking teachers for the advanced running classes. One of the directors button-holed me about all the good teachers in our group. We certainly had Sue, Baxter, Peter, Iain and myself. The money was great, with accommodation and food. Unfortunately Iain had to go to a important race in Courchevel. An opportunity missed. We could have made enough bread between all of us to live *high off the hog!* You can't win them all.

It is not every skier who gets to ski in St Moritz with friends, especially friends who skied so well. The shame was that the snow at the time was very poor. St Moritz in good conditions is a delight. We left St Moritz with Iain's wee yellow VW in convoy. A merry band. Iain wanted into the minibus so Hazel and Sue were stuck into the VW. We were off! Next stop Courchevel. Courchevel was the first custom built ski station in Europe. The man responsible for its design and location was the world famous French racer Emile Allais. I was looking forward to seeing just how well the great man had done his work and I was not disappointed.

When we arrived we found the resort had only been opened to accommodate the race. However, as we were with a British Racer we were made very welcome. And given free lift passes. The old karma. It was here I would meet a Toni Sailer, a man with six Gold Medals. A most impressive person, as I would find out in the near future. We also met a lovely wee Austrian ski teacher who had worked on Cairngorm, Norbert Uitz. He travelled the circuit for Koflach boots and Kastle skis. A great wee man, he speaks with a Carrbridge-English accent, which is musically quaint and very different. There was a slalom and a giant slalom. After the giant slalom was over, Norbert told me that Toni Sailer had a serious problem. There were 16 young men in the Austrian team with the same points in giant slalom, out of which he had to pick four for the next race. Some quandary, one that will not bother us in the immediate future.

One of the men who was involved with our men's team was in Courchevel at the time. He was Hugh Hunter-Gordon, who had done such a good job when he was in charge of the two weeks' racing in Cairngorm that same spring. Hugh and I had some long talks about where the team might be going. I don't know if Hugh remembers much about what was discussed, but I remember one item about why some of our team could not race the following week in the Première Neige in Val d'Isère. The reason for this decision was that, until the team improved their downhill points, they would not be entered into World Cup races. Even though we the Brits had, through the system at that time, some places in these events by right, for some perverse reason those in charge had taken this pointless decision. There was another Scot who was involved in this at the time, an ex-club-racer from the Dundee Ski Club, Ian Steven. How Ian was part of this thinking, with his background in skiing, went over my head. I include these incidents because they are very important details of how our teams were being handled at that time as I have done in describing how Richard Berry dealt with the two trainers who were, without a doubt, "horsing him about."

It comes back to me vividly that the night before we left Courchevel, I was staying in the same hotel as Toni Sailer, and he came and gave me the programmes for the Première Neige. He said, "this is for your son." Remember, Iain had been training under Toni's direction. When Norbert heard the reason Iain could not race in the Premiere Neige, he said that nothing has changed. Norbert having been a racer could see the daftness of this. These things do happen in life. It's at times like these that quotations come to mind.

John Henry Ford the First, to give him the title he gave himself, was a person that someone of my philosophy has little time for. He made this statement. "If you are having trouble in the running of your business, investigate management. If, after doing that, you are still having trouble, keep investigating management." There might be something in that. It may apply if you have complete control over all that concerns you. Few people have this luxury. He did. The most of our party were only concerned with the skiing and the conditions were nice and wintry. This was an added bonus of having been in their second major resort in a week. Now we were off to the mighty Val d'Isère. It wasn't too long since I'd been there. Like St Moritz, the snow was poor. The weather made up for that and up on the Grand Motte it was more than suitable for us Cairngorm skiers, who are more easily pleased than our Continental brethren.

Iain and I watched downhill practice runs for the Première Neige. Iain never said anything to me standing there watching young racers doing their non-stop training runs. Many with poorer points and less experience than Iain. This was a young man who had been ninth in the French National Championships, and had been to the Olympics. That would be the last time I would be involved in any way with a British team. Even if I'd been interested, I'm sure the establishment would not have been. The likes of me, in societies such as ours, are given a wide berth. Probably in any society! We all left "The Val" happy in spirit and the richer for having all been together over the last weeks. This was another skiing first, and like most of the good things, it all seemed to come together as one day followed the next. As if by pure chance.

Driving up through the Pass of Killiecrankie, new snow had made the country more beautiful. Baxter was playing his guitar, and McKee, who was a good singer, and the rest of us, sang most of the way home to Aviemore. Tommy and I sang old weekend songs. In the van there was a special feeling of camaraderie that was soft and gentle. It seemed to grow and, without the stimulus of alcohol, kept itself going all the way to Aviemore. I doubt if I've felt the same thing since. What a start to the new and coming season. With all that had taken place in the last two years, it would appear that skiing was becoming, for some of us, more or less a fulltime commitment, rather than a seasonal occupation. This was good for skiing. It was giving skiing a better chance for steady continuity.

BASI was steadily becoming a much more stable and viable entity. We had very smart uniforms. This was something I was personally proud of. We were reaching the stage where we had a bit more flexibility in our choice of trainers. I say this in no mean or bumptious way. It was a fact of life that, up to starting this period, the standard of our trainers was just keeping pace with the improving standard of candidates coming forward. For our country's experience in skiing, this was just about right. Having said that, we had still a long way to go. And *still* have. Satisfyingly, at that particular time, we were in the process of bringing into full membership young skiers like Hugh Clark, Peter Fuchs and Iain Finlayson. These all had considerable racing experience. At the same time we had other young skiers, male and female, who had been skiing since their school days. So the future seemed to have a much broader horizon. Something to look forward to.

Now, having run two BASI courses in Gotzens, I had arranged for a course to be held in Saas Fee, Switzerland, in Canton Valais. In 1973 it was still possible to undertake a project like this in Switzerland. To try such a thing today would beggar the imagination when you see the rate of exchange. I had never skied in Saas Fee. In the Swiss School Director's Courses I had made a number of friends of ski teachers from Saas Fee. Like Zermatt and Wengen, this village had many ski teachers who are mountain guides. Like Zermatt and Wengen, no cars were allowed in those villages. It must have taken a lot of determination for the local people to resist the pressure for that. At least Swiss locals seem to have the right to protect their birthrights. Something we, in this country, never seem to have enjoyed.

If I had been looking forward to the Gotzens course, I was more than keyed up about running this course in Switzerland. The freedom of not having the worry of paying the trainers, and being able to pay them reasonable wages. This stands out in my mind. What also stands out in my mind is how proud I was with our new uniforms. One of my close personal friends who had attended the first two Gotzens courses was an old Saas Fee hand. He was like a local. His name was Jack Wilson. So with my connections, and with Jack being almost like a local, the ship was fully trimmed. I fell in love with Saas Fee. It was a wee jewel lying under the Fee Glacier, with its narrow wee up and down walkways. It was more hemmed in than the Zermatt walkways. By pure accidental research, I discovered what Saas Fee might mean (between the Italian and German languages) "Rocky Pastures." They're as daft as the Celts. There is not too much pasture in those high places!

This was a fine time. It was here I started to find out what was starting to happen as far British ski teachers in Europe were concerned. I'd first taught out of Lauterbrunnen and Wengen in 1958. Ali Ross in Wengen in 1972. Few Brits. had made that step at that time. And here we were, running a BASI Course in the high hinterland of Switzerland. We even had two young Germans in their early twenties, who had asked to join in and undergo our Grade Three. This intrigued me as the Germans had a grading system of their own. I never really found out why they were at our Course. They did come to Scotland that spring and successfully take our Grade Two.

It came over strongly to me that they thought they skied better than they did! They were always on about going through the sticks. I explained that the "sticks" were not on their programme. To be fair, and give them their moment in the sun, I set up about thirty gates. It so happened Iain Finlayson was there for a few days off, between races. We had him demonstrate how to attack the gates. For someone still on circuit, Iain could make a feast of thirty gates. The two boys knew what Iain was. You could see them winding themselves up in the start gate. I had put a wee tricky bit in the middle on the course. Both of them blew right out of the course.

Naturally I was expected to go down the course. I was only 44 at the time and thirty gates are a lot different to 65 or 70. My time was quite good in relation to Iain's. We had another couple of goes at it. The results were the same. A salutary lesson, which the boys took in good humour. Not much else they could do. Their English was excellent enough to call me a fit old "Twisted Bastard," and I know exactly what they meant. Eric Langmuir the principal of Glenmore Lodge loved seeing these young boys getting a good humoured lesson. The rest of the candidates were delighted. This added a great deal to the feel-good factor and the morale of the course. I was pleased.

I was delighted how the courses were building up their own momentum. We were finding our way in and around what was needed to things simple. *Screwing up the ball game* in ski teaching is the easiest game in town. And the worst. I've always believed (and still do) that to lecture about ski technique puts the lecturer on dangerous ground. This is definitely a subject for another venue. Snow for example. As I said that when I was introducing this subject on our first BASI course in 1963, I personally used the "question and discussion" approach. This means the individual candidate can, from the anonymous safety of "the body of the Kirk," state their case as to how they think the "skis turn." And *stand in the sun*, as is their right. As individuals with the right to their own opinion on the matter, without having fancy badges and certificates. It also protects the would-be-lecturer from having to make absolute, dogmatic decisions as to how the skis turn, within *technique*. A pursuit more foolish, than religious, or political, debate.

Among all ski teaching communities you get the smart arses who love to stick it to you. An easy thing to achieve from the safety of a comfortable chair in a room which, unlike the snow slopes, is neutral, and where your performance cannot be judged. As I have said before, you never have knowledgable ski teachers involving themselves in the futility of splitting hairs. I know someone who will smile quietly to herself, when she reads this. Mrs Fiona Thomson once rightly accused me of doing just this. Of course, *I* was doing it with *style!* I bring this up because other trainers had to be brought in to contribute in this part of the course. And I know they were falling into this. I had seen it at the Swiss Director's Course. Anyway, I know for sure it's quite a problem in the BASI courses of today. That will ruffle a few feathers! But there is nothing wrong with facing up to any problems you may have. If you do, you can only improve.

Saas Fee turned out to be an excellent location for our course. Perhaps its ties with British climbers and skiers that went back to the turn of the century helped to ease our intrusion into this old fashioned, charming example of a high Alpine community. Jack Wilson, who I've mentioned was treated as local, had been teaching fulltime there for two years. With a modest BASI Three. It's who you know, not what you know, and if your face fits! I myself was a friend to the ski school boss and many of the mountain guides-come-ski teachers. This made our presence less intrusive.

There was one local ski teacher, a nasty piece of work, who gave me a wee bit of bother one day. The "young" Jimmy Smith asked me if he would sort this loud mouth out. That was easy, but not clever. Arnold Adermatin, the ski school boss, sorted it out. And that was the matter closed.

The course by this time was establishing regulars. Out of these there developed an identity and singleness of purpose. A fine rewarding thing for our Association. There developed classes of Grade Three and Two members who were preparing themselves for higher grading courses. Or who just wanted to ski in good company. I always took one of these classes. It went by the metaphor of the "Rubbish and Scrubbers." A very special group. Reasonable skiing was sufficient to get you into our class. However there were other talents needed. If you did not have them, there were experts in the class who could teach them as you went along. No extra charge!

A good friend of mine was taking the Grade Three examination at the end of the course. Our class of Rubbish and Scrubbers were in a bar having "lunch." In came Clive Freshwater and told us to come out to see something, This friend

Race Training – Self, Sue Dickson, Iain Finlayson

was doing the teaching for Grade Three. We were treated to an exhibition of teaching and class handling of the highest order. There we were, the "High Heid Yins," standing watching. Many would have buckled under less beady eyes. Not Hedley Wright from the Mull of Kintyre, Scotland. He was a brick made of sterner stuff. And a colourful character. Unfortunately Hedley's skiing did not match his other abilities. It would be another two seasons before he would proudly pin the BASI Grade Three badges on his jacket.

Before the season was over Iain Finlayson would give up racing. I was not too pleased about it. In his opinion there almost no support from the powers-that-be. Even less from management. I still never agreed that he should give up. He could have entered on his own. The old adage about taking a horse to water is, I'm afraid, true!

Back at home by this time we had been building up the Cairngorm Junior Training Squad. Sue Dickson and I had been working together on this for two seasons. Iain came in to the training and contributed the skills he had been learning and garnering since he won his first race, "the Bairn's Bucket," at six years of age. Sue was very suited for this work, something not many people are cut out for. This is where in ski teaching you can do almost irreparable damage. Those who are entrusted to this task should fully understand how the skis "turn." And a lot could be written about that.

Like many others, I am convinced serious damage was done on Cairngorm by the use of inexperienced poorly skilled, unsupervised kids as trainers, who were left to transfer all their own faults to the unfortunates that were entrusted to them. The blame for this, once again, must be placed at the feet of the administrators. I have spoken earlier about the choice of selecting suitably skilled persons for this critically important task. Allan Askins, another old friend of mine, joined the ranks of the Grade Ones. And he's still working away at it.

22. Summer Camp in the Rockies

When fortune is running well for you it can run loose and fast. For the last dozen years the world had been an oyster for our family. The winter mornings could not come quickly enough for me, no matter how bad our weather on Cairngorm was. As bad it can be, it never seemed to be the grind it can be of recent years. The constant perniciousness of Scottish mountain weather can be *hard to thole*.

The year 1974 got a fine start for me personally, with the BASI course back in Saas Fee. I had the lovely class I have already mentioned. They were Grade Threes. Trudi Bishop, the vivacious Swiss lady, who spoke English tidied up with a touch of the Dublin Irish. We had Michael O'Donaghay, a one hundred percent Dubliner. This was a man to be remembered. He'd charm all the birds out of all the trees without knowing he was doing it. There was an English lady by the name of Shelagh, and like Trudi, a charmer who made any man feel ten feet tall. The famous Hazel Bain, the general factotum for all BASI members over long years. And, of course, secretary. Jack Wilson, like Hazel, a very special friend of mine. Jack's particular skill was trouble. He could cause it in a monastery.

There was a younger girl from Speyside by the name of Chris Stoddart. She worked in our ski school in Aviemore. Chris was a BASI Grade Two. The reason she was in my class was to boost her skills in skiing and teaching, in preparation for her Grade One in spring. Chris became a demonstrator for the New Zealand Ski Teachers Association and demonstrated on their behalf in Japan in 1979. As you see, she became a *good* skier. She was very good to have in the class, but because of her skiing ability she inadvertently, at times, created some stress in the class.

As she improved I became more demanding of her performance. In her effort to come up to my demands she started to get bitchy with herself. This is the same as pressing the self-destruct button. As happens when a skier is crossing from almost good skiing, into *good* skiing, she ran into the invisible *blank wall*. She was a hard case and could be treated as such. I explained to her that the bitching was doing her no good, and that it was getting up the noses of the rest of the group. Being a good friend, I took her as close to the limit as was safe. I did point out to her that the class would give their eye teeth to ski half as well as she did. That lunchtime I used secret weapon number one. Two slugs of brandy slung down her throat knocked a hole in the blank wall, and through it she came. And in the process she skied the butt off me! There is a long steep slope below the Lange Fluh Hut. Chris and I started to short-swing down that slope. I pulled every lousy trick and stunt I knew. She was not allowed to lift her ski tails, as so many do, as they mistakenly say they are short-swinging. Short Swings are not every girl's cup of tea. They didn't seem to bother Stoddie. I kept having a look back, and this was my undoing. I fell right on my face! And Stoddie kept swinging away. That stopped the bitching. I did the same thing to my teacher, Werner Stager, in Zermatt not too many years before. Stoddie passed her Grade One handsomely in the spring of that year. Chris has a brother Peter who was one of the most gifted skiers I have ever had the pleasure to ski with. Yet, for one lucky enough to live in the mountains, he did nothing with his gift. What a dreadful waste.

With my other duties as Course Director most of my days finished at around seven in the evening. Trudi and Shelagh would have the class up to one of their rooms for pre-dinner snacks. Smoked salmon, caviar and other wee things to titivate the appetite. The ladies would have their long dresses on. They even had the wash-hand basin covered with a fur coat. After the first night the men took to wearing suits. It was all very proper and seemed to be in keeping with the quality of the people in the group. There were, of course, suitable wines served. This was without a doubt one of my outstanding memories. On my final night the class presented me with a pocket watch with matching silver fob. I had their names inscribed inside it. A possession dear to my heart. This was the class of the "Rubbish and Scrubbers" Some Scrubbers, some Rubbish!

There was another event that happened on that course. An Austrian, who had been teaching on Cairngorm since 1964, came and started to undertake the BASI course. This was a man who had the chance to take advantage of the special two week course in 1965. He would have passed and made himself a Full Member. He greatly regretted not having taken advantage of that special two week course. His name was Helmut Ehrenstrasser, a very gifted skier by nature. He could make any old set of skis make music. He could also speak Glaswegian. Helmut was a bundle of fun and good at getting into trouble.

On the second BASI Course in 1964 there was a Londoner by the name of Roy Ferris. He qualified as a Grade Two. He moved over to Vancouver where he managed to obtain the franchise for running the ski school on Whistler Mountain, the new ski area north of Vancouver in Garibaldi National Park. Now how a partly qualified, non-Canadian managed this I really can't remember, I doubt if that would be allowed under the conditions that prevail in Canada today. From this he established the Toni Sailer Summer Ski Camp. Roy had been asking me to come out and see his operation for a number of years. In early June Jeanie and I did just that.

I would imagine anyone making their first trip to that great mountain range that runs from Mexico to the Arctic tundra would be excited. I was one of those. The saying "it's a small world" is stained with truth. Sitting next to me on the plane to Toronto was a wee man from Newton Stewart, a salmon poacher, a scrawny wee fellah going out to visit some of the countless Scots who populate that part of Canada. I remember this well because he was dressed as if he had just come off the river after a night's poaching. He and I had a good time swapping stories about nights on the rivers. Plus a few drams!

Our first contact with the Canadian people on their own ground was very pleasant. We found them to be civil and helpful. On asking directions in Toronto Airport a young couple took Jeanie and me personally to the departure lounge for Vancouver. We found this to be normal throughout our stay in that fine country. The stopover at Calgary for an hour has stayed with me. It was as the sun was starting its descent before evening. Having had, like all of my age group, a healthy diet of badly made cowboy movies, I was treated to a wondrous example of the golden western sky at night. The big silver 707 took off and beat the coming darkness all the way to Vancouver. Or so it seemed.

The plane was almost empty leaving a choice of window seats. To my fertile way of thinking, and in the frame of mind to be easily impressed, what I saw below did not disappoint my already fired up imagination. We were moving over these terrific mountains. It was early June, yet it was like flying over the Alps in deep winter, there was so much snow. Great rivers ranged their courses through what looked like new fresh unspoiled country. There did not appear to be much in the way of habitation. It was as I expected it to be. The emptiness of the big flying machine meant the "room service" was prompt. It was the old *karma* working again. As we dropped down the flight path into Vancouver we were to be treated to a second helping of the golden western sunset. Not bad, two in the one day!

We received a king's welcome from my friend Roy. This is the kind of friend that mountain pursuits can bring you. Roy had booked Jeanie and me into a hotel. He apologised for not having room in his house as it was too small. I was delighted. It meant that we were free agents for the few days we'd be there. The hotel was the Park Royal. It sat on the side of a salmon river called the Capilano. Not bad, a salmon river right in the middle of a city! Quite a number of those in Scotland! With the summer snow-melt, the run-off made the Capilano run with tremendous power.

Toni Sailer was waiting in the hotel with Jane, Roy's wife. Jane was a lively, handsome lady of easy humour, who was comfortable and fun to be with. Toni, Jane and Roy were going out on the town. Roy insisted that we would be jet-lagged, so we'd want to get to bed. Jeanie was tired, but I was in no way jet-lagged. As we were being ushered up to our room, the sound of merry making came up from this stairwell. On enquiring as to what it may be, to my delight I found it was a place of entertainment and refreshment. After being on the go for twenty odd hours Jeanie went up to bed, and I made my way down to the land of the living. The place was jumping! There was a very good country and western singer doing a turn. I found a table with a spare seat, excused myself, and sat down. I quickly caught the serving-wench's eye and got a large Water of Life, with a beer chaser. Who needs jet-lag!

I was feeling the greatest ever world traveller. It took the Scottish explorer Sir Alexander MacKenzie years to find his way into this country overland from the east. The 707 from Prestwick took a few hours off that for me! Yes, I was feeling smug and full of myself. First time I'd been so far from home since 1950, in a foreign country where the language was English. The next turn was a solo singer and teller of stories. This was in broad Glaswegian. I was struck dumb. You can't escape them! However, he was very good. Praise from a Glasgow man! However, all that glitters is not gold. The performer turned out to be a German immigrant! It must have been his guttural German speech that enabled him to get the sound right. I got to speaking with two young Canadians at the table and I found it was refreshing to converse with them on their home ground. Sure I'd met many such people at home, but that's not in any way the same. From these two I got a wee insight of the psyche of the locals of this area. This gave me an idea as to the cast of their minds. And so ended what in anybody's life could only be called *a momentous day.*

The Park Royal dining room sits right by the side of the Capilano river. The wall overlooking this magnificent scene was mostly of glass. At around 7.30 am, sitting over my first coffee, and feeling like a million bucks, a fine looking Chinese waiter, who had served us our coffee, came back for the breakfast order. I decided to go deluxe, and ordered a large fillet steak and two eggs sunny-side up. Without a blink he said, "how would you like your steak, sir?" Quickly I

229

retorted, "rare!" This place was made for me. Here in the middle of a city, a salmon river. Like the salmon back in *my Kelvin*. The empty dining room seemed to accentuate all that was right about the place. The wholeness of the moment left you with a proud sense of gratitude for being where we were, and for the reason why. It would be around this time I would imagine the possibility of a canoe load of Capilano Indians paddling down past the window to the sea. That would have been too much. I think Jeanie said as much!

Jane Ferris came early to drive us round and give us the conducted tour. I won't go on about Vancouver. I will say, however, at that time it was an impressive place. And all of the different people that I met were of the solid opinion that they were fortunate to live in that part of the world.

That afternoon I was to golf with Toni Sailer. Toni would be an impressive person in any company. Tall, good looking, and with above average intelligence. Good to be with, and despite his outstanding achievements of six gold medals he is a person like you or me. What he was on the golf course was a low handicap golfer. We were given the use of the Capilano Golf and Country Club. Now I have golfed on most of Scotland's world famous tracts. Here, once again, what you expected is what you got. Its called one of North America's most beautiful. There was the proverbial Scots Pro in the Pro shop. We had a wee chat. His accent slipped back immediately.

I had met Toni in Courchevel, but I did not know him. If there is any place you can find out what kind of a person a man is quickly, it's on a golf course. Or on a mountain. Toni was great on the golf course. He was a ferocious competitor. My passage through life has been richly strewn with this particular type of animal, not all of them necessarily male. Having said that about Toni, in that first game, like many others I know, he kept both our scores. When the game was over, he worked through the scores carefully and announced, "next time you get one more stroke!" I nearly *had a stroke!* The Bandits I play with would not give themselves a stroke. Mind you, six gold medals might leave you with *a wee touch* of the milk of human kindness. What a tasty start to Vancouver, and we had only just arrived.

Roy and his partner Allan White were having a dinner party for the trainers and a few others. We were going to a French restaurant. The reason for this was Patrick Russell was here as trainer. The Canadian agent for Rossignol was involved in sponsoring the Camp. Patrick's dad was Export Director for Rossignol. He was a man I knew, a handsome man of the world and clever with it. Patrick had been one of the world's best slalom skiers. I admired his skiing very much. Not long before the Sapporo Olympics he broke his leg in a sad accident that was none of his fault. So that was his almost certain gold medal gone for that Olympics. Next day Roy drove me up to Whistler. We had a nice long ,private, old pals bull session. While driving we had some beers. Highly illegal!

I was amazed by the sheer scale of the country. The size of the trees. The rivers were enormous, with great newly uprooted trees causally drifting down to wherever they'd end up. Roy explained that it had snowed through most of May, and that so much snow was not normal. This was a special way to see the country. Late snow gives mountains an extra dimension. I mentioned this when we took wee Rudigoz down to Torridon. But in the wonderment of driving through British Columbia like this, it left me short on talk. I'll leave Mr Louis "Satchmo" Armstrong to speak for me in a song he sang so beautifully, *"What A Wonderful World."*

At the Ski Station, Whistler, 20 years past, they were only at the beginning of the development of what has become a very fine ski resort. The first flats were just being built. As a matter of interest, there's a wee enclave of Cairngorm ex pats ensconced in that happy place, and all doing very well. Our accommodations were small condominiums. These were excellent. They were spaced out among the trees on the side of Alta Lake, if I've got the name right. Food was served in the complex's restaurants. A trencher-man could have made a pig of himself, and I know one who did. Frith. There was unlimited food of the highest quality.

I was shocked to see the outrageous waste and abuse the kids made of this Bonanza. If I described how bad this was, you'd think I was raving. I mentioned it to Toni that my granny would turn in her grave if she had seen this. He said that so would his. These kids would load their plates with steaks and other goodies, fill two or three large glasses with pure fruit juices, have a pick from the plate, a sip from one the glasses, get fed up, then walk out and buy a coke and a Mars Bar! And enjoy themselves? I was not impressed with the *rich children* of North America. But, in fairness, they were not all like this. Summer Camps, I'm sure, were built up in the Rockies. Those who attended were referred to as kids. Their average age was between 14 and 18.

The Camp Directors were all people of the highest calibre. Advanced Racing, Toni Sailer. Six gold medals.Intermediate &. Novice Racing. Nancy Greene, another gold medallist. Free Style. Wayne Wong, American ballet champion. Free Style included, Ballet, Bumps, Aerials. Recreational Skiing. Wayne Booth. After dinner on the night of arrival Roy did his big thing, giving a welcoming introduction. This he did with skill. Mind you, he was a Londoner. Cities have a habit of producing *able-mouths!* When Roy introduced the trainers to the trainees, it showed just how well this training was staffed. He made a big thing about myself, and what he thought I had done in skiing at home. I had never thought of, or expected, that sort of thing.

Apart from the ones I've mentioned, there was Al Raine, Nancy Greene's husband, who was head trainer to the Canadian National Teams. One of his assistants, Don Lyon, an impressive, quiet, reticent man. He was with the Canadian girls. He was also on the staff. George Askvold, the current American Aerials Champion. Wayne Wilkie, the current American Bumps Champion. These would represent some of the best in the world at that time. impressive by any standard.

The Recreational classes were in the charge of Wayne Booth. He was Roy's Winter Ski School boss. He was a *big bear* and a top man in our profession. When you worked for him you did what he told you. He looked after yours truly up on Whistler Mountain. Later on I sent some good teachers out to work with him on Seymour outside Vancouver. One of these was a young Jimmy Smith. They became friends. There was a young Chamonix ski-teacher-come-mountain-guide working on the course as a race trainer, who was married to a Canadian girl. When we started to speak about Chamonix and other things, we became pals. They were some trainers, all of whom were pros.

231

After finding the quality of the trainers I was in for a big surprise when it came to the trainees. Most of them were not interested. To say they had been spoiled with the goodies of life would be an understatement. Not all of them, but most of them. Breakfast was at 6.00 am. This was necessary to get things moving and started for 7.30 am. Skiing later than noon and the snow becomes dangerous for the work we had to do. My surprise was how they managed to get some of the Stumble Bums out their kips for six am. I had nothing to do with the running of the show, so I never found out how they actually managed that.

Whistler, BC
left to right – Toni Sailer, 6 Gold Medals, Nancy Greene, 2 Gold Medals, Frith and Jeanie

232

Not long after I arrived there was a wee bit of banter between Toni, Allan, Roy and others. It was about how Nancy Greene and I would get on. They presumed we'd clash. Why should we? It seemed she was very forceful at speaking her mind and liked to get things her own way. So I explained that that was kind of normal in my world, and that I could not see any problem. As I was in Rome, that old saying still applies, "do as the Romans do." I managed that fine in the Schweiz for years. I'd learned in the hard school of the shipyards. And in the climbing world. Nancy was a Cracker. An' a no nonsense "broad." Mind you, taking her home a pay packet with a few bucks missing might cause you a wee touch of pain! She and I became buddies. Having said that, the first day up on Whistler Mountain I was to find out why Nancy had this reputation.

Whistler, like all ski areas, have mountain men who became mountain men by working for long years in winter on the mountains. There are no tests, no examinations. Patience plus servitude cuts it. On the first day, when all the wrinkles were being wrung out, and one of the long rope tows was to be located, two of these laconic stoics seemed to be conversing in nods and grunts. Oh Nancy! *Where angels fear to tread.* She stepped in and made it very clear where this uphill dragging contraption should be located. It was clear that Nancy was in muddy waters. Unbeknown to Nancy, bless her, the stoics were having a private nod and grunt conversation between themselves as to where the contraption *would* go. She was in a no win situation! A little later I mentioned to her that I thought she might not have gotten her way. I'm sure she "knew the score." She was not in the least put out.

The training set-up was new to me. We had around ten classes of Alpine. Each of these had their own short slalom course of about 30 gates, all of them visible. The trainer stood at the bottom, and when the skier came down the teacher spoke to them, or left them for a bit. It was a novel approach whether you agree with the rights or the wrongs of it. If it was the best system possible, you would need lot of heavy *bread* to pay for the *labour*. Apart from the money, if you were training a large squad, there would inevitably be ten different ways of thinking spread between your total squad of trainers. There's food for thought!

I have mentioned how the snow became dangerous by noon. This is caused by the early summer sun. Now here is where the organisers were clever. They had seed-spreaders. They were basin-like and fitted in front of your waist, held there by a broad strap round your neck. There was a crank handle near to the bottom of the basin. For the salt crystals, snow cement. You filled the basin, turned the handle and the crystals spread evenly over the width of your course. It did a first class job. Each noon you had to stamp out all your ruts, side-step the track, then use the spreader, and then carefully side-slip your course. Next morning you had a solid tract that lasted near enough through to the end of the morning. This should be an interesting item for those involved in late season training.

Whistler in good winter conditions must be fine place to ski. As I understand it, it's very extensively and well developed today. As the days passed I quietly fitted in. Naturally I kept my eyes open. I noticed Al Raine had a marvellous way in achieving results. Like myself he pushed those individuals who were able, as hard and long as they could maintain the pressure. I did notice he liked to have a good belt through the poles. Always a good sign. He had a good group. I should make it clear that all of these kids were club skiers.

233

As we were down off the hill by one pm, the day was young. Toni and I would sometimes go golfing. He took me down to Squamish where there was a new golf course. This course had been laid out in what had been an ancient spruce forest. Through it ran a river, deep, fast and wide. Too wide for Indians! In among the tall trees were the ruins of man's past activities. There were the stumps of trees long since felled. The stumps stood about ten feet above your head, some were twenty feet across. If ever man left "his mark of Cain" on the land, it's here to be seen. The bountiful hand of nature has new trees growing there. These are already big by European standards. Out of the middle of the roots of some these giants, there were new trees growing tall, a 100 feet or more. I never even tried to find out the history of the long departed trees. I prefer not to know as it might leave the memory less magic than I want it to be.

Wayne Booth and I played there against Toni and Don Lyon, the Canadian trainer. That was a mixed bunch. You could almost hear the screech of diamond cut diamond, for the strokes, and the five dollar double-or-nothing bets. Booth "the Bear" and I won. For quality, you can't beat the wandering Clydesider. There's them as would call the Red Clydesider, "the Great Unwashed." It would be around this time that I learned that it was expected that I would be old-fashioned and dressed in plus-fours. Well, you don't always get what you expect!

Before Jeanie and I were due to leave, Al Raine arranged for helicopter skiing. He asked me if I was interested! For fifty dollars we got a super long morning skiing much higher mountains than Whistler. Al had six friends to make up the group. We were getting around six thousand feet vertical descent. The slopes were completely buried, at the top we would have wind-blown, then powder, followed by spring snow and the inevitable slush. And here you *can* use the cliché "pristine", because *no one* had skied that snow! I skied through a long rough snow slide. That raised the eyebrows.

While on about the plus-fours, there's this story. That lovely young Frenchman from Chamonix had been at me for a race down the dual slalom. I pointed out the twenty-year age difference. He was determined to have this head-to-head. Well, he got his *day in the sun*. We were running dual slalom, class against class. Betsy Clifford, just out of the Canadian team, had been working with the kids. Her class was racing Nancy's, which was a few points ahead. I was working with Nancy, and Mr Chamonix was with Betsy. Betsy said to me, "you'll race Mr. Chamonix." I asked why. Sharp as a whip she said, "you can't beat him, so we'll win a point!" I said, "d'you think so?" I slipped Nancy *the wink*. I'm sorry to say I detected a lack of confidence in her!

Chamonix was champing at the bit. The kids were going bananas. I declared *pro rules*. The boy agreed. I didn't know what *pro rules* were! Nancy looked at me. She didn't know anything about *pro rules* either! Anyway, Mr. Chamonix was prime for plucking. In the gates we got the "ready, steady" for the countdown of 5 to 1. On the count of 4, I was out of the gate like a scalded cat! I could hear the boy shouting protests. I also heard Betsy shouting, telling him to move his arse. There were only thirty gates, and there was no way he could catch me! And, of course, he fell! I thought Nancy Greene was going to wet herself! Betsy did not miss the humour. The boy was back up at the start gates demanding disqualification. I claimed *Pro. rules*. That's when they found out what *pro rules* were. Five seconds' penalty for jumping the gun. I also informed the boy that the clock was still running for him, as he never finished the course. So much for plus-fours!

The three weeks were a feast of new and fresh experiences. Patrick Russell and I seemed to click! His skiing was a delight. We skied off the hill a few times. It's nice to ski beside a technique as good as Patrick's. He used to come to us for a *wee nip* and I don't know if he knew all that I said to him. Jeanie accused me of bull-shitting the young man. I wonder where she got that idea.

Coming back from the golf Toni took me to see the bears at the local garbage dump. There they were, getting stuck into the goodies! Close to the car was a wee baby bear. I thought it was quite big. Toni gets out of the motor, goes up close to it, messing about with a camera. Now, I understood that mama bears were usually nearby and are not keen on humanoids messing around their little babies. Frith sat in the car, with the door closed! Never push your luck unless there's a possible gain to be had. Wrestling big bears cannot show much of a profit, I would think!

I must mention Wayne Wong, the Ballet Champion. A good looking Chinese American. A million laughs and, above all, a Pied-Piper with the young ones in the training. That's a very special gifted talent for anyone to possess.

From all the very many happenings during these three weeks of long days starting at 6am, and seldom to bed before the wee hours in the morning, there was a special one. The night before we were due to go back down to Vancouver, Nancy and Al held a staff party. They had built a large Swiss-type chalet deep in timber, near some small lakes. Like all these parties, it did not take much to fire it up. Maybe the load of booze gave the fire a good start. I was surprised - we ran out of booze!

There was a fair mix of different nationalities. All were expected to give a song from the country of their origin. The novelty turn came from a Japanese ski teacher. He naturally sang in his own language. He was a striking looking character, tall for his race. Of course, there may have been a wee touch of something else in there. His face reminded me of a Samurai warrior, only he seemed to smile all the time. It seems he was a good ski teacher. We never knew a word he sang, but the whole party were wetting themselves. He could really communicate. Toni naturally gave a Tyrolean number. Jeanie and I sang a Highland song together. *"The Tay Boat Song."* This is a lovely song from our central Highlands. This received much acclaim. Toni Sailer and the Samurai sang a duet, "in Japanese." This raised the roof. Toni managed to look like a very tall Japanese when he was singing, stretching his eyes into slits with his fingers. Toni was very famous in Japan. That, however, is another yarn. The time we spent on and around Whistler was full of activity and not much sleep. The time was too precious to waste sleeping! So that final night is how Jeanie and I remember the 1974 Toni Sailer Summer Ski Camp on Whistler.

When the Purves brothers and I were wandering round *our* Loch Lomond as fourteen year olds, we'd romanticise about the great North West of Canada. It never crossed my mind at the time that I'd ever get to see it, let alone in the capacity in which I was now visiting it! What I was very pleased to find out, was how much control the Provincial government were applying to conserving their wild places.

23. Cervinia

By the time the season of 1975 settled in, things that were at one time new and novel to us became part of a routine. I am not for a moment suggesting they were in anyway mundane. Not so. In our junior race training we had worked out how to utilise the juniors' skiing ability, such as it was at that time. Out of Speyside we were getting good numbers of youngsters from 10 to 15. Not beginners, but not racers. The Chairlift Company paid for most of their training. We had Sue Dickson and Iain Finlayson. Between us we had a good balance of teaching skills and racing experience. The good thing with these kids was no one had been screwing up their natural stance. In most cases they came to us "clean."

We taught them to turn their skis with their feet and to leave their bodies still. We did this without making a big deal out it. One thing we did insist on was that they behaved themselves in the lift queues and on the hill. Any really bad behaviour could result in permanent expulsion from the training. This did happen to a son of a good friend of mine.

There's no point having firm rules and not using them if they have been breached badly enough. Our training lasted for a few more years until the local club took over the direct running of it. As I have said previously, it is impossible for skilled professionals to work under the directions of part-time weekend skiers. This does not function successfully anywhere in the world. The years I was involved in training on Cairngorm were richly rewarding.

We went through a period when many of the would-be-trainees behaved as if the hill and all the facilities on it had been put there for their private use. This was the fault of the people in charge of them. Once again, that is another story. For a number of years there seemed to be droves of kids skiing on the Cairngorm. Parents seemed desperate to have their kids involved in what they thought was "race-training." Race-training is not suitable for all children. This foolishness seems to have tapered off which is much more beneficial for the kids and lets them get on with their own skiing. Race-training is really meant for skilled skiers, be they kids or juniors.

Kids will gain more benefit skiing in small groups, under good supervision. Skiing, by all means, *hell for leather*. This creates unpressured competition that is better than filling their heads with the nonsense that they are racers before they can turn their skis reasonably well. If you allow this to happen it will inhibit them from developing their own natural "way" of skiing. Anyone who says this is *even* controversial, lacks a knowledge of ski teaching of any kind in my opinion. A curse many juniors over the years have paid for!

At the same time as the competitive side of skiing was maturing, finding its feet and stabilising, the recreational skiers were making their place in the ski world. Unbeknownst to me, a lovely mixture of skiers from around the country was developing. They came from different strata of our society. This gave its colour, its strength and character. We seemed to gather into a corner of the old Sheiling at the middle station on Cairngorm. Strangers thought it was a reserved area. We had terrific unplanned parties in that corner! Skiing is a great mixer of people, like good whisky and water. In the right quantities and in the right places they are fine. It's getting the mix right that's the trick.

One of the special people, Andy Stirling, a headmaster and Clydesider, used this corner most weekends. Andy and I met through BASI. One December he was on a Ski Party Leaders course in Glenmore Lodge. I was in charge. He was with two other Glaswegians. For some reason they were up at the Lodge without a car. Not too clever! Of course, there was a good excuse for them being daft. They were school teachers, and worse, headmasters! They were not *that* daft. They conned the director of training into bringing two bottles of malt whisky to the Lodge each morning. After I'd suggested a kind of sober week might be good during the course! I'll do anything for a glass of malt!

The cheek of them! Between the three of them, they could never have made a skier in thousand years. They skied like humpy backed crabs. And not the bonniest looking ones either. They looked so pathetic I did not have the heart to deny them entrance to the course. Because of their crap skiing I had to give them a trainer to themselves. Headmasters! Their subject must have been teaching "conmanship." Brian Hall, who got them to teach, was taking his first BASI class. Talk about "in the deep end!" Or was it being "lumbered?" They looked after him. They had him gassed one night before dinner. That's what the two bottles were for. I had a few slugs myself. Brian was a nice, quiet, reserved, English boy. A fulltime staff member of Glenmore Lodge. This would be a good wee part of his *learning curve*. I know he remembers it with great fondness. Andy Stirling for a good number of years used to spend Christmas and New Year in our home. He was a good hand in the kitchen.

From then up into the early eighties these weekends were exciting and fresh, then they quickly ended. The reason for this I never gave much thought to. Things change, otherwise life would be a uninteresting and dull experience. Skiing, and all that goes with it, still dominates my life. Glad am I for the day on Meall a' Bhuiridh that John Cunningham put me on his skis!

January 1975 saw BASI in the high Italian resort of Cervinia. This was a marvellous village for our programme. As usual we introduced ourselves to the village Ski School, where we received a warm welcome. I have always found the mountain folks of Italy the easiest people to get on with. The Ski School boss appreciated the bottle of malt. The water of life is always a good way of starting a new relationship. Cervinia lies above 6,800 ft. The runs from Platta Rosa back to the village are long and simple, with plenty of room where you can keep out of everybody's way. Cervinia is the Italian name for the Matterhorn. You can ski to Zermatt. This is a fine day out. The surrounding feast of mountains must be one of the most impressive in scope and scale in Europe. Monte Rosa, the second highest mountain in Europe, and the Matterhorn facing over to the Monte Rosa, Weisshorn, Dom and the Taschhorn are all around 4,550 metres. To the north, the giants of the Bernese Oberland. To the west, the Mont Blanc Massif. All this plus some of the best skiing the world can present to you. It's truly a magic place, if mountains are a big thing for you.

These courses throw up numerous funny incidents, some of which can be a way above average. Across the street from our hotel was a local pub. This suited us just fine. It was one of those watering holes that, by law, have to close by one in the morning. Hugh Clark was making his first appearance as a trainer-come-examiner. He was the first local-born Speysider to do this. He'd be in his early twenties and not as worldly as he is today. The locals learned that he was a farmer from a "Ski Station." This made him one of their own. Being an engaging young man, they made a great fuss of him and led him into the ways of strong drink. He would stand at the bar and, with his Boat of Garten English way of speaking, hold forth with the locals. They, in turn, boisterously in their Italian way, would gabble away in their local dialect. They seemed to be having no bother in communicating. It must have been in the farming blood. Hugh liked that place and it seemed he used it regularly.

One night the bar was still open a long time after it should have been closed. In came two policemen. A wee bit different from ours, with 9 mm pistols. And those wee machine-guns, hanging from their shoulders. They fined the owners on the spot, along with all the Italians who were drinking. They frog-marched Hughie across the street with his arms up his back, and ordered the hotel doorman not to let him out again that night! It was the next night that I found out about the event. When I asked Hughie if he was worried about the guns, his reply was that he was more worried that, if he had been locked up, he would have missed turning up for work, and then he would need to have faced me! Here was a nice touch of humour. At least he had priorities right!

Bob Clyde had decided to take his BASI Three. A bold undertaking. Bob, being the general manager on Cairngorm, did not get much time for skiing, though he was an able performer. He was in his forties. But, being who he was, the examiners would show no quarter. If anything, *they would screw him*. This seemed to happen when a prominent skier came on our courses. They did it to his daughter three years later. June skied quite well, but they bumped her on her teaching. June, a tough nut, wise in the ways of the world, came back and passed. She had done her homework. There's no way *clout* could influence these results.

In Bob's group were three others. Between the four of them it was at best an "Unholy Alliance." Peter Simpson, whom I've mentioned before, was the trainer. It needed a man of Peter's guile to deal with these four. Apart from Bob there was one called Bing Crosby, his real name, Hedley Wright, a whisky distiller from Mull of Kintyre. Jack Wilson, a trader of motor cars, many motor cars. Aberdeen is the town guilty of producing Jack! Bing was an older man. A quiet, solid Englishman. The others, if given the chance, would and did make merry long into the night. I know. I was with them often when they did! I had used Peter in difficult groups before. He never ever gave me any thanks for these little *perks!* I more than likely got his *lip*. They all passed except Jack. He should have passed more easily than the others. I understand Clyde and he had been rowing just before the examination. Jack must have taken his temper to the examination. I hope I've got that story right. It is not often you get four so diversely different men as those in one class. Bing Crosby I only knew from Saas Fee, the others were close friends. It was classes like these that added character to early courses run by BASI.

During these two weeks, BASI had a team at Interski, in Czechoslovakia. John Cunningham went as our photographer. He said the country was corrupt under the totalitarian communist regime. John, being a Clydesider, and as such was a very clear thinker. Like most of his breed, he was hard to impress, and slow to criticise. In his opinion, the totalitarian administration had no control over the "police state." A young New Zealander on the New Zealand delegation got badly beaten up one night. He was drunk. But that can be no excuse for the state police's action!

1975 Interski – BASI Team in Czechoslovakia
left to right – Hans Kuwall, Doug Godlington, Ingie Christofersen, Kenny Dickson,
Carl Luttenberger, Ali Ross

John told me the whole system appeared to be run to suit those in power. He said everyone was constantly being ripped off, and when leaving the country you could not take out the local money, or cash it in. You *could* buy the junk from their gift shop. So much for the "total control system." The famous American, Thomas Jefferson, signatory to the American Constitution, said on the subject of Government, and I quote:-*"God forbid we should ever be twenty years without rebellion. What country can preserve its liberties if their rulers are not warned from time to time that their people preserve the spirit of resistance. Let them take up arms!"* Maybe there is a wee message here for all of our politicians? We all know what happened in Czechoslovakia. And in others, eventually. You can kid some of the some people some of the time. But you can't kid all of the people all of the time.

The following year, 1976, we were back in Cervinia with the BASI. This was highlighted by high winds. For two weeks the wind blew over most of the slopes we needed for our work. We were limited to very restricted skiing near the village. Bob Clyde, the new BASI Grade Three from the previous year, was back skiing for fun with the Course. Now, if you know Cairngorm weather, you will understand wind is part and parcel of the scenario. From the first day Bob Clyde opened the first chairlift on Cairngorm, people who should know better plagued him by complaining about the wind. Now, Clyde was not keen on people who went over the top in what he thought was unfair criticism of *his* Cairngorm. Oh yes! He thought the Cairngorm was his, alright! The wind persisted throughout the two weeks, and Bob loved every moment of watching the long faces and listening to the whining. Despite the fact this was ruining his two weeks, he took a twisted delight in watching the painful tableau work itself out with no respite to the bitter end. He rubbed it into me. I don't know why I was always on his side as far as Our Mountain was concerned. Cairngorm wind gave big problems, especially when you were running a ski school.

What amused me was that there were, on that course, people who had on many occasions given Bob earache about our weather. He could not wait for the next time they came to him complaining about Cairngorm wind. It was no worse than the one which was raging down off the Matterhorn. Bob could be a capricious bastard at times! Luckily, most of the time he was just a Pussy Cat. Those who knew him will recognise how typical of him this behaviour was in situations such as this. This one I liked!

Those who were close to BASI's centre will remember that this present course would be the first BASI training that I had not directed. The change had been at my suggestion. After fifteen years of my being in charge it was due a change. At a meeting in Pitlochry the previous September, it was decided that a new National Director and two assistant directors to be appointed. This would create a workable situation. Up to this time in our existence we did not have the numbers of trainers with the skills to make this sort of improvement. I proposed that Hans Kuwall be the new National Director, that John Hynes be one of the assistant directors, and that I should stay on for a period of two years only as one of the assistant directors. This was very warmly accepted as a good way to find our way along the path that the growing skiing industry was taking. It presented a good way to end something that started from nothing and came through the very difficult times of lack of money, plus the long period of the severe lack of skiing skills. Anyway, that first course under "New Management" worked well, despite the Cairngorm weather. Back home the spring Course had grown in numbers. So things in the new garden seemed to be coming on nicely.

In the next season, 1977, we were back at Gotzens. There seemed to be a change of atmosphere here. It got off to a bad start. We were crowded into a hotel too small for our purpose. Dinner the first night was a disaster in every way. The hotel specialised in school parties, which meant everything was cut to the bone. The first night they ran out of beer straight off. The chairman, Jack Thomson, and his wife, were given a room over the disco. I changed with them. The noise in the wee hours was almost *physical*. How the owners had the effrontery to put anyone in that room was beyond me. In changing rooms I gained the noise and lost my bath. But, where there's bad there's good! Sue Dickson and Kenny offered their room with bath. It's good to remember certain things. I never took their room. Why should *two* suffer? A bad start, but not the end of the world. I've had much poorer accommodations.

What followed later was the fault of BASI. Now, what I'm going to say is important. Others may not agree, but that is up to them. At Gotzens, unlike Cervinia and Saas Fee, you had to take a coach up to Lizum, where the skiing was. On previous BASI courses the morning starting time was to be sacrosanct. This was made very clear at the introduction talk. It was also clearly stated on the daily programme. On the first Gotzens course, the candidates called it the Hate Thirty Bus. I called it the 8.30 am. It was all in great fun. After a few mornings on this course it was very noticeable that the bus was late in leaving. It was even more noticeable that some senior trainers were responsible for keeping the candidates waiting.

This went on for most of the first week. As an assistant director (and being me), I confronted the Director, Hans, as to why this was taking place. There was no explanation. I was bluntly told, "this is not the Army." And I was an Assistant Director of Training? I did suggest he clear up what it said on the notice board about the starting time, and the matter was dropped. For the moment! I had a word with Jack Thomson about this. He well knew about it, as he had had to stand and wait with the candidates at the convenience of the late comers. And he Chairman! Jack reckoned that, with Hans being the Director, it was up to him how he ran things. I was amazed at Jack. He was a stickler for "doing it right!" I knew then that the "Wind of Change" was starting to blow.

We all know there must be changes in how things are run under new management in all collective enterprises. However, to allow slackness in a simple thing like time keeping, whether it's a deliberate policy, or you don't think it's important, you will end up suffering from what is popularly called "The British Disease." And I, as a Red Clydesider, agree. The tenet of good time keeping is an absolute fact where good successful collective enterprises flourish! There is another principle when you are dealing directly with the public. You must not keep them waiting, particularly if you are working at a professional level. It has nothing at all to do with "the Army."

There seemed to be no consideration for the intelligence of those waiting, though there would be none of those waiting who would be missing what was happening. On average they would be fairly cute. Or should I say, "astute?" To have the resources to ski well enough to reach the standard to attend a BASI course, candidates knew when they saw these particular trainers keeping them waiting, that those trainers were abusing their *clout*. This was unnecessarily stupid, and certainly not *playing the game!* It's easy to misuse any kind of power. It is not, however, impressive in any way.

The saving grace was that those waiting could see that not all of the trainers were abusing their position in the pecking order. It was obvious to the candidates that our Chairman was always on time. The last time the BASI Course was held in Gotzens this could never have happened. I never ever figured out why this was happening. Was it a new way of doing things? Was there some obscure reason for it that was my going over my head? I never thought I was *that* thick! There's one thing for sure, it was way out of line as far the as the candidates were concerned and a poor way to run anything, let alone the national training and grading course for Britain! I am sure that this was the beginning of what was the saddest and most unnecessary episode in the life of BASI. An episode which none of us who were in the heart of it came out of with a shred of dignity. Having watched BASI over the years since, I'm sure we damaged BASI. We will come back to this.

As for the hill part of the course, candidates coming through were better skiers. This was most satisfying. It was easier to balance the Grade Threes and Twos. The whole course looked fine, compared to our early days. We, like others, had to start somewhere. It's worth pointing out that this was the result of 14 years' work. It never happened overnight, as some seem to think. I'm sure BASI was lucky in its beginnings. It had a new *frontier* on which to operate. A wonderful untested opportunity. We also had some very fine members, not all of them top skiers. Some of them had special skills that the average ski teachers did not possess. That most certainly helped us to arrive at where we were at this particular time in our development.

Speaking of development, the demand for ski teacher training was such that Hans Kuwall was sending Jimmy Smith and myself home two days early to run another Grade Three Course on Cairngorm. Iain Finlayson would be the third member of our wee team. These helpers would do me just fine. And I could see no problems. Maybe the wind would blow, but we had lived with that before. Before I left, Hans gave me strict instructions that I take all the best skiers. That

Jimmy Smith,
A Truly International Ski Teacher

was a good one. Me who had carried BASI to where it stood at that exact time in space! I had every intention of doing just that. No way had Jimmy or Iain, with his twenty third place in the Olympic Slalom, have enough experience to handle some of the animals I knew were coming on the course. But Jimmy and I had a lot of ground to cover before we sorted out who got which class on Cairngorm on Sunday coming.

Jimmy and I knew each other. There is a big difference between that and just being casual friends. We'd worked together in my ski school. Being a friend takes a long Scotch Country Mile. By the time we arrived in the Winkie Owl that

night from Gotzens, we had both crossed the friendship Rubicon. It was a marvellous journey of blunders, recoveries, stunts and other outrageous joviality.

The first trick was me mislaying our air line tickets in Munich. Now, it must be understood that we had taken strong refreshment on the night before. When I told Jimmy about our bit of bother, he didn't seem too impressed. I told him to hold my beer and my schnapps. I breezed up to the rep. handling the BASI travel. I explained that we were told by his man in Gotzens that tickets would be waiting for Jimmy and me. The man was dumbfounded. They get so much hassle. I just presumed we looked important, sunburned, one young and the other handsomely matured. Up came two tickets. When in doubt, always push your luck. That must have impressed Smithy. There was more where that came from. He passed me back my beer and schnapps as we were heading for the plane. I felt smugly pleased with myself. I was sure I'd impressed "the boy." I put my hand in my pocket and out came the two original tickets! I said to Jimmy, "not bad, eh?" I wish I'd had a camera. And we were only starting. Can you imagine not being able to find tickets in your pockets?

On the plane, just after it took off, I said to Jimmy, who was sitting next to the passage, to get us some gins and tonic. The hostess, who was a tall blond, did not seem to notice, so Jimmy told me. I suggested he nip the hem of her skirt as she passed by. I said, "that'll stop her!" Stop her it did. Like a young man who does what he is told. When she spun round, he flashed her the sunburned smiling face, disarmed her, and ordered four gin and tonics. We had a few more!

We had to transfer to another airport for the Inverness plane. We were very tight for time. We picked a real Cockney taxi driver. I said, "there's twenty in it if you get over in time for our plane!" It was a great drive. When we arrived, our plane was delayed. What's twenty quid? In the bar I said to Jimmy, "that driver did alright, with the bung!" Jimmy looked a bit sheepish. He said, "he sure did, I left my duty free fags and vodka in the back seat!" The driver was lucky, Christmas twice! Not bad, these Scots boys, when drunk! By this time I was running short of *the readies*. I had to pay for the two tickets with the plastic. I had trouble signing the credit card slip, or should I say, *seeing* it! Just as well it was the London Inverness plane. People who take strong refreshment travel on that plane regularly. Nobody pays any attention to them. And you don't have to wait long for a libation on that fine aircraft! We arrived home, as I said, at the Winkie Owl, after walking our first long Scotch Country Mile together.

For some reason I had been looking forward to working on this course with Jimmy and Iain. The prospect excited me. I was not disappointed, and I still remember it *fine!* In the writing of these words I have had to think back to analysis and to extrapolate what at that time was important and how it affected how I went about my life in skiing. Hindsight is a wonder and a powerful stimulant to your thinking and, if you're honest with yourself, a humbling experience when you discover just how crassly you may have behaved. Would we want to change the human psyche to all be similar, let alone the same? If so, writing and reading would be pointless.

Even worse, there would be no uncertainty in the world and consequently no excitement. Nothing to talk about. What a dull place! The world's fine as it is. I'll take it as it comes, straight! And live with the trouble we produce from time to time. When thinking back you get a second and clearer look at how you conducted yourself. Like the game of golf, it does you a power of good and straightens up your thinking. What came out of this course that Jimmy Iain and I were about to run for BASI, was that it would be the last one I would be involved in that gave me any pleasure.

It was to be all the more memorable because of the weather and the snow conditions. On the introduction talk I explained to the candidates who had no experience in Cairngorm just how bad our weather could be. The first day the snow was as good as you could have hoped for. This gave the course a great start. That evening, at the debrief of the day's work, some of the course made so bold as to suggest that I had painted an unfair picture of Cairngorm's weather. I assured them that it had been a fluke of a day and not to look for too many of those. I was wrong. We had two weeks of the same! We skied in sweaters many days, and, as a result, the progress of most of the candidates was above average.

Acting on Hans Kuwall's instructions that I take all the good skiers, I did just that, with one exception. There was a young man, David Lyndsay, who lived in Meribel, France. His father had been a moving figure in developing that great ski area. David was a first class skier in any company. When I saw him ski, I put him in with Iain Finlayson. At the trainer's meeting it transpired that David was being a handful. Iain said the young man was not conforming to class discipline, and asked me to take him. Iain could easily handle his skiing. The "boy" was out to impress everyone. Good for him, and how nicely normal! There is the guile and the cunning, and that wee touch of experience needed to handle such situations.

It just so happened that in our class were a number of *bears*. We knew each other, and *they knew the score*. One was New Zealander Nigel Palmer. He became a good skier. Another was a big worthy called Tree. And there were some others. Now what David was doing was not staying in line, in the fast free skiing. He was cutting in and out of the class, upsetting the others who were less skilful than he was. I tried to explain that there were ground rules. He was young, full of life and cocky with it. No different from most other young men. But he had to be curtailed, and in the curtailing, be left with his feathers not *too* ruffled. This we would do through skiing.

We skied fast over to the top of the Headwall Coire na Ciste. He was right up my backside. I turned at speed into the Saas Struggie, turning hard right. He never made the turn. He blew it! He was air borne, face first all the way down to the bottom of gully. He should have paid more attention to where I was going, and less attention to impressing the others in the class. He took it well. What else? He was none the worse for it. He was a treat to have in any group. He was impish, impetuous, and aggressive in his skiing. Best of all, he was modest in his demeanour.

Later that season I would have a long slide face first down that very steep slope. We were running race training for the Glasgow University Ski Club. I was adjusting the heel binding for Gordon Crawford, now a Glasgow doctor. I kept my face too close to one of his boots, and had him try to and release it. This he did. Out it came and caught me right on the mouth. It was a big black Lange, and left my mouth in a fair mess. As we were at the top of the Headwall in Coire na Ciste I ended up at the bottom. This gave a lot of people much amusement!

Rossignol Team
left to right –Fraser Clyde, Willie McKenna, Ian Baxter, Iain Finlayson, FF

The excellent snow and weather conditions made this course very easy to work on. Working with skiers like Jimmy and Iain was another plus. We had a high pass rate. The conditions would have helped make this possible. Because of the small numbers on the course we decided to debrief those who failed. What came out of this was what little so many had put into their thinking about how they skied. It stated clearly on the application form that you had to ski to a high parallel standard. This is a very much misunderstood description. We had one man who failed badly. He had obviously not skied much. He could not accept the fact that he had failed. If you put your head on the Block of Chance, you *can* lose. Life's like that. I remember Jimmy Smith commenting on this particular case. Young David Lyndsay came through the course successfully. We all remember him with fondness. We could do with a lot more of these.

Around about this time we had started pro Dual Slalom racing on Cairngorm. There was a fair bit of cash for the winners. I was the manager of the Rossignol team. This was recognised as the most accomplished of the teams as well they should have been. The team was Bridget "Newall" Clyde, Fraser Clyde, Iain Finlayson from the British teams and Ian Baxter, Jimmy Smith, and Willie McKenna. It usually ended up by them racing it out between themselves. We had an arrangement where the winnings were lumped together and divided equally between the team members. I myself took nothing from the kitty.

24. The "Wind of Change"

These last summers had been spent playing golf most days, that is to say, whenever it suited us. There were a few who could play more or less when we wanted. We were so well organised that if we were held up by other players on the courses we played we felt that we were being messed about. So much for our self-professed liberal outlook on life! Skiing in winter on your own terms. Golfing in summer under the same terms. There are few people anywhere, who have that standard of living. I played a lot of my golf with a young man born to Speyside. He was a natural golfer. He was also another gifted natural skier. Like many I've known he unfortunately did nothing about his talent. What a shame! Surrounded by some of the best ski teachers you could find anywhere he never bothered to take advantage of this unique situation. His name is Donny MacDonald. A man who also has the talent to sing well! Anyway, Donny and I played unlimited golf. That was the sort of life that some of us were enjoying. Some of our friends who had fulltime jobs still had a pretty full outdoor life. During this period we got to play some of Scotland's famous courses. Life was sweet and fulsome.

It was back to Gotzens in the winter of 1978 for the BASI course. It was here that the path of life would change for me. How it would have turned out otherwise, no one will ever know. After so much time to reflect back on what happened, I think I now know what transpired. I will try to the best of my honesty to tell how I saw these events start to unfold. Events took place which would end up with me being expelled from my membership in BASI. There are very few people who will know what transpired to allow this extraordinary thing to take place. Out of the Gotzens course came the situation which definitely was the starter for what was to follow.

The course seemed to work under the new regime, and once again there was an improvement in the standard of the candidates. This improvement was among the younger skiers who were coming forward in growing numbers. I had a class of free skiers, skiers who were not undertaking any kind of examination. We all knew each other, in some cases very well. After the first day I had been going through the advanced snowplough exercises in difficult terrain, leading up to fast stem-swings and parallels. This leads into more difficult snow and terrain and, in turn, leads to better all round skiing.

One of my class, David Johnston, a bar owner from Aviemore, made a remark to one of the class that he didn't fancy the snowplough turning etc. David had nothing to do with ski teaching. He just wanted to go skiing as fast as he could manage, a natural outlook as a skier. David was not interested in all the rigmarole about ski teaching. Nor were any of the others, as they were all BASI members already. Next day I skied the class much faster. The class knew it was thanks to David. What I did, was I pulled out the stops, as far as I could for a class at that level. A normal practice when classes are up to it. This was not a school class. It was a small group given to me to take, and improve their own skiing.

There was a girl in the class who, as it turned out, was very keen on going forward to start training in the BASI system. I'm sure this was our first meeting. Her name was Liz. She should have been in the Grade Three group. I found these things out later. It would be from these first two days that the start of the trouble to come would have its roots. History is stowed full of sad tales that had their beginnings in less innocuous circumstances. To add to this, I developed the flu. I am able to write these simple facts because shortly after these events I had very serious reasons for taking notes as to how things had panned out during that last period of time. I was to learn over the next 18 months or so how poor most people's memories can be. It is also interesting how poor these same memories can be in matters of great importance.

The first Saturday of the course was the day off. Ali Ross wanted me to go through to Switzerland to Lax and Flims to visit with a friend who had a new chalet, where we could ski for a day. I told Ali that was I feeling so bad that the thought of serious skiing was the last thing in my mind. He more or less told me he wanted me to go. He had a lovely Range Rover, so I went with him. It's to be remembered that Ali and I had more than a fair rapport going. For a ski teacher he is a most uncommon animal. He was tight lipped, and he never got involved in gossip. In this respect he is a real Highlander. He told me, when we were driving through Liechtenstein, that I should pull the pin and get out of these courses. He said there were those who bore me no good will. Ali never went on about it, that was not his way. I was surprised he had brought the matter up. I explained that this was my last course. I had declared that two years back. He advised me to keep my eyes open. Maybe because I was feeling so lousy, my brain did not register what he said.

Lax was what you would call a Swiss custom-built resort. It links with Flims, a fine place to ski. The chalet we stayed in was a Hollywood production. I'm sure none of those magnificent houses would be used for package holidays. All the houses were new, or in the process of being constructed. There were some bigger than one we stayed in! The new lift system was excellent, the skiing superb. It's a pity I was not in better shape to appreciate it. We returned the next afternoon, stopping off at the Bahnhof Bar in St Anton. This is where a lot of British skiers went for drinks. Ali wanted to try and meet someone. We did meet a number of Cairngorm skiers. St Anton was one of the *in places* in those days.

It was here I saw, for the first time, "Ski Bums" in their true light. They seemed to come from America, Australia and the UK, and in my opinion "ski bums" was the right name for them! We suffered from them on Cairngorm. I'm glad to say they are long gone. I remember Jim Currie, of the Scottish Ski Club, telling me how much they bothered him. After St Anton, and our experience on Cairngorm, I fully understood what Jim meant.

On the last day of the course, most of the classes gathered at the top of the long run down to Gotzens, where drinks were taken by all and sundry. Our group started down to Gotzens. About halfway down to Gotzens I started having serious trouble with my legs and breathing, so much so that the class had to more or less get me down off the hill. A number of my close friends turned up and helped to get me down off the hill. Naturally it was presumed I was drunk! If so, it was the first time I was that bad with drink, that I could not get myself off the mountain. At the time *I* thought it was the drink. Mind you, I could not figure out how this could be. I remember clearly, later that evening, at the end of course party, feeling like death heated up. If that was a hangover I'd have sworn off of drink for life. That trip back home was long and miserable.

When I got back to Aviemore I saw my own doctor. I explained to him exactly what happened. There was no use trying to bullshit him as he had known me as a friend for some 15 years. He suggested that, at that time, I had been verging on pulmonary oedema. I got the biggest fright of my life. He put it straight to me that "I do not want to see you out of the house for a month." Neil MacDonald does not mince his words.

The next week a BASI course started on Cairngorm. Jimmy Smith and Iain Finlayson were the trainers. On the first morning I received a phone call from the two trainers. They seemed to think they needed another trainer because the group was of a mixed standard of skiers. There was something like 26 or 27 candidates in total. Now, in those days, the economy of the courses did not justify another trainer. It's natural to see how two young trainers would want to balance their classes exactly. Unfortunately we must cut our cloth to suit our means.

I warned them that this had better be *kosher*, as I was not supposed be out, far less up a mountain! I sneaked out of the house wrapped up like a mummy. On the hill the weather was Arctic. Hiding out of the cold at the middle station, waiting for the trainers, who finds me but the good Dr McDonald. He walked up and called me a "stupid bastard." I hadn't a leg to stand on. As a matter of fact, standing in the physical condition I was in, was difficult. After Neil had his say he stomped off. He never ever brought the matter up again. I had then to go up the hill and ski off and sort out the candidates. I put them into two groups, then left Jimmy and Iain to get on with their job. That should illustrate the state of my fitness, the week after returning from Gotzens. On looking back, I remember I was not even responsible for that course. Jimmy and Iain probably took it for granted that I was.

A few days after this Jack Thomson came to see me. It was obvious he was very uncomfortable. I knew what it was about. If only it could have been someone other than Jack. A lousy job for him, as Jack and I were too close. But he was the Chairman and this was his responsibility. When he got started what he said surprised me. He said he'd been asked to ask me not to train again, or words to that effect. That was not what I expected. I asked for the reason. The answer was obscure at best. It seems I was not teaching the BASI method. That confused me. Actually, it dumbfounded me. Me who had been there at the beginning of any method that BASI may or may not have had! *I was fit to be tied!*

So I asked Jack how I had not been teaching the "BASI Method," when I had a free- running class. That class was supposed to be advanced skiers. At that time BASI did not have any detailed written information on skiing beyond parallel. As it does not appear to have yet! Jack knew too much about skiing to wish to become involved in the futile pros and cons of that contentious part of skiing. With his usual quiet way of thinking and of doing things, he sat and listened to me explaining that the accusation could not be true. I explained that I taught in my usual way, the only way I had ever taught. He understood that, and that is what he would have expected of me. I suggested we stop beating about the bush and asked if what was behind this situation, was me supposed to have been drunk when skiing down Gotzens. If that was the real case, then let's get to it. I then explained about what I have just been writing. I even went as far as saying Neil McDonald could, if asked to, confirm what had taken place between Neil and myself. Jack in his old fashioned manner told me that he did not need to verify any thing. "I had told him." I then told him that I had no intention of giving up my right to be a trainer, for that reason, of not teaching the "BASI Method." If the reason was that of being drunk at work, that would be another matter. But let's have it out in the open.

I went on to describe some of the events that had transpired over past years on BASI courses that have been run abroad.

The first year in Cervinia three well known trainers missed the examiners' meeting one night because they were drunk. One of them had even smashed up a piece of furniture. BASI paid for it. "A prank." There were other things involving trainers, trainers who had been involved in making this arbitrary decision about me. A decision about what I was supposed not to have done, "teach the BASI Way."

On the previous course we had a trainer who was having a torrid affair with one of his class. When the matter was raised at the trainers' meeting, no one seemed to think there was anything amiss. Now don't get me wrong, I'm not old fashioned. I don't care who's "doing" who, but there are some proprieties which must be observed, and they in turn become rules, which must be applied across the board. But to say I was not teaching "the BASI method." If that was an attempt to let me gently off the hook, I'd rather have the hook up through my upper lip. I made it clear to Jack that in no way I was accommodating this back-door escapism. But I'd think about it, then decide what to do when my mind was clearer. Between this and the changes taking place in the training, it was obvious that there was more bother to come. I decided to get out for the time being and wait and see how things panned out. I then resigned from the committee. Jack asked me to reconsider. He was determined that I stay in the committee. I did stay on a sub-committee for organising BASI going to Japan to attend the International Ski Instructors Congress. I thought that was my due after a long tough 15 years of total effort on behalf of BASI. Something dear to my heart and that I was more than proud of.

The trouble I had with my lungs was something that could have stayed with me for the rest of my life, or so I was told. I remember well the day I walked with Alasdair Watson, our ski school manager, to the top of Cairngorm. I was chary of making the walk in case I could not finish it. Nothing to do with pride. Pride! That is something I never gave much thought to. Or so I thought. Alasdair was born to Speyside, and we got on like the proverbial house on fire. Half way to the top I found was I walking loose and breathing well. It was like a new start in life. The world was wonderful again. Alasdair said, with feeling, "we should shoot you, you old bastard!" Not a bad compliment. You can always depend on your friends to be nice to you!

Now there was a bizarre event between myself and the two directors of BASI training, John Hynes and Hans Kuwall. They came to see me. What they asked me to do I could never have guessed in a thousand years. Before I go any further, it is to Hans' and John's great credit that they did what they did. This happened just prior to the BASI spring course. What they did took a great deal of, what is now a well used statement in our spoken language, "balls." They walked into my office and bearded the Angry Bear, and angry I was!

The spring course had over two hundred candidates, and a hundred and thirty of these were Grade Threes. Without any messing about they asked me to

249

take over the running of the Grade Threes. They never said it was for BASI. No plea, just a straight forward request that would put paid to any snide anger I may have been harbouring. Any normal person would be disarmed in this situation. There was no room for recriminations or resentment. Here was a job, a substantial job to be done. And they wanted me to do it. They had me "taped"!

But you had to hand it to these two. Here they were, deeply involved in wanting me not to train again, rightly or wrongly, but still they were prepared to take the chance of me telling them where to go! I have always admired them for doing that, at that time. It took a great deal of courage. Maybe they knew I could not walk away from this responsibility to BASI. Our association should be pleased that two stiff-backed men like these were prepared to take a large bite of *crow pie* for the good of our association. It marks the timbre of their backbone. And of the clearness of their thinking. The mere fact that there were nearly two hundred people coming to trust us with one of the most important things that would happen in their skiing life left no room for senior members' personal problems or clashes of personality. BASI was bigger than that. Without rancour I did ask how you could be in charge of a hundred and thirty Grade Threes when you are not on the trainers "list." John Hynes, a blunt Clydesider, said "come on Frith!" There's not much room for stupidity or anger when someone puts it as simply as that.

If this sort of thinking and common sense had been used at the offset, this serious problem, which I was the centrepiece of, could have been resolved by now. Being just a normal human being (?) I did say that I would expect to pick a good corps of available trainers for "my Grade Threes." I could see the two of them looking at each other, and I could almost hear them thinking, "you bastard, Finlayson!" John Hynes, with his quick Glasgow mind for this sort of manoeuvring, saw its humour. He casually said, "try and leave Hans and me a few senior trainers so we can staff the Grade Ones and Twos!" A good note to finish on. Now this event could have cured the rift that had developed in our BASI. I never thought about it at the time but it came to me later.

But peace was not to be. Eventually BASI would have real serious trouble which, when it started, lumbered on to an end which would shame all who were involved. And I mean *all* of us. When I told Jack Thomson what had transpired I could see he was delighted though he never said so. This pleased me. Jack, like myself, had most of his adult life invested in what BASI was about. The numbers who had come forward to this course was testament to the success of what we had been doing since 1963. True to their agreement Hans and John let me have the trainers I asked for.

The only senior trainer I asked for was Alasdair Ross. There was Jimmy Smith and Iain Finlayson. The rest were all new to the training, but they were a bunch of beauties. Gustav Fischnaller from Glenshee. Ingrid Christofersen, Patsy Field and Keith Geddes from Glenmore Lodge. I don't remember the names of the other four. I am very sorry and apologise for this. Before we started, I asked Ali Ross if he would take the most difficult group, not the best group, which by dint of all his good work in the past, he was entitled. Being the supreme pro his reply was, "I will take any class you give me, Frith."

The snow cover for this course was wonderful. I remember going up the White Lady T-bar with this mass of skiers. The excitement of the moment, of the power generated by all of the candidates, all of whom were hyped up by the importance of the start of their first BASI course. You could feel it building up. I skied down to the T-bar with Ali first. As we looked up, the trainers and the candidates started skiing down. We could see then how the standard of skiing was progressing in the UK. The sun was splitting the sky. A glorious start to the course. The scene seemed to temper me down and set me up for the work at hand.

Going up on the lift Ali never mentioned anything about the nonsense taking place in the background, and for this I was thankful. What had been taking place was very wearing on me. Contrary to what many people think, confrontation was something I never enjoyed. It has never ceased to amaze me how wild some of the tales were that were credited to me in this matter.

It being a Sunday, the hill was full of weekend skiers. There was a fine promenade of many good weekend skiers. The activity could be felt. It was good to be part of what was a Great Event for BASI. We skied over to the top to the Ptarmigan lift. There had been a deep snow fall the night before. At least a foot of untracked *gunk* was waiting for us on the right-hand side of the lift. This was just the place to sort out the groups. It must have been an impressive sight, a hundred and forty-odd skiers all waiting for the kick off!

There were mutterings in the ranks. All of these skiers knew that this snow was a *bastard*, a real test of anyone's ability. I skied down doing short-swings, no hopping, continued them right onto the flat at the bottom of the lift. By the time the trainers came down the snow was left in a terrible condition. Much more difficult than before it was skied on. Well, *"that's how the cookie crumbles!"* You win and you lose. The whole hill was watching this. My friend Andy Stirling had seen the whole spectacle. He said it was a tremendous sight. It was surprising how well some of the candidates managed to ski in that junkie crap, character-building snow!

Gustav Fischnaller is a class skier with a long distinguished background in all facets of skiing. As was Ingrid Christofersen. They were given the two top groups. Ingie was delighted. Jimmy Smith and Iain Finlayson were given two of the other difficult groups because they had more experience than the new trainers. The course settled down. By the next morning the classes were well balanced. Life was sweet, things were coasting along.

Shortly after this Jack Thomson came to me and insisted I attend a special committee meeting he had convened. It was his intention that I would be back on the committee and at this meeting he would have the whole mess sorted out. Only Jack could have made me attend that meeting. You see, I *do* suffer from pride! It was convened for the night before the examination at the end of course.

But alas, peace was not to be. Before the meeting got started I was grossly insulted. Dougie Godlington, who heard what happened, was appalled. It does not now matter who insulted me. The only thing that would do at that meeting, was if Jack, as Chairman, had dealt with the one who insulted me. He did not. Then I was insulted again. Being insulted is not the end of the world, I've thicker skin than that. It was then I left. There was no way I could sit through that sort of anarchy. Having gone there in good faith and being treated like that! Jack should have ordered the perpetrator out of the room. But because Jack was my special friend, that may have made it look bad. I would have put him out of the room, if I had been in the Chair. In my mind, I know that would have saved BASI from a more than embarrassing episode in its past.

I turned up on the hill next day for work. I was so upset by what had taken place the night before I lost all interest in what the course was about. My work was done. I explained to Hans how I felt. He understood and let me go off the hill. That was my days in BASI courses finished. What a sad way to go.

The only contact I retained with the committee was to do with fund raising for a BASI demonstration team that we were sending to Japan for the International Ski Instructors Association meeting. Two friends of mine, who were also Grade Three members, had undertaken to raise the money for this enterprise. The estimated cost back in 1979 was around eight thousand pounds. Eventually the costs would be a good bit more. There was to be a team of 8 demonstrators and 4 officials. It was going very well.

The job of picking the demonstration team was given to Kenny Dickson and myself. By late November Kenny and I had produced our two lists of names. We met in Kenny's office in Aviemore with Hazel Bain and Jack Wilson, one of the sponsors, to finalise the list of demonstrators. Both Kenny's list and mine almost tallied. After a short discussion we agreed on who would be in the team. To confirm this we phoned Hans Kuwall in Edinburgh to inform him who it had been agreed would be in the team. Hans was in accord with what we had come up with.

No matter what we had done in regard to picking that team, we could not in a month of Sundays have pleased everyone. That was why we had taken the trouble to meet in Kenny's office, and then phone Hans to get his opinion and agreement to the members of the finalised team. Later that week I arrived at Jack Wilson's house in Aberdeen on the way out to the Alps for some early skiing. It was there that I learned that the committee had added another name to the list. Kenny Dickson and I produced more than eight names each, and it was from our two lists that the team of eight was agreed. The extra one that was added had not been on either Kenny's list or mine. He was, however, a member of the committee and was also a trainer.

This would look highly irregular to anyone. I could not believe they could be so daft. Because you are a member of a committee, influence can be brought to change the agreed arrangements of the national body. If this was not an abuse of position, I don't what it could be called. There were very many long standing members who thought they should be going out to Japan. Possibly they were right.... Attentive non committee members would have picked it up instantly. And justifiably *created Cain*. Besides that, it was out of order.

There was already a very strong body of opinion that BASI was being run for the convenience of those at the top of the pecking order. In other words, the trainers, of whom there were many on the committee. There are strong feelings today that this is still the case. I was never in agreement with this point of view. But decisions as daft as this one could make you change your mind. When I returned from the Alps I asked our Chairman how the committee could in common sense have made this decision. I had the strong impression he was not comfortable with the situation. I also got the impression that it had been a most contentious meeting. Jack was on the cleft stick. It was then I told Jack that I would not be involved with our efforts in going to Interski in Japan under these circumstances. At the end of the day Jack Thomson did not take up his rightful place on the Interski delegation. This is a trip I knew he was really looking forward to in a very special way. Something he had richly deserved and had earned.

As we will see later in this narrative, approximately ten years on, the trainers, some of them extremely experienced, threatened to withdraw their labour if they did not receive a very substantial pay rise. *This attitude is strong among most of today's trainers.* All this information is available in the minutes and newsletters produced by the BASI office. This was an unhealthy period in BASI's life.

What eventually happened on the 31st May 1990, when accounts were made public, a loss in excess of sixty two thousand pounds was shown. Some turn-up for the book! We did not even own our office. We will come back to this, at the correct time in the story. In our determination to stop what we thought was a very serious mistake, Hedley Wright and myself applied for an *interim interdict* to stop the Committee using the Association's funds to finance this trip. This would be necessary as the sponsors Jack Wilson and Hedley Wright had withdrawn their support. They were both BASI members.

For those readers who have personal knowledge of these events, I'll make it very clear that I in no way influenced these two men in their decision in this matter. Anyone knowing these two men will know they are not "camp followers," or yes-men. The opposite would apply. My part in the *interim interdict* was a desperate effort to stop an act which, to me, was very wrong and offensive. We never got our *interdict*. We did, however, get expelled from the Association for "conduct detrimental to the good name of the British Association of Ski Instructors"!

25. Expulsion and Limbo

The first thing you find out about yourself when you become trapped in something as serious as this was just how important your part in it had been to you. In my case, that was, and still is the "The Ski World." Writing about this close to the event would not have been possible for me. It would have been hopelessly clouded, by at best anger and most probably by spite. That would have shamed me and made a sad story, much sadder than it already was.

There's another thing you learn. People who you thought were friends, for some reason or other, turn out not really to be what you thought them to be. As it turned out, it was my old friends from Glencoe who maintained confidence in what I was. Now, being as normal as most of us get to be, the natural reaction to those who voted against you, who you thought they were friends, is that conversation with them becomes at best uncomfortable. Anything that you may have in common with them went with their vote. For those who you had little in common with, there was no loss. What surprised me was their reaction to my not wanting to have conversation with any of them. The world I was reared in was obviously a lot less forgiving than their one. They make a tremendous decision about your life, and, rightly or wrongly, you would need to be a bit thick, or a two-faced clown, to maintain the *status quo* after that!

Now having had more than enough time to think of what took place back in 1979, I ask the question, "would I do it again?" The answer is, "*yes!*" As this story unfolds, you may see through my understanding of what I believe took place. *From my point of view.*

At the AGM it became obvious that there had been a lot of leg-work and background effort put into ratifying this expulsion by the committee and friends of the committee. BASI rules that then applied meant that, before the expulsion of a member, the committee needed to have a 100% agreement. A very difficult decision for any committee to achieve! The main objection that I had to make was their use of BASI's funds, the day to day money. It was promised this would not be done. To go into the pros and cons of it at this late day would be pointless.

By the day of the AGM the "bits and pieces" of the drama had lost any importance to the issue at hand. What was obvious was the determination of the committee at their table to have the expulsion ratified. You could smell it. I wondered where all this enmity emanated from. The thing was palpable. There was not a shred of dignity left in the room. It was sad.

They were so hyped up they missed a smart move that if their minds had not been so clouded, they would have clocked it. When it happened I was astounded. I had no idea what was coming. Hedley Wright, the other member who was "up for expulsion," worked it on the chairman. When the motion for expulsion came up, Hedley requested his case taken separately. If I was astounded, the committee were all the more so. It was then they made their second blunder. Their first blunder was turning this into a personal contest, between the committee and me. After a wee whispered confab at the table, the new chairman, Clive Freshwater, said that this would be in order.

The vote for Hedley was taken first. The members did not ratify his expulsion. You would have thought that would have changed the conduct of the meeting. They then proceeded to start the vote on my situation. David

Dalrymple, a full member, and no friend of mine at that time, then proposed that, as the members had already voted on this in a positive way, there was no reason to take another vote. The Chair decided to take the second vote. The result was 6 or 7 votes majority for expulsion. There were so many friends of mine who never attended' the meeting. If they had, the expulsion could not have been ratified. The profound old fashioned saying. *We deserve the government we get.* How true! As said by Thomas Jefferson? When the meeting was over, David Dalrymple said how much he disagreed with all that had happened. This was a man whom I had fired as a BASI trainer for being untidy. I have often wondered if David Dalrymple's common sense had prevailed at that meeting, would BASI be any different today?

It was amazing how many informed non-BASI onlookers could not understand how two people committing the same "offence," so to speak, could then be treated so completely differently. A curious way to go about such a serious business, as this certainly was. And how anyone can describe a fully franchised member of any democratic organisation, who challenges their elected leaders in how they the run the affairs of *their* organisation, however strongly, as "detrimental to the good name of the association," goes over my head.

The affair was quoted in our local Press and Journal newspaper in June 18th 1979. The reporter was Ian McKerrow. Mr McKerrow had written a very accurate account of what happened at our "private AGM." This was printed on the front page. In his report he stated that it was a BASI member who gave him the formation. But Ian McKerrow got one part of the information wrong. He said that I could not be contacted. He believed I was away Ireland on holiday. But that was not true, I had been at home and could easily have been contacted.

Someone from the Press and Journal phoned me the evening after their article appeared. He wanted to know if I had any comment to make. I offered to make a deal with him. Give me the name of the member who gave the information, and, in return, I would give him my full account of what happened. Also, put my name to it. He was not a very bold fellow. He refused. BASI might then have had valid reason for the expulsion of the member who gave them the story, and by any standard, was way out of order!

Once again the frailty of the average scale of human thinking comes into this equation. For most of those who got the plane to Japan were not concerned with what was going on. All that mattered to them was to get onto the plane for a free trip to Japan. There was only one man on that committee who I thought was on the committee for the same reasons as myself, and that was Jack Thomson. I have mentioned earlier that Jack had put his job on the line in pursuit of BASI's interests. Once again he put principle before personal considerations. He never got onto the plane to Japan. He voted against me, he also made this gesture. I knew he had been looking forward to heading our delegation on such a grand occasion. Of all of BASI's members he was the most worthy of going. There are men and there are men.

It was number of years before I would have another conversation with Jack Thomson. It happened at John Cunningham's Memorial Service. I was feeling dreadful after John got killed. Among all those well know mountain people, Jack walked over and made me shake his hand. The barrier was down. The hand of friendship is impossible to refuse. As I said before somewhere, Jack was not just big in stature. There were those there who knew how things stood. They were pleased to see the handshake.

There was Jimmy Smith, who expected to get to Japan on merit, who never got to Japan. He was on *my* list. The withdrawal of people of my like mind left three or four booked seats on the plane that had been paid for. Jimmy Smith was approached and asked to fill one of these seats. To his credit he refused. There are some people who do have strong principles and pride. Jimmy eventually went to Japan as a top, highly regarded, international ski teacher under his own steam.

My sacrifice was that I lost the right to participate in, and be part of, something very dear to me. In the years to come I'd watch BASI develop. Being reasonably normal, I did not always agree with some of what took place, as you will see. I suppose you could say I was in a sort of wilderness. That's the Piper wanting his pay again! Not being at the centre the hierocracy, and I mean hierocracy, meant there was no influence I could bring to bear on how our professional future would turn out. Before I finish I will give a clear resumé of how I see BASI as it is today.

Some time after things had settled down, one of the committee, whom I really thought would have seen things differently, came to me and tried to explain to me the reason why he had voted with the committee. I told him in no uncertain manner that what he did he should stand by. Don't make excuses for your thinking, considering the tremendous consequences it had for someone's future! I was in no way interested. Or if he was being insincere to me, it would have been inexcusable. Fortunately we don't all behave the same, or the world would be short on ambition.

During the immediate years running up to this dreadful period, I had been working in the making of TV ski type movies. The first was with that very fine Scottish actor, Paul Young. A most entertaining typical Scot. For three weeks we had great fun. Hazel Bain was the love interest in this *Major Epic*. Hazel took some stick over this. A lesser person would have collapsed under the stress of the expert slagging she took. It was great fun.

Over a much longer period of time I was responsible for the skiing in another TV series. It was a bigger commitment. Part of this was done in Europe. This series was called "Wilkie in Winter," depicting David Wilkie, the Olympic Gold Medal swimmer, learning to ski. It was here I got to have a go in the British Four Man Bob. This was without a doubt, one of the most exciting things I've ever done!

Not having involvement in BASI's activities left a big hole in how I spent a lot of my winter time. To fill the void I took all my energies and tried to transfer them into a more physical type of personal skiing. This is something that is difficult to do, when your mind is tied into something as serious as being involved in teaching ski teachers to improve their craft, as I had been with BASI. When the new season of 1980 started, after the turmoil of 1979, I was now in the position to try to see if it was possible, at the age of fifty, to get power and some speed back into my skiing.

For a long number of days I worked on sharpening up all the elementary turns up to parallel. At the same time increasing the speed until the running position became unstable. This takes you *to the wire* and builds up your stamina and, more importantly, your confidence. I'm sure it was a kind of effort to work some of the anger out of my system, which is not a very healthy emotion to carry around with you. I don't remember if that part worked, but I do know it sharpened up my skiing to a remarkable degree. It was a self-taught lesson. I found my way into this years before as, if it works for the pupils, it works for yourself. When the mood takes hold to ski well, it's a good way to *kick off!* When I did this deliberately back in 1980, I am sure that decision still effects how I ski today. It was probably the best "lesson," of any kind, I'm ever likely to have. In the same year of 1980, Jeanie and I went back to ski in Wengen. It had been fifteen years since we had been there.

How I looked forward to seeing the old place again. Going up on the mountain train from Lauterbrunnen, I was so excited I could hardly sit still. Coming off the train I naturally went into Eiger Café. The first one I met was Ali Ross. He was sitting with Chris Brasher. Chris had done an article about Ali and myself some years before, called "The New Highlanders." Wengen was all that I remembered it to be. At that time, almost all of the local people whom I had known were still there and remembered me. Jeanie had invited Frau Stager for lunch one day. We met her off the Lauterbrunnen train and Jeanie greeted the grand lady with traditional flowers. She is one of those ageless persons, or is it all in the eyes of the beholder?

We had an old friendship lunch in a traditional Swiss hotel. With great charm she treated me just like the callow young man she knew from the middle 1950s. Jeanie was still referred to as Madam Finlayson. We spoke of times past, she told me how Werner had died. She managed this without recourse to emotion, despite her closeness to Werner. This took me back. Nostalgic memories lived again. I felt so pleased and comfortable just being there and as if the fifteen year gap had not been.

Frau Stager was having a starter of garlic snails. I mentioned that her breath would be rather strong. With richness in the ways of the world, her reply was "but I have no one to go home to." I thought I detected a wee touch of pathos. This from a very strong lady. We are not all made of stone, as some foolish people may presume! On paying the bill I gave the waitress, who was local, a rather good tip. Frau Janet Stager remonstrated with me, saying that Werner and I were always stupid with our money. This was one of *her Bonnet Bees.*

We took our leave of each other and as she walked away, I thought how splendid she looked. And how kind she'd been to me in the past, this Matriarch of Switzerland and at a time when I had needed a wee bit of support in Lauterbrunnen in the late 1950s. When she was gone, Jeanie said to me that she had treated me as if the last 15 years had not been! Feeling pleased with the success of the reunion, skiing was abandoned for the afternoon.

At the time it went through my mind, as such things do, that all the crap that had taken place with BASI was not all that important when I had places and people like this that I could call my own. Not too many have had such good fortune to have lived through and experienced such growth and change that had taken place in the ski world in general. What had happened at home would, perhaps, sort itself out in time.

It was during this holiday I had a phone call from home at 7.30 am. It was my son. The call was to tell us that John Cunningham had been killed, while teaching climbing. This was a terrible time for Jeanie and me. The holiday was going so well. That was it finished.

I went back to Wengen the next two Januarys, where I taught a little. One night at dinner I was called to the phone. Someone was trying to get in touch with Ali Ross for lessons. He was away teaching for BASI. They heard that I was there and wondered if I could take them. It was a girl who was arranging this for her husband and his friend. We made arrangements to meet in the Eiger Café. They wanted to know how they'd recognise me, was I tall dark and handsome? I explained this was not the case and gave them a true description.

That night Jack Wilson and I were sitting in the Eiger Café, waiting to meet these young people. We overheard these two lovely young girls talking and wondering what this "Frith Finlayson" would be like. Jack Wilson said to me in his usual snide manner, "Boy, are they going to get a disappointment!" What are friends for? Jack, the little pig, took it on himself to introduce me to the lovely girls with all his usual *bull*. I apologised for Jack listening in to their private conversation. It was obvious I'd made a big impression. As I told Jack later, you can't hide class. Jack ordered a correct wine, and we soon had them at their ease and laughing. Then their men came in. They must have wondered who the two Freaks were.

As it turned out their two husbands were a pair of tough nuts. When skiing with them it was possible to push them as hard as you needed. They skied quite well and were easy to teach. The pity was they had only one day left, otherwise more lessons would have been arranged. I invited them to ski with Jack Wilson and another, Willie Wilson, "Smiler" by nick name. The two young men had a great day. They commented on how much Jack and Smiler's skiing resembled mine. They were right. Smiler's and Jack's resembled mine with one difference, my mistakes were much more *polished* than theirs! I'm sure that I never let Ali down in any way and that the lesson was up to the full standard that Ali would have approved.

The following January, while sitting on the train going up to Kleine Scheidegg, a lady came over to me and asked if I was Frith Finlayson. When she learned I was, she replied by saying that her Granny's second name was Frith. Being a *bullshit merchant*, I asked her if her Granny came from Enniskillen. "Yes!" she said. I then said, "well, your Granny and mine were sisters!" You would not believe it...it turned out they were! The woman was red headed and the right age, at around forty five. She spoke with a well educated Glasgow accent. She was also a very handsome lady. The reason this was possible was that, around 1880, two sisters from Enniskillen went to Glasgow to work as house maids. There they married Scots men. It sure is a small world! My grandfather was a Skye man. Now there's a fine line of Celtic blood to be proud of, Irish and Scots!

She and her husband had a lesson with me. We had a pleasant day and, as it turned out, I found they both skied not too badly for holiday skiers. It's stimulating to look back and think of how fortunate you have been in having had some of the world's special gifts. This was one of mine.

The next two or three years were very painful. I wandered about bored. I hit the bottle. That's the only way to describe what happened. Too much money and a brain that was switched off. By the way, that's not an excuse, its a fact! It would

258

surprise you how many people, who are considered successful, have had a drink problem at some time or another. And, strangely enough, most of them get over the excesses of it. After all, the world would be a queer place without the "Water of Life." Slowly, the people I estranged myself from came to terms with what turned out to be a pointless exercise.

I cannot say all was forgotten. That would be a bit much. I am sure some of those involved never gave the consequences of what happened any consideration whatsoever. With that attitude they leave nothing in their passing and are remembered as such.

That is a thought.

26. Home and Abroad

In the years from 1980 onwards the changes in the ski world would increase. The number of skiers kept increasing, and many of these would want to be involved in ski instructing. This first showed up when I took charge of that number of 140 Grade Threes in 1979. The demand for BASI courses grew. With this the need for trainers also grew. There was a serious problem however. The UK was not producing enough *good* skiers to fill that bill properly. Because of this, trainers started to appear who were well below the standard that was required. That for me is putting it mildly!

Contrary to what many people may think, not everyone who passes the Grade One necessarily makes a trainer. A full driving licence does not make an advanced driving instructor. That is a very simple simile. To point out the pitfalls of making any Grade One into a trainer, consider the fact that we have a trainer of long standing who took more than one attempt to pass his Grade Three, his Grade Two *and* his Grade One! It was actually very much worse than that. I hope this is not me bringing our Association back into disrepute again! One meaning of "disrepute" being "of doubtful certainty." That was an exceptional case. It would be true to say, however, that the average Grade One does not make a trainer. This can be understood. This really should preclude them from being involved in teaching at the top end of performance in skiing. Their own skiing cannot be skilful enough to demonstrate the physical side of skiing at this level. It also makes it impossible for them to understand the feeling that good skiing affords to the performer. How can they, if they have never *experienced* how it feels? Unlike a lecturer in a room, they need to be able to demonstrate at the highest possible level. This level is not available to every skier, even though they may happen to be Grade Ones.

Anyway, that is what happened. We have trainers who do not ski well enough to be trainers. An opinion of many respected BASI trainers. We have had Grade Ones who had not really worked as fulltime ski teachers who became trainers. An undesirable situation. Actually, it is an intolerable situation. This was unnecessary. If BASI had kept raising their standards, as we had been doing, we would have kept pace. Better still, we would have got ahead of our needs. The moment you plateau out in any human endeavour, your progress is at an end. There are no shortcuts to the best possible goals.

Here is a part of the end product of this thinking. In the Ski Instructors Race in 1994, on Cairngorm, a nearly fifty-year-old ski teacher won the race. An apprentice teacher, with not too much experience, came second, An ex-ski-teacher-come-shopkeeper was third. That would have been impossible ten years ago. It certainly could not happen in any Alpine country at this time. The time was, when to win "Our" Ski Teachers Race, you had to be near enough British Team standard. No one who has pride in skiing can say that the quality of skiing among the bulk of those working as ski teachers on our hills is what it should, or could be. It cannot be, when a near fifty year old is capable of winning the Scottish Ski Teachers Race.

This is not all the fault of the younger skiers in the profession. We will not be justified in calling it a profession if we keep letting the skiing standard of those working as instructors slip away to the extent that the good weekend skiers are remarking how poorly most of the instructors are skiing. And it's not only on

Cairngorm. BASI must take the bulk of the blame for this lowering of standards. If you do not keep striving to boost the physical side of the skiing at the top end of the grades, and indeed, all grades, you stop progressing! If it's left like that, at best your standard stands still. From there, if it goes anywhere, it goes *downwards!*

It is about twelve years since BASI eased off the attainable standard to accommodate what they thought was the need for trainers. That was not the way to go about the illusory problem if there was a problem. I have already said, we were on the right road. "O ye of little faith." The result is self evident! It can be seen skiing about on our slopes at present. Let it be clearly defined, this is not the dodderings of some old fart! It's vibrant. It is clearly understood to be a fact in the fabric of the skiing of too many BASI members today. To keep any standard up is the same as competing. Front runners must carry the ball. The front runners in our case are those in charge of the training. If you keep dropping the ball, you might not get it back! Seeing this from the outside, with more than average knowledge of professional skiing, I think this is where BASI took a poor turn on the road to their future.

There were other things that took place in the mid-1960s that I am sure did damage to professional skiing, which we suffer from today. First "We" in BASI established Grade Threes. This was done because the standard of skiing of those coming forward was so poor that we in our wisdom thought a one week's training would prepare the people coming forward to understand what was required of them. We later found one week was of no value and changed it to two weeks. We meant to phase it out later when the base of candidates skiing coming forward had improved. The mistake was, we never phased it out.

The next mistake we made was that we agreed to help the Scottish National Ski Council establish Ski Party Leaders. We even agreed to them having a development officer, Hans Kuwall, who was one of our committee. Neither of these two things was popular with most of us. If ever there was an anomaly, it was the fact that one of our committee was the Development Officer of SNSC. Were we ever so tolerant! What has been said here is without malice, it was needing said. It was not long before Ski Party Leaders were calling themselves Grade Fours. A gross misnomer. Nothing to do with BASI. I understand that "Assistant Ski Party Leaders" are now in use. Also, "Assistant Artificial Slope Instructors." Will wonders never cease?

What we wanted was that the Scottish National Ski Council adopt our Grade Three. They maintained that this standard was too high. If they had adopted Grade Three, UK Instruction would now be so much better than it is today. In Scotland they could have achieved that as a *norm*. Not as quickly as the no value Ski Party Leader. People can achieve much higher standards if they are handled well. And are set correct, achievable goals. The British Ski Federation would have followed. We might not have had the Artificial Slope Instructor. Grade Threes would have fitted in there very nicely. Budding Slope Instructors would have risen to the standard required. But the responsibility for the patience in achieving such goals is invested in those who are the leaders!

This was part of the reason the British Ski Instruction Council was done away with in the Crown & Mitre Hotel, Carlisle, on June 11th 1973. We in BASI knew exactly what was taking place at the time by the would-be powers-that-be.

They had neither the patience nor the foresight to let time make it happen. What a tidy package of ski teaching for the public of UK to be able to use. Simple and solid. And something to be proud of. But no, as always, it was the usual small minds burrowing away in the background for their own narrow ends. And skiing ends up with a mixed up conglomerate of *nothing*. Who really suffered from all this useless duplication of effort, apart from the users of instruction, in all its different shapes and forms? It is the present day fulltime Ski Teacher, be they Grade Three, Two, or One. There have been many very fine ski teachers who over the long years looked after their pupils, not "punters," to the highest of standards. Stan Davis, of the Scottish Norwegian Ski School, did it for thirty years. He *is* a ski teacher. Tommy McKee and Hazel Bain, of Ski School D'Ecosse, were also affected. These were Grade Three.

This is for all you newer ski teachers who wonder why it's so difficult to become a ski teacher and so expensive. And at the end of the day not able to find a decent day's pay for your hard earned skilled qualification. Particularly if you are a Grade One, trying to earn a living on a Scottish mountain. What I've said above is a big part of the reason, but certainly not all of it.

To get back to standards. The carrot must be hard to get hold of. Easy prizes are fools' rewards. Unfortunately, ski instruction in its physical make-up, and with its easy access to those who pursue it, lends itself to having far too many adherents, and for many of the wrong reasons. It is incredible how many skiers are desperate to stand in front of reasonably good fellow skiers and spout off how these pupils who, in many cases, are equally skilled performers, should be enjoying their skiing– under the instruction of such as themselves! Many of these same type skiers are used by some ski package operators, in the Alps, fulltime. They are a poor advert for our skiing. Fortunately there is a number of top class British ski teachers working in major resorts. Some have been established for years. Like all good professionals, they make their own mark, with the quality of their work. Something to be proud of. However, it is not those we'll speak of.

Around 1976, during the BASI spring course on Cairngorm at a trainers meeting in Glenmore Lodge, Ali Ross brought up the subject of the growing number of "Brits," as he called them trying to get teaching jobs in Europe. I was still the director of training at that time. I remember remarking that it was a good thing. Ali had been working since 1973 with the Wengen Ski School and he was not so sure. He went on to explain that numbers of BASI Grade Threes had been moving about trying to pass themselves off as fully qualified. I pointed out that they needed a current International Stamp on their licence, which was only issued to Grade Ones. He seemed to think there was a lot people trying work this *oracle*. They must have been thick. The Swiss were very involved in the International Ski Instructors Association and were fully conversant with what an International Stamp was. And what a *good* skier was. Having worked in Wengen, I could not see anyone among those Bernese Oberlanders who could not spot a phoney a mile away. Ali went on to say that it was common knowledge in the profession in Europe that this was being tried on. There would be much more trouble to come out of this in Europe in the not too distant future.

Having highlighted the manifestation of the misgiving of the ski schools in Europe I'll quickly itemise what I think causes our European fellow ski teachers to be rightly concerned. The next few sentences should highlight where their concern was coming from. They determined not to allow British ski teaching to take permanent root in *their villages*. They already had experience of travel companies using the Profession of Ski Teaching to help subsidise the selling of package holidays. Ski teachers in Europe have a very strong political lobby working in their favour. Lucky them! They have no intention of letting foreign ski schools or ski teachers work in their country, without strict controls. They fully understand that once any outside interests get a toe hold they could upset the *status quo*. In their efforts to hold back any encroachment, they suggest that BASI standards are below their own standards. With the above events in mind, who could blame them? Well, the present standards of BASI, sad to say, in the opinion of many of our own experienced ski teachers of long standing, are not as they should be. Particularly at the Grade One level. Also, the overall standard is lower than it should be, for the following reasons.

Around twelve years past, BASI made ropy Grade Twos, into poor Grade Ones. And then compounded this felony by making them trainers. Nothing but a recipe for the lowering of our standards for the future. As it certainly did. There may be some substance in what our Alpine brethren think. Those were some of the pros and cons of the goings on in the background. Now to carry on...

In the past, when a candidate had bare pass marks plus a poor trainer's report, they were told not to apply again for further examination for a specific period of time in the future. This was especially important at Grade Three level and set a clear standard aimed to be carried through all the training Grades. Over the years I've heard it said, "it's only Grade Three." What a negative thing to say! What a negative way to think! How many hundreds of smiling faces, ecstatic, rich in contentment, have I seen when they received their hard earned "Threes." If the most important time in a beginner's skiing is their first introduction to skiing, surely the same applies to the débutante in learning to be a ski teacher. Striving to keep this to as high a standard is well worth the while. That's what a Grade Three should be! Stiffen up the skiing side of the Threes, as the talent is there to absorb this. Do this and the ropy Grade Twos and Ones will lessen within two seasons. After all, it's from the Threes that they come. If our foundations are not sound, how can we expect to have a good end-product? *There is nothing for nothing.* An age-old axiom that stands as true today as when it was first quoted. It is no bad thing to take a long caustic look at yourself and your responsibilities to the ski teaching system and public in general.

Becoming fully qualified at the present time has became a highly complicated and very expensive undertaking. Before I criticise this, I'd like to point out that by the time I had gained my Swiss Ski School Director's Licence, over a period of four seasons, it was very expensive. But it must be remembered that, here in the UK at that time, there was no BASI to look after such needs. It still does not follow that it need be as expensive as it is. The main reason for the heavy expense is the amount of steps that must be taken to get you all the way through to National Ski Teacher. Total Time Required seems excessive, by any standard. Check recent BASI news letters. 460 hours teaching experience. 444 hours training, over a period of 60 days. This information comes from a BASI Newsletter. Issue 38. Winter 1995. On the face of this, it may not seem a lot for a qualification at a national level.

However, few Ski Teachers get a full four months employment in any one winter. Working six days, teaching 6 hours per day, might earn up to approximately, seven thousand pounds, in a ski school, which would almost certainly be in the Alps. I doubt if there are many, if any, earning that out of ski teaching on our mountains. However, it could be done comfortably if teachers were properly organised. Teachers working on Cairngorm could not finance their courses from incomes at presently being earned. Having a National Ski Teacher's licence on Cairngorm makes little difference to your income. To utilise a Grade One Licence to its possibility, you would need to work in the Alps.

I mentioned on earlier pages how Ali Ross was concerned about Grade Threes trying to pass themselves off as qualified. In Europe, qualified means Grade One. And nothing else. As far back as 1976 Ali was right. Since then, what Ali forecast has happened. It is now very difficult to work in the Alps. Before the troubles we have now, to teach in the Alps was no problem. The International Ski Instructors Association Stamp on your Grade One licence opened most doors. We were all satisfied with that arrangement. It was very uncomplicated.

Around 1988 the build up of the number of package holidays from UK seemed to explode in Europe, and particularly in France. The travel companies who ran these holidays started to include ski instruction as part of the arrangements. It was then the shit started to hit the fan!

Once again people who had no idea of what teaching skiing is about, became involved in employing ski teachers. Unfortunately, they did not use Grade Ones. At best it was Grade Three. In their amateur efforts to look professional they fitted up their teaching staff with very obvious uniforms. They stuck out like sore thumbs. As did their skiing! Naturally, when needs must in busy times, they used anyone who worked for them, or anyone they knew who skied. I have seen this at Les Deux Alpes and Serre Chevalier. Observing it with a clinical, if not jaundiced eye and it was awful to see such an abuse of honesty for what was seen as British ski teaching.

With an Old Compadrie,
Gordon Bruce

Then it was made worse when, somehow, a new phenomenon was created. It went by the name of "ski guides." If you know anything about Alpine mountain people, you'll understand the designation "guide" has special connotations for them. It means you can guide people through, up and over the high mountains. To be a guide in these mountains is special. I think it's *special* in our mountains too. It was around this time that the French really took a very strong line with what was happening. Mountain people all over the world tend to be *cannie* folk. They're careful. They can also be awkward! It's only in the last 20 years or so that their natural resource, their mountains, has started to bear the fine fruit it does today. When I lived with the Stagers in Lauterbrunnen, I learned much of their frugal ways and their outlook on life as it had been in the past. Life is easier now, but the old culture still dominates. Our own Highlanders are of a similar disposition, and if you do not go carefully in dealing with them, they become difficult to deal with. If not impossible!

The Alpine valleys, unlike ours, have healthy populations. There are many young people wanting into ski teaching. Waiting in the wings so to say. My son introduced me to many of them in Serre Cheavlier, and pointed out to me that there were apprentices and that they never got much work. He himself was well employed, fully qualified, and, with 23 FIS points in slalom, he fitted in well as a professional ski teacher speaking their language.

Iain also pointed out that this was becoming a very serious contentious problem with the local population. Well, we all know what the French are like, even when they are wrong. In my opinion in this case they are one hundred percent correct. I agree with them and how they handled their problem. Why should tour companies from this country use cheap, semi-skilled and for the most part unskilled labour to subsidise their operation?

The French have taken severe steps to contain this situation. Despite its severity quite a number of our highly skilled Grade Ones have conformed. They are now supplying their international talents in the same French resorts where the trouble started. They are highly respected and are a credit to British ski teaching. They are also earning money in keeping with their professional ability. Something they can't do here. The Austrians have produced training which is set up to cater for the English speaking people wishing to teach in Austria. The Swiss make no arrangements. If any ski school wants you, they will get a work permit for you, qualification or not. The Italians allow BASI members to work 15 days per season, Grades One to Three. Before this trouble, there were no restrictions.

All this trouble because of *greed and need*. The *greed* was on part of the tour companies, in their efforts to keep their costs down. Instead of facing up to the real cost of local ski school tariffs, they tried to shortcut those costs. This stirred up a hornet's nest. In the end it got them nowhere. It made the French, Italians and Austrian national ski teaching bodies organise for the future. The *need* was on the behalf of Grade Threes, and others, in their desperation to get skiing in the Alps for the winter on the cheap, or as they may have thought, free. Nothing is free! That became very clear in this case. This has been cleared up by the Brits having had to adjust to Alpine requirements. How simple! In all truth you cannot blame the would be instructors. Who I do blame are the poorly run tour operators who always seem to get into these situations, not only in skiing. Maybe they've done us a favour!

We at Cairngorm as ski teachers are cursed with a similar problem. Weekend organisations bring large groups at the weekends. They start off with one ski school, and, after a season or so, they start punting around for cheaper deals for instruction. Once again with no regard to the quality of the instruction. I'm sure the time is not far away when this will be dealt with at a much higher level, for the general good of all concerned. It will improve the standard of ski teaching. And, very importantly, greatly improve the income of ski teachers without any increase in the cost to the public. If the income of genuine ski teachers is not improved dramatically, ski teaching as an art will be replaced by inferior instruction from *part time handy men*. These changes are closer than most people who are involved may think.

I'm explaining these behind-the-scene problems that ski teachers are having because I'm sure it will be of interest to the general public to understand that ski teachers are ordinary workers, despite the fancy jackets and airs and graces some of them put on at times! People using schools will understand that well paid contented teachers will most certainly be much better motivated than if they are struggling to make ends meet. The manifestation of these prevailing conditions is that the bulk of our better up-and-coming younger members are working in the Alps. Indeed there are a number of our very experienced members finding their way to the French Alps where they teach during winter. This is bad for good ski teaching on our mountains. How we get out of the *bind* is another matter. You cannot take that much quality out of the middle of a living entity such as a cadre of ski teachers like we have on Cairngorm, or anywhere in Scotland, and not have deterioration in the overall picture.

What of BASI as it is today and what it might be in the not too distant future? My way of seeing the way forward is as follows. BASI's only function at present is to train and grade teachers in the UK. I say "at present" because I'm convinced that BASI must sooner rather than later take an interest in how their members are remunerated for their work. If they do not, they will not be able to demand the ever increasing requirements of the National Ski Teacher. Once again this is another subject. The only people who get any real return out of BASI at present are trainers. They work for very good wages and this is correct and right. If we expect the lot of teachers working in the open market to be fair, we must start inside our *own house*.

However, whether we agree or not, to the bulk of BASI's membership it would appear that the Association is oriented towards the trainers, who seem to think they are an elite group that make training possible. How wrong can they be. The *membership* is the body of the dog, not the *tail*. The auld Scots saying means the same. It's the congregation that's the "Body o the Kirk," not the building. One of the big mistakes that was made, was the production of the trainer's badge. To my mind this separated the trainers from Grade Ones who were not on the trainers list. It actually looks like we have another tier and tends to highlight a *variance* between Grade Ones and those using trainers badges. These badges should be discontinued. Have they unwittingly established a separate *hierarchy?* Another question that is worth looking at.

It's also disgraceful to see some trainers and Grade Ones who do not display their BASI badges, but do wear International Ski Instructors Association (ISIA) badges. Not bad when the are being paid by BASI! This must be stopped. I have made verbal complaint to the Chief Executive on this very serious matter.

There is another turn of events which I'm sure is obvious to other members. That is that the bulk of our Grade One members now work in the Alps. This was bound to have transpired. What it could bring about is a split, or even a break away of some sort. After all, they for the most part conform to the requirements of their Alpine hosts! These members may decide they would be better served by having their affairs looked after in Europe. After all that's where they work. Being absorbed into an Alpine nation is possible. I did it back in 1962 without an organisation like BASI to represent me!

There is another possibility. That is that members of all grades working in Scotland may start to feel that they are not getting enough out of BASI as it is presently working. And may find that they want to go their own way and run their own qualification at a cost in keeping with their income from skiing here in

Scotland. It would not be very difficult for this to happen. Nor would it be difficult to set up and organise. The lift companies would certainly cooperate with a properly set up organisation. The catalyst for this would be the right "Leader."

It would be worth taking into account that there's much muttering and very reasonable cribbing about the cost of becoming qualified in BASI. It must be remembered that being BASI qualified does not automatically let you work in Europe. Even Grade Ones do not have this right. I would suggest these two possibilities be seriously taken into consideration. It was not easy to build BASI up to what it is today. It's taken long years. If given enough reason, fragmenting could happen much more quickly than may seem possible. I personally would regret this deeply. If I was involved in BASI's management, I would pay a lot of attention to these observations.

Loyalty in these modern times is fragile and illusory. Altruism, sadly, is old fashioned and a thing of the past! I hope I am not being too sanguine in thinking that BASI's leaders are aware of *mutterings on the lower decks*. If you are on the bridge, you are in the firing line. It goes with the territory. And it can be very heady wine. But remember, "the sheep of the fold are capable of thinking for themselves."

27. Our Loss

As I draw near the end of telling this story of what is really about the many different people I was involved with since 1956 when skiing really started for me in Glencoe, it has meant me taking a deep, serious, long and honest look at myself. I've learned since starting that what I thought I had done at certain times, is what I really did do. As a consequence I have tried to be as blunt about myself as my ego will allow, at the same time being as circumspect as my natural honesty will allow! I know for certain, that some of my actions and behaviour has been very poor, or even bad. There's not much that can be done about it now. If we had all lived sanitised lives, we would have made poor companions, been dull company and, as a result, someone like myself would have had nothing to write about. That is not an apology. Writing this narrative has been the most exciting thing I have achieved in my above average, interesting and eventful life!

Even after all the long years, during which I have been gifted to have skied with some of the world's notable skiers, and also met and associated with other notable persons from all walks of life in the colourful world we live in, special events still occur. The most recent one I have enjoyed happened on the 14th of February 1995 at 8.30am. That morning, I happened to meet Jimmy Smith at the carpark T-bar on Cairngorm. He asked me to ski with his group for the day. Skiing with Jimmy is always a pleasure. His group was ten British, fully qualified Mountain Guides. Let it be clearly understood; our Mountain Guides stand head and shoulder equal to guides anywhere in the world.

Skiing with Jimmy's group gave me a great boost. When I started skiing, all my companions, men and women, were mountain people. To ski with a group as fit and able as this took me back in time. Their ability to assimilate ski information, plus their energy, enthusiasm and commitment to what they were about was stimulating. All of these men would have made first class ski teachers. As indeed some of them are. When the day was over, I thanked them for having had me in their group. I was greatly pleasured when they replied that it had been their pleasure also. Watching Jimmy working with these highly skilled, discerning, professionals was very educational. I have always taken great pleasure in watching well intentioned young up-and-coming ski teachers. Not that Jimmy is "up-and-coming." He served his time years ago. Keeping your eyes open and, of course, your mind, will keep your own learning process in good working order, and, with luck, present opportunities to learn new and fresh wee gems about ski teaching.

There were other memories and thoughts that came to mind in the writing of this. I had to remember Werner Stager and my times with the man and, in particular, the three weeks I spent with him when I crossed my Rubicon in skiing. He pushed me up to what he thought was my limit, and then some. I don't know to this day if he knew what he was doing. It's only lately that I think I understand *what he was about!* But at no time did he get me near to *my limit.* Werner was without a doubt a cornerstone in my skiing. He made it possible for me to attend the Swiss Ski School Directors Course. This in turn gave me a solid grounding and the confidence to help in the formation of BASI and to get it established. It was a great shame that he died when he was still comparatively young. I would have taken much pleasure in bringing him to Cairngorm to see the good work we had done in establishing the British ski teacher training system. I'm sure he would have been pleased.

One of the most important things I learned from the Swiss was how to describe what a top class skier was. They simply referred to them as *good* skiers! How often do you hear the statement about how fantastic this one or that one is, when, in reality, the person being described is really a run-of-the-mill skier. People working in fulltime skiing should know what a *good* skier is! Within the ranks of the people working as ski teachers we seem to have too many who have an over-valued opinion of how well they ski. This is almost always a male fault. The result of this kind of thinking is that the "thinker's" personal skiing stands still. It comes to a plateau where they get stuck.

During this period in my learning time, which is never ending, I have found that practice of all the elementary ski movements is an absolute necessity to keep my skiing *tight*. It is something I have always found deeply satisfying. While doing it, I find that every move I make in practice must be carried out with my full and careful attention, that being my best possible effort. Otherwise my results would be less than I am capable of. As Gary Player said when someone said how lucky he was getting out the bunkers, "the more I practice the luckier I get." If your turn gives you a kick of adrenalin, you've got it right. Unfortunately, it does not always work that way. And maybe that's the way it should be. You never hear a *good* skier shooting the bull about their own skiing. What they all do when they've got it going well, is try a lot harder and, in so doing, they inadvertently play to the gallery. The gallery like this. That's the cream on the pie!

One memory from near the end of my first full season's skiing, was when we were walking down in South Ballachulish one day. We had been stormed off Meall a' Bhuiridh. The thought came to me that this freedom, of skiing all winter, was about to end. It was a feeling of almost physical proportions. It was the thought that I might not get to have any more of these unbelievable full winters of skiing. How strange this should be and so starkly sharp in my mind after so many years. The impact of the end of the season was to stay with me for long years, particularly after a good season. There is still a fair touch of sadness in it. However, it would be fair to say we are rather used to having the seasons running one after the other, considering how much water has run under the bridge. I'm writing this now because we have just had two very satisfying seasons. At this moment, in 1995, we are nearly finished our season. For some reason I have the feeling of complete ebullience. I'm like "the cat that's nicked the cream," replete in having enjoyed my own skiing. My own skiing is still the main driving force in my psyche. So this has got my old friend, my memory, reminding me of how good the world and Lady Luck has been to me.

Having said that, it reminds me of something John Young said to me as far back as 1965/66. John was the one who skied with the "Hanging Judge," and our first close friend to die. He had a talent for looking to the future. He could anticipate problems to come. At that time I was moving through the ski world noisily and with a great deal of determination. So much so that, behind my back, I was called "Stramash." A Glasgow description for a person who constantly and noisily stirs things up. A fair description! *And a fair cop!* John put it to me all those years ago, "what will you do when all these young fellows start catching you in their skiing?" I was on the crest of a high wave and I certainly had not been thinking of such eventualities. I told John that when the time came I would face up to it. Inevitably it happened. In skiing I've successfully adjusted to the demands that nature has physically placed on me. That's positive thinking. There's is not much else you can do about it! Success is when you know you have done well. Sound experience should let you *know* if you have done well. Mind you, back in the early sixties there were other good young skiers coming up. Our group had its share of them. So I knew then what was to come.

I have just met a man I have not seen for thirty years. He was one of three male school teachers BASI ran a special Grade Three course for. This course was run from the forestry houses in Glenmore. Cosily, in the small living room, we held the simple lectures that seemed to be all that were necessary in those days. To be honest, it was probably all we knew. This is an obscure wee bit of BASI's background. While we are on about ageing professional skiers, and I am certainly one of those, for the likes of us the main problem is trying to ski at speed. When you try to ski very fast, you automatically become apprehensive. It does not matter if you have been used to skiing fast and ski well, your brain will turn on the built-in safety devices. Your ageing body will not respond to what is demanded of it. You will stiffen up, sit back and become afraid. That is the cost of having enjoyed becoming *mature*. The piper must be paid!

Once I was teaching a violinist from a symphony orchestra. He was a private pupil. He was a short-arsed, gutsy, good humoured man. I kept asking him about his life and work. I should have been paying *him!* We spoke of the cost of houses in London. I asked if he had a house in London. His reply was that he'd buy one when he possessed his own instrument. What a wonderful answer. It's people like this who renew my faith in humankind. Like things you read that stay with you. Here are some...

> Time is ticking "Beauty" away.
> Someone went away and left an "Empty Space."
> Love is a "User" who demands a High Rate of Interest.
> To describe something special, "Rowan Full." I hope Robert Burns wrote that?
> A special place, "A place of Whispers."
> To quote Ginny Cox, that female Rascal! "It always snowed at Christmas."

I quote something Rudyard Kipling wrote to describe how we might feel about close dear friends.

> Oh East is East and West is West,
> Till Earth and Sky stand presently at God's
> Great Judgement Seat,
> But there is neither East nor West, Border, nor
> Breed, nor Birth,
> When two strong men stand face to face, though they come from the ends
> of the Earth.

This of course would include the Ladies! That was a look at a few of the many good and lasting reading experiences in my life. There is always a side of living that runs hand and glove with all of life's joys and achievements. That is the losing of these nearest to you. It must eventually happen.

As I mentioned early on, in 1966 we lost John Young. Then, much later, we lost John Cunningham in a climbing accident. At the time of these happenings, we were all grieved and deeply affected. Our son moved out to live in Les Deux Alpes in the Dauphine Alps, France, around December 1989. After a time he started to work as a ski teacher. He spoke French, with his international background in skiing he fitted in with local French people.

Tommy Paul, the general manager of Cairngorm Ski Area, Willie Smith and myself drove out in Tommy's car for a visit, in January 1990. Tommy and Willie were as much Iain's friends as they were mine. He grew up in their company at weekends and on holidays. As Iain was learning to ski as a three-year-old these were two of the many who took an interest in what he was doing. Like many others in our close-knit Glencoe clique, they helped to get him up and onto the hill. As a three-year-old the going was rough and all such help made the task seem simple. At that time Iain was the only child skiing in Glencoe. In later years he worked in skiing alongside them, and they learned to respect each other as men. In the process they grew closer as equals, despite a large age gap. This became apparent to me during our stay with Iain's family in Les Deux Alpes. Iain's wife Mary made dinner each night. Liberal pre-dinner drinks were served, and Mary's dinners needed large appetites to make any headway with what was on the table. The atmosphere in the small flat was one of warmth and of soft private intimacy. Our two grandsons helped to turn the gathering into the closeness of a family holiday outing. We met some of Iain's new friends, Peter and Lyn, two Londoners, and their next door neighbours, where we put our heads down. The first morning we skied with Iain, Peter and Lyn. The couple skied quite well. I got on very well with them. They liked *dogs!* Skiing with Iain, as always, pleasured me, as was skiing in a new Ski Station for the first time. To get onto the Dome de Puy-Sallé at 3425m so quickly was impressive.

Kevin and Craig, my grandsons, and I had a day's skiing on our own. I was vexed to see their skiing was not what I thought it should have been. We stayed up on the hill all day. They had picked up the Alpine way of skiing very fast and, alas, the bad habits that can go with it. I was determined to improve their skiing. Youngsters who think they are skiing well don't take kindly to changing from something they believe they are good at. It is very much against their young male ingrained chauvinism. It is something that the experience of living in our world will surely temper out of most male chauvinists! I had caught bigger fish and skinned wilder cats than these two. We skied all day, almost till 6pm. It was near the last hour before I had them standing square and swinging clean. I don't go big on telling pupils how well they are doing. I leave that to their brains. They should *feel it*. As we came down near to the village they were now by my side. I spotted their Dad and his fellow ski teacher Rocky, an Englishman teaching there. Rocky had worked with me on Cairngorm. I pointed out to these two Finlaysons that they were now on parade. We cut a line down through Iain and Rocky's classes. The boys did themselves proud. Their dad was delighted. No more than I. *This I remember*. And I even told the boys how well they had skied!

I skied one afternoon with a girl Iain had been teaching. She was a smart lady who worked for a well known travel company. Her name was Annie Barker. Improving her skiing was a cake-walk. She could soak up information and turn it into almost instant improvement. She was one of those lucky ones I have spoken about, who have an extra little bit of talent with which you can cross any Rubicon! She was a no-nonsense very able lady. There was a smart-mouth who made a snide sexual remark in Smokey Joe's bar late one afternoon. She verbally gutted him down to his socks. I thought he was a nasty piece of crap. Well done Annie!

271

Willie, Tommy, Iain and I skied Serre Chevalier. It was the first time we had all skied together for fun, for long years. It had been 1969. since I'd last skied there. It's a fine Ski Station today, with marvellous timbered runs. The conditions were perfect. I also remember how well we all skied that day. That season, as it turned out, was notable in that it started well before Christmas with excellent snow at home. In the company of old friends with my son's family, we enjoyed a holiday in skiing that had a reason to be remembered. The rest of the season at home turned out to be the cream on the top of a memorable winter.

Before we left, Iain told me he had something big in the pipeline for the future as far as Les Deux Alpes was concerned. He wanted to settle there. His two boys were enjoying their school. They, of course, were learning French. The younger one had a natural talent for languages. Mary, Iain's wife, loved the place. Iain himself was working at learning Italian, as another string to his bow in teaching skiing. They were becoming part of the New Europe. All was well. It turned out that the "something big," was that Mary and he were to rent a new chalet with the object to buy. This was in Mont de Lans, a little below Les Deux Alpes. Access was by a chairlift. The chalet could take 8 to 10 guests. There was a beautiful view of the valley from the chalet. It was "A place of Whispers." Needless to say they were excited about their future in this fine part of the world.

Mary and Iain came home to Aviemore to collect some of their personal household things for the chalet, prior to first guests, before Christmas 1991. Iain and I spoke about me getting a small studio flat in Les Deux Alpes. It was planned I would teach skiing at busy times and enjoy winter in the high Alps. This would be a pleasant, fine way to enjoy the coming winter seasons. One night after dinner in early December, enjoying a glass of wine, I was contentedly musing in my mind's eye the coming winter. Dreaming is not the private realm of the young. I'm sure the older you get, the sweeter the musing becomes. And with maturity we learn the value of dreams that come true. If we lose the energy to dream we lose the skill to use our imagination. What, then, will we have to look forward to?

A phone call from France ended all my dreams. When the phone calls were over, my son was dead. Iain's wife was on the phone telling me Iain had collapsed. In her terrible state I asked her to put someone else on the phone. A young girl's voice came on. She explained that they were just back from skiing when this happened. She said that there was a doctor there and he was looking after Iain. I remember saying to her that she would be phoning me back within minutes, with good news, or very bad news. I immediately phoned Neil McDonald, our doctor, and told him. He said I could only wait for the call. Very shortly the return call told me the most painful thing of my life. I had no time for grief, my first thoughts were for my wife, and how would I tell her. She was out at her Tuesday night curling. Before I went to tell Jeanie I phoned Neil McDonald, then made a call to Carol Simpson, Jeanie's close friend.

Up to the moment when I actually spoke to Jeanie at the ice rink, I had no idea how to go about it. When the time came, I just told her what had happened. What else could you do? She was shocked, but being the person she is, her personal dignity carried her through those first moments. Her first thoughts were for Mary and her two grandsons. Being so far from them seemed to compound the tragedy. Personally, this affected me deeply, the thought of being of no use.

It was surprising how many friends turned up that night to our house to share our grief. I am now in the position to appreciate how much support and comfort that gave me personally. We flew out on the second day after the news. Allan McKenzie, one of my early racing pupils, had been in Aviemore at the time, and stayed over to drive us to Glasgow airport on the Thursday. Allan had been a younger racer than Iain. He's also a dear family friend who my wife has always been more than fond of. With a born talent for entertaining you, he made what should have been a miserable journey, an almost pleasant diversion.

At Glasgow airport my sister Carol met us. Carol is one of the world's sweethearts. Iain had always been "her wee boy." Sandy Greaves, of Greaves Sports, Glasgow, turned up to pay his respects. This all helped at a time when help was needed. This is something I found out later. We all need help. At times. The flight to Lyons on the second day was quiet and tranquil. We had little conversation. This was understandable and possibly a good thing. We were met at the airport by Rocky, Iain's friend, and our grandsons.

The drive up into the high Dauphine Alps was in the pre-dawn. Low in the valley it was damp and miserable, as it tends to be in deep Alpine valleys at that time of the year. We arrived at the new chalet in the coming of the dawn. It was when we went into the chalet that the power of what had happened struck me. The hallway was decorated with all of Iain's memorabilia from his racing career. I had not realised how extensive and varied this had been, nor had I previously thought about it. The scene impacted on me at that moment the finality of what had taken place and struck me like physical blow. That part of our life was now over. Mary's two brothers had managed to get a flight on the first day. This must have been a tremendous help to Mary. The brothers, Allan and Jim, were towers of strength and very able men. On arriving, Jim told me that Iain was upstairs, and asked if would I like see him. I said no, as did Jeanie. The last time I had seen my son he had been in the prime of his life. That is how I still remember him.

On the morning of the funeral I walked about outside the new chalet. It was now a place of "Sad Whispers." The beauty of the early morning added greater poignancy to what was happening. The local ski school made arrangements for the funeral. They did it in a simple and practical way. Iain's coffin was put into the back of a normal estate car. We were in ordinary cars. The graveyard was only some minutes from the chalet. It was small and butted out on a high escarpment hanging over the steep valley. A small, ancient church graced the beautiful place. A more suitable place of peace for someone who loved mountains could not be found. One of Mary's brothers paid eloquent tribute to the "good French people of Les Deux Alpes" for having welcomed Iain and his family into their community so warmly. He said this in English. Rocky, speaking in French on behalf of Mary and the boys, had difficulty with his emotions. I felt sorry for the young man. He had admired Iain so much, and his task was the harder for this. Four ski teachers using old climbing rope lowered Iain into his grave. This somehow or other touched me, as being in keeping with how things were taking place.It was gratifying to see how many locals were there paying their respects. All the local Brits who lived there attended. For myself I was moved by the practical, simple dignity of how the Good People of Les Deux Alpes buried our son. Later I wrote to the local paper to thank them.

When the ceremony was over I wanted to be on my own, and I walked into Mont De Lans, which has only a handful of houses. Here I found a small bar. It was empty. I had a few drinks. As I left the middle aged lady who served the bar asked me if I was Mr Finlayson. When I left the bar I went back into the churchyard. Unfortunately, I arrived as they were filling in the grave. I could have well done without seeing that. I left, being even more upset. Back in the chalet Mary had food and a bar set up for anyone who wanted to come. This had been done well despite the occasion.

By this time we had found the circumstances leading up to Iain's passing. A dinner party to celebrate the house warming of the chalet had been arranged. Prior to this, a day's skiing with their friends. The local doctor was part of the party. He had been there when Iain had his heart attack. Its seems there was nothing anyone could have done, no matter where they had been. The doctor had arranged for lunch after the funeral for family and close friends. The meal was in a fine mountain restaurant. I sat beside the doctor, during the meal. He was in his forties. He was an impressive man who spoke our language fluently. The lunch was his idea to relax the family after the funeral. The act of a sensitive, thinking person. I remember speaking to him of General De Gaulle and how he gave France back its self respect after the war. He seemed pleased that, in my opinion, De Gaulle had been good for France. Is not the world a "Queer Place."

I came home the second morning. Jeanie and Mary over the years had become very close, so it was natural that Jeanie stayed on to be company for Mary during the bad days that were to follow. I flew out of Lyons feeling terrible, saying goodbye to Craig, our eldest grandson, at the airport. Like the morning of our arrival, cold damp fog filled the low valleys. This, as on the morning we arrived, seemed to suit the occasion. The plane was almost empty, which suited my frame of mind. As it climbed, we came into the coming dawn. Two mornings, two days, and so much had changed in the inbetween! In the light of a clearing sky, almost at once out of the East climbed the heights of Mont Blanc. Back came the memory of Jeanie and I climbing there, back in 1950. How much had happened, in the intervening years, to Jeanie and me. Possibly the climbing of the Mont Blanc was the start of all the wonderful successful adventures we had been party to. And here was I looking down in sadness on a mighty mountain where our success in life got a good part of its start. This was passing through my mind as the Blanc dropped out of sight and the plane made its high passage to the north west.

In Glasgow I visited Sandy Greaves of Greaves Sports. He was very interested to hear what I had to say about how things worked out in Les Deux Alpes. He made an observation that two of our best skiers were gone. He was taking about Peter Fuchs. Peter had been killed sometime past. He was right, they *were* two of the best.Walking from the Greaves shop to the bus station in the centre of Glasgow, I stepped in front of a car. It almost hit me. I never saw it. Nor I was I bothered, one way or another. The pain came in the quiet of long lonely nights. In recent years night had became a private place to me. Reading in its quietness was a soothing pleasure. Its tranquillity had became a friend. Now the quietness seemed to stalk me. Like a vacuum, it was empty. Real sleep became impossible. Reading, another friend to me, was impossible. Long walking, in the quiet darkness around our home during the night, did nothing to ease the confusion that was racking through me. It was good that Jeanie was still in Les Deux Alpes. I had my own company in which to nurse my anger. And at the same time try and sort myself out.

Soon after I returned, Andy Stirling had me out to dinner, with Joan, an old dear friend of Andy's. A no nonsense direct person who I've always communicated well with. At the table she quietly asked me how I felt about what had happened. Without having to think, I replied "Anger," and anger it was. It was a terrible thing. It was eating into me like a canker. Because she had asked me the question so well, I explained to her that the anger was frightening, and I was not proud of it. But it was mine to live with. I remember that I did not mind the question. I think I welcomed it. You find you have lost something for good that you have taken for granted. It is very, very private. And to yourself. People like myself appear to take the fine precious gifts of life for granted, as if they are ours by right. Not so! We learned early on in life what is precious. We don't make a fuss about our Dear Ones. That's the difference. I have only one regret. I never ever told my son how proud I was of how he lived his life. And especially how he looked after his family.

People like myself are guilty of being wasteful. What shame, we don't even know how wasteful we are being! In the first weeks, meeting people and having to speak about Iain was difficult, particularly if they were close friends. When I met Willie Smith and described how things had gone at Les Deux Alpes, I was extremely upset, as was he. I told him about the climbing rope. I thought he saw the rightness of that. Meeting Hazel Bain was another difficult one. Hazel had been more than close to our family.

There are things in life which we must face up to responsibly. I have never made much of what happened. There was a great deal to think of. This I am sure I have done reasonably well. The answering of all the letters to all the many people from many distant places. I would do this in the *sma' hoors* of the night. This was the most difficult task I have ever had to face up to in my life. I feel this must be part of this story! Our son, by circumstance of birth, had a life that would be the desire of any right thinking person, and hard to make to order. In this we, his parents, are content. To his living memory are two fine young men, Kevin near to 18, Craig 21 years. Since that sad night the boys, as they were then, have grown into fine young men their Dad would be proud of. I have had a great deal of difficulty in writing these words. It is, however, an important part of the story.

28. The Finale

I mentioned Hazel Bain as being a close family friend. In the year following Iain's loss, she became ill, and she was ill for a long time. The illness was very severe on her, and, as the effects of it started to show, she behaved and conducted herself with dignity. When I visited, she would offer to make me the fine Indian tea she took pride in serving, even when it was difficult for her to move about. I would let her. Her friend Issy Dickson from Carrbridge became Hazel's caring angel. She looked after Hazel in a soft, gentle, understanding way. Hazel lost what she had struggled so hard to preserve, and in Raigmore Hospital, before Christmas 1992, she passed away. If there would be a place to go when we are finished here, she should be in Valhalla with all the rest of the warriors, where I'm sure she will equal the company she finds herself in!

Next we lost Bob Clyde. He had been very ill for years. Unlike Hazel, he passed away peacefully. He did this in winter. He was buried by the side of Loch Inch, with the snow falling. He even arranged to have the hill stormed off, in his effort to have a full turnout at his funeral. Or so it was remarked, in the best of taste, by an old friend at Bob's grave!

Shortly after Bob, we lost Jack Thomson. Like Bob, he had been not well for a long time. By freak of chance, Jack lies in the beautiful Loch Inch churchyard alongside his old boyhood friend Bob. There would appear to be a fairness in our world after all! I won't use the hackneyed term "pioneers," as it's used too loosely, and applied where it's not been earned. But here were two men who had contributed enormously to what Scottish Skiing is today.

Chris Lyons of Glencoe, of whom I have spoken extensively, was lost in December 1994.

We also lost Calum Finlayson in the same year. Calum took some eighty plus good years from this world with him. Well done, Calum! Chris and Calum are mentioned in Chapter 1, on the list of honour.

We also lost Tommy McKee. Tommy and I worked for the best part of thirty years teaching skiing together. He worked in John Brown's, Clydebank, as a boiler maker on the Royal Yacht. That means he worked steel into different shapes and sizes. A highly skilled job. He worked on installing the steel work on the Royal Yacht in what became the Queen's bathroom. The bathroom was spoken about in less reverend terms than that. In recognition of this special achievement "We" appointed him Boiler Maker to Her Majesty the Queen. Not bad for a Red Clydesider. These men are mentioned through the narrative. They have been an example to all who have known them, in how to live productive and creative lives, without halt or hinder to those around them. Unlike Hazel and Iain, they had more or less achieved the proverbial three score and ten. Part of the price of growing comfortably older is that you start to lose those who are dear to you. When it starts to happen you have the arrogance to feel "ill-done-to." How dare nature treat us so!

Is it not peculiar that it's in the psyche of the Scot not to appreciate the good qualities of their able people until after they have gone? Are we not all guilty of this? Maybe not. The era, or should I say "eras," when this story was in the making, are over. The world today is so dramatically different that it almost in no way relates to the world as it was then. Having said that, I am now of an age

276

when, on Mondays, I hurry to the Post Office to collect my state pension in my grubby grasping hand, and many of my friends are surprised that I lasted long enough and made it far enough to collect it! I can't argue with that. What I find is how rich and rewarding life still is. There are many reasons for this. One of these I attribute to new friends in skiing, who unknowingly help to keep me trying to ski well. This works if you try hard, and is certainly a source of deep satisfaction. That is the skiing side. Even though this takes all of my attention in winter, this leaves the other half of the year. Living in this idyllic part of our world, summer offers unlimited opportunities for outdoor-type people, at all levels. Even for those not interested in anyway with outdoor activity, living in the country that surrounds us would still be difficult to match. Even for those who "do nothing."

Around seven years past, we moved out of the centre of Aviemore to a smaller house. This is located in a birch wood, near to the river Spey. Our front windows have an unobstructed view of Cairngorm. Around us the woods abound with wildlife. In the quiet of the early morning, it can be "a place of whispers." Most of the houses are holiday homes. It did not take long for natural selection to take place. From out of these holiday homes Jeanie and I made good friendships with couples a fair bit younger than ourselves. Younger in as much as their children were still at school. At weekends and holidays, over these past years, we have all got to know each other, and, in doing so, established an important part of our lives for the future. While this was happening, some of their children became mature teenagers, this indicating that the years are moving on untrammelled and unconcerned as to whether it suits us or not. Suit us or not, it's an inexorable fact of nature, we are all getting older! However, these new younger friends help to keep the likes of us in the middle of *the main track*.

How often I have I been asked by people I've not seen for years, "are you still skiing!" When I say, "yes!" many reply, " how do you manage at your age?" Now, what can you do with that sort of thinking. There is no answer. All of my compadres from the days of our youth still do most of what they have always done. There is no hard or fast rules as to when you only wear slippers! This, like my peers, I refuse to do. When the interest dries up and I lose the will to get up and go, I will sit back, contented in the life I've been fortunate to have had. If, however, the lack of reasonable mobility came into play, the die would be cast. And I'm sure that our Old Faithful, the "World" would come up trumps again, and give me another kick at the ball! Be it a different ball.

In the beginning of this story I said that one of the reasons for writing it was the ill health of many of the main players who had made it possible. Iain Finlayson was the only one we had lost before I started writing. I did not start writing this for that reason. It may have been a signal. But that was not the reason. As we have seen, not too long after I started writing, the dying started. The wee bit of sadness is that these fine people cannot read what has been said about them. I am so glad I have undertaken the responsibility for doing this. I will get satisfaction when I know my friends approve of what I have written about their dear departed lifelong friends, known as the "The Boys." The story has been seen and told through the eyes of a true Scot. A Scot who has seen tremendous changes over a long period of time. Changes in all the mountain sports. The mountains in Europe, in all their ancient strongholds, have given up their secret places to ever increasing numbers of climbers and skiers, who now have comparatively easy access to most of these mountain places. We now have Ski Boarders, whose numbers are rocketing. Where it will all end, who can guess? I have seen the coming of all the lifts and ski facilities in the UK, in particular in Scotland, and am proud to have been a part of what it is today. I really hope to see Scotland's first mountain railway. If I see that, I will witness the start of the rebuilding of Cairngorm. That is one of my "Wee Dreams."

Writing this has been like travelling through the main part of my life again. It generated a new excitement for me. It gave me a clear look at what I think I've been all about. Some of what came out did not suit me. This can happen if you take an honest look at yourself, and you are reasonably normal. That is how life pans out. Without the contributions of friends, associates, or passers-by, conscious or otherwise, no one could make their mark in this world we live in. Painters of pictures, singers of songs, sculptors in stone, writers of words that sing. At the end of the day, the world needs such contributions, even if they only seem to disagree with what you have been saying or doing.

Part of what I have written is how I've seen skiing develop during the long period from the early 1950s up to 1995, in particular British professional skiing. What happens now? Firstly, no one can plan a life really, or what or how they want their future to be. The young ones? Maybe. No matter how cute man's technology becomes, what will be, will be. "The best laid plans" do not always pan out!

I now quote another "last memory." In our early twenties we were all full of the arrogance of youth and knew full well we were indestructible. We would be young forever. We were certain of this. Hamish McInnes, he of great climbing fame, went so far as to say that, rather than start to age, we should all be put down at the age of thirty. How strange. The last time I spoke to Hamish a year or so past, in Glencoe, he was hale and hearty and he's well past thirty! So much for forward planning! I do look forward to the future and, with luck, will go on skiing with friends, meeting new people in skiing and others. My life has always been enriched by "others." If I had the chance to go round again. I'll play safe and go for the return ticket. "Valhalla" can wait for me.

Yours Aye in skiing,

Frith Finlayson.

Aviemore, Scotland. 9.30 pm. 3rd May 1995.